Our little systems have their day;
They have their day and cease to be:
They are but broken lights of Thee,
And Thou, O Lord, art more than they.

Alfred Tennyson, *In Memoriam*

A Comprehensive Christian Appraisal

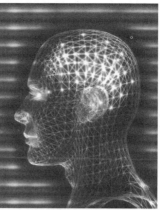

MODERN PSYCHOTHERAPIES

STANTON L. JONES

& RICHARD E. BUTMAN

IVP Academic

An imprint of InterVarsity Press
Downers Grove, Illinois

InterVarsity Press
P.O. Box 1400, Downers Grove, IL 60515-1426
World Wide Web: www.ivpress.com
E-mail: email@ivpress.com

InterVarsity Press® is the book-publishing division of InterVarsity Christian Fellowship/USA®, a student movement active on campus at hundreds of universities, colleges and schools of nursing in the United States of America, and a member movement of the International Fellowship of Evangelical Students. For information about local and regional activities, write Public Relations Dept., InterVarsity Christian Fellowship/USA, 6400 Schroeder Rd., P.O. Box 7895, Madison, WI 53707-7895, or visit the IVCF website at <www.intervarsity.org>.

All Scripture quotations, unless otherwise indicated, are taken from the Holy Bible, New International Version®. NIV®. Copyright ©1973, 1978, 1984 by International Bible Society. Used by permission of Zondervan Publishing House. All rights reserved.

Design: Cindy Kiple

Images: Chad Baker/Getty Images

ISBN 978-0-8308-1775-7

Printed in the United States of America ∞

Library of Congress Cataloging-in-Publication Data

Jones, Stanton L.
    Modern psychotherapies: a comprehensive Christian appraisal/
Stanton L. Jones and Richard E. Butman
        p. cm.
    Includes bibliographical references and index.
    ISBN 0-8308-1775-1
    1. Psychotherapy—Religious aspects—Christianity.
2. Christianity—Psychology. 3. Pastoral psychology. I. Butman,
Richard E., 1951-. II. Title.
BV4012.J65 1991
261.5'15—dc20

91-10470
CIP

P	32	31	30	29	28	27	26	25	24	23	22	21	20	19	18	17
Y	22	21	20	19	18	17	16	15	14	13	12	11	10	09	08	

To
Jenny, the gentle spirit;
Brandon, full of sensitive brightness;
and Lindsay, an effervescent sprite—
in hopes that
you will each grow up to know
the fullness of God's love.

And to
Ashley Elizabeth, aglow with wonder—
in hopes that you will continue to manifest God's grace
in the lives of those you touch.

Acknowledgments   7

Introduction   9

1 The Integration of Christianity and Psychology   17

2 A Christian View of Persons   39

The Dynamic Psychologies   63

3 Classic Psychoanalysis   65

4 Contemporary Psychodynamic Psychotherapies
written with Michael W. Mangis   92

5 Jungian Therapy   119

The Behavioral Psychologies   143

6 Behavior Therapy   145

7 Rational Emotive Therapy   173

8 Cognitive-Behavioral Therapy   196

9 Adlerian and Reality Therapies   226

The Humanistic Psychologies   253

10 Person-Centered Therapy   255

11 Existential Therapy   *278*

12 Gestalt Therapy   *303*

13 Transactional Analysis   *324*

The Family System Psychologies   *347*

14 Family Therapy   *349*

Toward Christian Psychologies   *377*

15 Responsible Eclecticism   *379*

16 Christian Psychotherapy   *401*

Subject Index   *419*

Author Index   422

Acknowledgments

Reformed Christian thinkers often assert that in pursuing truth, we attempt to "think God's thoughts after him." We cannot be so confident to claim that we are presenting "God's thoughts" in this book, but it has been exciting to pursue that goal in this project. As we wrote, we were acutely aware of those who have been mentors to us in some form or another along the paths of our development. In some sense, much of what might be good in all that follows is due to their influence—we have been thinking "their thoughts" as well as God's thoughts. What is inadequate in what follows is due to our own weaknesses.

Our thanks go out in a special way to C. Stephen Evans and Alan Tjeltveit, who read the first draft of this manuscript in its entirety, even though it was in very rough shape. Their suggestions were always helpful, thoughtful and honest, and their insights have significantly advanced our thinking and so made this a better book.

We are deeply thankful for the help offered by Michael Mangis of Wheaton College, who did the initial draft of chapter four (Contemporary Psychodynamic Psychotherapies) for us. We were out of our depths on many areas of current psychodynamic thinking, and his expertise in this area is outstanding.

Dennis Okholm, Frances J. White, Siang Yang Tan, Robert Roberts, H. Newton Malony, Kirk Farnsworth, Don Bosch, Drew Loizeaux, Brian Van Dragt and Jon Peterson contributed substantially to our work by offering critiques of individual chapters at various stages of development. We are indebted to many of our colleagues at Wheaton College who make that institution a rich place to think and work. We wish to thank Michael Maudlin, our first editor at InterVarsity Press, whose initial enthusiasm and encouragement meant a lot. Finally, we thank our principal editor at InterVarsity, Rodney Clapp, whose commitment to Jesus Christ has been so evident, and whose skills as a thinker and writer are always in evidence.

Our secretaries at Wheaton College, Carol Blauwkamp and Geraldine Carlson, have been of terrific assistance in the process of finishing this project, as they so often are in all other areas. Over the years, a number of research assistants have contributed to greater or lesser degrees to this project; we would like to extend our thanks especially to Karen Crow Blankenship, and to Joel Arp, Rose Buier, David Dodd, Michael Gillis, Kathy Hobson, Todd Keylock, Kathleen Lattea, Stephen Moroney, Grace Ann Robertson, Lauren Strickler, Trudy Walk, Elizabeth Watson, Don Workman and Chris Zang. Special thanks to David Wilcox for preparing the index and proofreading the manuscript.

Figure 1.1, picturing the historical roots of the major psychotherapy approaches, is from the manual for the "Theories and Principles of Counseling" Extension Studies course, Wheaton College Graduate School, copyright Stanton L. Jones, Ph.D., 1986. Used by permission. This figure is based on an earlier chart by Dave Benner, now of Redeemer College.

Portions of chapters six and eight are based on S. Jones (1988), "A religious critique of behavior therapy," in W. Miller and J. Martin (Eds.), *Behavior therapy and religion* (pp. 139-170), Newbury Park, CA: Sage; used by permission. Portions of chapter seven were based on S. Jones (1989), "Rational-emotive therapy in Christian perspective," *Journal of Psychology and Theology, 17*(2), 110-120; used by permission.

Figure 7.1, used with permission, is from *Reason and psychotherapy,* by Albert Ellis, Ph.D. (© 1962 by the Institute for Rational Living, Inc.; published by arrangement with Carol Publishing Group; a Citadel Press Book).

Our thanks go out to Don Browning and the faculty of the University of Chicago Divinity School for extending to Stan Jones the status of post- doctoral fellow and use of their marvelous library (heaven-on-earth for a bookworm) for the academic year 1988-89. Our thanks also go out to H. Newton Malony and the faculty, students and staff of the Graduate School of Psychology at Fuller Theological Seminary for hosting Rich Butman for a very rewarding sabbatical during the fall of 1987.

Handling the issue of gender in writing is an ever-troublesome matter. We have chosen to use inclusive terms wherever it did not torture the language to do so. In places where it was not stylistically pleasing to use neutered terms, we have attempted to alternate references to females and males. We were not compulsive in the process, so some unintentional inequities may remain, but we hope not.

To our wives, Brenna and Deb, we offer our appreciation and most profound gratitude for their support, love and encouragement, without which this book would never have been done. Thank you for being excellent in all that you do.

INTRODUCTION

✛

*T*his book attempts to appraise each of the current major psychotherapy theories in the mental-health field from the perspective of evangelical Christianity. It is a "dialog" between the supposedly nonreligious therapeutic psychologies and the religious Christian tradition. But it is a dialog where one side of the conversation, that of the Christian faith, is presumed to have the ultimate standing as truth. Nevertheless, we presume that the various psychologies have much to teach us, and may in fact lead us to see certain truths of the Christian tradition in a different light.

In 1977, one of us was in graduate school and came across a book written in the 1950s relating Christian faith to the field of psychology. It was authored by one of the most eminent scholars in the field of clinical psychology today. An enthusiastic letter was soon written to this scholar, asking him if he had written more in this area. He graciously replied, saying that he was no longer a Christian; he was not sure where he stood religiously, but it was probably closest to Zen Buddhism. But he also added that while he no longer had a personal commitment to the presuppositions from which he wrote in the 1950s, he nevertheless felt that the earlier book was logically sound; that is, the form and content of his analysis stood even though he no longer believed the foundations for what he wrote at that time.

Because of our presumption of the truth of the orthodox Christian tradition, this book may be perceived as "parochial" by some, as it represents only one religious tradition. Our intended audience is students, pastors, mental-health professionals, and interested and informed lay persons in the evangelical Christian tradition. But in line with the story of the scholar above, we would argue that the form of our analysis stands even if one is not an evangelical Christian. Christians of other stripes, and perhaps even those of other, non-Christian faith traditions, will, we hope, find this book helpful in outlining the religious implications of the various psychotherapy traditions and in suggesting how religious faith might interact with and revise the way in which we think about personality and psychotherapy.

We are certainly not the first to write in this vein. Vande Kemp (1984) has compiled a detailed and annotated list of books relating religious thought and psychology published between 1672 and 1965. Among these are many that took specific psychologies and explored their relationship with religious belief. The works by Browning (1987) and Hurding (1985) are excellent recent examples of such works. Further, in each chapter, we cite recent literature that examines the particular issues and psychotherapies we are addressing. In composing this book we have been able to build upon the work of many able scholars, to whom we are heavily indebted.

Before embarking upon our study, we will briefly examine the nature of psychotherapy and counseling, since it is vital to have a general picture of the nature of what we are appraising before we focus on the details.

What Is Psychotherapy and Counseling?

The topics we will examine in this book are germane to the concerns not just of professional psychologists, but to all mental-health workers, pastoral counselors and pastors, and indeed to the concerns of informed laypeople who desire to be effective in their interpersonal ministries. But despite the number of people involved in this endeavor, defining psychotherapy and counseling is quite complicated.

The Problem of Diversity

Psychotherapy is a generic term that covers a wide variety of theories and techniques, all of which have articulate spokespersons and supporters, and make claims of success. The varied theories and techniques are derived, for the most part, from clinical experience and reflection rather than systematic empirical research. This helps to explain the proliferation of therapy approaches. They emerge from each theorist's unique experiences of the type of people he or she has seen for counseling, the types of problems they manifest, the cultural context of the therapist, his or her assumptions about how people change, and the core beliefs that shape the therapist's life philosophy. This understandably leaves wide room for diverse approaches to people helping.

And there really are an incredible array of approaches. Not only are there numerous major theories, but each seems to have a number of variations as well. A recent work identified 260 distinct schools of psychotherapy (Strupp and Binder, 1984). Certainly, many of these are "kissing cousins" rather than truly unique approaches.

Since many approaches to psychotherapy claim impressive results, it is difficult to evaluate critically the ultimate worth of a particular theory or technique. One must get the broad perspective when assessing the value of a specific system: Who is working with whom, under what conditions and assumptions, and on what particular problems and concerns? There is an ever-present danger of the overenthusiastic extrapolation of a theory or technique to client populations or problems for which it was never intended, or for which there is little or no reason to suggest its effectiveness (see Goldenberg, 1983). For example, the unquestionable effectiveness of behavior modification with autistic children (Lovaas, 1987) has little bearing on its use with adults struggling with the meaning of life. Likewise, counselors should be appropriately humble in their pronouncements about their theories and techniques, though we don't know of a single counseling approach that hasn't in some form claimed to be the true and best way.

Defining Psychotherapy and Counseling

In light of all this diversity, it is not surprising that academicians, clinicians and researchers have found it difficult to agree on a specific definition of *counseling* and *psychotherapy*. As London (1964) has noted, many find it easier to practice the art and science of people-helping than to describe it.

Still, across theories and techniques, there appear to be some common features. In fact, many theoreticians and researchers today argue that these common factors influence, or even determine, the likelihood of a successful therapeutic outcome. The common techniques that all psychotherapists seem to use (though with differing frequencies) include (1) offering reassurance and support, (2) desensitizing the client to distress, (3) encouraging adaptive functioning and (4) offering understanding and insight (Garfield, 1980). (There is evidence, however, that suggests these factors are not all there is to effective psychotherapy [Jones, Cumming, and Horowitz, 1988].) Understanding these common features can be helpful as one tries to define *counseling.*

We would describe individual counseling or psychotherapy as a dyadic (two-way) interaction between a client who is distressed, and perhaps confused and frightened, and a professional helper whose helping skills are recognized and accepted by the client. The two engage in an ongoing, private, collaborative encounter that is structured as to time, place and overall purpose in a way that informal friendships are not. The relationship is likely to rely heavily on verbal communication of the client's thoughts, feelings, attitudes and behaviors. The client comes to believe in and develop hope from what happens in therapy, in part because the therapist appears to have a theory for understanding and explaining the client's distress as well as having intervention techniques for reducing it. In a supportive atmosphere with an empathetic and caring therapist, the client begins to disclose and re-evaluate feelings and behavior patterns, to understand and accept previously rejected aspects of herself, to take risks, to become more open and honest about herself, to learn new methods of living with self and others and to gain new satisfactions from life. With the client having less need for the psychotherapy, the process is usually terminated by mutual consent with the therapist (adapted from Frank, 1973; Garfield, 1980; and particularly Goldenberg, 1983, pp. 172ff.).

Given that counseling and psychotherapy is so intensely personal, and yet is regarded as a professional rather than personal relationship, how is psychotherapy and counseling different from friendship? As is commonly observed, a lot of good counseling goes on over cups of coffee, in the barber shop, or over a back-yard fence; perhaps a lot more than goes on in any given day in the offices of psychotherapists (Matarazzo and Wiens, 1972).

There are some important differences, though. Ideally, the therapist is able to avoid undue emotional involvement with the client so as to be more objective, allowing the client to more freely communicate his thoughts and feelings (Copans and Singer, 1978). The therapist's personal qualities and the environment she creates encourage risk-taking and facilitate the acquisition of skills and sensitivities that will foster the development of health and wholeness. Perhaps the most important distinction between psychotherapy and friendship is that the former is by definition a one-way relationship emotionally and psychologically—it is the client who is supposed to derive good from the interchange. The growth and healing of the therapist is not the purpose of this limited and purposeful relationship (Korchin, 1976). Friendships, on the other hand, are ideally mutually beneficial emotionally and psychologically, and are not structured intentionally for the benefit of only one of the parties involved. It is obvious, though, that we cannot say that psychotherapists derive no benefit from the therapeutic relationship, as financial and social benefits certainly can and do accrue to the psychotherapist who is effective.

Are Psychotherapy and Counseling Different?

An important and often hotly debated question is how psychotherapy and counseling are to be differentiated (McLemore, 1974). The traditional distinction has been that counseling is done by less comprehensively and intensively trained professionals (e.g., pastors, school guidance counselors) and by paraprofessionals (lay counselors or mental-health volunteers). It is done with less seriously disturbed groups of persons, such as those struggling with decisions of what career to pursue, whether or not to get married, and so forth. Counseling has often been regarded as relying heavily on the giving of wise advice as a major mode of intervention.

Historically, psychotherapy was thought to be more appropriate for "deeper" problems and was most often done by more highly trained and/or certified therapists. The focus was on significant personality change rather than adjustment to situational and life problems. It is sometimes said that psychotherapy attempts significantly to change the personality of clients, often paying less attention to specific current life problems, while counseling works within existing personality structures to help people adjust to the current demands on them.

Although some authors still prefer to make a distinction between counseling and psychotherapy, we have chosen to use the terms interchangeably in this text for two main reasons. The first is that clinical and counseling psychology, which were once substantially different disciplines and arose out of different historical roots, have grown closer together over the last several decades. The distinctions between the two subdisciplines are hard to make out today (see Altmaier, 1985). Perhaps more importantly, we will not make the distinctions here because the very same theories are utilized as guides for the change process by psychotherapists and counselors. Survey textbooks for counseling theories and methods and for psychotherapy theories and methods contain almost identical content. While there can be different emphases in books to the two professional populations, the basic theories are not different.

Structure of the Book

Our perspective in this book is decidedly psychological and "spiritual." In taking this perspective, we do not wish to minimize the clear importance of the biological/physical perspective on mental health, nor of the sociological/sociocultural perspective. But our focus of attention will be on the current interactional psychotherapies. We believe that a careful critique of these approaches is important for the Christian world today.

We also believe that psychologists do not have the final word in understanding humanness, suffering and growth. If anything, psychologists have been saying too much and the populace has been listening too much. It is no wonder that many today describe psychologists as the "secular priests" of our age. We believe that the centrality of religious reflection must be reasserted, as well as the value of philosophical, artistic, literary and other facets of our human ways of knowing.

Psychotherapy has assumed a position of high visibility and importance in many sectors of our American society. Our goal is to come to a new understanding of this field in order that we might more effectively participate in the work that God is doing in and through his church. The needs of contemporary society are creating new and potentially challenging roles for Christians who desire to minister in the name of Christ to a hurting world. We believe strongly that a greater awareness and knowledge of both the assets and liabilities of the major psychotherapy can contribute in a significant way to the larger mission and work of the church.

This book is structured in three parts. In the two introductory chapters we have outlined a summary of our view of what it means to relate or "integrate" the Christian faith with a field like psychology or psychotherapy theory. Chapter one discusses this process in general terms and deals with some important and frequently expressed objections (at least in conservative circles) to such an approach. Since an examination of psychotherapy from a Christian perspective must proceed from a foundational Christian understanding of persons, chapter two focuses specifically on the broad strokes of our Christian view of persons. Having clarified our method and the Christian view of persons, we then proceed into the heart of our appraisal.

Chapters three through fourteen cover a variety of approaches to psychotherapy. The four major paradigms in the field today are the psychodynamic, the cognitive-behavioral, the humanistic and the family approaches. The most important representatives of each of these traditions are examined from our Christian perspective. Each chapter will begin with a summary presentation of each model; the interested reader can get a more exhaustive presentation of these approaches by consulting the volumes suggested "for further reading" at the end of this introduction and at the end of each chapter.

The book will conclude with an examination of how one can profitably draw from more than one approach in elaborating one's approach to counseling (chapter fifteen) and a discussion of what it means to be a Christian counselor (chapter sixteen). Our main premise in these concluding chapters is that there are many ways to counsel Christianly. But it is not and cannot be the case that "anything goes." We hope that our suggestions in these concluding chapters will help the process of "putting it all together" for the reader.

For Further Reading

Corey, G. (1990). *Theory and practice of counseling and psychotherapy* (4th ed.). Monterey, CA: Brooks/Cole.

Corsini, R., and Wedding, D. (Eds.). (1989). *Current psychotherapies* (4th ed.). Itasca, IL: F. E. Peacock.

Prochaska, J. (1984). *Psychotherapy: A transtheoretical analysis* (2nd ed.). Chicago: Dorsey.

These are three of the more readable overviews of psychotherapy and counseling systems. They will be cited in many of the chapters to follow. Keep these titles in mind as possible resources for further reading in each of the therapy chapters to follow.

References

Altmaier, E. (1985). Counseling psychology. In D. Benner (Ed.), *Baker encyclopedia of psychology* (pp. 252-254). Grand Rapids, MI: Baker.

Browning, D. (1987). *Religious thought and the modern psychologies.* Philadelphia: Fortress.

Copans, S., and Singer, T. (1978). *Who's the patient here?* New York: Oxford.

Frank, J. (1973). *Persuasion and healing* (rev. ed.). Baltimore: Johns Hopkins University Press.

Garfield, S. (1980). *Psychotherapy: An eclectic approach.* New York: Wiley-Interscience.

Goldenberg, D. (1983). *Contemporary clinical psychology* (2d ed.). Monterey, CA: Brooks/Cole.

Hurding, R. (1985). *Roots and shoots.* London: Hodder and Stoughton.

Jones, E.; Cumming, J.; and Horowitz, M. (1988). Another look at the nonspecific hypothesis of therapeutic effectiveness. *Journal of Consulting and Clinical Psychology, 56*(1), 48-55.

Korchin, S. (1976). *Modern clinical psychology.* New York: Basic Books.

London, P. (1964). *The modes and morals of psychotherapy.* Washington: Hemisphere.

Lovaas, O. (1987). Behavioral treatment and normal educational and intellectual functioning in young autistic children. *Journal of Consulting and Clinical Psychology, 55*(1), 3-9.

McLemore, C. W. (1974). *Clergyman's psychological handbook.* Grand Rapids, MI: Eerdmans.

Matarazzo, J., and Wiens, A. (1972). *The interview: Research on its anatomy and structure.* Chicago: Aldine.

Strupp, H. and Binder, D. (1984). *Psychotherapy in a new key.* New York: Basic Books.

Vande Kemp, H. (1984). *Psychology and theology in Western thought (1672-1965): A historical and annotated bibliography.* Mill Wood, NY: Kraus.

1

THE INTEGRATION
OF CHRISTIANITY
AND PSYCHOLOGY

✣

*C*hristian counselors and psychotherapists are vitally concerned with understanding and improving human functioning. Our field has arisen in a time when it is painfully
obvious that improving our standard of living and our physical health
docs not guarantee one a sense of personal well-being. Far too many
people are in emotional, mental or spiritual pain.

It is out of a desire to alleviate such suffering that many Christians
today are interested in the mental-health field. There is a strong desire
to enrich Christian ministry by drawing upon the resources of the
developing field of psychology and its related disciplines. What
thoughtful pastor or counselor would not want to use all available
knowledge and techniques to make his or her people-helping as
effective as possible?

But there is also considerable ambivalence about, and outright opposition to, drawing upon the strengths of psychology among conservative Christians. Some describe the field of psychotherapy as "Satanic" or "completely secularized" and "unredeemable." While in graduate school, one of us spoke to Jay Adams, a well-known writer in the field of Christian counseling. Asked if he had any words of guidance for Christians studying psychology, Adams responded, in essence, "Drop out of graduate school. If you want to serve God as a counselor, you can only do so by going to seminary, studying the Word of God rather than the words of men, and becoming a pastor."

Neither one of us took Dr. Adams's advice. We have, however, tried to maintain our foundational commitments to Jesus Christ in our work as psychologists. This book is the fruit of the working-out of that goal. It covers the intellectual aspect of what we believe it means to be a Christian psychologist, mental-health professional, counselor or psychotherapist.

This book is about thinking Christianly about the modern approaches to psychotherapy. We strongly believe that it is not enough simply to pray for clients, or to refrain from discouraging their spiritual sensitivities, or to have high ethical standards.

Every theory or method of people-helping carries with it a system of beliefs, a way of seeing or understanding people: who they are, why they experience what they do, how they can change and what they should be aiming for in life. These theoretical suppositions may or may not conflict with direct assertions of the Christian faith or with more indirect implications of the faith. *It is because we feel that these theories of psychotherapy have often been either summarily dismissed or uncritically embraced by Christians that we have attempted to provide a balanced appraisal of these views from a Christian perspective.*

In this first chapter, we want to set our foundations by grappling with the core of how a religious faith should interact with the seemingly "scientific" field of psychotherapy. Since this task has come to be called "the integration of psychology and Christianity" or of "psychology and theology," the core of this chapter is a discussion of what *integration* means. We will conclude with a discussion of the specific integration methodology we will use to appraise or critique the various approaches to psychotherapy.

How Does Christianity Relate to Psychology?

Being a Christian is easy when faith is contained in a tiny "spiritual" corner of one's life. But the living God has a mind of his own. Not being content with such limits, he often breaks out into the rest of our lives and lays claim to territory we had not yet thought about deeding over to him.

Often he first lays claim to our moral lives, with the result that we discover that being a Christian entails confronting and struggling with our selfishness, jealousy, pettiness or rebelliousness. This often has implications for our vocational lives—such as when we must curtail unethical practices or when we must reassess the values that have energized us for years.

But God can lay claim to our thought lives as well. Do we need to think differently about politics, science, art, philosophy and indeed all areas of life as a result of our faith? Indeed we do. The claims of the gospel are all-inclusive, spanning every dimension of our private and public lives, because Christ has been declared the Lord of all (Col 1:15-20).

But what does it mean for sincere Christians to relate their religious beliefs and faith to an area not overtly or obviously religious or theological? There is a Christian position on the nature of salvation, but is there one, correct Christian position on literary criticism, on thermodynamics, on the fundamental motivations of human personality, or on the nature of depression? Answering this general question on the relation of faith and scholarship and/or science has absorbed the energies of many Christian thinkers over the centuries.

As we mentioned earlier, in conservative Christian psychological circles in the last two decades, this task has come to be called *integration*. We will continue to use this term, even though we regard it as problematic. The word implies that things that don't naturally mix must willfully be brought into connection, to be integrated. This is surely not the vision of faith and scholarship that we are advocating, as we believe that faith and scholarship naturally and inevitably interrelate.

We will not often refer to the integration of *psychology* and *theology*, because this implies that the goal is the fusing together of what are and should properly be two distinct conceptual disciplines. Surely integration is misguided if it is directed at creating a new academic discipline, such as "psychotheology" or "theopsychology."

There are a number of different approaches to understanding the integration of Christian faith with the discipline of psychology.[1] Jones

---

[1]Much of the discussion of these issues of integration has been influenced by recent de-

(1986) has characterized the main three of these as (1) *ethical integration,* the application of religious moral principles to the practice of science (in this case, to the field of psychotherapy); (2) *perspectival integration,* the view that scientific and religious views of any aspect of reality are independent, with the result that scientific/psychological views and religious understandings complement but don't really affect each other (e.g., Jeeves, 1976); or (3) *humanizer or Christianizer of science integration,* an approach that involves the explicit incorporation of religiously based beliefs as the control beliefs that shape the perceptions of facts, theories and methods in social science (e.g., Evans, 1977, 1989; or Van Leeuwen, 1985). We will use this last view as our framework for examining psychotherapy theories.

Thus the task of the Christian scholar is "to study reality in the light of biblical revelation" (Greidanus, 1982, p. 147). Because the claims of the gospel are all-inclusive and the gospel should penetrate to the core of all who claim the name Christian, the task of integration is that of being distinctively Christian in an appropriate and responsible fashion in one's scholarly pursuits.

Destructive and Constructive Modes of Integration

Integration can be performed with either an essentially destructive or constructive stance toward relating the Christian faith to the life of the mind, with very different results.

Many opponents of integration (such as Adams, 1979; Bobgan and Bobgan, 1979, 1987; Hunt, 1987; Hunt and McMahon, 1985; Kilpatrick, 1985) assume a destructive stance toward non-Christian thought in psychology, feeling this is the only viable option. They approach the study of psychotherapy theories with the assumption that each therapy model is a vision of human nature that is in direct competition with the Christian faith. Thus the theory must be disproved by finding

---

velopments in the philosophy of science. We wish to acknowledge immediately that the field of psychotherapy does not conform in all ways to the common meaning of the term *science.* In other words, we are not treating the terms *science, psychology* and *psychotherapy* as equivalent. But we would argue, on the other hand, that the most central issues in relating religious faith to a putatively nonreligious area of scholarship have been illuminated by discussions of the hardest case, that of science, since science is supposedly the human activity with the least to do with other ways of human knowing. What we are after in this section are the lessons that have been learned about the general character of integration from the dialog about relating faith to science generally and the scientific discipline of psychology in particular. These lessons will form the context for our specific discussion of psychotherapy.

critical flaws in it so that it can be rejected. This certainly appeared to be the main method of Adams (1970) in *Competent to Counsel* where he dismissed the theories of Freud and Rogers after showing that the assumptions on which they are built were in places incompatible with Christian faith.

The "destructive" mode of functioning is vital for Christians today. There are times when the best response of the Christian is to "demolish arguments and every pretension that sets itself up against the knowledge of God" (2 Cor 10:5). But we contend that the appropriate time for such apologetic efforts is when the views actually are raised up *against* God. In other words, when the views of romantic humanist Carl Rogers, for instance, are presented *as ultimately satisfying answers to the major questions of life,* the right Christian response is to point out critical flaws in the approach and to reject his views. This is what we appreciate about the critics of psychotherapy—they take matters of faith so seriously that they are zealous to protect the faith from distortion or perversion. Surely it is right and good to have such a concern.

But there is a constructive side of relating Christian faith to human scholarship that is unrecognized by the critics of psychotherapy (from Stoker, 1971). A believer who strives to stand upon a distinctive commitment to the truths of the living Christian faith and build an understanding of persons that is true, broad and more complete can validly engage in a constructive dialog with the psychotherapy theories. The Bible, although containing God-inspired revelation that is infallible and authoritative, is nevertheless of limited scope (i.e., Scripture doesn't cover everything). Thus it is not unfaithful to search out how to reasonably expand our understanding beyond what God chose to reveal in the Bible.

Christian theologians engage in this sort of constructive interaction when they gain enlightenment from secular philosophers for resolving nagging theological problems (e.g., Allen, 1985). In fact, Christian theologians sometimes even derive benefit from the study of other religions! The late Anglican bishop and theologian Stephen Neill (1984) summarized a respected position on this matter: "The Christian faith may learn much from other faiths; but it is universal in its claims; in the end Christ must be acknowledged as Lord of all" (p. 284). We can profitably learn from other thought systems that are not explicitly Christian if we retain the distinctiveness of our faith commitments to Christ in the process.

Yet, even this constructive approach should embody some elements of the more "critical spirit" of the destructive approach. While appropriating what is good in a particular theory, we must also discern the erroneous baggage it carries. Christians who get naively excited about some superficial compatibilities of a psychotherapy theory with the faith and turn off their critical faculties will often be led astray. Christians examining the psychotherapy theories with a constructive motive (as we will try to do) should retain an attitude of careful criticism, and should note problems encountered in order not to fall prey to error. But neither should they summarily dismiss an entire system because of the problems encountered.

In summary, if our goal is, for instance, to show how Skinnerian behaviorism is an inadequate life philosophy, then our stance must be destructive, showing how the Skinnerian metaphysical system is an impoverished and unsatisfying materialistic deception. But if our task is a constructive one of building the truest distinctively Christian view of psychotherapy possible, we would look at and learn from Skinnerian behaviorism, after taking a firm stand on the foundation of the orthodox Christian faith and tradition. This would be especially the case if God had given us a burden for a population where behavioral methods have been shown to be effective.

The Two Stages of Constructive Integration

There are two stages in constructively integrating Christian scholarship with secular thought. The first is *critical evaluation*, where we engage in a dialog with secular thought to find what may be of value in models that are not easily and obviously compatible with a Christian stance. This phase is essentially one of sorting through the approaches of others to retain the good and discharge the bad. We must recognize, however, that the end product of this phase alone will be a rather disjointed conglomeration of useful insights and helpful tidbits that hardly form a powerful and cohesive system of thought.

Critical evaluation needs to be followed up with the second stage, *theory-building*. After Christian scholars have discerned the advantages of secular models with which they have interacted in the critical-evaluation phase, they need to develop new and different theories to incorporate these insights. They need to propose new hypotheses and theories for scholarly examination, ones which bear the imprint of the Christian presuppositions. We would contend that good "integrators" must not only review research, but do research as well. This implies active involvement in the process of doing science, informed by enlightened notions of philosophy of science (Evans, 1989). Good integrators must be committed to evaluation and assessment of their endeavors. Currently, the community of Christian psychologists is weak in this area.

Our hope is to contribute eventually to the theory-building enterprise from a Christian presuppositional base. This is critical because, as we will argue in chapter fifteen, the work of the mental-health field significantly overlaps with the healing and reconciling work of the church. It is vital that Christian scholars develop thoroughly Christian approaches to counseling. The work of the church has suffered from those who promote either hastily "baptized" versions of secular models or superficial renderings of "biblical" models.

While developing a tested Christian psychotherapy theory is our dream, we know that this book represents only the first stage, the critical-evaluation phase, of constructive scholarship. We do not offer a powerful new theory, but hope to encourage the development of thoroughly Christian thinking by offering a critique of existing secular theories. In other words, we believe the place to start is to appraise the thinking of the secular theorists who have gone before us. We believe that carefully listening to them from the perspective of the Christian tradition is an essential first step.

We anticipate that a thoughtful reader will find this book inadequate, in that we will end with finding none of the approaches adequate for understanding human nature, while pointing out many benefits of most of the approaches. We challenge such a thoughtful reader to join in the dialog of developing the comprehensive Christian approach that we all so need!

The Dangers of Integration

The process of integration is complicated in part because in many areas, and especially in psychology, adequate scholarship requires interacting with scientific theories and clinical models that are questionable from a Christian standpoint. We believe that the field of psychology in general, and psychotherapy in particular, can be a "slippery path" for Christians to walk. Why do we regard the study and practice of psychotherapy as a different and riskier endeavor compared to other areas such as forestry, dentistry or physics?

First, many of the major proponents of secular approaches to psychotherapy were (or are) non-Christian thinkers, with many having large axes to grind against religion generally and Christianity in particular. In this field of study, one inevitably encounters direct and indirect "jabs" against the Christian faith. Some of the major psychotherapy systems have been set up as competing "life views" that are religious in scope and content. (In our chapter on Transactional Analysis, for instance, we criticize the "messianic" pronouncements of some of its proponents.) Research has shown that psychologists as a group tend to be socially and politically more liberal and less traditionally religious than the general population (Lovinger, 1984, chap. 1). Thus it is not uncommon to have the type of encounter one of us had when he began his graduate studies: In the opening moments of the first class the professor gave a five-minute diatribe against Christianity!

More often, the antagonism against Christianity is subtle, demonstrated more in the silence about religion in psychology texts, papers and classes than in open antagonism. Kirkpatrick and Spilka (1989), for instance, have documented the almost total neglect of religion as a meaningful human phenomenon in major psychology texts. We are convinced that this conspiracy of silence about things spiritual can be more deadly than open antagonism. Christians are seduced into lowering their guard and being lulled into a secular mindset where faith is neither good nor bad, true nor false, but simply irrelevant. (This has not always been the case. In the first half-century of American psychology—1880-1930—religion was a major area of investigation for the field [Spilka, Hood, and Gorsuch, 1985].)

Second, we believe that psychology in general and psychotherapy in particular are especially prone to subtle "errors" or departures from truth. As theologian Emil Brunner (1946) has suggested, sin biases and distorts not only our moral behavior, but also biases and distorts our thoughts (this is called the noetic effect of sin by theologians). Brunner went on to argue that sin would have a more subtle and profoundly disturbing effect on belief the closer one gets to the "center of existence," where one is struggling with the core truths of human life. Proportionally, the further one is away from this core, the less the influence of sin upon thought. Thus when one is studying the nocturnal migration behavior of the notch-winged red-bellied thrush, one is not grappling with quite the same core issues that one encounters in grappling with the central motivations and needs of human life.

Also, the closer one gets to this core of existence, the further one gets from the "facts" or data of experience and the more one depends on speculation. Data can be seen as a restraint upon speculation (being held accountable to clear and irrefutable facts); in the absence of such close restraint, when the scholar is attempting to propose a grand theory of personality and therapy, one may be freer to drift from the facts into pure speculation and hence error. We are not, however, arguing that science can only function with pure facts or that Christians should only deal with pure facts; actually, contemporary philosophers of science have shown that there really is no such thing as a pure fact. All "facts" rest in a web of interpretation of some kind; it is simply the case that some human assertions are more interpretation than others (see Wolterstorff, 1984).

Third, as we will develop more fully in our last two chapters, we believe that there are some very seductive elements of the profession of psychotherapy that can ensnare the immature or unwise Christian. Psychotherapists take great pride in being in a "people-helping" profession and, in most circles, are accorded respect for their skills and professional activities. One can subtly begin to believe that helping people on an interpersonal dimension is all there is to caring for others. It is all too easy to become enamored with the powerful position one occupies in relation to one's clients and to the financial rewards possible in the field (though these have been greatly exaggerated), which can open the door to great error.

We have offered these points as what we feel are realistic warnings about some dangers of the task of integration. Critics of integration, those we call the "psychology bashers," go beyond these warnings to voice concerns they claim render the entire task of integration illegitimate. We will summarize their core concerns below, showing that every concern has a kernel of truth, but has been exaggerated beyond reasonable and biblical bounds.

Criticisms of the Task of Integration

There are four core arguments that have been advanced against the integration of Christianity and psychotherapy. They are:

1. The assertion that the Bible declares itself (in passages such as 2 Tim 3:16-17 and 2 Pet 1:4; 3:14-18) to be sufficient to meet all human needs. Thus to argue that one could or should study anything other than the Bible (such as psychology) in order to better meet human needs is tantamount to declaring the Holy Scriptures to be inadequate to equip the servant of God and also to rejecting God's own claims for his revelation (Bobgan and Bobgan, 1987, p. 11; Adams 1979, p. 46).

2. The belief that there are two sources of counsel in this world, God and Satan. Further, "The Bible's position is that all counsel that is

not revelational (biblical), or based upon God's revelation, is Satanic" (Adams, 1979, p. 4; see also Bobgan and Bobgan, 1987, p. 32). Thus to decide to listen to and learn from a non-Christian in an area where God has revealed his will (i.e., in psychology) is to "walk in the counsel of the wicked" (Ps 1:1).

3. The argument that psychology is bad science. If we are to accept truth from any quarter, surely (it is argued) it should only be on the assurance that we are accepting true truth, real truth. Surely the vain speculations and philosophies of mere humans (2 Cor 10:5) do not merit a place in our beliefs alongside God's Word (Swaggart, 1986, pp. 6-7; Bobgan and Bobgan, 1987, pp. 29-30).

4. The argument that integration is amalgamation or syncretism. This argument of the anti-integrationists, simply put, is that "combining Christianity and psychotherapy is joining two or more religious systems" (Bobgan and Bobgan, 1987, p. 23). This position assumes first that psychotherapy systems are religious systems ("Psychotherapy . . . is not only a substitute method of helping troubled souls, it is a surrogate religion" [Bobgan & Bobgan, 1987, p. 15]) and second that "the goal is to integrate or amalgamate the truth of Scripture with the so-called truth of psychology to produce a hybrid that is superior to the truth of each" (Bobgan & Bobgan, 1987, p. 33).

We cannot take the time here thoroughly to refute all of these arguments, but we will summarize our responses.

First, we affirm the sufficiency of the Bible. At the same time, we must remember that it is God, not the Bible itself, who is declared to be *all*-sufficient, to provide all that pertains unto life. Christians should courageously claim and proclaim whatever authority and power that the Scriptures declare for themselves—no less and no more.

On this basis, let us look at 2 Timothy 3:16-17: "All Scripture is God-breathed and is useful for teaching, rebuking, correcting and training in righteousness, so that the man of God may be thoroughly equipped for every good work."

Note that, while inspired ("God-breathed"), Scripture is not declared to be the only and all-sufficient source for every word ever needed anytime by anyone for any purpose related to human need; rather, it is called "useful." In other words, we do not look to Scripture for guidance for plumbing; nor should we for distinguishing schizophrenia from a character disorder. Also, Paul teaches that Scripture is essential to the forming of our core character, which, if shaped and molded by God's living Word, can prepare us for beginning any good work—though the accomplishment of that good work may well also depend on the mastery of other key skills.

The Bible is thus an essential foundation for a Christian approach to psychotherapy and is very relevant to this field. Nevertheless, while the Bible provides us with life's most important and ultimate answers as well as the starting points for knowledge of the human condition, it is not an all-sufficient guide for the discipline of counseling. The Bible is inspired and precious, but it is also a revelation of limited scope, the main concern of which is religious in its presentation of God's redemptive plan for his people and the great doctrines of the faith. The Bible doesn't claim to reveal everything that human beings might want to know.

Second, all truth is from above (Jas 1:17). Correspondingly, Satan is the father of lies, ranging from out-and-out fabrications (e.g., atheism) to lies that are subtle twists and perversions of the truth (e.g., cults based on distortions of scriptural revelation).

In addition, people are fallible, fallen and finite. Thus our theologies, our confessional heritages, our Bible teachings (not the Bible itself) and our prayers are filled with subtle and sometimes blatant falsehoods and imperfections. We are not right in all that we believe, though by God's grace through the Holy Spirit and the influence of the body of Christ, we are guided into sufficient truth to be able to actually relate to God and understand something of his nature, and to even be able to proclaim our faith as the truth.

The flip side is that Christians are not the sole possessors of truth. Just as the rain falls on the just and the unjust, so too does truth, by the process that theologians call God's common grace. Romans 1 speaks of God even revealing central truths about his nature to unbelievers (v. 19). John Calvin, the courageous defender and expositor of the Scriptures who was so central to the Protestant Reformation, stated it well when he said, "The human mind, however much fallen and perverted from its original integrity, is still adorned and invested with admirable gifts from its Creator. . . . We will be careful . . . not to reject or condemn truth wherever it appears" (*Institutes of the Christian Religion,* 2.2.15).

There are two sources of counsel in the world, God's and Satan's, and we should follow God's counsel. But God's counsel is not always synonymous with the counsel of a Christian, and Satan's counsel is not synonymous with the counsel of a non-Christian. Rather, we would identify God's counsel with the truth, and Satan's counsel with falsehood. Thus sometimes a so-called secular approach to understanding a given topic may be nearer the truth than the distorted understanding of a particular Christian person. If we understand God's counsel to be truth, we will be committed to pursuing truth wherever we find it. And we may sometimes find it in the careful and insightful writings of unbelievers.

Third, responding to the charge that psychology is "bad science," let us first cut to the heart of this argument. We deny the fundamental premise that Christians can only derive knowledge from two sources, authoritative revelation or science. It is the Bible that is infallible, not the human beings who read it. Thus, while the Scriptures are infallible, any given human interpretation of the Bible may be fraught with problems. Further, science is a human activity, and since humans are fallible, science is fallible.

Revelation merits the most prominent place among human ways of knowing, and science also merits a place as well. In fact, properly understood, all human routes to knowledge deserve an appropriate place in the cognitive life of the believer. Authority (including revelation), experience, intuition and reason—the four commonly described ways of knowing—all have legitimate roles to play (Foster and Ledbetter, 1987). On the basis of the foregoing, then, we reject the simplistic assertion that Christians need heed only authoritative revelation and science. If only life were that simple!

The second part of the argument is the assertion that psychology is "bad science." This argument is usually pressed on the basis of misrepresentative quotations and misperceptions. A major historian and philosopher of psychology, Sigmund Koch, is often quoted correctly by psychology-bashers regarding his conclusions that "psychology cannot be a coherent science" (Koch, 1981, p. 262), but this statement is taken to mean that psychological research is incoherent or that psychologists are incoherent. What Koch was actually arguing, however, was that psychology covers too broad a span of reality (from the neurons of insects to the psychology of human communities) to ever have one model of scientific methodology govern all areas of study. Thus if the requirement for coherence as a science is a uniform methodology, then psychology will never be a coherent science. We must use different methods to study neurons and multiple personalities.

Koch is also often quoted as saying that some areas of psychological inquiry "cannot be properly labeled scientific" (quoted in Bobgan and Bobgan, 1979, p. 44). This is interpreted by the Bobgans and others as asserting that some areas of psychology are nonsense, fiction or fantasy.

Far from it! Koch was arguing that investigators in some areas of study should *properly* distance themselves from the rigidly empirical methods traditionally associated with "hard science," such as physics and chemistry, if these investigators are to do justice to their areas of study. In these areas, psychologists may properly use methods traditionally associated with history, anthropology or even literary scholarship in their pursuit of truth. In other words, being "nonscientific" in some areas of psychology is a virtue to Koch, and the area of psychotherapy theory is probably one such area (see also Evans, 1989; Van Leeuwen, 1985). Koch would argue, and we would agree, that psychology is an amazingly broad discipline that cannot be easily defined by one model of science, and that suffers from confusion and lack of clarity regarding standards for properly scientific methodology (see Koch and Leary, 1985).

In summary, then, psychology is not necessarily "bad science." In any case, Christians should carefully look at any way of knowing that helps us better understand the human condition, even if that way of knowing does not conform to some narrow definition of "good science." On the other hand, we must acknowledge that some areas of psychotherapy are neither good science nor good reason, good intuition or anything else; they are rather examples of slipshod argumentation and speculation. Some psychology, and some psychotherapy writings, are simply good-for-nothing. A similar conclusion might be drawn about some writings by psychology-bashers, and perhaps even about some of what passes for Christian theology!

Finally, in response to the charge of syncretism, the key assertion here is that integration is the blending of psychology and Christianity. We simply reject that this is the case. We know of no major writers in the area of integration whose "recipe" for integration is to "take equal parts psychology and Christianity and mix in a blender until all you have left is a sticky, unappealing mishmash of beliefs." We will admit that some Christian psychologists doing integration have not been above sloppy biblical interpretation and farfetched theological speculation.

The critics of integration do not have to look far to find examples of unsubstantiated clinical speculation, sloppy logic, careless biblical interpretation, theological naivete or feideism, and unbridled self-promotion. In many of the chapters to follow where we examine the merits and drawbacks of therapy theories, we will be forced to criticize statements made by Christian mental health professionals regarding the merits of different approaches. Christians doing integration have deserved much of the criticism they have received from the psychology-bashers.

Methodology for Christian Appraisal

As we have seen, what we need in evaluating models of counseling and psychotherapy is clear thinking about our presuppositions, our views of humanity, and our moral standards and how to apply these to real situations. While we must be careful about being overly dogmatic and rigid, good evaluation is brutally honest about the realities of the human condition in all their tragic complexities.

We need guidelines on how to think clearly, critically and courageously. The following are the major guidelines we intend to pursue in critiquing the theories in this book.[2]

Philosophical Assumptions
We begin with the vitally important task of looking carefully at the philosophical assumptions or presuppositions that undergird an approach to counseling. Ideas about human character and personality do not arise in a philosophical vacuum. As Browning (1987, p. 95) has said, "the modern psychologies function within larger contexts of meaning about the way the world is." The approaches we will examine vary widely in terms of how explicitly the influence of philosophical assumptions are acknowledged. Behavior modification has been an easy target for Christian critique over the years because Skinner has been so transparent about his assumptions (see chapter six). The originators of some other approaches have not been so explicit, resulting in the need for careful work in unearthing their presuppositions.

---

[2]Our colleague at Wheaton, Robert C. Roberts, has derived independently criteria for the evaluation of therapy systems which are similar to our own. Roberts (1985, 1987) has argued for what he calls the "virtues approach to integration." He starts the examination of an approach to psychotherapy by looking at the virtues that the approach strives to cultivate. This is similar to our criterion of a model's vision of ideal humanness or wholeness. Roberts argues in turn that each virtue is embedded in a network of assumptions that he calls the "grammar" of the virtue (alluding to the way that verbal ideas are nested in linguistic grammar systems). Minimally, this grammar system includes a concept of human nature (similar to our criterion of the view of personality), an explanation for the failure to achieve virtue (a theory of abnormality), and some ideas for how change toward the development of the virtues of the system can be facilitated (prescriptions for change).

No common philosophy unifies the many diverse and varied approaches. Each has a different view of reality, truth, purpose, personhood and the like. These assumptions and presuppositions are of crucial importance for the Christian academician, clinician or researcher, especially those that pertain to our notions of personhood and philosophy of science. These convictions directly or indirectly affect every phase of science and the people-helping process. In short, theory significantly affects practice whether or not this relationship is acknowledged.

It might be helpful for the reader to get some sense for the history or "roots" of the various theories and models of psychotherapy. The roots of the four major traditions—humanistic-existential, dynamic, cognitive-behavioral and family systems—are deeply imbedded in certain world views and control beliefs, especially about the nature of persons and the way good science proceeds. In figure 1.1, the reader can see a very brief outline of the "parentage" of the major psychotherapy systems.

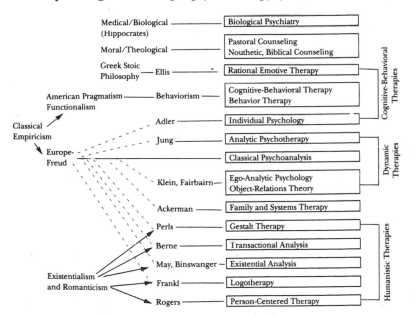

Figure 1.1 From S. Jones (1986), "Theories and Principles of Counseling" extension course, Wheaton College Graduate School Extension Studies

A distinctively Christian approach to counseling and psychotherapy will have theological and philosophical underpinnings compatible with Christian faith; this will be most clearly reflected in its notions of personhood and philosophy of science. It will look at the task of the psychotherapist from both eternal and temporal perspectives and will fully acknowledge the reality of the supernatural. Sin and the consequences of the Fall will be taken seriously, as well as the reality of human and supernatural evil.

Model of Personality

We must also examine the personality theory or model of humanity upon which an approach is built. Every theory must build upon an understanding of what determines human character and action, and these theories vary widely in terms of their understandings of human motivations, personality structure and core characteristics. As Tjeltveit (1989, p. 1) said, "Models of human beings—explicit or implicit, complex or simple, internally consistent or inconsistent, . . . open to change or static—shape society, the actions of every human being, and every individual's worldview. . . . [They are] part of every psychotherapy session."

Our understanding of persons and personhood must be grounded in the words of Scripture and in Christian experience in the context of confessional communities (Farnsworth, 1985). It is inadequate to look to the Scriptures and/or religious experience alone to develop one's personality theory. The purpose of Scripture is to present a record of God's redemptive dealings with persons throughout history, to present a plan of salvation and discipleship, and to provide us with the knowledge necessary to guide us into productive life. The Scriptures were never intended to be a textbook of all psychological conditions and disorders, although they should anchor and condition our metaphysical and ontological assertions about persons and provide a practical foundation for moral guidance.

So at the start we begin by asking if the theory of personality is compatible with Christian truth. Further, is it clear yet comprehensive? Does it do justice to what is known about human behavior and experience, and does it reflect diverse gender, socioeconomic and sociocultural contexts? Is the personality theory concerned with all dimensions of human behavior and experience—cognitive, affective, interpersonal, spiritual, physical and behavioral? (Counseling methodologies often tend to focus on one dimension of human experience, giving other dimensions short shrift. Christians, in particular, should expect their theory or theories to respect and acknowledge all dimensions of personhood, and not overemphasize any dimension of human experience.) Is the theory elegant and parsimonious, given the complexity of the subject? Does it generate serious research and study? Does it directly inform clinical practice and theory? In short, is the theory valuable at multiple levels of inquiry (i.e., theory, research and practice)?

Model of Abnormality

We should look carefully at a theory's core understanding of *human abnormality*. To discuss a theory of personality is usually to presume that one also understands deviations from normal personality development. To suggest how one can change human action is to presume that one has some understanding as to the processes that explain how it came to need changing in the first place.

How compatible is the view of abnormality with the Christian faith? Are core concepts like human accountability, responsibility and sinfulness compatible with the model? Is faith itself classified as a pathology? Are the virtues that Christians are to cultivate and express viewed as abnormal? Is there a balance between personal causation of distress ("because of my sins") and system causation of distress ("because I live in a fallen world")?

Model of Health

Related to the last point, every theory seems to have a *vision of human wholeness* which complements its view of abnormality. To discuss abnormality and the change one intends to work in the client's life is to presume a direction that one is going to move in, a goal one is moving toward. Even theoreticians who are aiming to be "value neutral" by saying that they are just trying to decrease pain are working from an implicit hypothesis that minimizing pain is part of human wholeness.

The goals and views of normalcy within a particular psychotherapy tradition should be closely examined. What does the theory propose the truly healthy individual will be like? What are the explicit and implicit notions of maturity, wellness, holiness, wholeness or health being advocated? Methods of therapy are often intimately intertwined with the theory of normalcy of the approach. For instance, a therapist may use emotional catharsis ("discharge") techniques because the therapist's view of normalcy includes emotional expressiveness as one of the criteria for health. Further, unless theorists or therapists are clear about where they are headed, therapy tends to become directionless and unfocused, heavily affected by whatever popular technique the change-agent has been exposed to lately. Such goals need to be explicit from the start. Ideally, these should be communicated to clients at the beginning of therapy.

Model of Psychotherapy

Next we need to look at the methods of change themselves to gauge their essential credibility. Some proposed change methods are quite similar to intuitive or lay understandings of the process of growth (e.g., the rational discourse of Rational Emotive Therapy [chapter seven] or the loving support of Person-Centered Therapy [chapter ten]), while others are so radically different as to require substantial support merely to make them look credible (e.g., the role-playing of Psychodrama or the "body-work" of Bioenergetics, which we will not be able to cover in this book). Do the counseling processes and techniques provide real resources for healing? Are the techniques proposed ethical and moral? One critical question is the ethical context of healing: Is that context the church or the mental-health profession? Is the clinician seen as a value-neutral technician or as a disciple, shaped by the rituals and discernment of Christian community (see Dueck, 1986)?

As Tan (1987) has observed, a distinctively Christian approach to people-helping will emphasize the primacy of warm, empathic and genuine relationships, stressing the relevance of *agape* love. Such compassion should extend to the clinician's personal and professional relationships with others. A distinctively Christian approach will take the role of the Holy Spirit seriously, as well as the many spiritual resources available to the Christian counselor (see chapters fifteen and sixteen). Large contextual factors like familial, societal, religious and cultural influences will not be minimized, and appropriate community and church resources will be mobilized when necessary. We have to be more than pragmatists (using whatever works), being sure to employ only those techniques that are consistent with biblical truth and the wisdom and discernment of the confessional community.

Demonstrated Effectiveness

Finally, as a matter of Christian stewardship, it behooves us to look not merely at the five more "conceptual" criteria listed above, but also at what the scientific research says about the effectiveness of a particular approach. We should add that we are using *scientific* in the broad sense discussed earlier, which we take to include the standard empirical methods of traditional American psychology and those nontraditional methods that are variously known as phenomenological, "human-science" or humanistic (Evans, 1989; Farnsworth, 1985; Van Leeuwen, 1985).

Research literature on the empirical evaluation of psychotherapy and counseling is emerging and deserves the serious consideration of the would-be Christian people-helper. A full-fledged literature review of effectiveness studies for every approach is surely beyond the scope of the present volume, but we will try at least to provide the reader with a feel for the state of the empirical literature on each major approach today. Because solid data of any kind are often missing for many of the approaches, we will put our discussion of demonstrated effectiveness in one section in chapter fifteen. The other five criteria will be discussed in each chapter.

Conclusion

The business of evaluating psychotherapy theories is very complex, and healthy (but not paranoiac) caution is in order. We are concerned that the reader recognizes that what at first seem like clear compatibilities between faith and a particular theory can hide radical incompatibilities. On the other hand, superficial incompatibilities can often distract the Christian learner from perceiving what are actually some rather deep and striking areas of compatibility between the faith and the theory.

To give two quick examples: On the one hand, many Christians have uncritically accepted Rogerian person-centered therapy (chapter ten) because its techniques of counseling superficially resemble one understanding of *agape* love, thus missing the deeper system of thought of Rogers which is radically incommensurate with the faith. On the other hand, the offensive atheism and hedonism of Albert Ellis, the founder of Rational Emotive Therapy (chapter seven), have led many Christians to an overly quick dismissal of the theory, thus causing them to miss some of the areas of compatibility between RET and Christianity in the understanding of the place of rationality in human emotional life. We would urge all readers to bear with us in our attempt to engage each of these theories in a thoughtful and deep fashion. Only sustained analysis can save us from triteness.

Evaluating the merit of a particular approach boils down to a choice. We need the "facts" to make a decision. We need to face the reality that all facts are interpreted facts, and that most facts are felt facts (Smedes, 1987). Proponents of particular approaches care passionately about the validity of their positions. Not only do we need to see the facts for ourselves, but we need to get to know how others see the facts, and we can only get that sense by reading their writings or by talking to them directly. If we want the whole truth, we will let others tell us why they see what we don't see and why they hear what we don't hear. Good evaluation will be done in the context of dialog and community.

But genuine listening is risky. If we really listen, we may have to adjust our view of the facts, revise our sense of their relevance, qualify our interpretations of them and modulate our feelings about them. But the truth about facts is that if we look at them through our own eyes only, we may miss their meanings. And if we look at them with other people, people we respect and listen to, we might have a better sense of seeing them right and a much better chance of making good judgments about their relevance and appropriateness (Smedes, 1987, pp. 40-42).

For Further Reading

Browning, D. (1987). *Religious thought and the modern psychologies*. Philadelphia: Fortress.

Though written from a nonevangelical Christian perspective and requiring much theological sophistication to fully digest, this is an extremely valuable work exploring the religious implications of most of the major therapy systems we will examine in this book.

Collins, G. (1989). *Can you trust psychology?* Downers Grove, IL: InterVarsity Press.

A readable and reasonable response to the "psychology-bashers."

Evans, C. (1977). *Preserving the person*. Grand Rapids, MI: Baker.

Evans, C. (1989). *Wisdom and humanness in psychology*. Grand Rapids, MI: Baker.

The work of Evans in exploring the shape of a Christian understanding of the social sciences is the most understandable and important available for the evangelical Christian reader.

Hurding, R. (1985). *Roots and shoots*. London: Hodder and Stoughton.

This is an excellent work attempting the same sort of appraisal we engage in here. Hurding's book differs in offering somewhat more condensed critiques of a slightly more abbreviated list of therapies. We will offer much more coverage of pastoral and "Christian" counseling approaches. *Roots and shoots* was published in Britain, and we will quote throughout from the British edition. The book was more recently published in the U.S. under the title *The tree of healing* (Zondervan).

Jones, S. (Ed.). (1986). *Psychology and the Christian faith*. Grand Rapids, MI: Baker.

A readable sampler of ways to approach integration in the various subdisciplines of academic psychology.

Koch, S., & Leary, D. (Eds.). (1985). *A century of psychology as science.* New York: McGraw-Hill.

A massive and challenging overview of the status of psychology as a discipline. Probably not readable by the nonpsychologist, it has inadequate coverage of applied psychology, especially the area of psychotherapy.

Van Leeuwen, M. (1985). *The person in psychology.* Grand Rapids, MI: Eerdmans.

One of the more comprehensive attempts to critique the range of the paradigms of contemporary psychology (e.g., behaviorism, cognitive psychology, etc.) from a Christian perspective. Essential reading.

Wolterstorff, N. (1984). *Reason within the bounds of religion* (2d ed.). Grand Rapids, MI: Eerdmans.

A readable and intriguing discussion of contemporary philosophy of science from a Christian perspective.

References

Adams, J. (1970). *Competent to counsel.* Grand Rapids, MI: Baker.

Adams, J. (1979). *More than redemption: A theology of Christian counseling.* Phillipsburg, NJ: Presbyterian and Reformed.

Allen, D. (1985). *Philosophy for understanding theology.* Atlanta: John Knox.

Bobgan, M. and Bobgan, D. (1979). *The psychological way/The spiritual way.* Minneapolis: Bethany Fellowship.

Bobgan, M. and Bobgan, D. (1987). *Psychoheresy: The psychological seduction of Christianity.* Santa Barbara, CA: Eastgate.

Browning, D. (1987). *Religious thought and the modern psychologies.* Philadelphia: Fortress.

Brunner, E. (1946). *Revelation and reason* (O. Wyon, Trans.). Philadelphia: Westminster. (Original work published 1938).

Dueck, A. (1986, January). The ethical context of healing. Paper presented at the J. G. Finch lecture series at Fuller Theological Seminary, Pasadena, CA.

Evans, C. (1977). *Preserving the person.* Grand Rapids, MI: Baker.

Evans, C. (1989). *Wisdom and humanness in psychology.* Grand Rapids, MI: Baker.

Farnsworth, K. (1985). *Whole-hearted integration.* Grand Rapids, MI: Baker.

Foster, J., and Ledbetter, M. (1987). Christian anti-psychology and the scientific method. *Journal of Psychology and Theology, 15,* 10-18.

Greidanus, S. (1982). The use of the Bible in Christian scholarship. *Christian Scholar's Review, 11,* 138-147.

Hunt, D. (1987). *Beyond seduction.* Eugene, OR: Harvest House

Hunt, D. and McMahon, T. (1985). *The seduction of Christianity.* Eugene, OR: Harvest House.

Jeeves, M. (1976). *Psychology and Christianity: The view both ways.* Downers Grove, IL: InterVarsity Press.

Jones, S. (1986). Relating the Christian faith to psychology. In S. Jones (Ed.), *Psychology and the Christian faith* (pp. 15-34). Grand Rapids, MI: Baker.

Kilpatrick, W. (1985). *The emperor's new clothes: The naked truth about the new psychology.* Westchester, IL: Crossway.

Kirkpatrick, L., and Spilka, B. (1989, August). Treatment of religion in psychology texts. Paper presented at the annual convention of the American Psychological Association, New Orleans.

Koch, S. (1981). The nature and limits of psychological knowledge. *American Psychologist, 36,* 257-269.

Koch, S., and Leary, D. (Eds.) (1985). *A century of psychology as science.* New York: McGraw-Hill.

Lovinger, R. (1984). *Working with religious issues in therapy.* New York: Jason Aronson.

Neill, S. (1984). *Christian faith and other faiths.* Downers Grove, IL.: InterVarsity Press.

Roberts, R. (1985). Carl Rogers and Christian virtues. *Journal of Psychology and Theology, 13*(4), 263-273.

Roberts, R. (1987). Psychotherapeutic virtues and the grammar of faith. *Journal of Psychology and Theology, 15*(3), 191-204.

Smedes, L. (1987). *Choices.* New York: Harper & Row.

Spilka, B., Hood, R., and Gorsuch, R. (1985). *The psychology of religion: An empirical approach.* Englewood Cliffs, NJ: Prentice-Hall.

Stoker, H. (1971). Reconnoitering the theory of knowledge of Professor Dr. Cornelius Van Til. In E. Geehan (Ed.), *Jerusalem and Athens* (pp. 25-70). Phillipsburg, NJ: Presbyterian and Reformed.

Swaggart, J. (1986, November). Christian psychology? *The Evangelist,* pp. 4-9.

Tan, S. (1987). Intrapersonal integration: The servant's spirituality. *Journal of Psychology and Christianity, 6,* 34-39.

Tjeltveit, A. (1989). The ubiquity of models of human beings in psychotherapy: The need for rigorous reflection. *Psychotherapy, 26,* 1-10.

Van Leeuwen, M. (1985). *The person in psychology.* Grand Rapids, MI: Eerdmans.

Wolterstorff, N. (1984). *Reason within the bounds of religion* (2d ed.). Grand Rapids, MI: Eerdmans.

2

A CHRISTIAN VIEW
OF PERSONS

✤

*O*ur task is to critically evaluate the major secular psychotherapy theories in light of Christian revelation and faith.
But what is the Christian view by which we are going to
grade the secular psychotherapy approaches? Is there a Christian
personality theory hidden in the pages of the Bible?

The purpose of this chapter is to highlight what we believe the
Christian Scriptures assert about human beings, as these beliefs will be
the backdrop or plumbline against which all else will be evaluated. It
is our contention that the Scriptures and Christian theology do not
teach a theory of personality as understood by contemporary psychology. These sources teach us a great deal more than that. They teach us
the way to eternal fellowship with the Creator-God and everything we
need to know about ourselves and our predicament to obtain salvation
and to grow as persons. They record God's redemptive dealings with

his people throughout the ages. But they teach us less than we need to know to understand why individual persons have the characteristics they do (for instance, why a particular person struggles with obsessive tendencies or another is blessed with incredible strength of character). And they teach us less than we need to know in order to help many individuals move beyond the pain and confusion they feel.

What the Scripture does teach about persons lacks the specificity and precision necessary for qualifying either as a formal scientific theory of personality or as a clinically useful heuristic model for understanding personality functioning. ("The general judgment of theologians has been that the Bible gives us no scientific teaching on man, no anthropology, which should or could concur with scientific anthropological research on man" [Berkouwer, 1962, p. 194]). Even in ancient times, pastoral theologians found it necessary to develop models for understanding personality that were built upon, but went beyond, scriptural revelation in order to develop guidelines for pastoral care. In doing this, Christian pastoral thinkers have frequently turned to contemporary nonreligious scholarship about dimensions of personhood to construct more complete models of ministry (Clebsch and Jaekle, 1975; Oden, 1984). While some seem to regard this as heresy (e.g., Adams, 1979), as discussed in the previous chapter, we regard this as a strength as long as the distinctives of the Christian faith are preserved and given pre-eminence.

But if we are not searching for a personality theory, what in the Scriptures is it reasonable to expect to find? In brief, we believe that our foray into theological and biblical anthropology will give us the essential foundation for a more true and more complete understanding of persons by giving us "control beliefs" (Wolterstorff, 1984) or presuppositions. These control beliefs are the "givens," the assumptions that control or shape all other thought. We can then use these control beliefs to build a theory of personality with greater Christian distinctiveness.

Before embarking on this task, we would endorse a number of basic hermeneutical principles (from Greidanus, 1982) that undergird orthodox biblical interpretation.

First, since God is the Creator, there can be no ultimate conflict between knowledge from special revelation (what the Bible says) and creation (also known as "general revelation," what nature says). There can and often has been, however, conflict between interpretations of special revelation and interpretations about the facts of the created order. In such cases of conflict, the interpretation of either special or general revelation can be wrong, or possibly both.

Second, "the Bible is the Word of God addressed to the heart of man" (Greidanus, 1982, p. 140). Hence a sincere submission to the Lord who speaks through the Scriptures and is revealed in them enables us to see reality, however imperfectly, from God's perspective, the only proper perspective. Special revelation is *special*, and that is why Calvin suggested that the Scriptures can function as spectacles that correct our vision of God's creation when sin has distorted our understanding.

Third, the Bible is a historical book written first of all to a particular people in their culture at a certain time, answering their questions and meeting their needs. Thus the biblical message to us today cannot be understood properly without understanding its historical and cultural context. With a proper appreciation of these factors, we can confidently expect that we will hear God's voice speak to us through his words to ancient peoples.

Fourth, the Bible was written in nonscientific, everyday language that sometimes used (or assumed) commonly held "scientific" concepts of that time but which we now know to be false. But this does not mean that the Bible teaches those concepts. For example, Exodus 20:4 ("You shall not make for yourself a graven image, or any likeness of anything . . . that is in the water under the earth" [RSV]) reflects the ancient cosmological belief that the earth was flat and floated on water, but the Bible does not teach authoritatively that view; rather, the purpose of the verse is to prohibit idolatry and not to teach a cosmology.

Similarly, many of the verses often cited as teaching formal psychological concepts cannot responsibly be interpreted in that way. The folk psychology in the verses is merely a vehicle by which to teach the main point of the verse. For instance, Paul's use of "spirit, soul and body" (1 Thess 5:23) connotes the whole person, every aspect of the believer, and cannot necessarily be taken to mean that Paul was authoritatively teaching a tripartite (three-part) view of personhood (see further discussion of this matter later in this chapter). The danger here is expecting from Scripture something God did not intend to provide.

Fifth, biblical passages must be understood in light of the author's intention or meaning, and in the light of the totality of the biblical revelation. It is especially important to remember that obscure or unclear biblical passages are to be interpreted in light of clearer, more unequivocal passages, and deference must be given to the cumulative weight of many passages over one seemingly clear text if there is apparent conflict.

Humanity in Its Created State

Intelligibility, Meaning and Value

"In the beginning God created the heavens and the earth" (Gen 1:1). The historic Christian doctrine of creation *ex nihilo* (creation from or out of nothing) is derived from the first chapters of the Bible and has assumed a place of priority in all the historic creeds (e.g., the Apostles Creed: "I believe in God, the Father Almighty, Maker of heaven and earth").

The first biblical information we have about humanity occurs later in the creation story, where we find, "Then God said, 'Let us make man in our image, in our likeness'" (Gen 1:26). Humanity and the entire created order were made by the intentional actions of the Sovereign God of the universe. Far from being the chance products of blind causal forces, with lives that are thereby unintelligible and meaningless, we were created intentionally. Our understanding of ourselves begins here. Our basic identity will remain confused until we see ourselves as part of God's creation.

In his book *Maker of Heaven and Earth*, theologian Langdon Gilkey (1985) examines the myriad implications of this central Christian doctrine. Prominent among these implications is the notion that being created, rather than having simply come to exist by naturalistic processes operating without purpose or meaning, is the foundation of intelligibility and meaning for our lives. Our lives are intelligible precisely because we can have faith that our existence is the result of the actions of an all-knowing, intelligent God. Our lives have meaning because God meant or intended for us to be. His plan or purpose remains sovereign throughout history.

In addition to having meaning we accrue *value* in at least three ways. First, being the creation of the all-perfect Lord imputes value to us in the same way that all creation has value; we are the work of the Lord, and all of God's works have value. It would be contempt toward God to suggest that any of his creations are without value (as is said in our vernacular, "God doesn't make junk"). Second, we have special value in that we are the only aspect of creation specifically said to be created in God's "image." Finally, and getting a bit ahead of ourselves, we have value because God chose to make his Son a human like us and to die for us. Surely, God would not waste the life of his dear Son on beings that are without value, and we further gained value through the acts of the Incarnation, the death and resurrection of Jesus Christ. Thus God's mighty works both give us value and show that we had and have value. These realities form the basis for our psychological perception of value.

As one final implication of being created, we should note that if we were made by God out of nothing, then *we are different from and separate from God*, though we are continually dependent on him as the ultimate ground of our very being. As Gilkey (1985, pp. 58ff.) has noted, it is an undeniable implication of Eastern monism (the doctrine that the universe is of one indivisible essence; everything is God) and pantheism (God is everything) that humans are part of God and thus finiteness (being less than God) and individuality (being a creature separate from others, including God) are illusory and evil.

For Christians, separateness from God and others is real and good. We belong in relationship to God and others, but this relatedness is not meant to consume and destroy our separateness. Union with God is a theme of Scripture, but nowhere are we taught that we cease being ourselves in the process of this union. As in marriage two persons become one without the loss of their personal identities, so it is with our union with God. The image of heaven as the time when we will merge and become one with the Godhead, losing our individuality in the process, is a perversion of the Christian view of heaven; it is based on non-Christian Eastern religions. Such thinking is pervasive in many of the "New Age" views so common today.

The Image of God

What does it mean to be created "in God's image"? This complex question has been the subject of some of the most diverse biblical and theological study in the history of Christian thought.

As summarized by McDonald (1982) and Plantinga (1988), the concept has, over time, been interpreted to mean many different things, and interpreters have taken fundamentally different approaches to the problem. Some have taken the approach of asserting that we are the image of God because what we are mirrors what God is. A widely argued version of this tradition is the argument that we image God in being *personal beings*. Another widely accepted version of this view is the notion that we have an immaterial, spiritual soul and thus are at our core spiritual beings like God.   ·

Others emphasize the work or activities that we can perform that mirror God's work. The most common form of this view focuses on the fact that we exercise responsible dominion over a portion of the universe, just as God exercises dominion over it all. God rules over all, and has designated persons to rule over the earthly component of his kingdom as his stewards (Gen 1:28) as a direct reflection of his own activity. Another example would be the assertion that we image God when we manifest his perfect virtues. In so doing we function in the world as a manifestation of God's character just as his Son, the perfect image of the Father, did and does.

An even broader presentation of this idea would say that we image God in living out the gospel message in our lives, through suffering as well as triumph. Authentic life is to image God ever more closely by becoming like Jesus Christ, the expressed image of Father. In our suffering we are called to be open to the wounds of the world. We were created with the capacity to feel the pain of the other, and to "weep with those who weep." In some profound and mysterious way we have the potential to be wounded by the wounds of others and thus reflect the work of God (adapted from Wolterstorff, 1987, p. 86).

Yet another approach points out that we image or mirror God in our possession of certain distinct capacities that set us off from the rest of creation. The classic Reformed teaching that human beings image God in their capacity for *rationality and morality* is an example (these two capacities will be very important as we engage in our dialog with the therapy theories). Another version is that of Jewett (1975) who followed the lead of Barth in locating the image of God in being diversified genders, male and female (Gen 1:27), who can relate to and become one with one another; in this union, we can bear fruit (pro-creation) in a reflection of God's creativity which flows from his innerrelatedness. In exercising this capacity for relatedness, we mirror God's diversity within unity as manifested within the Godhead.

As McDonald (1982) and Plantinga (1988) have argued, it seems judicious at this time to not fight for an exclusive meaning of the image, but rather to conclude that being created in the image of God means all this and more. As Plantinga put it, "The image of God may plausibly be said to consist . . . in the whole set of these (and many more) likenesses. . . . The image will thus emerge as a rich, multi-faceted reality, comprising acts, relations, capacities, virtues, dispositions, and even emotions" (p. 52).

Compound Beings

A debate has raged for centuries about the essential elements of our identity. There are those who argue that the Scriptures teach a "tripartite" (three-part) understanding of humanity. Drawing on such verses as 1 Thessalonians 5:23 ("spirit, soul and body"), this view suggests that we are formed of three distinct parts: the physical body with its passions; the soul, which is the basis of human rationality and will; and the spirit, wherein reside those aspects of the person that are distinctively Godlike and attuned to the spiritual realm. Some go on to argue that the main difference between Christians and non-Christians is that the spirit part of the person is dead before salvation but enlivened when the person is saved.

Supporters of a bipartite view argue that despite occasional tripartite language in the Bible, the Scriptures only really make a distinction between two aspects of the person, the material and immaterial, "body and soul-spirit" (McDonald, 1982, p. 78). Being overly literal in interpreting passages such as 1 Thessalonians 5:23 would lead us to propose four parts to the person based on Mark 12:30 (heart, soul, mind and strength) or a different three elements (heart, soul and might) based on Deuteronomy 6:5, or only two elements (soul and body) based on Matthew 10:28.

With this diverse presentation of divisions in these and many other Scriptures, we are driven to think theologically rather than literalistically on the biblical evidence. Based on such reasoning, McDonald (1982, p. 77) concludes that the weight of the evidence seems to favor the bipartite side. Through our physical being, we are placed in, and are part of, nature, but by virtue of our immaterial being, we have a certain degree of freedom from the temporal order and are responsive to and responsible before God.

Three important facets of this matter deserve special emphasis. First, though the biblical data do support a bipartite view, the biblical emphasis is always on the unity of the person. As McDonald (1982, p. 78) says, persons are "constituted of a unity of these two entities," and hence it is not true that one aspect (the soul-spirit or the body) is the real person and the other part an add-on. We are embodied soul-beings. This is why the term *bipartite,* and not the term *dichotomous,* was used for this view; the latter term might imply that the two elements are fundamentally opposed and irreducibly separate and noninteracting. The former term, however, implies that while the two elements are distinguishable in the human person, full human identity is vested in the union of the two aspects. We can never say, "That was my body that did that, not my spirit," or vice versa.

Often biblical words for the various aspects of our being are used to refer to the whole person from a certain perspective. But there is a center to our persons, and biblically the term *heart* (cf. Mt 15:18; Lk 16:15; Acts 14:17; 2 Cor 5:12) is most consistently used to describe this core of what psychologists and philosophers often call our self. The scriptural emphasis on *heart* teaches us the importance of understanding ourselves as a unity.

Second, this recognition of two distinct essences cannot be used to make a hard differentiation in value between the two essences (most Christians are exposed to teachings emphasizing soul over body). In spite of passages suggesting that our temporal existence is of lesser importance (e.g., Mt 10:28; 2 Cor 12:3), ultimately people are their bodies and soul-spirits in unity. The value of bodily existence is unquestionably assumed in the creation (God made us bodily beings), the Incarnation (God became a bodily being) and in our resurrection (through which we will remain bodily beings, albeit perfected bodies, for eternity). As McDonald said, "Thus does the biblical view of man represent him as consisting of two principles, the cosmical and the holy, which unite the individual into a free and personal oneness of being" (1982, p. 78).

Finally, one tendency that can be quickly noted among secular (and Christian) thinkers is that of exaggerating one end or the other of our compound natures (Evans, 1990). Some so emphasize or exaggerate the immaterial side of our being as to deify humanity and deny that we are inevitably conditioned by our physical existence. We will see this tendency among the humanistic psychologists (chapter ten). The other extreme is to emphasize or exaggerate our temporal existence so as to make us mere physical machines that are just another biological phenomenon caught up in the grand mechanistic universe. Behavioral and classical psychoanalytic thought make this mistake (chapters three and six).

A Christian view of the person balances these two diverse aspects of personhood, respecting that we are both *embodied* spirits and embodied *spirits,* embodied souls and ensouled bodies.

Personhood and Agency

As we put together the diverse elements that we have uncovered so far concerning our essential natures, we begin to see an emerging pattern of humans as persons with capacities and qualities unique among the created order. One of the premier capacities of personhood merits special attention, that of responsibility, limited freedom, or agency.

Evans (1977, p. 144) put it well in saying that "human beings are first and foremost agents. Their lives do not merely consist of a string of happenings or events, but constitute a series of choices and decisions about what they will do." C. S. Lewis (1963, p. 50), in discussing this matter, said, "Yet, for us rational creatures, to be created also means 'to be made agents.' We have nothing that we have not received; but part of what we have received is the power of being something more than receptacles."

To be a human being is to reflect God in our capacity to act responsibly, which logically entails the capacity to have acted other than we did. It is not necessary to a Christian view of freedom to argue that a person always and in every instance reacts with complete and unbounded freedom. Some events in our lives may be so powerful as to cause us to react involuntarily, as may occur when a young woman sexually abused since childhood reacts with fear and revulsion when approached by an aggressive young man interested in a date. In such instances, she may have practically no freedom to respond as she might rationally choose. At other times, we may be characterized as having limited freedom, as when the abused woman has struggled with and reflected on her experience and can make some choices of thought and action as an adult that will at least partially reshape her responses to men. Finally, there may be some instances wherein people act with almost total freedom, when they have few powerful forces impinging on their choices and they freely choose their actions. A pastor whose marriage is relatively stable but who chooses to have an affair to experience the excitement of rebellion against "rules and regulations" might be such an example.

The Christian view of persons requires that people have some responsibility in life, not that we always act without influence or constraint. Precisely how this influence interacts with human responsibility and agency is a profound mystery. The fact that we are so profoundly influenced by our biological inheritance, our families, our communities, our cultures and by the idiosyncratic events that happen in the course of life only adds to the mystery.

Human Motivations

The Bible gives no direct message about the nature of human motivation, but that does not mean that we are left drifting on this important point. We find it highly instructive to study carefully the first two chapters of the Bible to see the tasks that the first persons were assigned in the beginning. If we believe that God created us in a perfect match for the role that we were intended to fill in the garden, then perhaps part of the matching would be that we are "motivated" at a fundamental level to live out the tasks assigned to us.

In Genesis 1:26 we read that we were made to *rule* over all of creation. We were also made male and female, and in being blessed by God, we were instructed to be "fruitful and increase in number" (1:28). God then repeated the instruction that we are to rule over all living things, plant and animal. In Genesis 2 the charge to rule reoccurs in the instruction to cultivate and keep the Garden of Eden (2:15). Further, Old Testament scholars point out the additional significance of Adam naming the animals, since naming was a function of authority in ancient times, of one who owns or controls. In the creation of Eve, we learn that God himself uttered the words that "it is not good for the man to be alone" (2:18). We learn that it was God's creational intent to provide a partner for the man, one for whom he was to separate from his family, to whom he was to cleave and with whom he was to become one flesh.

Two themes emerge. The first is the theme of *responsible dominion.* Humans were meant to rule in God's behalf. Our vocations, our callings, are a primary vehicle through which we rule. Even seemingly mundane work such as gardening is a manifestation of our capacity for exercising dominion. We are God's stewards in this world, and all persons are meant to live out their Godlikeness in exercising responsible dominion over their part of the created order. Our contention is that this command entailed a human need for purposeful activity in life, a need for meaningful work and the realization of purpose outside of ourselves.

The second theme is that of *loving relatedness*. God related to himself before we were created (God said to himself, "Let us make man"). We image God in his inner oneness by our capacity to become one with another who is separate and different from us, our spouse. Our relational capacity is also reflected in the rich possibilities of celibate friendship, through which the single person can live a life of love and sharing in the community of the people of God. Such relatedness with the brothers and sisters is as vital for the married person as for the single. We also image God in having the capacity for procreation, a reflection of God's much more profound capacity for creativity and generativity. Having children anchors us in crossgenerational relationships of loving acceptance and discipline. Obviously, generating biological children is not the only means of our reproducing ourselves. Adoption and crossgenerational ministry are among the many profound ways of passing on one's riches to the next generation.

It is clear that we were created for fellowship with God. Human beings are intrinsically relational and social beings. God's greatest gift to us at the beginning was not the order of creation or the beauty of the Garden, but the fellowship of his own person and the capability to enter into that fellowship—though God himself said that this relationship with him was not enough, that it was not good for Adam to be alone. The Scriptures talk about our relationship with him in terms of a covenant or marriage contract. So the web of relatedness intended by God reaches to the sovereign Lord, to the spouse with which we become one, to the children which come from the marital union, and to all the people of God with whom we are in family relationships because of our mutual adoption into "God's family."

It bears special emphasis in these times that a Christian view of persons will emphasize family as fundamental to what it means to be human. Families are webs of relationships in which we are imbedded throughout life, for better or for worse, in much the same way that God who created us remains in relationship with us, his fallen and wayward people. And family is a profound metaphor for our interrelating in Christ. This creation mandate of relatedness suggests that a fundamental human motive will be the establishment and maintenance of meaningful relationships characterized by intimacy and unity even while we celebrate our uniqueness.

Humanity in Its Fallen State

Though we were created for dominion and relatedness, we managed to pervert both capacities in the Fall. First, we were given the task of accountable dominion over the earth and were given the freedom and the abilities to discharge those responsibilities. But there were limits to the dominion marked by God, and we violated those guidelines in prideful disobedience. Second, though created to be in loving relationship with the Father, we betrayed his faithfulness and love toward us with our rebellion and deceitfulness. We betrayed the loving Father who had only our good in his heart. Created to be open and responsive to God, we became willful, accountable rebels against God, and as Hubbard (1979, p. 78) said, "at that moment God's scepter of glory became his gavel of justice."

This is seen as unpopular and harsh language in certain evangelical circles, but biblical realism takes sin seriously, and we must do the same. Because we are fallen and under divine wrath, we became alienated from God and disoriented within ourselves—twin facets of the Fall. As Peck (1983) has so capably written, we are "people of the lie," as is especially evident in the unhealthy ways we deal with money, sex and power (Foster, 1985). We all have a rather predictable tendency to deceive ourselves and others, and often attempt to deceive our Creator. Perhaps the most powerful literary rendering of this capacity and tendency for self-deceit is C. S. Lewis's (1956) brilliant novel *Till We Have Faces,* in which the main character, who had spent her whole life justifying her actions, realizes her unreadiness to confront her Judge and asks rhetorically, "How can they meet us face to face till we have faces?" (p. 294). In other words, how can we meet God face to face when we spend so much of our lives deceiving ourselves about who and what we really are and hiding our true faces from ourselves and God?

The divine wrath that we are under is not only an expression of God's justice and dignity; it is an expression of his love. Where such vast capacity for fellowship exists, the capacity for hurt is enormous, not unlike that of a broken marital covenant. "What we were made to do and what we were best at doing are now our sharpest and clearest failures" (Hubbard, 1979, p. 79).

The Nature of Sin

Sin as state and act. Sin is dealt with in very complex ways in the Scriptures, and getting a clear handle on this slippery concept is difficult. Christians often think of sin as isolated acts that violate moral standards. In the Gospels sin is presented as willful disobedience (McDonald, 1982, p. 8). But left by itself, this view becomes a legalistic definition of sin that can trivialize it.

Sin also refers to a state of being. Individual sins testify that we have a "sin nature," which predisposes us to individual acts of violation against God's law (cf. Mk 7:20-23, which states that individual acts proceed out of a heart of corruption). As Bloesch (1984, p. 1012) stated, "Sin is not just a conscious transgression of the law but a debilitating ongoing state of enmity with God." Yet sin is even more than a disposition in our natures; it is "a power that holds us in bondage" (Morris, 1986, p. 57). Paul especially among the New Testament writers seems at times to reify sin as a transpersonal "force" acting against God and his purposes (cf. Rom 6—7). So sin is at once acts of transgression, a nature or disposition, and a force in opposition to God.

Rebellion or anxiety? What is the nature of our sinfulness? Why do we commit sins and/or have a sinful nature? The classic orthodox answer to this question has been to highlight our human rebelliousness against God. Bloesch (1984, p. 1012) states that "in Reformed theology, the core of sin is unbelief. . . . Hardness of heart, which is closely related to unbelief, . . . means refusing to repent and believe the promises of God (Ps 95:8; Heb 3:8, 15; 4:7). It connotes . . . stubborn unwillingness to open ourselves to the love of God (2 Chr 36:13; Eph 4:18)." In this formulation sin is a culpable rejection by humans of their rightful submission to God's sovereignty. It is a willful abuse of the freedom God imparted to us.

The other major current understanding of the nature of sin might be characterized as "neo-orthodox." Originating with Niebuhr and Tillich, this view suggests that sin originates in the "union between man's dependence as a creature and his free spiritual life" (Gilkey, 1985, p. 231). Confronted with the awesome responsibility of managing the tension between our human finiteness and contingency (dependence upon God for our very existence), on the one hand, and our capacity for freedom and transcendence, on the other, we experience anxiety of an existential nature. We don't want to be dominated by our temporal existence, but neither do we want the responsibility of choice. The righteous response to this dilemma is to balance the tension and choose to live in humble submission to the Creator as a dependent being with responsible choice. But the sinful response is to evade the human responsibility of managing this tension by either denying our freedom and living life dominated by the cares of this world (plunging oneself into sensuality with the cry "I can't help myself," for example), or denying our dependence on God and trying to become gods unto ourselves (thus rebelling against God's laws and saying, "No one is going to legislate my life for me!"). Both of these imbalanced responses are regarded as sin, as both shrink from responsibly living out life in the way God created it to be.

There are actually many other understandings of sin (see Bloesch, 1984). Liberation theology, for example, rightly recognizing that sin can and often does become institutionalized, emphasizes the exploitative, oppressive, greedy nature of corporate sin. And many of these views are not mutually exclusive; it is not hard, for instance, to see the Reformed and neo-orthodox views as complementary truths.

A Christian understanding of sin that is truly biblical must maintain a balance between seeing sin as a violation of law and as a violation of relationship, of sin as individual and sin as corporate, of sin as driven by rebellion and sin as driven by anxiety, of sin as something we are in bondage to and are yet responsible for.

Moral evil, natural evil and finitude. Ethicists commonly make the distinction between *moral* and *natural* evil. Moral evil is the result of moral choice—such as intentional theft, for instance. Some things, though, are bad, but are not the result of a culpable choice. The accidental injury of a young child who falls down a set of stairs is such a natural evil, as are most instances of disease, decay and death. They may be no one's fault, but they are bad nevertheless.

We can also distinguish moral and natural evil from our *finitude,* our limitedness as human beings. Our human limitations exist because we are not gods, and thus finitude existed in creation prior to either moral or natural evil. There is much that is beyond our possible reach physically, mentally, emotionally and spiritually. Adam could not run a two-minute mile, will immediate emotional changes, know the future or in any way exceed the capacities God had given him. Humans must confront their finitude and achieve some reconciliation with their limitations. Many limitations are not flaws or sins; they are simply the limits of the raw material from which we are to forge who we are and who we are to become.

These distinctions become important when sorting out our understanding of human problems. Some human difficulties are due exclusively to human moral evil, sometimes our own, sometimes that of others, but most often both. If we deceive ourselves and engage in immoral behavior, we will bear the consequences.

But many human problems are essentially natural evils rather than moral evils. Chemical brain imbalances appear to be predisposing factors in such disorders as manic-depressive illness, and are probable factors in other serious disorders. Not limited to biochemical problems, natural evil also occurs when people endure deprived or traumatic childhood environments and so suffer psychologically in adulthood for what they failed to receive as children.

Finally, we may experience problems because of our finitude without that problem being a sin. The college student struggling with the difficulty of making decisions about careers is confronting the reality of her finitude—no one knows the answers to all the questions one could ask about careers and the future, and it is no sin not to know these answers and to struggle with the decision.

The matter gets more complex when we begin to interrelate moral and natural evil and finitude. Some can have problems because of the moral evils inflicted on them. For instance, research suggests that an extremely high percentage of persons with multiple personality disorder have experienced Satanic or occult abuse as very young children (Friesen, 1988). Such persons have been victimized by the moral evils inflicted on them, but their adult psychological troubles may have originated from their childhood overreliance on dissociative defense mechanisms (the splitting of part of one's consciousness off as a way of coping), which began at an early age because no other defenses were available to respond to those moral evils. The coping mechanism of dissociation might be seen as a result of human finitude, and the overdevelopment of that capacity might be seen as a natural evil resulting from the child never having been helped to develop other coping mechanisms.

We can also respond with moral evil to the occurrence of natural evil (e.g., cursing God because a disastrous storm destroyed your home) or to our finitude (e.g., plunging into envy and bitterness because one has not been blessed with physical beauty or robust health).

Johnson (1987) suggested the designation of "moral fault" to describe instances where both moral evil and "weakness" (his term for what we are calling *finitude*) are involved. We prefer a three-component designation as developed above, but his concept of moral fault is a good one that suggests that often, perhaps almost always, problems involve all three components.

We must also mention another significant instance of moral evil, that of the active opposition against God's purposes and goodness by the "forces of wickedness" and darkness (Eph 6:12). Satanic and demonic evil are real, as we are becoming increasingly aware in our time. Police officials in many communities are encountering ever more brazen criminal acts committed in the name of Satan. Psychopathology researchers are finding occult torture and oppression to be among the crimes committed in child-abuse cases and in the backgrounds of a significant number of the severely psychologically impaired. Inpatient treatment programs for children and adults involved in Satanism are beginning to appear on the professional scene. The personal evil of the supernatural forces in rebellion against God must be taken seriously by all Christian mental-health workers.

Yet influence of Satanic forces must not be limited to the obviously occult. Shuster (1987) has argued that there is a demonic element to all evil and that Scripture suggests that these personal forces of evil have infiltrated all aspects of human life. This further complicates our understanding of moral evil, natural evil and finitude when we grapple with how the forces of darkness corrupt our experience and contribute to the evil we are exposed to and commit. Usually, all these elements—the moral evil of ourselves and those about us and of the demonic world, natural evil and human finitude—are involved in the problems of the person who comes for psychotherapy.

Sin and Human Freedom

We need to briefly address a topic of mind-boggling complexity, the state of human freedom after the Fall.

Humanity is now burdened with an impaired capacity for freedom, in that sin now infuses our very being and clouds our every choice. The desperate cries of Paul in Romans 7 are repeated by all Christians who find their desire to follow God in righteousness frustrated by a continual bondage of the will to sin. We can all testify to our impotence to obey God perfectly and to follow him wholeheartedly. And yet God holds us responsible for our disobedience. In short, we have the dual experience of choice versus bondage, culpability versus an incapacity to do otherwise. This experience matches the scriptural puzzle of our seeming inability not to sin coupled with our undeniable culpability for sinning.

We can offer no easy resolutions to this matter (see McDonald, 1982, pp. 57-67, 92-100). We would note that theological discussion of the matter of free will has usually centered upon the person's choice to become a Christian, with Calvinists asserting that such an action is wholly the work of God through his grace, and that to believe that any element of being born again is attributable to the person's choice diminishes God's sovereignty and makes faith a "work" and thus Christianity a religion of works rather than grace. Arminians, on the other hand, assert that there is an element of choice or human freedom in becoming a believer, and that to assert otherwise is to make humans into moral robots and God into the grand puppet-master. They do not, however, deny our bondage to sin nor the central importance of God's work in freeing us from that bondage.

For our purposes here we are *not* so concerned with the decision of becoming a Christian as we are with the capacity for human freedom in the give-and-take of everyday life. Suffice it to say that in the give and take of everyday life, humans may not, on a moment-to-moment basis, be free to choose the perfect good. Most often this appears beyond our grasp. But the inaccessibility of that choice does not render nonexistent other choices that we can make. For example, we may not be able to choose to be perfectly honest, but we have real choices day by day of particular instances where we can be either honest or deceitful.

God in his sovereignty may shape human choices to insure the triumph of his grace and of his redemptive plan for humanity, but human choice is nonetheless real. For example, one of our children may be destined by God to some work of critical importance to God's purposes on earth, and as such he may be guiding our actions toward them, drawing them toward him, either through our good example and discipline or through the poverty and pathos of our hypocrisy. In either case, we still make choices of how to deal with them and are accountable to God for those actions. There are, from eternity's perspective, no small decisions and no unimportant persons.

Human Motivations

Earlier we addressed human motivations implied in the creation narrative. There are also implications for our understanding of human motivation to be drawn from the saga of humanity's Fall.

Rebellion against God, the desire to be gods ourselves, now becomes an operative motive in all that we do. Also, to the extent that sin is rooted in the ontological anxiety of grappling with our freedom in light of our limitations, the desire to run away from this burdensome responsibility now operates as an ever-present motivation as well. The story of the Fall makes it clear that Adam and Eve tried to cover up their sin by first avoiding God and then attempting to shift blame and abrogate personal responsibility. This awareness of divine judgment, and the desire to avoid that righteous judgment, now colors all that we do.

This immeasurably complicates our understanding of human motivation. Humans experience compound and conflicting motivations as part of their essential unredeemed natures (and redeemed natures too). For example, as we approach dating and marriage, we may desire another with the good motive of desiring intimacy and the bad motive of desiring someone to exercise power over. In summary, the constellation of our motivations is vastly complicated by our rebellion against God. Our motivations are seldom pure and never simple.

Humanity in Its Redeemed State

Using covenant terminology (after Anderson, 1987), we might say that in the midst of the devastation of the Fall, the marriage between human-ity and God had been shattered, but from one side only. Grace for reconciliation is needed. God has promised restoration in the life, death and resurrection of Jesus Christ, the pivotal events in all of history and the only source for our hope and salvation. Receiving this grace may lead to significant transformations in the lives of ordinary people through believing and acting on the truths of the faith.

Life between the Beginning and the End

Roberta Hestenes has observed that the experiences of the Hebrews in being redeemed from Egypt by the Lord (Exodus through Deutero-nomy) is a powerful model of our own redemption process. While the Israelites were oppressed, God raised up for them a savior, Moses (a type of Christ). God through Moses freed them from their bondage and servitude to an alien master, and initially they exuberantly cele-brated their freedom. But release from captivity was not immediately followed by entering the Promised Land. Rather, the Israelites had to wander in the wilderness for many years before being ushered into the "land of milk and honey."

Christians similarly live between the day of emancipation and the day of final deliverance. A battle has been won but the war is not over. Brunner (1939, p. 114 and throughout) calls this "life in contradic-tion"—living life suspended between our fallen and redeemed natures.

We live between the kingdom of God which is present, and the kingdom of God which is to come. We must navigate the struggles and tensions of this "in-between" life by depending on God and others who share this journey. We do this by becoming part of a covenant people, by becoming deeply involved with a local body of believers. Only in the context of a healing community can we learn to cultivate and express the fruits of the Spirit, which along with a deep concern and compas-sion for others should epitomize mature, committed Christians.

The Goal of the Redeemed Life

Paul's central prayer for the Philippians expresses well the central goal of life in Jesus Christ:

> I consider everything a loss compared to the surpassing greatness of knowing Christ Jesus my Lord, for whose sake I have lost all things. I consider them rubbish, that I may gain Christ and be found in him, not having a righteousness of my own that comes from the law, but that which is through faith in Christ—the righteousness that comes from God and is by faith. I want to know Christ and the power of his resurrection and the fellowship of sharing in his sufferings, becoming like him in his death, and so, somehow, to attain to the resurrection from the dead. (3:8-11)

According to the apostle Paul, the goal of the Christian life is to know Christ, which entails having a righteousness based on faith, being conformed to (or in some way identifying with) Christ's sufferings and death, and finally attaining eternal fellowship with Christ through the resurrection of the dead.

On our contemporary scene, much has been written about emotional wholeness and Christian holiness. Some authors seem to regard the two as essentially identical. Surely growth in Christ means to become more like Jesus, and the more we are like him, the more holy and whole we must be.

Yet wholeness and holiness are actually very different. We live in a fallen world. It is easy for our conceptions of wholeness to become contaminated with sub-Christian notions of well-being, especially those that emphasize easy accommodation with the world. All too often in psychology, the goals for clients are to become well adjusted and do one's best at a purely human level, rather than radical realignment of one's life to the claims of Christ.

In contrast to such ideals as minimizing conflict, total emotional awareness and expression, maximizing life satisfaction and pleasure, and living up to our innate potential, note that Paul prescribes the goals of becoming conformed to Christ's suffering, death and resurrection. Such a calling certainly includes a number of personal experiences that are far from secular psychology's ideals for well-adjusted human living. In short, we are called to a way of life that is often at odds with the ways of the world, a way of life where suffering and pain are an inevitable part of our lot in life, where being *holy*, which literally means being set apart to God's purposes and manifesting his righteous character, can be difficult and even despised by the world.

McLemore (1982) cautions that it is quite possible for an individual to be a paragon of mental health, as it is traditionally defined in psychology, yet be living without faith in God through Christ. The peaceful practitioner of Zen Buddhism, unruffled by life's demands as he retreats into an inner world, might be supremely healthy by the definition of some. On the other hand, a "saint" in the local church may be living a life of emotional pain and interpersonal estrangement as she faithfully follows God's calling, thus living a life of holiness that is far from the current psychological understanding of wholeness.

Thus, while there may be much that overlaps between *wholeness* and *holiness* (especially as both are embodied in the concept of Christlikeness), and the two concepts may not be contradictory in any way, we must be exceedingly careful when we discuss the two terms. The chief danger is that the pursuit of wholeness is so easily and widely approved of in the Western world that it would be easy for Christians to pursue "growth" as defined by some therapy approach while deluding themselves that they are thus pursuing holiness as well.

Christian clinicians need to think carefully, critically and courageously about the goals that they are advocating in the context of counseling and psychotherapy, to think in the light of what it means for a believer to be "salt and light" in the world and to be "bearing the marks of Christ." It is imperative that these goals include considerations of Christian faith and experience.

Conclusion

It is essential for Christian pastors, academicians, clinicians and researchers to take Christian world views and control beliefs seriously. As McDonald (1986, p. 138) has noted, there is no purely psychological theory of personality that can give an effective account of all the ethical and religious concerns of the human individual. What we have covered above does not constitute a personality theory, but it does form a vision of personhood that should undergird a personality theory acceptable to Christians.

No such theory exists today. Christian psychologists must therefore tentatively work within incomplete personality systems while striving for development of a full-bodied Christian view. As Brunner (1939, p. 62) has argued, there can be no Christian psychology if by that we mean a theory of elemental sensory processes or memory. But when we move to the level of a comprehensive understanding of the "person," then there will be a distinctively Christian approach to psychology.

Does the faith have implications for how we intervene with persons?

Does it specify modes of counseling with troubled people? From surveying the writings of Christian counselors, one sometimes gets the idea that God specifies one and only one way of dealing with all problems and difficulties. The problem is that each of the Christian counselors specifies a different technique, claiming that his or hers is the one endorsed by Scripture. One emphasizes exhortation to behavior change, another a change to biblical thinking, another healing prayer, another supernatural intervention and yet another the casting out of demons.

Our position on this matter is that we have much to learn from various forms of pastoral intervention recommended and utilized in the Scriptures. In 1 Thessalonians 5:14, the apostle Paul says, "And we urge you, brothers, warn those who are idle, encourage the timid, help the weak, be patient with everyone." Paul's admonition shows that different types of human problems call for different types of responses from counselors. Many other types of interpersonal helping responses are specified in the Bible, including loving, forgiving, providing material charity, teaching, comforting, grieving with, rebuking, excommunicating and so forth. Clearly what is needed is a flexible repertoire of approaches, grounded in coherent theory and deeply respectful of the complexity and profundity of human struggles.

Almost any form of counseling interaction in the Bible can find its counterpart in the practice of secular psychotherapy. It is interesting, though, that each major school of psychotherapy tends to build its identity around a rather limited number of styles of therapist-client interactions—so that cognitive therapists are teachers, person-centered therapists are accepting, psychoanalytic therapists are distant and interpretive, and so forth. No counseling model we know of embodies the diversity of interaction styles that seem to be recommended in Scripture. So, as the Christian therapist moves beyond a secular theory, one needed area of growth is an expanded vision of technique that incorporates the eclecticism found in Scripture.

As a final note, we would raise the issue of the curious place of those few secular theories (and Christian theories as well) that propose styles of healing interactions for which there is absolutely no parallel in those sections of Scripture that offer pastoral advice on change and growth. The two most obvious examples are the theories that call for the client to go about re-experiencing specific life events, most notably the birth trauma (as in secular and Christian versions of primal therapy—Janov and Lake respectively—which we have not included in this book) and the theories that call for bodily interventions for the purpose of releasing pent-up emotional responses (such as the "body-work" massages of bioenergetic therapy—also not included in this book).

These types of interventions depart from the "normal" patterns of interpersonal relating that are modeled and lauded in the Scriptures and are also on the "outskirts" of the psychotherapy establishment. Given this, we feel a need for special caution as the Christian approaches these types of therapies. We would not argue for a naive biblical literalism of saying that a technique must be specifically suggested in the Bible for a therapist to use it ("*Transference* isn't in my concordance so I'm against it!"), but we would suggest that the further removed a mode of psychological intervention becomes from normal patterns of human interaction, the greater the need for a strong theoretical rationale for its use, for empirical documentation of its potential helpfulness and for a high degree of humility about its applicability.

For Further Reading

Berkouwer, G. (1962). *Man: The image of God* (D. Jellema, Trans.). Grand Rapids, MI: Eerdmans. (Originally published n.d.).
An excellent Reformed study of theological anthropology, emphasizing the image of God.

Brunner, E. (1939). *Man in revolt* (O. Wyon, Trans.). Philadelphia: Westminster. (Originally published 1937).
A challenging and insightful study from a neo-orthodox perspective.

Clebsch, W., and Jaekle, C. (1975). *Pastoral care in historical perspective.* New York: Jason Aronson.
One of the best studies of the history of the pastoral care tradition, including "exhibits" of original writings in pastoral care from throughout history.

Lewis, C. S. (1946). *The great divorce.* New York: Macmillan.
A moving and thought-provoking depiction of physical existence after the resurrection.

McDonald, H. (1982). *The Christian view of man.* Westchester, IL: Crossway.
An excellent overview of Christian anthropology

References

Adams, J. (1979). *More than redemption: A theology of Christian counseling.* Phillipsburg, NJ: Presbyterian and Reformed.

Anderson, R. (1987). *For those who counsel.* Unpublished manuscript, Fuller Theological Seminary, Pasadena, CA.

Berkouwer, G. (1962). *Man: The image of God* (D. Jellema, Trans.). Grand Rapids, MI: Eerdmans. (Originally published n.d.).

Bloesch, D. (1984). Sin. In W. Elwell (Ed.), *Evangelical dictionary of theology* (pp. 1012-1016). Grand Rapids, MI: Baker.

Brunner, E. (1939). *Man in revolt* (O. Wyon, Trans.). Philadelphia: Westminster. (Originally published 1937).

Clebsch, W., and Jaekle, C. (1975). *Pastoral care in historical perspective.* New York: Jason Aronson.

Evans, C. (1977). *Preserving the person: A look at the human sciences.* Grand Rapids, MI: Baker.

Evans, C. (1990). *Søren Kierkegaard's Christian psychology.* Grand Rapids, MI: Zondervan.

Foster, R. (1985). *Money, sex, and power: The challenge of the disciplined life.* San Francisco: Harper & Row.

Friesen, J. (1988). Treatment for multiple personality disorder. Workshop presented at the International Congress on Christian Counseling, Atlanta, GA.

Gilkey, L. (1985). *Maker of heaven and earth.* Lanham, MD: University Press. (Originally published 1959).

Greidanus, S. (1982). The use of the Bible in Christian scholarship. *Christian Scholar's Review, 11,* 138-147.

Hubbard, D. (1979). *What we evangelicals believe.* Pasadena, CA: Fuller Theological Seminary.

Jewett, P. (1975). *Man as man and female.* Grand Rapids, MI: Eerdmans.

Johnson, E. (1987). Sin, weakness, and psychopathology. *Journal of Psychology and Theology, 15,* 218-226.

Lewis, C. S. (1956). *Till we have faces.* New York: Harcourt Brace Jovanovich.

Lewis, C. S. (1963). *Letters to Malcolm: Chiefly on prayer.* New York: Harcourt Brace Jovanovich.

McDonald, H. (1982). *The Christian view of man.* Westchester, IL: Crossway.

McDonald, H. (1986). Biblical teaching on personality. In S. Jones (Ed.), *Psychology and the Christian faith: An introductory reader* (pp. 118-140). Grand Rapids, MI: Baker.

McLemore, C. (1982). *The scandal of psychotherapy.* Wheaton, IL: Tyndale.

Morris, L. (1986). *New Testament theology.* Grand Rapids, MI: Zondervan.

Oden, T. (1984). *Care of souls in the classic tradition.* Philadelphia: Fortress.

Peck, M. (1983). *People of the lie.* New York: Simon and Schuster.

Plantinga, C. (1988). Images of God. In M. Noll and D. Wells (Eds.), *Christian faith and practice in the modern world* (pp. 51-67). Grand Rapids, MI: Eerdmans.

Shuster, M. (1987). *Power, pathology, and paradox: The dynamics of good and evil.* Grand Rapids, MI: Zondervan.

Webber, R. (1986). *The church in the world.* Grand Rapids, MI: Zondervan.

Wolterstorff, N. (1984). *Reason within the bounds of religion* (2d ed.). Grand Rapids, MI: Eerdmans.

Wolterstorff, N. (1987). *Lament for a son.* Grand Rapids, MI: Eerdmans.

THE DYNAMIC
PSYCHOLOGIES

3

CLASSIC
PSYCHOANALYSIS

✠

*A*lthough psychoanalysis is the grandparent of all psychotherapeutic methods, it tends to be unpopular in conservative Christian circles. The specific concerns focus around three troubling themes in psychoanalysis: (1) the emphasis on sex and aggression as motivational bases for behavior; (2) the deterministic and naturalistic assumptions of the model; and (3) the direct attacks on religion Freud made in his later writings.

Despite these reservations, many Christian mental-health professionals have a profound respect for this tradition (see, for example, Crabb, 1988; McLemore, 1984; Narramore, 1984; or Peck, 1983). Certainly the reservations are legitimate, but to dismiss psychoanalysis as irrelevant to the real problems of life is to fail to see its potential significance for the church and the society (cf. Browning, 1987, p. 32).

Psychoanalysis[1] is certainly the "most comprehensive and far-reaching conceptualization of personality, psychopathology, and psychotherapy in existence" (Korchin, 1976, p. 332). The influence of Freudian thought in the Western world has been profound, and in spite of legitimate Christian objections, we seriously doubt that all the influence has been negative. Our endorsement is less enthusiastic than that of McLemore (1982, p. 164), who asserts "that a well-conducted psychoanalysis is still the best way by which to come to understand oneself." Still, the direct impact of this system can be seen in nearly all academic disciplines, including history, literature and philosophy. The more indirect influence on the larger public consciousness can hardly be overestimated (Jones and Wilson, 1987).

Given the brevity of our treatment, we cannot analyze the development of psychoanalytic thought over time. Freud's thinking evolved over his productive years; the most striking example of this is his gradual move away from a harshly biological approach to his subject matter, and his widening of his understanding of motivation to include not just the sexual drive but the aggressive/death drive as well. For the sake of economy, we will present Freud's system as a static whole, though we recognize that this is not wholly accurate. We will appraise contemporary derivatives of the analytic tradition (called psychodynamic theories) in the next chapter.

Descriptive Survey

Philosophical Assumptions and Model of Personality
Classic psychoanalysis assumes that all human behavior is determined by psychic energy and early childhood experiences. In order to make sense of a person's current behavioral patterns, it is necessary to understand the behavior's roots in largely unconscious conflicts and motives. The forces that "move" us are irrational and strong, and most often related to aggressive or sexual impulses. Consequently, the goal

---

[1]A word about terminology is necessary. The words *psychoanalysis* and *psychoanalytic* are potentially ambiguous. At the most restrictive level, they refer to a classical or distinctively Freudian approach to psychological research, study or treatment. At a somewhat broader level, they refer to specific models of personality, psychopathology or psychotherapy. At the broadest level, they can refer to a comprehensive and well-articulated world view (cf. Van Leeuwen, 1985). Indeed, it is at this final level, often referred to as a metapsychology, that we want to focus much of our attention. We will reserve the word *psychodynamic*, which is usually also used in reference to psychoanalysis, to refer only to the post-Freudian approaches we will discuss in chapter four.

is to illuminate critical life events in the formative childhood years in order to resolve the "problems in living" that emerge throughout the remainder of the life span. Only through greater self-knowledge and self-control can mature adults increase their capacity "to love and work" effectively.

Philosophically speaking, psychoanalysis reflects the influence of classical empiricism as well as the Enlightenment tradition (cf. Rychlak, 1973). Freud adopted a materialistic, or naturalistic, world view as the backdrop for his model. It makes at least five core assumptions about persons (Brenner, 1973; Arlow, 1984): (1) the topographical, (2) the genetic, (3) the dynamic, (4) the structural and (5) the economic assumptions.

The *topographical assumption* asserts that there are three levels of consciousness: (a) the conscious experiences of which we are aware (e.g., thoughts you have as you read this page); (b) the preconscious experiences which we can voluntarily recall but are not currently cognizant of (e.g., the memory of your best experience in the fifth grade); and (c) the unconscious experiences that are the primary determinant of psychic life but which are not directly accessible to conscious examination (e.g., unresolved conflicts from your childhood). All behavior is assumed to have largely unconscious determinants. Although we may be aware of our conscious motives for writing this book (e.g., contributing to the work of the church), at a somewhat deeper and perhaps more powerful level, we may be unconsciously looking for approval from parents or significant others.

The *genetic assumption* essentially asserts that current behavior and experience is a product of past events. All the influences that we believe to be shaping us in the present (e.g., conflict with a supervisor at work or our love for a spouse) have their real power through the unresolved issues of our past (e.g., conflict with a parental figure that was strictly authoritarian or overly permissive). In other words, current events largely derive their meaning from activating unresolved difficulties from the formative years of childhood. Consequently, psychoanalysis has a strong historical as well as deterministic bias (cf. Ford and Urban, 1963).

The *dynamic assumption* contends that all behavior is ultimately dependent on the interaction of two fundamental human drives. The *libidinal drive* is largely "erotic" or "sexual" in nature. Broadly defined, the libido focuses on far more than genital sexual release—it includes the desire or urge to create, to develop or maintain intimacy, to love self and/or others, and more (Munroe, 1955). The other major drive

is primarily oriented around the twin themes of *aggression* and *death*.
Both drives have creative or destructive potential (Prochaska, 1979).
Both drives can be understood as deterministic at the intrapsychic,
interpersonal or societal levels. These "life instincts" and "death instincts" are at the core of the Freudian view of human nature.

The *structural assumption* asserts that the psychic apparatus can best
be understood in terms of three separate but interdependent entities
known as the *id, ego* and *superego*. The *id* is the repository for our most
primitive sexual and aggressive drives and urges. Id processes are
assumed to be present at birth and to be largely unconscious, illogical,
demanding and relentlessly driving toward personal gratification (this
is called the *pleasure principle*). The *ego* is reality-based and develops as
an individual interacts with the external world. The ego is largely
conscious and serves a vital role in mediating the primitive urges of the
id with the constraints or opportunities of reality. Finally, the *superego*
places restrictive demands on both the id and the ego. It is generally
understood as a split-off from the ego and as the repository of the
moralistic standards one has absorbed from "significant others," most
often parents and society. Often seen as a kind of "conscience," the
superego is assumed to be only partially conscious.

Finally, the *economic assumption* asserts that human personality can
best be understood as a closed or quasi-hydraulic system. In other
words, a certain amount of energy is introduced into the system in the
form of the basic drives. Since this energy must be released, ways must
be found to disperse it in a direct or transformed manner. This is
"economic" in the sense that energy is neither gained nor lost; the bank
account always balances. The goal of psychoanalytic treatment is to
develop the capacity for the release of energy in socially acceptable and
appropriate ways. In contrast, psychopathology is understood as disper-
sion of energy without regard to the constraints of reality or external
social norms (e.g., psychotic regression).

For Freud, consciousness was only a small part of the total psyche.
Although it can't be studied directly, the existence of the unconscious
can be inferred from direct observation of behavior or through conscious experiences such as dreams, "slips of the tongue" or material
derived from free association. Freud hypothesized that all the stored
experiences, memories and repressed material of a lifetime can be
found in the unconscious. Since unconscious material influences all
behavior, the deeper contents of the mind must be explored at some
level to achieve any significant measure of health and wholeness.

Awareness and insight of this material alone isn't curative—it must be "worked through," ideally in the context of a psychotherapeutic relationship.

In the absence of such working through, however, means must be found to deal with the anxiety that develops out of the conflict between the id, ego and superego over the control of the available psychic energy. Ideally, the ego can control the anxiety through direct and rational means, but more often than not the largely unconscious and often primitive *ego defense mechanisms* must be utilized. These defense mechanisms transform the threatening anxiety into some alternate form the person can deal with, and thus help one cope with threatening unconscious conflicts. The more primitive defense mechanisms often result in marginal coping. Most abnormal psychology, personality or psychotherapy textbooks contain summaries of the most important defense mechanisms. The main lesson to be learned about defense mechanisms is that overt behavior rarely means what it seems to, because in transforming the anxiety caused by unconscious conflicts, the true reasons for our behavior become largely inaccessible.

The classic Freudian understanding of the development of personality asserts the existence of a series of *psychosexual stages*. According to this perspective, the personal and social development that occurs in these critical stages of infancy, childhood and adolescence lays the foundation on which further maturation can be built. Both healthy and unhealthy personality development reflect the manner in which the relevant tasks were accomplished. Each stage is distinguished by the focal area of the body where the gratification of libidinal impulses is concentrated.

The *oral stage* (first year of life) is foundational to later personality development. The caregiver's focus is on the feeding and nurturing of the infant, and gratification for the baby centers on the mouth; sucking and chewing are primary. Failure to get one's needs met potentially leads to greediness or an unhealthy preoccupation with possessions in later life.

The *anal stage* (ages one to three) centers around the child's experience of parental demands, discipline and expectations, especially as they relate to toilet training. Psychic gratification centers on retention and expulsion of feces. Unresolved issues at this stage potentially lead to unhealthy attitudes about the body or bodily functions. Extremes of orderliness or messiness are also assumed to be related to unresolved issues in this period.

In the *phallic stage* (ages three to six) the focus for gratification moves away from the mouth and anus to the genitals. It is during this stage that the child learns much about sex-role identity and develops an interest in sexual matters. Parental attitudes in particular are communicated verbally or nonverbally, and negative experiences can affect feelings about sexuality throughout the remainder of the life span.

The phallic stage is assumed to be the period in which *Oedipal* (for boys) or *Electra* (for girls) conflicts emerge, in which the child develops threatening, erotically charged feelings for the parent of the opposite sex. Freud developed his notions of what happens at this stage for boys to a much greater extent than for girls, so we will focus on those. (The Oedipal crisis was named after the famous Oedipus myth in which Oedipus was destined to murder his father and marry his mother.)

The boy, Freud proposed, comes to experience vague libidinal longings for union with his mother. These are rarely experienced consciously. These feelings are often exhibited by intense attachments to mother, jealousy for her attention and so forth. Realizing that the father is a competitor for the love of the mother, the boy first experiences an angry competitiveness with the father, followed by a fearful realization that he cannot, as a child, hope to compete for the attention of the mother (assuming the basic health of the parental relationship). The healthiest resolution to this terrible dilemma is for the boy to identify with the father and actually absorb parts of the father's personality, so that at least the boy can have some sense of special attachment to the mother on a vicarious level by being like the father.

In the *latency stage* (ages six to twelve), increased socialization with other children typically replaces the inwardness of the phallic period. Coupled with new interests in others, the child develops academic, athletic, interpersonal or recreational competencies. These social themes are predominant throughout the prepubescence period.

In adolescence the child moves into the *genital stage* (ages twelve to eighteen) where again sexual impulses become predominant. Interest in the opposite sex develops, often with some sexual experimentation. Ideally, libidinal energies are redirected in socially appropriate activities (e.g., dating friendships). The genital stage is assumed to continue throughout the remainder of life as one searches for a healthy balance between love, work and play.[2]

---

[2]Somewhat parallel but complementary understandings of these stages can be found in the work of Erikson (1982) or other major developmental theorists (cf. Berger, 1988).

Even the most ardent critic of psychoanalysis would agree that the approach is comprehensive and that its model of personality has heuristic value (Ryckman, 1985). Unfortunately, the theory all too often lacks precision and testability, and runs the risk of leading to "nothing-but," or reductionistic, interpretations of behavior (e.g., everything becomes the result of aggressive or sexual drives). Still, as Silverman (1976) has observed, aspects of psychosexual theory can be clinically demonstrated. For example, several studies suggest that persons with primitive defenses against aggressive and sexual impulses do seem to exhibit greater rates of neurotic psychopathology, an observation consistent with Freudian theory.

Model of Health

In the psychoanalytic tradition, healthy individuals are ones who have enough conscious awareness of their basic issues to have self-control (as Freud reportedly said, "Where id was, let ego be"). Earlier painful and traumatic experiences have largely been "worked through" and are no longer denied or distorted. To a meaningful and significant degree, aspects of the unconscious have been made conscious. Important dimensions of the personality structure have been reconstructed as neurotic processes have been undone, thereby facilitating greater movement toward maturity.

The healthy person is one who has good ego-strength. Destructive impulses exert less pressure on the individual so that he or she is increasingly able to make responsible decisions about how to deal with the tasks of everyday living. The clash between the biological urges and the demands of social reality is still there, but effective compromises, choices and commitments have been made. Self-knowledge about these and other tensions are of supreme importance in this tradition, so much so that it is often viewed as a necessary, if not sufficient, condition for growth toward an autonomous and productive life (Korchin, 1976, pp. 326-332).

Maturation, then, is seen as a lifelong process of increasing the capacity to understand and regulate one's life. Obviously, this will require a high level of self-awareness and intelligence, a fair degree of willingness for painfully honest self-assessment, and a strong motivation for change and growth in one's life. Perfection is impossible to reach.

Model of Abnormality

According to this tradition, everyone is pathological, to a greater or lesser degree, due to the inevitable conflicts and fixations that develop in our formative years. The specific symptoms that develop reflect both the psychosexual stage in which the conflicts and fixations first developed and the particular manner in which immature or primitive ego defense mechanisms are utilized to deal with the resulting anxiety. In other words, psychoanalysis assumes that "problems in living" are universal, since nobody proceeds through the developmental stages without difficulty. At the intrapsychic level, all symptoms "work," in that they help us cope with the demands of everyday living, even though the symptoms may be self-defeating and perhaps self-destructive.

The model is thoroughly psychosocial in its assessment of the etiology and maintenance of emotional difficulties. The more intense the conflicts and fixations are, the more severe the psychopathology. Given sufficient environmental or internal stress, the defenses can be overwhelmed and symptoms emerge. These internal threats are typically avoided rather than dealt with directly, and the person is highly motivated to keep unacceptable impulses or childish anxieties out of direct consciousness at whatever cost. When the avoidance strategy is coupled with often well-meaning attention from family and friends—which helps continue the unhealthy way of dealing with the conflict—the cycle of avoidance can become a deeply ingrained pattern (what has come to be designated "the neurotic nucleus").

In short, stress makes the person anxious; the anxiety is avoided at all costs (which can be highly reinforcing); and a vicious habit becomes established. A more direct strategy of resolving the conflict is not adopted because the deeper unconscious "primary process" is nonlogical (irrational) and atemporal (makes no differentiation with respect to time) (cf. Prochaska, 1979, pp. 34-35).

According to the model, conflict is not incidental to being human. Rather, conflict is intrinsic to human nature and forms the core of our being. The key psychic drives inevitably conflict because the aggressive and erotic drives do not naturally complement each other. The structures conflict also: id and superego battle, like two powerful horses, with the relatively impotent ego astride them both. Consequently, conflict is as much a part of normalcy as it is of pathology.

Anxiety is at the core of all psychopathology, operating largely at the unconscious level. Generally speaking, the person has no awareness of the deeper significance of immediate precipitating events and how they affect the underlying impulses or unresolved conflicts and fixations. As the largely unconscious anxiety intrudes on consciousness, the person tends to panic. Depending on where these conflicts and fixations first developed psychosexually, and the specific ego defenses mechanism utilized to "bind" the anxiety, the full spectrum of psychopathology takes shape. Obviously, certain responses to immediate precipitating events are more healthy than others. But at some level all symptoms are gratifying, even to highly functioning individuals. This inevitable tendency to deny and distort reality is apparently generic to the human condition (cf. Munroe, 1955, for an especially insightful treatment of these themes).

Model of Psychotherapy

The ultimate goal of psychoanalysis is the total reconstruction of the basic personality (which is the highest and most difficult goal of any system of psychotherapy). In order to accomplish this goal, psychoanalysts argue that it is necessary to "relive" certain painful childhood experiences and work them through. This process is called *abreaction* or *catharsis*. In making the unconscious conscious, the ego is strengthened, thereby facilitating a greater capacity for managing the demands of the instinctual urges within the constraints of reality. The resulting self-awareness and insight is more than merely intellectual—it is deeply felt and experienced after an agonizingly difficult and often painful process of change.

Standard psychoanalysis usually involves multiple appointments every week for at least two or three years, and often more. Obviously, this can be an expensive and demanding commitment. In actual practice, analysts work in diverse and varied ways, depending on their personal styles and the needs of their clients. Despite these differences, concerned analysts early recognized the need to reduce the length of the standard treatment, without sacrificing the technique's unique properties (Korchin, 1976, p. 325).

But it is precisely because of the length and intensity of the treatment that psychoanalysis is so widely disparaged in both lay and professional circles. Specifically, it is asserted that psychoanalysis is an elitist therapy, geared toward the rich and self-indulgent who find that talking about themselves to a highly trained analyst a great deal promotes their own sense of well-being. In their defense, psychoanalysts assert that promoting lasting and significant change is of necessity a difficult and time-consuming process. Not only do clients need to unlearn self-defeating coping strategies, but they must also develop new and more effective ones. Further, change is resisted because these same patterns have historically worked for the client, in that they bind anxiety and often lead to attention from others. As Korchin (1976, p. 325) has summarized it, "the process of character reorganization . . . is about on par with learning a new language to replace one's mother tongue, particularly if the student is ambivalent in his motivation, fighting the new experience while seeking it."

Psychoanalysts usually agree that they should remain relatively aloof and anonymous to their clients. They assert that more directive and supportive approaches have limited value, in that they tend to promote dependency rather than autonomy. Further, psychoanalysts assert that these therapies run the risk of becoming "antidevelopmental," in that they tend to lessen the necessity of the "legitimate suffering" that will occur when the client works at self-exploration. Only deep self-aware-ness and understanding can lead to the kind of insight needed to promote lasting change (see Meissner, 1985).

The most basic tool of psychoanalysis is *free association.* Clients are asked to minimize conscious control and tell everything that comes to their minds, with the expectation that more and more significant unconscious material will emerge. This "basic rule" of psychoanalysis is exceedingly difficult to follow even with the best of intentions. Most of us are loathe to speak directly and truthfully, even in the best of situations. This is especially pronounced in the context of a clinical relationship, where difficult and often painful material must be ex-plored and worked through. Resistance to free association often builds in direct proportion to the psychic significance of the unconscious material emerging. Indeed, Freudians assert that the forces that are striving toward recovery are usually met with equally strong opposing ones. And it is the analysis of these blocks or disruptions in free association that often give the analyst clues as to the nature of psychic conflicts and fixations. If they can be brought to awareness and effec-tively dealt with, increased insight can result.

Another major theme in this tradition is the analysis of the *transfer-ence* relationship that occurs between the therapist and the client. Strong, personal feelings of both a positive and a negative nature usually develop between client and therapist that go beyond the actual clinical relationship. Specifically, both client and therapist bring to the current relationship issues that are brought forward (transferred) from earlier relationships with significant others. Assuming that the analyst has dealt with his or her own "countertransference" issues (basic conflicts that might be transformed into feelings toward the client), the focus can be on bringing the client's hidden and repressed conflicts or feelings from the past, which are transferred into feelings about the therapist, into the present where they can be examined, understood and resolved. Thus client reactions toward the therapist are vitally important. Indeed, they can develop to the point where a "transference neurosis" will emerge, which then becomes the major focus of therapy. Also, a potential transition between illness and health becomes possible if the deeper meaning of the neurotic origins of the expressed feelings can be explored and worked through in the context of the client's current difficulties and needs.

Interpreting the client's resistances and defensive maneuvers is another fundamental strategy utilized in psychoanalysis. Good interpretations are appropriate in timing, tact and sensitivity. Specifically, they must be given at the level at which the client can hear them, understand them, appreciate them and incorporate them. If the interpretations are premature or inappropriate, they only lead to greater resistance. If they are well-suited, they can contribute to greater understanding and perhaps relief. Ideally, good interpretations help the client to make sense of current behavior in light of the past.

Psychoanalysts assert that *dream analysis* is especially helpful in uncovering important unconscious material. During dreams, normal conscious controls are relaxed, perhaps even more deeply then they are in free association. Through inquiry, inference and eventually interpretation, the meanings of both current and long-standing conflicts or difficulties can be explored and worked through. Although Freud once described dreams as "the royal road to the unconscious," they are "hardly a freeway with unlimited visibility, nor do hidden meanings roll forth with simple clarity" (Korchin, 1976, p. 328). As with free association, resistance and transference, working through the material is hard work that takes time and an extremely high degree of commitment on the part of the psychoanalyst and patient.

In summary, psychoanalysis consists of a variety of methods to make the unconscious conscious so that it can be worked through in the context of the psychotherapeutic relationship. In particular, the conflicts and fixations of the formative years of childhood and early adolescence are explored. These must be "reconstructed, discussed, interpreted, and analyzed" (Corey, 1986, p. 38) if any hope of lasting change is going to occur. Since the therapeutic goals are so high and difficult to obtain, and the self-defeating patterns so deeply established with the client, it is inevitable that treatment be intensive and long-term.

Few clinicians alive today can deny that they have felt the impact of Freudian thought. Hardly any well-developed approach to people-helping lacks a conception of an unconscious, an appreciation of the role of early childhood development, or an understanding of the relevance of such clinical concepts as transference and countertransference, resistance or the ego defense mechanisms. The model stresses biological and instinctual factors to the neglect of other psychosocial or sociocultural factors, but it does speak broadly and deeply to certain dimensions of the human experience. On the other hand, as Alston has noted (1967, p. 516), psychoanalytic concepts need to be more explicitly stated and anchored in objective criteria if they are going to be the basis for further interdisciplinary dialog. The works of Hackett (1986), Oakland (1977) and Walters (1973) are good initial examples of such interdisciplinary work.

While we will discuss the documented effectiveness of psychoanalysis in chapter fourteen, we note that the perceived effectiveness of Freud's psychoanalysis was enhanced by the evident clinical insightfulness he demonstrated in his writings. But according to Storr (1989, pp. 100ff.), while Freud mentioned 133 cases in his writings, he only provided extensive reports on six cases. Of these six, he only saw two for over six months, and only one for a full course of psychoanalysis. This case, the famous "Wolf Man," was "not quite the advertisement for psychoanalysis which Freud might have hoped for" (pp. 106-107). Apparently while Freud reported his analysis to be a complete success, a follow-up study suggested that the Wolf Man's analysis with Freud was only somewhat helpful, allowing him to live a life of moderate maladjustment.

Christian Critique

As might be evident from the previous section, Freudian thought has come under fire from many sectors. As Hurding (1985, p. 70) notes, Freud receives criticism "from the academic psychologists for being unscientific, from humanistic and theistic psychologists for being too reductionistic, and from the behaviourists for not being reductionistic enough." Still, a balanced and fair assessment would recognize that we owe much to Freud in assisting us in our efforts to make sense of the often bewildering complexity of our psychospiritual natures.

Philosophical Assumptions

Freud is perhaps best known in religious circles for his attacks on religion. Psychoanalysis is essentially an agnostic or atheistic system, since religion is treated as an illusion. Genuine religious motivation and the spiritual life are ignored or treated negatively in psychoanalysis (Vitz, 1987, p. 66). Exemplified in works like *The Future of an Illusion, Civilization and Its Discontents,* and *Moses and Monotheism,* the essence of Freud's argument is that the religious believer in adolescence or adulthood comes face to face with a cold, ambiguous and threatening universe in which annihilation, isolation or meaninglessness are seen as likely options. This creates overwhelming anxiety. In a primitive, self-protecting gesture, we create for ourselves a comforting illusion with which to shield ourselves. The illusion we embrace stems from real or distorted memories of our childhood years, when as weak and vulnerable persons we felt nurtured and protected by what we perceived to be omnipotent, omniscient and loving parents, specifically a father.

In a desperate attempt to maintain that sense of security and well-being and meet our adult needs and wants, we embrace some form of religion, creating an imaginary deity, a divine father-figure. Freud specifically argued that religion fulfilled three needs: "[The gods people believe in] must exorcise the terrors of nature, they must reconcile men to the cruelty of Fate, and . . . they must compensate them for the sufferings which a civilized life in common has imposed upon them" (quoted in Storr, 1989, p. 89). Indeed, the illusions we create for ourselves can also serve as a symbolic means to meet unfulfilled childhood longings as well. From the psychoanalytic perspective religion is seen as a kind of universal neurosis that civilization substitutes for a more authentic personal reality based on scientific knowledge.

In light of Vitz's (1988) treatment of the deeper motives for Freud's rejection of religion, it seems reasonable to assert that important events in his own life contributed to his antipathy toward matters of faith. In fact, Freud's profound ambivalence about Christianity in particular appears to be as much a function of his own projective tendencies as it is the logical outcome of his theorizing. Vitz suggests, for instance, that the traumatic early loss of a nanny who may have been a devout Catholic believer could have complicated Freud's feeling about religion. Vitz also documents Freud's possible dabbling in matters of the occult. There is apparently more to Freud's contention that religion lacked integrity than his "adulation of the scientific method of the day" (Hurding, 1985, p. 73). His attitudes about Christianity reflected his complex hostility and attraction to a faith that meant something to him at a deeply personal level, at the level of *Freud's* unconscious.

The analysis by Vitz and Gartner (1984a, 1984b) of Freud's understanding of religion also reveals some interesting weaknesses in the theory. They argue that if one presumes God is an illusion, then the "projection of a father figure" understanding of religion makes sense. But if one starts with a presupposition that God exists, psychoanalysis does equally well in explaining atheism!

How would the denial of a real God happen psychologically if psychoanalysis is true? If God is a heavenly "father," then disbelief in God must clearly be attributable to the Oedipal period of development. During this period, the child feels infantile rage at the same-sex parent who competes with the child for the love of the opposite-sex parent. If the child does not adequately resolve that unconscious rage at the parent during the genital stage, the unconscious rage might be played out as atheism in adulthood—what better way to get back at (or murder) a father figure than to simply not believe in him! Since one can only go so far in rejecting the earthly parent, a deeper rage, an even more primitive aggressive impulse, can be vented on God by denying his very existence.

While interesting in itself, we can also see in this brief sketch that one frequently noted problem of the theory of psychoanalysis is its very adaptability. Psychoanalysis can literally explain anything! This is quite a conundrum, in that a true and comprehensive theory would have to explain all facets of human experience, but a theory that is so flexible that it is impossible to come up with any human facts that refute the theory ceases to be a theory and achieves the status of a world view or dogma.

This case study of Freud's view of religion also highlights the epistemological problems latent in the theory. Because the theory is deemed to explain everything, and because all human experiencing (including rational reflection on truth) is viewed as shaped and determined by irrational, unconscious forces, it follows that we are ultimately locked in a closed system where everything that humans think or believe can be rendered as a function of early childhood factors. If atheism can be explained in as facile and convincing a fashion as religion, then there is no ultimate hope of ever knowing anything truly. We can all point at each other and say, "Well you believe 'X' because of your unresolved issues with your mother and father." Such an all-encompassing "psychologizing" of our capacity to know is repugnant to Christians, who believe that we are capable of knowing truly, at least at some level. Positively, it is an asset of psychoanalysis that it deeply understands our profound capacities for self-deception (which we will develop below).

Further, psychoanalysis tends to be thoroughly mechanistic and naturalistic in terms of its core hypotheses, in that it assumes that all mental events are ultimately biological and instinctual in origin. This inevitably leads to reductionistic explanations about religious matters and indeed about all that we regard as distinctively human. Freud is consistent in asserting that biological and physical laws determine every important aspect of human existence. And naturalism was not just a working hypothesis for him: "Freud was dogmatic about it" (Browning, 1987, p. 37).

Such a philosophical and scientific commitment allows no room for anything supernatural, for the kind of general or special revelation so central to the Christian faith, nor for a more constructive perspective about our spiritual urgings for deeper meaning and significance in life. Freud's system is a closed system of cause and effect with no room for a transcendent reality. It is at this point that there is no possible reconciliation with the fundamental assertions of the Christian tradition and the dictates of Freudian psychoanalysis. We concur with Hurding (1985, pp. 74-75), who states:

> The Christian believes in a creator God who brought all that exists into being and who sustains the universe by his power and love; he also declares a redeemer God who has intervened in history in countless ways but supremely in the incarnation, life, death and resurrection of His Son, and in the sending of the Holy Spirit. This is a God who calls man, both individually and corporately, to choose good rather than evil, life rather than death, the Lord's way rather than the Enemy's. This blend of divine determinism . . . and man's freedom to choose . . . is at the heart of biblical revelation and is a far cry from Freud's naturalistic world view.[3]

Model of Personality

Narramore (1985) argues that the personality concepts in psychoanalysis should stand or fall on whether or not they enable us to make sense of the complexity of human nature in light of biblical revelation and

---

[3]Other helpful treatments from a variety of perspectives on the philosophical tensions between psychoanalysis and Christian theology can be found in Browning (1987), Burnham (1985), Irwin (1975), Kristol (1970), Robinson (1985), Wallace (1983) and Wood (1980).

human experience. As with nearly every major theory we will discuss in this book, we contend that it would be a mistake to reject hypothetical constructs because their exact equivalent cannot be found directly in the Scriptures.

Our perspectives on some of the Freudian notions of psychosexual development have changed since our initial exposure to these concepts as undergraduates. Initially, we were quite skeptical, but our experiences since with our own children and clients have taught us that, broadly understood, these developmental themes have contemporary relevance. As we listen to the struggles of our clients and students, certain themes often emerge, including powerful "feelings towards parents of the opposite sex, . . . guilt over sexual feelings and actions, fears related to sexual intimacy and loving, fears of abandonment, struggles in the area of defining one's own sexual identity, anger and rage in not getting what one wanted as a child, and love/hate conflicts" (Corey, 1986, p. 39). Psychoanalysis speaks directly and deeply to the roots of these concerns. One does not need to accept all the tenets of orthodox psychoanalysis to appreciate the potential contribution of these emphases for our awareness and understanding of our client's difficulties.

Psychoanalytic thought is certainly a unifying perspective that stresses the developmental, historical and unconscious dimensions of the human experience. Although we find the approach to be overly deterministic, we share Korchin's (1976, p. 332) assessment that many of the central tenets of Freud's intrapsychic theory are perhaps less biological and universal than originally posited, and more overtly interpersonal or sociocultural.

Browning (1987) summarizes several scholars who suggest that Freud himself was actually quite torn on this point, writing sometimes in a mechanistic, deterministic vein, but at other times in an "intersubjective or . . . dialogical one" (p. 39). It is from an emphasis on the nonmechanistic aspects of Freud that the broad popularity of the contemporary psychodynamic theories has grown. There is certainly more possibility for Christian appreciation of psychoanalytic thought when theorists move away from the mechanistic aspects of psychoanalysis; we shall find this to be precisely the case in the next chapter.

Freud made his understanding of personality the backdrop for understanding all of existence. By doing so, he presented Christians with an unsatisfactory scheme for understanding the foundations for life. As Browning (1987, pp. 43-44) says, "By taking the position that the psychobiological realm is the only relevant context for human action he has indeed elevated eros [libido drive] and death [aggression drive] to metaphors of ultimacy, that is, to metaphors which represent the only effective and relevant ultimate context of experience."

Are eros/libido and death/aggression the ultimate motivational context for life? These id-drives could be described as aberrant and distorted reflections of the relational and dominion motivations we gleaned from Genesis 1—2 in chapter two. Biblically, we are seen to be positively motivated to procreate, to create and to love, and certainly the biblical attention paid to the distorted and evil sexual motivations we experience also suggests some centrality to sexual motivation in life. Further, the Scriptures assert very clearly that sinful humanity is bent on death and self-destruction. Aggression is sometimes understood as an aspect of control, making it possible that Freud's "darker drive" is a depraved version of our dominion drive.

We also note (with Van Leeuwen, 1985) that Freud's description of humans as having two intrinsically opposed core motivations places conflict as central and endemic to being human. Unlike the humanistic theories which say that humans are basically good but "messed up" by external influences, psychoanalysis says that to be human is to be torn by conflict. This darker reading of the human plight is much closer to biblical reality than romantic humanism. Christianity does not paint the conflict in the same way, but suggests that our conflict is most fundamentally between longing for God and being in rebellion against him. A Christian point of view is not completely incompatible, however, with the psychoanalytic view of motivation.

We appreciate Freud's stress on the reality of unconscious mental processes. Certainly there is a reality beyond that which we are immediately aware, perhaps most directly evident in the content of our dreams. In the clinical context, both free association and other psychoanalytic techniques strongly suggest that there is a level of thinking and feeling beyond direct consciousness. These assertions are not inconsistent with the scriptural understanding of persons.

We share the widespread appreciation for the psychoanalytic understanding of the defense mechanisms, especially as they are developed in clinical treatments (e.g., Meissner, 1985). The Scriptures speak directly to our tendencies to be deceitful to self and others and to avoid facing painful realities (cf. Jer 17:9). As Narramore (1985, p. 900) says, psychoanalysis's "understanding of the role of the defense mechanisms . . . goes beyond scriptural descriptions of how we avoid facing painful reality but is consistent with that scripturally described process."

Psychoanalysis can contribute much to our awareness of both the unhealthy and healthy ways that conflict and sin can be dealt with in the context of our religious communities. Indeed, the language of the ego defense mechanisms has so widely and thoroughly permeated contemporary Western culture that it is difficult to imagine how we could discuss our avoidant tendencies without such terminology. Psychoanalysis asserts that we can learn more adaptive and task-oriented means of managing anxiety. The limitation, however, of the psychoanalytic approach is that there are serious constraints on that potential due to our sinful nature (i.e., we are in need of divine intervention; we can't heal ourselves).

Psychoanalysis essentially contends that all behavior is purposeful and motivated. This assertion is not inconsistent with scriptural teachings about the nature of human beings. Nor is the assumption about the crucial importance of early childhood experience. Indeed, the Scriptures assert that the parenting relationship, like the marital relationship, ought to reflect the divine-human encounter (cf. Narramore, 1979; Prov 22:6), with all the inherent risks and responsibilities. The psychoanalytic assertion of the importance of familial, early life experiences alone does not, however, constitute a substantial contact point with Christianity, as any reasonable understanding of human life would emphasize these primary relationships as formative.

Model of Health

It should be evident from the earlier section on Freudian notions of health that the model stresses individualism over and against interdependence. We find this to be a matter of deep concern, since our understanding of the Christian tradition emphasizes a deep awareness of our utter dependence on God and the absolute necessity of developing meaningful and significant relationships with others, both within the body of Christ and in the broader community and society in which we live. Our concern is that the insight and self-awareness so deeply valued in the psychoanalytic tradition won't necessarily translate into appropriate other-directed behaviors. Rather, it will remain largely self-directed or self-serving.

Psychoanalysis is actually so oriented to understanding the person as a self-contained psychological system that even for the healthy person, "relationships with other human beings are of value only in so far as they facilitate instinctual gratification" (Storr, 1989, p. 91).

Browning (1987) noted that a literal interpretation of Freudian thought would inevitably make us skeptical about whether or not there is such a thing as authentic and legitimate altruistic service toward others that is free of self-serving gain. How could Freudian thought, for example, account for the sacrificial service of Mother Teresa in the slums of Calcutta?

A clearly articulated, stable ethical system is lacking in psychoanalysis (Browning, 1987, pp. 48ff.), though like all systems, it actually contains an implicit system in its view of health. The best description of its implicit ethic might be that of a "cautious but fair reciprocity" (p. 49). It is a reciprocity system because Freud recognized that if each person ultimately cares only about his or her own gratification, then we must each trade gratifications to keep everyone satisfied. It is cautious because Freud believed that libidinal energies are ultimately for our own satisfaction. We cautiously give to others so that we can get what we want.

But the stance of "cautious reciprocity" stands in stark contrast to the kind of costly discipleship and risk-taking inherent in Christian morality. Authentic love for the other *(agape)* is not based on reciprocity, but on our common family membership, on Christ's example, and on the Spirit's enablement. Granted, many of our efforts to be "loving" or distinctively and decidedly "Christian" in our compassion are less than noble or pure. But the assumption in psychoanalysis is that there is no normative basis for responsible ethical decision-making and action. In particular, psychoanalysis is profoundly ambivalent about whether or not there can be any genuine commitment to an absolute like the love of God or the love of one's neighbor. Psychoanalysis is brutally honest about our propensity toward extrinsic motivation, but asserts that intrinsic motivation, especially in a religious context, is largely an illusion.

Another concern about the Freudian notion of wellness is its extreme emphasis on subjectivism. Self-awareness tends to become a major goal of the maturation process. Our fear is whether a preoccupation with the "inner reality" of one's psychic life will replace any appropriate concern about the "outer reality" of God or the necessary obligations to the local church and community. Our worst fear is that the psychoanalytic mindset become so all-consuming that it breed an unhealthy narcissism and self-absorption that removes one from engaging with the world of everyday living. No doubt there is a need for greater self-awareness and understanding in our Christian communities, but this should not develop into an escape from active involvement in the local church or with the lives of suffering persons. Obviously, a healthy balance between escape and engagement is essential. The need to "know thyself" must not replace the command to "love God and others."

What is desperately needed in our Christian communities today are persons who can balance a desire and willingness to know self with an equally strong passion to know God. This accords marvelously with John Calvin's discussion in the first chapter of his *Institutes of the Christian Religion* (1.1.1-2):

> Our wisdom, in so far as it ought to be deemed true and solid wisdom, consists almost entirely of two parts: the knowledge of God and of ourselves. But as these are connected together by many ties, it is not easy to determine which of the two precedes, and gives birth to the other. For, in the first place, no man can survey himself without forthwith turning his thoughts toward God in whom he lives and moves. . . . On the other hand, it is evident that man never attains to a true self-knowledge until he has previously contemplated the face of God, and come down after such contemplation to look into himself.

A final fear relates to our concern about the ultimate direction of the maturation process in psychoanalysis. As Christians, we must continually remind ourselves that our ultimate salvation comes from without, not from within. There is the distinct danger in psychoanalysis of a kind of gnosticism where self-knowledge is seen as a means to self-salvation (cf. Vitz, 1987, p. 73). Specifically, the cultivation and expression of the Christian virtues (Roberts, 1982, 1984) should be seen as the apex of sanctification for the committed believer, not self-awareness and insight. The search for psychological wholeness ought not to replace our desire to know God or pursue authentic holiness.

A wonderfully helpful example of how concerned and committed Christian theoreticians can correct some of these inadequacies can be found in two articles by Vitz and Gartner (1984a, 1984b). At the core of the Freudian critique of Christianity is the assertion that unresolved Oedipal issues are foundational in the formation of one's superego (e.g., the son tries to take over the role of the father). In contrast, a more theologically informed understanding of the sacrificial love of the Son for the Father and how the obedient death of the Son brings ultimate redemption, can illustrate how the life of Jesus becomes a needed corrective for the unresolved issues of the "unredeemed self" caught in unresolved Oedipal tensions. In short, Jesus serves as a kind of "anti-Oedipus" who finds life by obediently doing his Father's will rather than trying to destroy the Father. Part of the "good news" of the gospel, then, is the potential power that comes when the perpetual fear and self-hatred of the Father due to the Oedipal crisis can be replaced by a thorough transformation of the mind through conversion and Christian commitment. The "unredeemed self" studied by Freud can be changed into a "redeemed self" in Christ through the mystery of belief in the Incarnation, crucifixion and resurrection of Jesus.

Model of Abnormality

The psychoanalytic approach speaks deeply and meaningfully to the origins and functions of symptoms. It seems foolish to disregard the impact of critical life events in the formative years or to neglect the role of the ego defense mechanisms in the etiology and maintenance of "problems in living." On the other hand, it does not necessarily follow that one must dwell exclusively on these matters in order to help clients make sense of the roots of their difficulties.

Psychoanalysis contends that the root of much of our psychopathology can be found in aberrant psychosexual development. In particular, aggressive or sexual impulses are major determinants of our neurotic tendencies. This is not consistent with the thrust of Scripture, where our own drive to be autonomous and godlike (i.e., pride) is seen as a more basic source of maladjustment and sin (Narramore, 1985, p. 900). Sexual impulses are troublesome but have become so because of our rebellion against God.

The Freudian tradition is prone to reductionistic interpretations of the etiology and maintenance of symptoms. This is inconsistent with the thrust of contemporary thought in the human sciences, where etiology is more accurately seen as a function of multiple factors for almost all disorders. Despite its strong emphasis on the biological and instinctual bases for behaviors, Freudian thought has very little to say about more recent advances in biological psychiatry and medicine (e.g., neurotransmitters, chemical imbalances, genetic predispositions and so on). In its defense, psychoanalysis was originally focused on the concerns of reasonably high-functioning neurotics in a particular cultural and historical context. But the scope of psychoanalytic practice has been considerably broadened since its inception.

Traditional psychoanalysis needs a much broader base of social motivations and dynamics to be closer to a more biblical understanding of persons. The more one views psychoanalysis as not just a tool in the therapist's armamentarium, but as a world view as well, the more difficult it seems to reconcile psychoanalysis and legitimate religious concerns (Wallace, 1983).

Model of Psychotherapy

Responsible eclectic therapists find psychodynamic concepts like resistance, transference and countertransference, and the ego defense mechanisms to be extremely useful in exploring current difficulties in a client's life. Further, awareness of the psychoanalytic distinctives probably helps these same clinicians to have a greater depth of awareness and understanding in their efforts to assist their clients. Broadly understood, Freudian thought can be a powerful model for understanding behavior.

Psychoanalysis, when practiced in its strict classical form, is widely perceived as impractical for the majority of mental-health settings in this country or abroad. This is due to the time and expense that is involved and the limited availability of highly trained psychoanalysts. Few potential clients have the necessary financial and personal resources (e.g., introspective and verbal skills) and fewer still are willing to make the kind of commitment of those resources that would be necessary for a successful analysis. The lofty goal of personality reconstruction is probably inappropriate and unrealistic for the vast majority of suffering persons.

But there might be ways to transcend certain of these limitations. Klein (1970), for example, suggests that society should underwrite part of the cost of psychoanalysis for truly needy clients as well as a limited number of future psychotherapists. He suggests that this would contribute much to the continued development of the mental-health movement and to the direct well-being of the persons involved. The Institute for Psychoanalysis in Chicago (Desruisseaux, 1983) has been exemplary in offering low-cost psychoanalytic training and treatment to human-service providers (e.g., teachers, child-care workers, etc.). By investing in the lives of those persons "in the trenches," they are making a long-term contribution to the mental and emotional well-being of the lives their clients will touch.

We respect the emphasis of this tradition on the training and supervision of future therapists. No major system of psychotherapy takes the personal development of the clinician more seriously than does psychoanalysis. Only after years of personal therapy, specialized coursework and careful supervision of select cases can the psychoanalyst become "certified." Historically, these individuals have been trained initially as medical doctors and psychiatrists, but recently the way has been cleared for members of other mental-health professions to become certified analysts. With the incredible proliferation of people-helpers in our society, the careful and meticulous preparation of the psychoanalyst is certainly to be commended.

Such training, however, is not without its risks. Psychoanalysis is often accused of being a professional guild. But even within that establishment many articulate and vocal critics can be found (e.g., Robert Coles, a committed Christian psychiatrist and Harvard professor). But all too often the professional isolation remains, creating for all practical purposes rather exclusive clubs of the fully initiated, "true believers." This has done little to create good will with other traditions within the mental-health field.

We also have a concern that classic psychoanalytic treatment is not necessarily a good model for either clinical or personal relationships. Certainly there is a need for clinicians to listen attentively and respectfully to the verbalizations of their clients. But the risk is that the often cold, distant, anonymous style of the analyst can replace a more balanced and genuinely warm style that we more often associate with authentic Christian love and concern. The anonymous relationship that may be necessary for the formation of a transference neurosis can covertly or even overtly communicate deeper values about relationships in general. As Miller and Jackson (1985) have noted, notions of "ideal" clinical or personal relationships should be deeply informed by both societal standards and religious belief systems. Psychoanalytic therapy raises tough questions about what it means to care for others and be fully present to them. Specifically, it asserts that there is an essential place for the quiet receptivity of the psychoanalyst (Kovel, 1976). But whether or not it should be the primary relational modality of the psychoanalyst is a matter of intense debate both within and without psychoanalytic circles.

Finally, we sense a certain fatalism and pessimism in intensive and long-term psychoanalytic treatment. Obviously, a tremendous commitment of time, energy and expense is needed to bring about increased self- control and self-regulation through greater insight and self-awareness. Although we agree with Wheelis (1978) that change is all too often painfully slow and agonizingly difficult, the Christian faith commitment raises the possibility of quick, dramatic change in an individual's life (cf. McLemore, 1982). Granted, persons bring into their Christian conversion their "raw material," but the possibilities for change are certainly greater than psychoanalysis would have us believe, although perhaps less dramatic and sudden than many Christians would like to believe. Still, the belief in the possibility of the miraculous is at the root of some of the hope we have in our Creator-God.

Conclusion

Psychoanalysis deserves to be more than a whipping boy for conservative Christians. It is a comprehensive and exhaustive system of personality, psychopathology and psychotherapy that should be carefully considered by committed and thoughtful persons of faith. Our primary concerns have to do with some of the metapsychological assumptions of the Freudian world view.

In our judgment, psychoanalysis as a therapy is probably inappropriate and impractical for all but a very few carefully selected individuals. The model certainly needs to be more clearly articulated so that the central tenets are amenable to more rigorous clinical and empirical investigation. But we still assert that it is highly advisable to think, on occasion, in psychoanalytic terms so as to give greater structure and direction to our efforts to be effective change agents. On the other hand, the committed Christian needs to offer clearly articulated correctives to some of the deficiencies that can be found in this tradition, especially with reference to the overly deterministic and naturalistic assumptions. We fully suspect that classic psychoanalysis will serve as a springboard for discussion, debate and dialog for decades to come in Christian counseling circles. Perhaps its most enduring legacy will be that it gave birth to the approaches discussed in the next chapter.

For Further Reading

Basch, M. (1980). *Doing psychotherapy*. New York: Basic Books.
  An excellent contemporary introduction to the process of psychoanalytic psychotherapy.
Brenner, C. (1973). *An elementary textbook of psychoanalysis*. Garden City, NY: Anchor/Doubleday.
  A brief introduction to Freudian thought.
Gay, P. (1989). *The Freud reader*. New York: W. W. Norton.
  The best of the many edited readers available in print today. Gay is a highly respected Freud scholar.
Meissner, W. (1985). Theories of personality and psychopathology: Classical

psychoanalysis. In H. I. Kaplan and B. J. Sadock (Eds.), *Comprehensive textbook of psychiatry* (Vol. 4) (pp. 337-418). Baltimore, MD: Williams and Wilkins. A most useful synthesis for the serious student of Freudian thought by a psychiatrist who is also a Jesuit priest.

Storr, A. (1989). *Freud.* New York: Oxford.
A readable brief introduction to Freudian thought.

Vitz, P. (1988). *Sigmund Freud's Christian unconscious.* New York: Guilford.
A terrific stimulus for discussion and dialog about Freud's distaste for religious matters.

Wallace, E. (1983). Reflections on the relationship between psychoanalysis and Christianity. *Pastoral Psychology, 31,* 215-243.
One of the best of the many introductory articles available that speaks directly to integrative issues.

References

Alston, W. (1967). Psychoanalytic theories, logical status of. In P. Edwards (Ed.), *The encyclopedia of philosophy* (Vols. 5-6) (pp. 512-516). New York: Macmillan.

Arlow, J. (1984). Psychoanalysis. In R. Corsini (Ed.), *Current psychotherapies* (3d ed.) (pp. 14-55). Itasca, IL: F. E. Peacock.

Berger, K. (1988). *The developing person through the life span* (2d ed.). New York: Worth.

Brenner, C. (1973). *An elementary textbook of psychoanalysis.* Garden City, NY: Anchor/Doubleday.

Browning, D. (1987). *Religious thought and the modern psychologies.* Philadelphia: Fortress Press.

Burnham, J. (1985). The encounter of Christian theology with deterministic psychology and psychoanalysis. *Bulletin of the Menninger Clinic, 49,* 321-352.

Calvin, J. (1981). *Institutes of the Christian religion* (H. Beveridge, Trans.). Grand Rapids, MI: Eerdmans (original work published 1559).

Corey, G. (1986). *Theory and practice of counseling and psychotherapy* (3d ed.), Monterey, CA: Brooks/Cole.

Crabb, L. (1988). *Inside out.* Colorado Springs, CO: NavPress.

Desruisseaux, P. (1983, January 12). Psychoanalysis: Off the couch and into the streets of Chicago. *The Chronicle of Higher Education.*

Erikson, E. (1982). *The life cycle completed: A review.* New York: Norton.

Ford, D. , and Urban, H. (1963). *Systems of psychotherapy: A comparative study.* New York: Wiley.

Hackett, C. (1986). Psychoanalysis and theology: Two dialectics. *Journal of Religion and Health, 25,* 29-45.

Hurding, R. (1985). *Roots and shoots.* London: Hodder and Stoughton.

Irwin, J. (1975). Reinhold Neibuhr's critique of Freudian psychoanalysis. *Journal of Religion and Health, 14,* 242-254.

Jones, J., and Wilson, W. (1987). *An incomplete education.* New York: Ballantine.

Klein, G. (1970, August). Is psychoanalysis relevant? Paper presented at the annual convention of the American Psychological Association, Miami, FL.

Korchin, S. (1976). *Modern clinical psychology.* New York: Basic Books.

Kovel, J. (1976). *A complete guide to therapy.* New York: Pantheon.

Kristol, I. (1970). God and the psychoanalysts. In A. H. Cohen (Ed.), *Arguments and doctrines.* New York: Harper & Row.

McLemore, C. (1982). *The scandal of psychotherapy.* Wheaton, IL: Tyndale.

McLemore, C. (1984). *Honest Christianity.* Philadelphia: Westminister.

Meissner, W. (1985). Theories of personality and psychopathology: Classical psychoanalysis. In H. I. Kaplan and B. J. Sadock (Eds.), *Comprehensive textbook of psychiatry* (Vol. 4) (pp. 337-418). Baltimore, MD: Williams and Wilkins.

Miller, W., and Jackson, K. (1985). *Practical psychology for pastors.* Englewood Cliffs, NJ: Prentice-Hall.

Munroe, R. (1955). *Schools of psychoanalytic thought.* New York: Holt, Rinehart and Winston.

Narramore, S. (1979). *Parenting with love and limits.* Grand Rapids, MI: Zondervan.

Narramore, S. (1984). *No condemnation.* Grand Rapids, MI: Zondervan.

Narramore, S. (1985). Psychoanalytic psychotherapy. In D. G. Benner (Ed.), *Baker encyclopedia of psychology* (pp. 896-900). Grand Rapids, MI: Baker.

Oakland, J. (1977). The introjected and the intrinsic in psychology and Christianity. *Journal of Psychology and Theology, 5,* 91-94.

Peck, S. (1983). *People of the lie.* New York: Simon and Schuster.

Prochaska, J. (1979). *Systems of psychotherapy: A transtheoretical analysis.* Homewood, IL: Dorsey Press.

Roberts, R. (1982). *Spirituality and human emotion.* Grand Rapids, MI: Eerdmans.

Roberts, R. (1984). *The strengths of a Christian.* Philadelphia: Westminister.

Robinson, L. (1985). The illusion of no future: Psychoanalysis and religion. *Journal of the American Academy of Psychoanalysis, 13,* 211-228.

Rychlak, J. (1973). *Introduction to personality and psychotherapy.* Boston: Houghton Mifflin.

Ryckman, R. (1985). *Theories of personality* (3d ed.). Monterey, CA: Brooks/Cole.

Silverman, L. (1976). Psychoanalytic theory: The reports of my death are greatly exaggerated. *American Psychologist, 31,* 621-637.

Storr, A. (1989). *Freud.* New York: Oxford.

Van Leeuwen, M. (1985). *The person in psychology: A contemporary Christian appraisal.* Grand Rapids, MI: Eerdmans.

Vitz, P. (1987). Secular personality theories: A critical analysis. In T. J. Burke (Ed.), *Man and mind: A Christian theory of personality* (pp. 65-94). Hillsdale, MI: Hillsdale College Press.

Vitz, P. (1988). *Sigmund Freud's Christian unconscious.* New York: Guilford.

Vitz, P., and Gartner, J. (1984a). Christianity and psychoanalysis, part I: Jesus as the anti-Oedipus. *Journal of Psychology and Theology, 12,* 4-14.

Vitz, P., and Gartner, J. (1984b). Christianity and psychoanalysis, part II: Jesus as the transformer of the superego. *Journal of Psychology and Theology, 12,* 82-90.

Wallace, E. (1983). Reflections on the relationship between psychoanalysis and

Christianity. *Pastoral Psychology, 31,* 215-243.

Walters, O. (1973). Psychodynamics in Tillich's theology. *Journal of Religion and Health, 12,* 342-353.

Wheelis, A. (1978). *How people change.* New York: Harper & Row.

Wood, B. (1980). The religion of psychoanalysis. *The American Journal of Psychoanalysis, 40,* 13-26.

4

CONTEMPORARY PSYCHODYNAMIC PSYCHOTHERAPIES

written with Michael W. Mangis

*T*he contemporary psychodynamic psychotherapies are those schools of thought influenced by Freud and classic psychoanalysis that have evolved substantially beyond orthodox analytic thought. Christians have not been alone in being dissatisfied with the deterministic and mechanistic assumptions of the Freudian system, which paint a picture of humans as isolated beings irrationally driven by biological, primitive drives welling up within them, their personalities molded by discrete psychic structures interacting mechanically and unconsciously to achieve compromises leading to drive gratification. Christians have also not been alone in seeing the rich possibilities of a system that seeks to understand the profound impact of early relationships upon our character, the mysterious way in which we are shaped by unconscious processes, and the pervasive presence of psychological conflict in our lives.

In fact, many argue that Freud himself led the way in attempting to resolve some of the mechanistic and deterministic problems in his own model. The focus of much of Freud's later work was on the ego as presented in *The Ego and the Id* (originally published 1923). In his earliest theorizing, when he was working from his "seduction theory," Freud emphasized interpersonal environment as the cause of pathology. He quickly moved away from that position to a more "scientific" view where psychological development was seen as an almost entirely internal and self-contained process. The person was seen as controlled by biological instincts and drives and by the actions and fantasies associated with those drives. The ego had little true efficacy. But in *The Ego and the Id*, Freud began to acknowledge again the role of the environment, of relationships, in the development of the internal workings of the mind.

Some theorists have suggested that Freud intended *The Ego and the Id* to be a major paradigm shift, a new direction in his thinking, but others vehemently disagree. The classical psychoanalytic school, described in the previous chapter, believes Freud was not overhauling his thought but fine-tuning it. They have remained true to the bulk of Freud's work and see psychological development as being entirely controlled by biological drives; the psychic structures of id, ego and superego; and the effects of psychosexual development. For the traditional psychoanalyst, the instinctual drive model was and continues to be the only viable focal point for understanding human nature.

Descriptive Survey

Whether it was his intent or not, Freud's new thinking about the ego did create a dramatic shift in some psychoanalytic circles, resulting in several new models and paradigms. These Neo-Freudian, or post-Freudian, theorists share an appreciation for the way traditional psychoanalysis illuminates the complexity of our conflicting motivations and the influence of unconscious processes. Their key differences with classic psychoanalysis have to do with the ways in which these intricate processes are explained. Generally speaking, their formulations are less biological and mechanistic, and more respectful of cognitive and interpersonal processes, precisely because they have shifted from Freud's emphasis on id and drive to an emphasis on ego, self and relationships. As Guntrip (1969, p. 326) has noted,

Emphasis has moved away from "instinct entities" and their control, on to the vital problem of how we begin to grow an ego, the core of a personal self, in infancy; and how this growth in personal reality is rooted in the baby's environment of personal relations, first with the mother, then the father, family, neighbours, school, and the ever-widening world around.

Contemporary psychodynamic thinking is usually divided into three camps (Pine, 1988): ego psychology, object-relations theories and self psychology.

Ego psychology, usually dubbed the "American school," stresses the development of personality across the life span. It does not deny that certain conflicts reflect id-impulses striving for immediate gratification, but it does assert that the ego strivings for adaptability, competency and mastery are at least as important. The model is mostly an adaptation of Freud's original thought with a heightened emphasis on ego and relationships. Beyond the tensions surrounding sex and aggression, issues of identity, intimacy and integrity become especially striking and salient in this tradition. Erik Erikson, Anna Freud, Heinz Hartmann, Rudolf Lowenstein and David Rapaport are among the major theoreticians in this tradition (cf. Korchin, 1976; Prochaska, 1984).

Object relations similarly emphasizes the outward focus of the ego, rejects Freud's narrow range of hypothesized instincts and de-emphasizes or ignores his main psychic structures. Collectively called the "British school," these theorists concentrate on those first few years of life where they believe the foundation of the personality is laid. Experiences and relationships in these early years, they assert, leave impressions on the personality that profoundly affect the individual throughout the life span. The main determinant of personality is presumed to be the internalized images that we each carry within us of the primary relational figures in our past ("objects" such as mother and father). Personality is then understood primarily in terms of the relationships among and characteristics of these internalized "objects." These internal images or objects then are the primary psychic structures, replacing id, ego and superego. The interrelations of the objects create our psychological drives, rather than them welling up from the id (Edkins, 1985). The drives themselves are deemed relational rather than crudely sexual and aggressive. Well-known theorists in this tradition include W. R. D. Fairbairn and Otto Kernberg.

Self psychology, established by Heinz Kohut and his followers, also emphasizes the experiences of the early years in the development of a sense of identity after a process of differentiation and integration (to be explained shortly). If early relationships are healthy and nurturing, a stable or "true" self will develop that is capable of mature relationships. If the early environment is characterized by deprivation, however, the resulting "false" self remains limited in its relationship capacity (i.e., the individual cannot value both autonomy and community). A more mature identity is one that is open to input from others without a competing fear of being overwhelmed. Whereas the object-relations school focuses on psychological relations between internalized objects, self psychology goes the further step of positing a strong entity of *self* that is not a separate psychic structure, but rather "might be said [to be] the sum of all these [intrapsychic] entities plus an unnamed integrating function" (Johnson, 1985, p. 1052). Such a cohesive and higher-order entity is quite a departure from Freud's original thought.

Greenberg and Mitchell (1983) point out that the three traditions share a common view of the primacy of cognitive and interpersonal processes as the building blocks of personality. The ego psychologists accommodate classic psychoanalysis by building upon it. They modify the classical id-drive model by emphasizing early, formative relationships. A more radical alternative strategy, adopted by the object-relations theorists, requires complete replacement of the drive concept with a strong interpersonal model. Greenberg and Mitchell suggest that a third category, one of model mixing, describes the self psychology of Heinz Kohut and his followers; they have adopted drive-model concepts and mixed them with the relational model.

Our focus in this chapter will be on the commonalities of the psychodynamic models. Because each of the three models, and indeed different theorists within the three traditions, can be radically different from one another, we will stay at a general level in our presentation. Because of the popularity of object-relations theory, we will discuss it more than the other models.

As should be evident from the previous chapter, many of the fundamental tenets of classic psychoanalysis are simply irreconcilable with an orthodox Christian world view. It is our judgment, however, that these contemporary variations on Freudian thought deserve a closer inspection because of their rich integrative potential. These contemporary psychodynamic movements have generally inherited the distrust of organized religion because of their roots in traditional psychoanalysis. But there seems to be considerably less overt hostility toward religion in general in the writings of these contemporary theorists than was true of Freud himself.

Further, psychodynamic psychotherapy has become enormously influential in recent decades. In the judgment of many academicians and clinicians, these approaches have been fertile ground for broad-ranging discussions about personality, psychopathology and psychotherapy. It is not surprising then that growing numbers of Christian mental-health professionals have found these ever-evolving formulations to be useful in relating their Christian faith and practice with their professional lives.[1] We suspect that the majority of Christian psychologists today would describe themselves as psychodynamic or at least "psychodynamically informed."

Philosophical Assumptions

Few if any of the psychodynamic theorists have made the kinds of broad dogmatic assertions that Freud did, and this makes it difficult to explicate any fundamental philosophical presuppositions in these models. Since all are revisions of Freudian thought, all are likely to share the naturalistic or materialistic assumptions of psychoanalysis. Yet all of the models have rejected the mechanistic metapsychology of Freud and have thus opened up the possibility for a more satisfactory resolution of the determinism/causality issue than was possible with Freud. Nevertheless, none of the models, to our knowledge, have explicitly embraced a limited human freedom stance compatible with Christian belief. We will develop in the critique below how this might, in fact, be attainable.

Workman (1988) convincingly argues that these models share what might be called a "subjective epistemology" that is congruent with contemporary thinking in philosophical epistemology. The core of this view is that knowable reality is a "function of the inner world of experience as perceived" by the person (p. 3). External reality is ultimately unknowable except through the intermediary of psychological experience.

---

[1]In fact, several approaches to Christian counseling have their roots in this tradition. The work of Lake (1966, 1986), called "clinical theology," is fundamentally a derivative from contemporary psychodynamic thought, specifically of the object-relations variety. The "healing of memories" phenomenon (e.g., Linn and Linn, 1978; Seamands, 1985) is best understood as a lay derivative of a psychodynamic understanding of persons, though it proposes a directly supernatural methodology for healing. Hurding (1985) has developed a thoughtful critique of the clinical-theology and healing-of-memories approaches. Kirwan (1984) has also developed a psychodynamic approach to Christian counseling that he claims is compatible with Christian belief.

Model of Personality

Object representations, or *introjects,* are intrapsychic structures that are significantly affected by interpersonal relations. More specifically, introjects are the mental representations of the self and others (the objects). As mentioned previously, the central tenet of psychoanalysis and of psychodynamic theories in general is that each individual has an internal world that is affected by the past and which, in turn, affects one's functioning in the present, external world. According to object-relations theories, the past affects us through internalized memories and images of events and relationships. We are usually not conscious of these imprints, but they influence our daily lives in profound and significant ways.

When we interact with a person we are relating not just to the real person that stands before us but to an internal representation or idea that we have of who that person is. It is seldom possible for that internalized representation of the person to be wholly based on the reality of who the person is. Rather, our perception is colored by past images of events and people. In a sense, we relate to real people through our internal representations of past relations. For example, a person may look like someone we once knew; or someone may be in a position of authority and therefore stir up memories of our parents; a person's mannerisms or tone of voice may set off other cues, and so forth. In short, we transfer parts of past images of people (often called *object representations*) onto others. If these past images are strong enough, and if our ability to sort out the distortions from the reality is weak enough, we may act and feel in quite unrealistic ways toward this person. We may feel resentful toward them when they have done nothing to anger us. We may feel dependent on them for no apparent reason. Our feelings may vary dramatically toward them in any given encounter or across time.

In addition to these internal representations of others, we have internal representations of ourselves. In our earliest interactions with the important people in our environment we form ideas of who we are. A common example is the "gleam in the mother's eye." When an infant gazes up into his mother's eyes, her expression provides the child with a mirror image of himself. These mirror images form the earliest perceptions of self. If we are treated with adequate nurturing and protection we will develop a whole and integrated sense of self. This representation will include a realistic awareness of both good and bad qualities coexisting. In an environment where the needs are not adequately met, however, this integrated sense of self cannot develop. Instead, an incomplete or inaccurate sense of who we are is formed.

The development of the mature, or integrated, self is thought to take place in several stages through the first few years of life. To adequately complete a stage, parents need to meet the needs of the child in a loving and consistent fashion. In their study of young children, Mahler (1968) and her associates (Mahler, Pine and Bergman, 1975) utilized object-relations theory to provide a model of the psychological birth of the child, which is considered to take place over the two years following the biological birth. They suggest that the self develops in three primary stages. From physical birth (or perhaps even within the womb) until approximately two months of age, the normal infant exists in the *autism stage,* characterized by what is called "absolute primary narcissism." During this phase, infants are aware only of physical sensations which they experience as globally pleasant or unpleasant. Children are not able to distinguish between self and external world; they have no sense of identity whatsoever.

In the *symbiotic stage,* from about two to six months, the infant experiences a sense of oneness or symbiosis with the primary caregiver. The child is presumed to be only aware of the functions that the parent serves in meeting the needs of the infant. Thus, the infant views the parent as something of an "object."

From six months to two years, the child is engaged in the process of *separation and individuation,* which has several stages. The child first begins to focus externally, rather than on her own bodily sensations. As she begins to move about and explore her world, and to be able to affect her world (by grabbing things, etc.), her sense of separateness or differentness from the external world is heightened. This usually results in ambivalence as the child is conflicted between feelings of independence and wonder, on the one hand, and fear, on the other, which results from the loss of the ever-present sense of the parent's reassuring presence. These feelings feed the infant's sense of the parent as good and loving but also bad and frustrating.

Similarly, the child begins in this stage to realize that she can also be good and bad. For normal development to occur, the parent must walk the fine line of both encouraging independence while continuing to serve as a source of protection and nurturance. Overemphasis on either extreme can result in personality disturbances. If this phase is successfully navigated, the child achieves the optimal resolution of being able to internalize mental representations of parent and self that are stable, realistic (recognizing good and bad in self and parent) and comforting (because the parent's love and protection are with the child even when separated from the parent). The child feels loved and lovable, and has a sense of her capacity for independence and interdependence.

Since we carry around internal images of ourselves and of others, relationships can become complicated events. Not only are two real people interacting, but one's internal image of oneself is relating to the internal image of the other person, and the same is happening in the other person as well. In a reasonably mature individual the internal objects, or representations of self and others, have been allowed to develop adequately and come close to external reality. In a person who has been subjected to inadequate or nonexistent parenting there is little ability to discriminate between the reality and the distorted internal objects; this person seems to be responding to an "inner agenda" rather than true interpersonal reality. This function of discriminating between the internal images and the external reality belongs to the ego, and this emphasis on the relation between the internal images and the external reality is the primary difference between contemporary psychoanalysis and its classical ancestry. (This interest in relationships is also what led to the establishment of an object-relations school of family therapy, as discussed in chapter fourteen.)

Model of Health
As just described, the infant begins the process of maturation essentially unaware of the existence of others. As the child develops, a process of learning to separate and individuate from others takes place. The child learns to differentiate self from other, and can carry on a healthy, interdependent relationship with another person. Such a relationship is characterized by a valuing of other persons for more than their usefulness in meeting needs and desires. Maturity is, then, "the realization of our full potentialities as persons in personal relationships" (Guntrip, 1969, p. 324).

One of the most refreshing aspects of contemporary psychodynamic psychology is its definition of health. This is somewhat ironic since it, like its psychoanalytic counterpart, is essentially a psychology of sickness. This focus on the abnormal is obvious in light of the way in which the previous discussion of personality theory turned quickly to a discussion of disruptions of development. Psychodynamic theory has been constructed through the clinical experiences of the theorists who practice therapy. Such a system is necessarily skewed toward finding pathology. Nevertheless, by extrapolating from the theories of pathology and by observing the health that is there, as well as the health that develops, a model of maturity can be developed.

The mature adult, according to the relational model, sees self and others in a constant way that deviates only minimally from reality. The adult is, as a result, capable of enjoyable and interdependent relationships. Such individuals have learned to value others for qualities beyond their usefulness (unlike the narcissistic person). They can also view self and others as having an integration of both good and bad qualities without having to either reject or idealize others on the basis of passing moods or pressing needs (unlike the person with a borderline personality disorder).

Since the mature individual perceives the world, and other people, accurately, there is no need for exaggerated psychological defenses. Defenses are built initially against the real hazards of the world—pain inflicted, accidentally or intentionally, by people or events of our childhood. Later, however, we continue to project the threats of pain onto the world or people in the world when, in reality, those threats do not exist. The mature individual trusts others but remains aware that at times of potential pain the self may need to be defended.

Model of Abnormality

Given an adequate environment where the parent nurtures the child and meets his needs, the process of maturation is thought to unfold naturally. But for many the necessary nurture is not provided and the resulting immature personality, deprived of such a relationship, remains stuck in the early phase of viewing others for their usefulness in meeting internal needs. The object-relations literature primarily focuses on categorizing and treating the disorders of the personality that can result when the needs of the developing self are not adequately met.

A fragmented internal sense of self most frequently occurs when the primary parent is not healthy enough to provide adequately for the psychological needs of the child. Such a parent never had those needs adequately met for himself or herself. The parent will provide either little or no love, inappropriately intimate attention, love in an unpredictable way, or love only when the child acts as the parent wants him or her to act. In such an environment, the child's internal sense of self can become distorted in many ways. One common example is an inability to "own" or experience as part of ourselves those aspects that our parents found unacceptable, as when a parent rejects a child when she is needy. This may result in a fragmented psychology wherein the "bad" parts are "split off" from the acceptable parts, and the person's sense of a coherent identity is damaged.

Freud essentially divided psychopathology into two categories, neurosis and psychosis. Psychosis, the inability of the ego to interact with the reality of the external world, was seen as largely untreatable through traditional psychoanalysis. Neurosis, however, reflected unresolved conflicts from the Oedipal period of development. The individual generally remained cognizant of reality, and had established the capacity to develop a transference relationship which was seen as essential for a successful course of psychoanalysis.

Other analysts, working with populations more diverse than those visiting Freud in Victorian Vienna, found that many nonpsychotic patients were untreatable using the techniques of classic psychoanalysis. These patients were not capable of sustaining a consistent sense of self or of others and were, therefore, unable to invest in the necessarily intense analytic relationship. The consistent variable in the personality of such patients was the focus on pre-Oedipal disturbances in their relationships, disturbances rooted in problems before the age of four. The existence of such patients suggested a realm of abnormality between neurosis and psychosis.

Initially, these patients were seen as walking a fine line between neurosis and psychosis, what some called a "borderline" state. In time, psychodynamically oriented clinicians began to view this state as an entirely separate cluster of syndromes, the "personality disorders," with features unlike either the neurotic or psychotic constellation of symptoms.

Disruptions in the early development of object relations are usually considered to lead to the formation of either *narcissistic* or *borderline* disorders. What any two theorists mean by either of these terms, however, can vary widely. Stone (1986), for example, has identified six different uses for the term *borderline* in describing personality dysfunction. While theorists may disagree as to the number, differentiation and organization of personality disorders, they consistently assert that disruptions in early relationships leave the personality in an immature or incomplete state, largely incapable of forming healthy and mature adult relationships. By definition, an individual with a personality disorder has remained "stuck" in pre-Oedipal development and is thus always looking for ways to "satisfy" unmet needs. A neurotic individual, by comparison, has a reasonably well-developed personality, but is still unable to effectively manage anxiety in his or her life.

There is disagreement as to whether the infant is born with a complete and unblemished ego or a fragmented ego in need of further development. Relational model theorists agree, however, that the adequate development of the personality depends on the care and nurture provided by the primary parental figure(s). The parent who adequately meets the child's needs, or to use Winnicott's (1965) term, the *good-enough parent,* provides the child with the necessary raw materials for the development of a consistent and healthy sense of self and the world. As mentioned earlier, the parent whose needs were not adequately met in her or his own childhood probably cannot adequately meet those needs for the child. Instead the child will be provided with conditional love and an inconsistent or negative sense of worth.

The relational model's emphasis on the effects of the behavior and motivations of the parent on the personality of the child has been criticized by feminists and others as "mother-bashing," particularly since the mother is typically the primary caregiver (cf. Van Leeuwen, 1990, pp. 125-143). Indeed, the responsibility for the adequacy of the child's personality is placed disproportionately on the shoulders of the parents. The child is not able to have much volitional control over the development or reparation of his or her personality until late adolescence at the earliest. This certainly places an awesome responsibility on the primary caregiver(s).

Model of Psychotherapy

One of the strengths of the psychodynamic model is the direct link between theory and therapy. The theory is derived from the clinical work of the theorists with their clients. Because we are fundamentally relational beings, healing can only come through relationships. The core assumption is that healthy relationships have therapeutic potential.

In the classical approach to psychoanalysis the patient-analyst relationship was defined by transference. The analyst is an anonymous and blank canvas on which the patient recreates the vicissitudes of his or her past. Any feelings or personal involvement on the part of the analyst are seen as countertransference, the therapist's own unresolved neurotic conflicts. Thus, it is fair to say that the classic analytic relationship is not a real relationship at all.

Greenberg and Mitchell (1983) argue that the relational psychodynamic models see therapy quite differently from the classical model. Therapy is a relationship. The analyst and the patient participate in a dynamic interaction. Transference is an important part but the therapist cannot be a blank canvas. Who she is as a person will necessarily influence the transference. Countertransference (the reaction of the therapist to the client) also plays an important part. Rather than being the immaturity or "unfinished business" of the therapist, it is an essential tool and empathetic guide to the patient's inner experience of the world. In a sense the transference and countertransference interact as in a dance, a mutual event. In all likelihood, therapy may be the first authentic or consistent intimacy that many patients have encountered. The impersonal and artificial methods of classical analysis had to be discarded, because in this model the only hope for real change for the client is through a real relationship, and not through technique:

> The task of the analyst is not to remain outside of a process which is unfolding from within the mind of the patient, because this is theoretically impossible in the terms of the model's basic premises, but to engage the patient, to intervene, to participate in, and to transform pathogenic patterns of relationship. (Greenberg and Mitchell, 1983, p. 390)

Object-relations theories do not prescribe techniques or exercises for therapy. On the contrary, the spontaneity and mutual exploration of the relationship constitute the healing process. The therapist does not keep the theory always in mind. It becomes second nature, "the invisible backdrop, the unseen framework, within which the analyst hears the patient's story" (Greenberg and Mitchell, 1983, p. 15). While the patient remains always the focus of the relationship (therapist self-disclosure is not a common practice), the clinician is present in a real and intense way for the patient. Through mirroring back to the patient the therapist's own experience of what the patient is saying, the therapist provides the patient the experience of being understood and valued.

In such a context, it is asserted that the vital internal representations of primary figures, which form the core of personality, will begin to emerge. Therapy will focus on past and present experiences to encourage this uncovering. What makes therapy different from other relationships (where internalized representations are just as operative) is that the trained therapist can recognize distortions based on maladaptive inner images and can maintain the relationship in such a way as to allow the client to begin to change these images and come to have a more accurate understanding of self and the interpersonal environment.

The countertransference, or responsive and reactive state of the therapist, is her or his primary tool. Therapy hinges on it. The subtle confrontations or interpretations of the patient's experience of the world are chosen and worded through the matrix of the therapist's experience of the world.

A healthy therapist will judge the maturity of the patient's behavior with reasonable effectiveness and accuracy. He can monitor the countertransference and separate much of what is his internal interpretation of reality from that of the patient. An immature therapist, however, can model a distorted sense of maturity and influence the client to develop according to the therapist's faulty perspective. Little possibility exists, in this theoretical framework, for the therapist leading the patient to a greater level of maturity than the therapist has personally attained.

Psychodynamic therapies are typically longer term and do not focus directly on problem resolution. A treatment course of twice weekly meetings over a three-to five-year period for those with personality disorders seems to be the norm. While insight is still often an important goal of the therapy process, it is not considered the primary goal. Through their relationship, client and therapist strive to develop the client's ability to relate to self and others in healthy ways unencumbered by painful relationships from the past. In a real sense this is a chance for meeting needs left unmet since childhood. This process is primarily experiential, although the client's ability to reflect on the experience and gain insight into these issues may play an important role.

As opposed to other approaches which we will cover later, there is little faith in the client's capacity to grapple directly and rationally with the true determinants of his or her problems. Rather, the therapist must work to cultivate change gradually, through skillfully guided explorations of the client-therapist relationship and other current relationships and their impact on the client. As insight grows and the relationship between client and therapist becomes more influential, the therapy session can actually become a powerful context for re-experiencing one's relationships with others in a way that is freeing and fruitful.

Christian Critique

Philosophical Assumptions

In reacting against the scientism and mechanism of classical drive theory, contemporary psychodynamic psychology has adopted a theoretical understanding of human nature based primarily on the analysis of human relationships. Object-relations theorists look first and foremost at the primary attachments made between children and the caregivers in the early developmental years. Other biological, psychosocial and sociocultural variables are deemed as less formative on later personality development and functioning. These influences are not seen as irrelevant, only less uniquely and fundamentally "human." Who we are and who we tend to become, they argue, can best be understood in the interpersonal context.

In basing the foundation of its psychology on the relational rather than biological components of personality, psychodynamic theory has essentially taken a step back into the phenomenological and philosophical realms in which psychology as a discipline began. In embracing such an emphasis and in moving away from a mechanistic model, psychodynamic theorists have removed many major obstacles for Christians who appreciate their model. Object-relations theory lends itself to questions of human nature, values and subjective experience. Not surprisingly, object relations has become a realm for creative discussion among theologians and Christian mental-health professionals.

Object-relations theorists claim that humans have an inherent capacity and need for relationships. Guntrip (1969), for example, suggests that "the universe has begotten us with an absolute need to be able to relate in fully personal terms to an environment that we feel relates beneficently to us" (p. 328). Such a statement is reminiscent of the discussion in chapter two about the relational nature of humankind and how some say this is the central feature of what it means to be created in the image of God. Vanderploeg (1981a, 1981b), White (1984), Greenlee (1986) and others have noted how this common ground—an emphasis on the centrality of relationships—provides a foundation for the integration of the relational model and Christian thought.

Further, the notion that we internalize our relationships, that they become part of us, corresponds with Christian belief in marital union (Eph 5), family relatedness in the body of Christ (1 Cor 12) and even the notion of God residing in our very being when we become his child.

Surely theirs is a purely psychological understanding of relatedness, but it is at least a step in the right direction.

Since the relational model addresses itself to that which is fundamental to human nature, the place of sin and particularly of original sin plays a prominent role in a Christian critique of its theories. Henderson (1975, 1977) points to a parallel between the object-relations view of the infant's earliest stage of primary narcissism, or egocentrism, with the Judeo-Christian view of original sin as selfishness, a sense of omnipotence or of viewing self as the center of the universe. He suggests, however, that "the approach of dynamic psychology, in contrast to that of theology, is to assist the individual ego to search for, discover and know its inherent quantum of badness in the view that a badness which is well-known and familiar is thereby rendered impotent" (1975, p. 114). Christianity, however, goes further by offering forgiveness for and victory over sin, rather than merely rendering it psychologically impotent. Again, though, this is a step in the right direction, and there are almost certainly helpful aspects of this psychodynamic understanding of how we come to overcome our own "badness."

One result of the classic psychoanalytic approach has been a gradual erosion of a concept of *sin*. What theology had ascribed to sin, Freud ascribed to symptoms of illness, especially to psychological defenses. A person is not "bad" but "ill." Henderson (1977) resists this tendency with the accurate rationale that such a view tends to steer us away from "individual human accountability for the human situation" (p. 427). He suggests that "psychotherapists should bring a concept of sin back into their work and emphasize personal moral culpability and accountability as vital to mental health" (p. 432). This is consistent with the view of psychodynamically oriented clinicians such as Peck (1983) and Menninger (1973), and is a move all Christians can applaud.

The importance of individual moral culpability notwithstanding, a psychodynamic perspective may have something to teach us about sin. To search for a psychological factor in some forms of sin does not require a corresponding diminution of personal accountability. Since early deprivation can leave the personality in an immature and vulnerable state, it seems feasible that some means of protecting the self could reflect our sinfulness. This would not equate sin with defense, but some sins could serve a defensive function. Sexual sins, for example, might, in some cases, be motivated by early unmet needs for intimacy. A propensity toward gossip might be motivated by an inner need to feel superior to others. This controversial area of human accountability may provide fertile ground for dialog between theologians and psycho-dynamically oriented clinicians. Specifically, greater awareness and understanding of the nature of sinful behavior may aid in more effective (albeit limited) interventions that address it. Obviously, human beings in and of themselves are powerless to ameliorate either the ultimate causes or effects of sin. But they can serve an important and vital role as being agents of reconciliation and renewal in human relationships.

Discussions concerning moral accountability inevitably raise philosophical questions as to the existence of free will. On first glance, contemporary psychodynamic thought, in abandoning or altering the emphasis on biological instincts and drives, appears to have rejected the accompanying assumptions of determinism. In an apparent rejection of determinism, Guntrip (1969, pp. 330-331) states that:

> We have non-dynamic behaviour theories describing human beings as just repertoires of behaviour patterns to be treated by techniques of reconditioning. . . . Over and against this is the dynamic psychology of the psychoanalytic and psychotherapeutic schools, standing for man's basic freedom and right not to be manipulated, but to be supported till he can find his own proper mature selfhood.

While proponents of the relational model may seem to have wholly accepted the concept of free will, it is more likely that most have, in Evans's (1984, 1989) terms, rejected a "hard" determinism, which acknowledges the incompatibility of psychological causation and human freedom, for a "soft" determinism, which simply redefines freedom to make it seemingly compatible with psychological determinism. In both cases, internal forces exert powerful influences on our thoughts, feelings and behaviors.

But the relational models are much more amenable to a "libertarian" perspective on personal responsibility than is classic analysis. Evans (1984) has, in fact, argued forcefully that contemporary psychodynamic theory really has no need to retain the deterministic assumption of psychoanalysis. Eliminating that assumption would eradicate a stumbling block for Christian utilization of this approach. He argues that these approaches are quite compatible with a type of "limited freedom." We exist in the context of our personal histories. We are certainly influenced in powerful and significant ways by past relationships. We do not have to assume, however, that this history "forces" us to behave in a predetermined way, but rather provides "probabilities" of how we will act. Within certain boundaries, we have freedom and are, therefore, still accountable for our actions.

Models of Personality and Abnormality

While the emphasis of object-relations theorists is on the parents' impact on the child's personality, they do stress that no parent can be perfect, only "good enough." Kohut even emphasizes the importance of occasional failures by the parents so as to aid the internalization of the child's sense of responsibility for the maintenance of her or his own self-image.

It is difficult to criticize the relational model for its emphasis on the importance of the relationship between parent and child for personality development. If the *imago dei* (the image of God) is at some level a need for relatedness, it follows that our healthy development would depend largely on the adequate meeting of that need, and that our earliest and most profound relationships would leave powerful impressions on us. Greenlee (1986) has pointed out that the dynamic of persons deprived of adequate caring in childhood in turn depriving their own children might be seen as a way in which the sins of the fathers are passed on to the succeeding generations (Ex 34:7). Certainly the notion of intergenerational sin and psychopathology deserves more serious attention in our religious circles in light of the alarmingly high rates of childhood trauma (e.g., physical and sexual abuse).

The view of *imago dei* as "need for relatedness" certainly is not restricted to relations with other humans such as parents. According to a Christian creational perspective, the need itself arises from the fact that humankind was created for relationship with God and others. It is not surprising, then, that being created for a relationship with God and being born into a world where we find only broken and fallible images of God, we should have difficulty finding adequate resources for the building of a mature self capable of healthy relationships. It is also not surprising that we should have just as much difficulty developing a healthy relationship with God as with other human beings. Though created for this relationship, we are nevertheless on this earth separated from God, and thus there will always be a hunger for a greater sense of connectedness with him.

This latter difficulty, that of relating to God, has been a prominent area of discourse between object-relations theorists and Christian theologians. The center of this discussion has been how individuals image or conceptualize God. This area of research developed out of the common and puzzling observation that people have radically different core views of God even within the same religious groups (e.g., God as Daddy, Judge, Distant Originating Cause, Buddy, Cosmic Vending Machine, etc.). Ana-Maria Rizzuto (1974, 1979) is probably best known for her work in this area. She draws on the object-relations concept of internal representations, developed in early childhood, which later influence our interactions with other people and our world. She suggests that in infancy, the child, dependent on the parents for the provision of even the most elemental needs, creates an idealized representation of the parent as God. While later development will lead to separate representations for the parents, this original God-image remains.

This concept is not new to psychodynamic thought. As discussed in chapter three, Freud saw the child's view of the parents as the origin of belief in God. He enjoyed a play on words of the Genesis account of God making humankind in his own image and suggested that, instead, humankind makes God in its own image. Freud saw God as an individual and corporate myth arising out of early relations with our own human fathers. The healthy adult must, therefore, abandon the infantile belief in a supreme being and resign herself or himself to the relative and impersonal nature of the universe.

The object-relations perspective of our image of God is decidedly more tolerant than that of Freud. Rizzuto sees one's image of God as a dynamic and creative part of the self which can grow and change, particularly as our perceptions of our parents, the original models for the God-image, grow and change. Guntrip (1969) argued that " 'religious experience' is the same kind of 'stuff' as human 'personal relations experience' " (p. 328), and that a relationship with God is the "personal heart of reality" (p. 331). Such a relationship, he suggests, can contribute to the maturation and integration of the developing personality. Rizzuto (1974, p. 98) did not take her interpretation this far but did suggest that

> such a systematic grasp of the sources and the adaptive or maladaptive potential of internalized God-images within the larger theory of object relations would be, I submit, a useful tool, not just in the hand of the clinician, but also in the hands of the minister, rabbi and priest in their pastoral work as well as in the religious education of children.

But there is still potential here for views that are destructive of true faith as conceived in orthodox Christianity. Guntrip, for example, regards

God as an "indefinable term" (1969, p. 331). Similarly, religion as a relationship with God is

> an overall way of experiencing life, of experiencing ourselves and our relationships together; an experience of growing personal integration or self-realization through communion with all that is around us, and finally our way of relating to the universe, the tota. reality which has, after all, evolved us with the intelligence and motivation to explore this problem: all that is meant by "experience of God." (p. 326)

An internal relationship with a more healthy image of God or the universe will remain, however, a *uni*directional relationship. It is relating to an illusion within. When we form an internal image or representation of our parent, on the other hand, it originates out of an attempt to relate to the real person of the parent. No matter how distorted that internal image of the parent is, the potential always exists for further interactions with the parent and further maturing of the self to lead to a more accurate and "reality-based" internal image. Such a relationship is *bi*directional. We can test aspects of our internal image against the real person and the real person can take action to attempt to alter our internal image of her or him.

A secular object-relations theory cannot conceive of an internal relationship with an internal image of God as bidirectional. In fact, any belief in a real supernatural world in which the real God exists would be interpreted as "out-of-date dogmas or inadequate symbolisms of worship" (Guntrip, 1969, p. 329), a projection of our own subjective beliefs onto an impersonal external world. If this view were true, then Christianity would subsist purely of personal or collective autobiography, representations and images of God as recorded by our ancestors, together with our individual inner images of God formed in the context of relationships with significant others. Obviously this runs the risk of developing into a theology of personal subjective experience only (see discussion of Jungian psychology in chapter five).

Such a perspective by a secular object-relations theorist could allow for our image of God and our religion to be healthy, important, even artistic and poetic, but could not see it as a real relationship with a real person. The temptation, of course, is to believe that the discovery of the source and the distortion of our image of God is the end, to conclude that "we have discovered God and he is us." It is tempting to see an "almost" relationship with our internal image of God as the same thing as a relationship with God, to confuse sentimentality about vague religious impulses with a true relationship. It seems plausible, after all, that our images of God could be distorted by our experiences with fallen people, especially parents, in a fallen world. The slope can be quite slippery from that point, however. Having "psychologized" our experience of God, it may then seem logical to conclude that what Christians often interpret as their experience of God is actually the work of the unconscious, and so, perhaps, we should worship the "God-image" in all of us. To counter this, more accurate concepts of the Creator-God must be shaped in the context of Christian worship, education, fellowship and service. We need the input of these external sources for corrective feedback against our subjective and projective tendencies.

The seductiveness of these arguments does not invalidate the possible helpfulness of the object-relations theories. Knowledge of early development may truly inform us about distortions in our images of God; this knowledge could serve to lead us to a truer and more intimate relationship with God and others, just as understanding how our spouse is in reality quite different from our internalized image of "Mommy" or "Daddy" can aid the maturation of our marriages. It can take on an important role in therapy, especially when we know that in Christ we have a current, two-way relationship with a living, objective God both through the Word in us and the written Word, "living and active, [s]harper than any double-edged sword" (Heb 4:12).

The relational model of contemporary psychodynamic psychology may also provide helpful insights into how our image of God can grow and become more healthy as our capacity for relationships goes through its necessary healing and maturing process.

We would note in closing that this notion of the God-image being profoundly shaped by parental images has been subjected to careful empirical assessment. Spilka, Hood and Gorsuch (1985, p. 81) summarize the results of this research by stating that the complexity and the subtlety of the hypothesis, and the difficult and challenging measurement issues involved, make this a very complicated question indeed. The existing data provide some modest support for the projective hypothesis, suggesting mild similarity in concepts of God and concepts of the same-sex or most-liked parent.

Theory of Health
According to psychodynamic theory, the mature individual values relationships and can maintain a commitment to them, even when the

other person is not present. Such maturity requires a valuing of self since our perceptions of others are highly dependent on our internal representation of self. This notion is certainly in accord with the commandment to "love your neighbor as yourself" (Mt 22:39). It is significant, in light of the object-relations view of God, that this is the *second* greatest commandment. Jesus said that it was like the greatest commandment to "love the Lord your God with all your heart and with all your soul and with all your mind" (Mt 22:37). Our greatest commandment, to love God, places love of self and other second, an impossibility if self and other are real while God is only an internal representation. Perhaps the primary point should be, though, that love is central to what God wants in us when we are fully human, and it is to their credit that these models put the kind of interpersonal bonding that might be called *love* at the very center of their model of normalcy.

The psychodynamic system, like all psychotherapy systems, contains an implicit ethical system embedded in its understanding of normalcy. Altruism and mutual dependence are valued within the contexts of close, especially family, relationships, but self-sacrifice, giving to the point of allowing pain to be inflicted on the self, would not be highly valued. The hidden ethical vision of this tradition "is that one has a moral obligation to do that which deep down one wants to do. Or to say it differently, it is morally justifiable to do what one is inclined to do because what one is inclined to do is also moral" (Browning, 1987, p. 225).

Because of our relational natures, we are inclined to care for those close to us because they care for us and nurture us. This view directly parallels that of classic psychoanalysis. Thus a self-sacrificial act would generally be thought of as a self-induced punishment for irrational guilt or the result of an inaccurate view that others are more worthy of love than oneself. While this is probably often true (e.g., the self-styled Christian "doormat"), this model has little place for the reality of Christ's unilateral sacrifice and our commandment to model ourselves after his example (cf. Smedes, 1988). Since contemporary psychodynamic psychology is agnostic regarding the existence of reality or truth outside of this temporal world, it cannot allow for choices or values which call for the sacrifice of the needs of the self. It cannot envision a relationship with a real God that could empower one to make a truly self-sacrificial act.

In calling for the importance of equal and trusting relationships, and in highly prizing inter-relatedness, however, it fares decidedly better than some theoretical systems which seem to actively embrace narcissism alone (Browning, 1987, chap. 8). Its ethic is still partial and incomplete, but it is an important improvement.

Model of Psychotherapy

Benner (1983), Workman (1988) and others have suggested provocative parallels between the process of psychodynamic psychotherapy and God's work of salvation and sanctification. Salvation and sanctification, it is argued, might be loosely understood as the process by which in intimate relationship with God we grow by the process of God himself, through Christ, taking upon himself our "badness." Through Christ's death, "he is open to receive all our sin, able to contain anything we can project onto him. In this relationship, we are offered the opportunity to become whole persons" (Workman, 1988, p. 21). These authors suggest this is an analog to the psychotherapy relationship wherein the therapist acts as a human mediator who accepts, on behalf of God, the "bad introjects," the "psychic split-offs," that the client must be rid of to become whole.

This conception does parallel our call to be "Christ's ambassadors" (2 Cor 5:20-21), reconciling sinners with God. These authors do not wish to stretch these analogies too far, and we would agree with this caution. The analogies are fascinating, but the dangers of rendering God's work into a purely psychological framework and of elevating the redemptive work of the therapist to a grandiose level are great.

The psychodynamic methods of therapy may also be criticized for their seeming lack of appreciation for methods for change *other than* having a curative relationship. The pastoral instruction of the New Testament gives a great deal of attention to removing the characterological barriers to good relationships. We are to lay aside jealousy, envy, malice and so forth. But there is also ample biblical attention paid to other functions such as correcting our thinking, disciplined prayer and seeking restoration of shattered relationships. In the psychodynamic camp, such interventions are often regarded as trivial or necessarily ineffectual. Further, these models are subtly humanistic in assuming that all will be well if the client has one really good relationship. The person will, as it were, be able to function autonomously through the direction of the ego once the bad internalized objects are straightened out. What is missing is an understanding of health that includes a long-term relationship with a living God and an appreciation for anchoring self in commitments to the church and God's revelation of himself in the Bible.

From a Christian perspective, the faith of the therapist is important, though not the only factor, in determining effectiveness in psychotherapy. The world view of a Christian will, presumably, be substantially different from that of a non-Christian therapist. A non-Christian therapist with a healthy capacity for relationships may do far more good toward the healing of the personality than an immature Christian therapist, and a mature Christian therapist could possibly lead a patient away from true Christlikeness. On the whole, however, the greatest capacity for healing must certainly come from a Christian therapist directed by the Holy Spirit. As people, and in a profound and sobering way as therapists, we are imagers of God. The more that the therapist can be an accurate imager of God and therefore direct the individual to a greater capacity for relationship with God, the more healing will take place. A Christian object-relations therapist would, therefore, realize the importance of a relationship between the patient and God in which God actively participates.

While the intimate connection between theory and therapy may be considered the strength of contemporary psychodynamic models, those who aspire to a more objective science of psychology will view it as a fatal weakness. Because all knowledge of internal dynamics comes from the therapy process, in which the therapist is intimately involved, all conclusions are subject to the interpretations and distortions of the therapist. This might help explain the substantial disagreements between psychodynamic theorists from different schools and different eras. It is impossible to separate the conclusions of the theorist from his or her own individual dynamics.

To the question, "Have the premises of contemporary psychoanalysis been adequately researched?" the answer can be yes or no depending on one's theoretical orientation. There is little experimental literature in support of central constructs of object-relations theory. On the other hand, the amount of written literature based on case conceptualizations and actual hours of therapy conducted in this tradition is impressive. With a growing and dynamic clinical database, the psychoanalytic literature may provide a wealth of important information.

There has been some movement toward the empirical testing of the psychodynamic model. Perhaps the foremost example is the positive showing of Klerman and Weissman's psychodynamically oriented interpersonal therapy for depression (Elkin et al., 1989), which was rigorously compared with the two other most effective treatments of depression, antidepressant tricyclic medication and Beck's cognitive therapy. In these comparisons, the short-term psychodynamic therapy fared as well as the other two approaches. This work can stand as a model of the adaptation of the psychodynamic approach to a shorter term format and to the challenges of empirical research. Hopefully, more such work with other problem areas will be forthcoming.

The evolving theoretical framework of contemporary psychoanalysis has been painfully devoid of Christian influence. The fact that psychoanalytic theory grows out of the personal interactions of theorists with their patients provides an urgent call for Christian psychodynamically oriented therapists. Since the individual perspective and dynamics of the theorist necessarily form his or her conceptualization of theory and practice, object-relations theories have been formed primarily with non-Christian underpinnings. The truth that is discovered will be no less true, but the unintentional distortions will skew the interpretation and application of the results, especially with regard to matters involving the supernatural, as we have seen.

Conclusion

The psychodynamic psychotherapies are among the broadest, most comprehensive systems in use today. In moving beyond Freud's narrow commitment to a biologically rooted, "scientific" theory, contemporary psychodynamic theorists have developed a system that does not present many of the problems to the committed Christian psychotherapist that classical analysis did.

These models are relational in nature, balance a cautious optimism with a deep appreciation of our capacity for self-deception and have a substantial (though secondary in emphasis) understanding of our rational capacities as humans. The values imbedded in the model are broadly compatible with Christian values, though of course there is not a perfect match.

The observant reader will note that our criticisms of this model were not "devastating." Rather, they took the form of *cautions*. We think it fitting that this is one of the models that many Christian therapists are embracing; it holds much promise as a possible foundation for future elaboration of a thoroughly Christian understanding of human personality.

For Further Reading

Browning, D. (1987). *Religious thought and the modern psychologies.* Philadelphia: Fortress.

Browning's sympathetic analysis of the potential contributions of Kohut and Erikson to a Christian understanding of persons in his chapter eight is a model of scholarly thoroughness, though in the mainline denominational rather than evangelical tradition.

Crabb, L. (1988). *Inside out.* Colorado Springs, CO: NavPress.

A recent work that reflects Crabb's movement toward psychodynamic thought.

Greenberg, J., and Mitchell, S. (1983). *Object-relations in psychoanalytic theory.* Cambridge, MA: Harvard University Press

Perhaps the definitive work in object-relations psychology to date.

Guntrip, H. (1971). *Psychoanalytic theory, therapy, and the self.* New York: Basic Books.

A readable general introduction to all of the psychodynamic models.

Lake, F. (1986). *Clinical theology* (Edited and abridged by M. Yeomans). New York: Crossroad.

A readable abridged introduction to the fascinating thought of a dedicated Christian expounding a thoroughly psychodynamic view of the counseling process.

Miller, A. (1981). *The drama of the gifted child.* New York: Basic Books.

A book accessible to the lay reader, applying psychodynamic psychology to the understanding of childhood experience.

St. Clair, M. (1986). *Object relations and self-psychology: An introduction.* Monterey, CA: Brooks/Cole.

A readable general introduction to all of the psychodynamic models.

Strupp, H. H., and Binder, J. L. (1984). *Psychotherapy in a new key: A guide to time-limited dynamic psychotherapy.* New York: Basic Books.

A fascinating discussion of how psychodynamic concepts can be adapted for contemporary application by two well-respected clinical psychologists.

References

Benner, D. (1983). The Incarnation as a metaphor for psychotherapy. *Journal of Psychology and Theology, 11,* 287-294.

Browning, D. (1987). *Religious thought and the modern psychologies.* Philadelphia: Fortress.

Edkins, W. (1985). Object relations theory. In D. Benner (Ed.), *Baker encyclopedia of psychology* (pp. 769-771). Grand Rapids, MI: Baker.

Elkin, I.; Shea, T.; Watkins, J.; Imber, S.; et al. (1989). National Institute of Mental Health treatment of depression collaborative research program. *Archives of General Psychiatry, 46,* 971-982.

Evans, C. S. (1984). Must psychoanalysis embrace determinism? Or can a psychologist be a libertarian? *Psychoanalysis and Contemporary Thought, 7,* 339-365.

Evans, C. (1989). *Wisdom and humanness in psychology.* Grand Rapids, MI: Baker.

Freud, S. (1961). *The ego and the id.* In J. Strachey (Ed. and Trans.), The standard edition of the complete psychological works of Sigmund Freud (pp. 3-66; Vol. 19). London: Hogarth Press. (Original work published 1923).

Greenberg, J., and Mitchell, S. (1983). *Object-relations in psychoanalytic theory.* Cambridge, MA: Harvard University Press.

Greenlee, L., Jr. (1986). Kohut's self psychology and theory of narcissism: Some implications regarding the fall and restoration of humanity. *Journal of Psychology and Theology, 14,* 110-116.

Guntrip, H. (1969). Religion in relation to personal integration. *British Journal of Medical Psychology,* 42, 323-333.

Henderson, J. (1975). Object relations and the doctrine of original sin. *International Review of Psychoanalysis, 2,* 107-120.

Henderson, J. (1977). Object relations and the psychotherapy of sin. *Canadian Psychiatric Association Journal, 22,* 427-433.

Hurding, R. (1985). *Roots and shoots.* London: Hodder and Stoughton.

Johnson, R. (1985). Self psychology. In D. Benner (Ed.), *Baker encyclopedia of psychology* (pp. 1051-1053). Grand Rapids, MI: Baker.

Kirwan, W. (1984). *Biblical concepts for Christian counseling.* Grand Rapids, MI: Baker.

Korchin, S. (1976). *Modern clinical psychology.* New York: Basic Books.

Lake, F. (1966). *Clinical theology.* London: Darton, Longman and Todd.

Lake, F. (1986). *Clinical theology* (Edited and abridged by M. Yeomans). New York: Crossroad.

Linn, M., and Linn, D. (1978). *Healing life's hurts: Healing memories through five stages of forgiveness.* New York: Paulist Press.

Mahler, M. (1968). *On human symbiosis and the vicissitudes of individuation.* New York: International Universities Press.

Mahler, M.; Pine, F.; and Bergman, A. (1975). *The psychological birth of the human infant.* New York: Basic.

Menninger, K. (1973). *Whatever became of sin?* New York: Hawthorne Books.

Peck, S. (1983). *People of the lie.* New York: Simon and Schuster.

Pine, F. (1988). The four psychologies of psychoanalysis and their place in clinical work. *Journal of the American Psychoanalytic Association, 36,* 571-596.

Prochaska, J. (1984). *Systems of psychotherapy* (2d ed.). Chicago: Dorsey.

Rizzuto, A. (1974). Object relations and the formulation of the image of God. *British Journal of Medical Psychology, 47,* 83-99.

Rizzuto, A. (1979). *The birth of the living God: A psychoanalytic study.* Chicago: University of Chicago.

Seamands, D. A. (1985). *Healing of memories.* Wheaton, IL: Victor Books.

Smedes, L. (1988). *Caring and commitment.* San Francisco: Harper & Row.

Spilka, B.; Hood, R.; and Gorsuch, R. (1985). *The psychology of religion: An empirical approach.* Englewood Cliffs, NJ: Prentice-Hall.

Stone, M. (1986). Borderline personality disorder. In A. Cooper, A. Frances, and M. Sacks (Eds.), Psychiatry: Vol. 1. *The Personality Disorders and Neuroses* (pp. 203-217). New York: Basic Books.

Vanderploeg, R. (1981a). Imago dei, creation as election: Foundations for psychotherapy. *Journal of Psychology and Theology, 9,* 209-215.

Vanderploeg, R. (1981b). Imago dei as foundational to psychotherapy: Integration versus segregation. *Journal of Psychology and Theology, 9,* 299-304.

Van Leeuwen, M., (1990). *Gender and grace.* Downers Grove, IL: InterVarsity Press.

White, S. (1984). Imago dei and object relations theory: Implications for a model of human development. *Journal of Psychology and Theology, 12,* 286-293.

Winnicott, D. (1965). *The maturational process and the facilitating environment.* New York: International Universities Press.

Workman, D. (1988, April). An analysis of object-relations theory. Paper presented at the Christian Association for Psychological Studies convention, Denver, CO.

5

JUNGIAN THERAPY

✦

I nterest in the *analytic psychology* of Carl Jung remains strong
in certain religious circles and shows signs of increasing.
According to Vitz (1987, p. 77), much of its enduring and
immediate appeal may be a function of the hybrid nature of Jungian
thought—it is a mixture of a formal, or "Catholic," psychoanalytic
psychology (with its appealing intellectualism) and a less formal, or
"Protestant," counseling psychology approach (with its appealing freedom of choice). In Vitz's analysis, this mixing of elements results in a
kind of "Episcopalian" psychological mindset. Indeed, two of the
foremost interpreters of Jungian thought for the ecumenical religious
audience, Morton Kelsey and John Sanford, are Episcopalians who
share a deep and abiding interest in aesthetics, ritual, symbolism and
the "depth" dimensions of religious experience.

Although only a small percentage of clinicians today would describe themselves as "Jungian," concepts central to analytic psychology have been widely disseminated. The professional literature on Jungian thought is impressive in itself, but aspects of analytic psychology have been widely interpreted through numerous popular books, workshops and media programs as well (e.g., the work of Campbell and Moyers, 1988, in *The Power of Myth,* a book and PBS video production, was fundamentally Jungian in thought).

This tradition, like existential psychology (chapter eleven), speaks directly to the questions of meaning in life. Indeed, Jung saw his most basic task as "the care of souls" *(cura animarum).* Profoundly disillusioned with what he perceived as the unwillingness of the church to take up this most basic task, Jung felt it imperative that clinicians see their role not only as healers of the mind, but as comforters of the whole psychological person or *soul,* including the "spiritual" aspect of the person, as well. But whether or not his proposed solution is distinctively or decidedly Christian is a matter of intense debate and discussion.

Carl Jung left a considerable legacy of written material to ponder (see the Collected Works), an intimidating corpus which is often difficult to understand. Ryckman (1985) has correctly described the system as "complex, esoteric, and obscure" (p. 62), and pointed out that it is extremely difficult to define the core concepts or to test them experimentally. Jungian insights often integrate several disciplines, including not only medicine, psychiatry and psychology, but nearly all the humanities, natural sciences and social sciences, including comparative religions! Jungian psychology is second only to Freudian psychology in terms of the sheer number and diversity of the phenomena it attempts to examine or explore. There is little debate that the approach is comprehensive. This makes it easier still to ignore or dismiss the Jungian perspective, since so few persons in this day of increasing specialization have the necessary background to assimilate or evaluate this incredible array of complex material. Even Jung's most ardent and harsh critics tend to affirm him for his intellectual risk-taking.

Descriptive Survey

Philosophical Assumptions
Although Jung's work resists summarization, there are certain underlying assumptions and values. Perhaps foremost among these is the belief in a *collective unconscious.*

Jung, like Freud, conceived of a *personal unconscious* that was inaccessible to conscious reflection and could be connected to observable behaviors, and he resisted the neo-Freudian or post-Freudian tendency (cf. chapter four) to collapse the unconscious into the conscious. But for Jung, the domain of the unconscious "only became interesting beyond the point where Freud's method left off" (Kovel, 1976, p. 93). For Jung, the individual life of the client, even the individual unconscious life, was only a small part of the picture. A complete understanding had to reflect also the *transpersonal*, the elements of existence that transcended the personal, that connected one with the history of the human species (and indeed the cosmic order) that had preceded an individual's limited existence. For Jung, "consciousness is but a small boat on the sea of the unconscious" (Kaufmann, 1984, p. 108), and the personal unconscious (that which is unique to a person and unconnected to others) is but a small part of the unconscious.

The most fundamental reality in Jung's psychology is the collective unconscious. It is our source of energy, and it shapes or structures the most fundamental dimensions of our experience. It is seen as the storehouse of all the latent memories of our human and prehuman ancestry. This deep and most inaccessible level of the person contains the "wisdom of the ages" and serves as a potential guide for human development. Some have explained this concept by analogy to a human hand submerged with the finger tips protruding above the water; the finger tips would be akin to the conscious experiences of different individuals; the submerged shafts of the fingers akin to the personal unconsciouses of different individuals; and the body of the hand akin to the collective unconscious which all persons share in common.

The analytic approach of Jung is certainly more open to the ineffable and mysterious than any other major approach to people-helping. Although it embraces aspects of the scientific approach, Jungian thought refuses to embrace the spirit of scientific objectification or reductionism. It repeatedly reminds us of mysteries beyond our current comprehension and understanding. "Faith" is very much alive in Jungian thought. The mystical, spiritual or transpersonal is granted an intellectual respectability that is on par with the results of more formal and traditional scientific endeavors. The spiritual world is not reduced to rationalistic formulations.

Such thinking naturally follows from an understanding of the collective unconscious as the wellspring of creativity and the ultimate source of direction in life (Corey, 1982). These thoughts point to the

outlines of an epistemology in Jungian psychology that values introspection and examination of the unconscious as the most important
ways of *knowing*. This valuing of the "spiritual" also partially explains
the positive reception of Jungian thought in religious circles. When
Jungian acceptance of spirituality is contrasted with the antagonism or
antipathy against religion of most twentieth-century psychologies, it
strikes a responsive chord in the religiously committed person.

Jungians combine an optimistic teleology with a deterministic view
of causality. From the Jungian perspective, we are not really "in control," but are ruled by powerful transpersonal unconscious forces of
which we have only limited awareness. But this system is not as pessimistic as classic psychoanalysis, because the Jungian perspective is a
decidedly forward-looking one, where we are shaped not only by our
immediate and inherited pasts, but also by our aspirations for the future.
We have a drive to grow and evolve toward even greater wholeness in body,
mind and spirit. A more complete self-realization is a distinct possibility
for the person who is willing to embrace fully the mysteries of life,
especially those of the depth dimension of his or her own psyche. To live
a full and meaningful existence we must come to understand something
of these mysteries beyond our immediate experience.

As McLemore (1982) has noted, Jung found Christianity psychologically useful but certainly did not take the gospel or Christian
theology seriously. Jung's father was a Protestant minister in the Calvinistic tradition. By his own telling, Jung (1961) was profoundly
affected by his father's vacillating and doubt-filled faith; Jung was also
influenced by personal and professional encounters with the occult.
His grandmother was a medium; his mother had psychic experiences;
his medical thesis was on occult phenomena; and he had repeated
mysterious encounters with "spirits" throughout his adult life. He was
a serious student of comparative religion, especially Eastern religions
and the occult.

For all the apparent spiritual affirmations in Jung, Kovel (1976)
asserts that Jungian thought is essentially worldly and tolerant.
Jung's ultimate criteria for truth is vague and undefined, but is
decidedly subjectivistic. The experiential nature of analytic psychology resists an external, authoritative understanding of truth, emphasizing, in contrast, the personal myth and story of the individual.
Thus the Christian reader of Jung and Jungian psychology must be
extremely cautious when encountering phrases and concepts bor-
rowed from Christian theology.

Model of Personality

The Jungian perspective understands personality in terms of several unique but interdependent structures. Collectively speaking, the total personality is called the *psyche,* a general entity that operates according to the principle of opposites and is undergirded by a general life-process energy and motivational force that is more than aggression or sexual libido.

The ego is a unifying force in the psyche and the center of consciousness. It is primarily concerned with thinking, feeling, perceiving and remembering.

The *personal unconscious* includes all of the forgotten experiences that have lost their accessibility to consciousness. When these experiences begin to cluster they tend to form *complexes.*

Within the collective unconscious, which we have already discussed, are the great *archetypes* that can be discovered through the symbolic interpretation of dreams, fantasies, myths, rituals and traditions. Therein lies the great potential sources of creativity, energy, guidance, wholeness and wisdom for living. Archetypes are best understood as universal mental structures or cognitive organizing principles that give shape to human psychic experience. They are the forms or molds through which our previously unformed energy passes. Thus the particular archetypes that are active form our psychological reality. Archetypes, though, must be "activated (or evoked) by an experiential reality" (Kaufmann, 1984, p. 111); and so while they form our reality, our experience of them is also influenced by what occurs in exterior reality. Jung determined the basic archetypes through introspection, clinical work with clients, and the study of mythology, literature and comparative religions.

Several of the archetypes are especially important in Jungian thought. The *persona* is the mask we wear in social situations. It is our public self, our psychological "skin," the part of ourselves we show in our daily routines.

Our unconsciously feminine side is our *anima,* and it is yielding, containing, nurturing, concrete and intuitive; our unconsciously masculine side is our *animus,* and it is driving, penetrating, aggressive and disciplined. Males and females have both anima and animus archetypes. Whole persons are willing to embrace both dimensions of their personhood (cf. Van Leeuwen, 1990, for a more contemporary discussion of this issue).

The *shadow* is the part of our personality we would rather not acknowledge, the so-called dark side of the person. Unless we have integrated the shadow, we tend not to recognize these attributes or traits, in ourselves and project them onto others. Although seen most often as our "evil side," it can be a source of creativity and spontaneity if it becomes appropriately controlled and responsibly expressed.

Finally, the *self* is perhaps the most important archetype, and only emerges when the other dimensions of personality develop in the direction of wholeness. For Jung, not until middle age does the necessary unity and stability potentially develop that can serve as a true basis for centeredness, increasingly pulling the person from ahead rather than pushing from behind (Corey, 1982, p. 35). Other archetypes include the *hero, death* and *rebirth* and *the wise old man.*

It is within the context of the collective unconscious that we form an all-powerful being that we call "God":

> God is an absolute, necessary function of an irrational nature, which has nothing to do with the question of God's existence. The human intellect can never answer this question of God's existence. The human intellect can never answer this question, still less give any proof of God. Moreover, such proof is superfluous, for the idea of an all-powerful divine Being is present everywhere, unconsciously if not consciously, because it is an archetype. (Jung, 1964b, p. 81)

In other words, the "idea of God has validity in a subjective or inner reality sense because it has its roots in human experience on a universal basis" (Ryckman, 1985, p. 67).

Finally, the basic personality attitudes in Jungian thought are *extroversion* and *introversion*. In briefest detail, the extroverted person is oriented toward the external and social world, whereas the introverted individual focuses more on the internal and subjective world. Beyond these broad dimensions, Jung posited an eightfold classification scheme of psychological types. Within these broad and basic attitudes of extroversion and introversion, he described four types: (1) the thinking type—logical, objective and rational; (2) the feeling type—oriented around affective and subjective experience; (3) the sensation type—organized around stimuli from the senses; and (4) the intuitive type—creative, imaginative and integrative. Using this basic typology, Jung developed complex notions of how dominant attitudes and functions can influence our actions and behaviors in everyday life.

Despite the lack of clarity and precision in certain core concepts, there is research evidence supporting certain aspects of the Jungian theory of psychological types. Much of the focus of these investigative efforts has centered around the Myers-Briggs Type Indicator (MBTI), a personality test that is loosely based on Jungian concepts (cf. Keirsey and Bates, 1984; Kaplan and Saccuzzo, 1989). The MBTI is used to identify introverts and extroverts as well as sensing, thinking, feeling and intuitive patterns. An impressive amount of technical work has been done on the MBTI (cf. reviews in any recent edition of the widely respected *Mental Measures Yearbook;* Buros, 1978), and a number of studies have utilized the MBTI to explore dimensions of the typology for a wide variety of purposes.

Unfortunately, the MBTI has probably been overutilized and perhaps misused in certain lay or professional settings (especially in overinterpreting the results of the test). This has lowered its credibility in the larger academic and research community, since its application has sometimes been inconsistent with widely understood psychometric or clinical imperatives (cf. *Standards for Educational and Psychological Testing,* American Education Research Association ct al., 1985). Still, research with the MBTI does suggest that it is possible to translate some complex Jungian concepts into empirically verifiable terminology.

Models of Health and Abnormality

Jung viewed personality development as a dynamic and evolving process across the life span. The movement toward selfhood and actualization is often a painful and difficult process as we increasingly attempt to organize and integrate internal processes and structures. By the middle years, and perhaps not even then, we may learn what it truly means to move toward greater degrees of self-realization and wholeness.[1] In Jungian psychology, self-realization is generally seen as the last stage of the lifelong process of individuation. It is an ideal to work toward rather than an actuality that can be achieved in the course of one's life. Psychological wholeness and spiritual wholeness appear to be the same thing in the Jungian perspective (Hughs, 1987). Whether this process is centered on or empowered by Jesus Christ is apparently a matter of personal choice in this highly experiential and subjective system of understanding human nature. Jungians trust the psyche to guide us in adapting to our social and

---

[1]For a more complete analysis of these complex themes, see especially the insightful treatments in Munroe's *Schools of Psychoanalytic Thought* (1955) or Rychlak's *Introduction to Personality and Psychotherapy* (1973).

physical environment, much like the humanistic psychologies. Jungians assert that we are born with the potential for achieving greater wholeness throughout the process of our lives. Further, we actually have a drive to achieve this wholeness, a drive toward individuation which pushes us to become our truest self. According to Jung,

> Personality is the supreme realization of the innate idiosyncrasy of a living being. It is an act of high courage flung in the face of life, the absolute affirmation of all that constitutes the individual, the most successful adaptation to the universal conditions of existence coupled with the greatest possible freedom for self-determination. (Jung, 1934, p. 171)

This instinct for individuation is central to the Jungian understanding of health and wholeness. As Vitz (1987) has observed, the chief aim of life appears to be "to know thyself" as an end in and of itself. The process of facilitating the emergence of the authentic self is a highly subjective and relativistic one.

In the end, the healthy person is the one who follows the urgings of the unconscious. Health can only come from becoming what one was meant to become, and this ideal self is actualized by becoming able to experience all of the archetypes in their proper balance. For example, the fulfilled person experiences both anima and animus in balance, emphasizing neither rigid or stereotyped forms of masculinity nor femininity. In experiencing the unconscious, the healthy person will inevitably be responsive to and appreciative of the mystical, transpersonal, spiritual aspects of life.

In the Jungian perspective, we all develop more or less one-sidedly. We suffer from a number of incompatible opposites that we generate in the process of living. Psychopathology can be understood as our unconscious attempt to compensate for a lack of balance in our lives, or the result of our inattention to the deeper messages we receive from our personal or collective unconscious. These are most often expressed in terms of the specific complexes that form in our conscious ego and inhibit the emergence of the true self. When filtered through their characteristic attitudes and tendencies (e.g., extroverted-feeling type), the full range of functional psychopathology can be seen. The depth of the psychopathology is determined by the intensity of the repressed forces in the unconscious, which is in turn a function of the degree to which an individual is avoiding fulfilling the urgings of the unconscious. Overall, the Jungian view of abnormality is sketchy.

Model of Psychotherapy

For Jungians, hope for the alleviation of symptomatology lies in the acceptance and integration of the content of their personal and collective unconscious. Awareness can be best facilitated by recognizing the tendencies of the distressed or disturbed individual to project aspects of unconscious experience into daily experience. Finding new meaning through symbols that increasingly emerge into the conscious ego is the ultimate hope for releasing the creative and growth-producing potential of the archetypes stored in the collective unconscious. Meaning can only be found when we are willing to confront that which we don't fully know or understand from the greater depths of our being. If we are going to live a more complete and whole existence, we need to learn how to effectively deal with the dualities, polarities and contradictions of our existence. When we recognize and develop these different "sides," we will become more effective in our process of individuation and live with our opposites in a more integrated fashion.

Jung himself did not prescribe any set treatment methodology (Kaufmann, 1984; Sanford, 1985). Many methods are used, but the core principle is to help the unconscious become conscious, and for the therapist to affirm whatever direction and guidance the unconscious is providing, especially through the self archetype. Jungian therapists tend to be a rather diverse and eclectic group, drawing on the broad existential, humanistic or psychodynamic traditions. Jungian therapists have a profound respect for relationship between the therapist and the client. They see the maturational and personal attributes of both the analyst and client as major variables in the process of change. Consequently, standards for certification at formal Jungian training institutes in major cities around the world are rigorous and demanding. A common theme is a deep appreciation for how clinical techniques need to be adjusted or modified depending on the psychological type of the client; therapy needs to be a highly individualized and personalized encounter.

Jungian analysts tend to see dreams in a far more optimistic light than do Freudians, who view dreams as representations of unacceptable aggressive or sexual impulses, repressed or as disguised manifestations of conflicts. Unlike their more suspicious counterparts, Jungians assert that dreams need to be taken somewhat more literally. They are enormously difficult to decipher since they often draw on unconscious archetypes and symbols. The meanings of dreams are meant to be uncovered; they are messages from the unconscious that map out the road to wholeness. Interpreted in sequence over a period of time (rather than in isolation), they are typically central to effective psychotherapeutic process. The issues and themes they raise can help the unconscious become conscious if they are successfully explored in the context of the psychotherapeutic relationship.[2]

Jungian therapy tends to be long-term, typically lasting over a year or more. Jungians usually work individually with a highly select population of well-educated and high-functioning persons. Experiencing is valued far more than understanding. Although Jungians assert that their method has broad application, the "ideal" client appears to be the relatively normal or moderately dissatisfied or maladjusted, middle-aged individual seeking greater wisdom or enlightenment. In short, Jungian therapy tends to be viewed as a "growth therapy" by most clinicians.

Christian Critique

Philosophical Assumptions

Jungian thought has had enormous appeal for many religious persons.[3] As we mentioned earlier, we suspect that much of its appeal for Christians today is that it speaks forcefully of the centrality of the spiritual and to the need for *cura animarum*—the care of souls (Hempelmann, 1986). The Christian psychologist thirsty for a spiritually minded approach to therapy, and tired of the religious antipathy or apathy of other systems, can warm to Jungian thought because it is profoundly religious in its outlook. Jung saw himself as a "lover of the soul," and it deeply pained him that he was largely ignored before his death. He felt that the institutional religion of his day was not meeting the deeper needs of individuals, although historically it had supplied meaning through worship, fellowship

---

[2]Hall and Lindzey (1985) have an especially helpful summary of the Jungian perspective on dreams and dream analysis.

[3]Among the more interesting and helpful contemporary religious discussions of Jungian thought are Bryant's *Jung and the Christian Way* (1983); Johnson's three-book series *We* (1985), *He* (1989) and *She* (1989); Kelsey's *Christo-Psychology* (1968) or *The Other Side of Silence* (1977); Moore's edited volume *Carl Jung and Christian Spirituality* (1988); O'Connor's *Understanding Jung, Understanding Yourself* (1985); Sanford's *Dreams: God's Forgotten Language* (1989), *Between People* (1982), *The Invisible Partners* (1980), or *The Kingdom Within* (1987); or Stein's *Jung's Treatment of Christianity* (1985). Hurding (1985) does an excellent job critiquing several of these approaches that attempt to harmonize Jungian psychology and orthodox Christianity.

and service. He meant his psychology to fill this breach.

But this is precisely what is most disturbing about Jungian psychology. Of all the systems, Jungian psychology (and perhaps existential psychology, chapter twelve) comes closest to being a rival religion. It is comprehensive in its claim to explain the totality of human psychological and religious experience. In grounding his analysis of archetypes in the analysis of mythology and comparative religions, Jung psychologized religious experience much as Freud did. He looked to explain the psychological realities behind the vagaries of different types of religious experience. It was thus inevitable that his would be a relativistic understanding of the functional value of different "religious mythologies."

Jung's use of religious terminology and concepts can lead the less discerning reader to imagine him to be in closer allegiance with the faith than is justified. Jung seemed to find Christianity useful in promoting the larger quest for meaning, but he clearly did not embrace the cross and the resurrection as historical facts. As Browning (1987) observed, Jung supposed that overt material expression was needed for covert psychic realities and thereby came to view important religious symbols as having great significance and meaning as "mystified" psychic projections. The notion of a God who loves and forgives or a God who died for us and rose again to give us eternal life are the symbolic representations of deep archetypal, and thus purely psychological, realities. Thus historic realities are interpreted as projections of psychological needs.

Jung reasoned from the recurrence across religions of certain motifs, such as death and rebirth or atonement, that these motifs represent or reflect underlying archetypes. This is a psychological explanation of religious commonalities. But it is vital to realize that this is not the only possible explanation of such commonalities. A dogmatic understanding could, for example, propose the enduring historic truthfulness of one religion, Christianity, and suggest that commonalities shared with other religions represent the residual of shared truth still left with us after the human fragmentation and alienation of the Fall. This appears to have been C. S. Lewis's working model in *The Abolition of Man*, which closes with Lewis's listing of what he called "the Tao," the shared moral foundation of all the world's great religions. In other words, commonalities between religions could either mean that all religions are partially true and all represent projections of psychological realities or needs, or they could mean that one religion is true and others still share commonalities with the true faith to varying degrees. Jung's explanation works best if one has made an a priori commitment to some sort of psychological universalism in explaining religion.

This leads us to ask if there is a Christian objection to the idea of a collective unconscious. Frankly, we perceive that many Christians react negatively with knee-jerk rapidity to the very idea of the unconscious, but with no apparent rational basis. They often are concerned about determination of all psychological reality by the unconscious, but this is an objection to determinism, not to the idea of an unconscious per se. It may in fact be true that the unconscious exists as Jung asserts, and further that to know ourselves and hence be whole we must know more about what is in our unconscious. But it is Jung's profound trust of the unconscious that is questionable. We have no warrant as Christians to regard any aspect of our being as untouched by the Fall and hence an inerrant guide for life and growth toward wholeness.

Further, we have no warrant from a Christian perspective to accept or deny the idea of a collective unconscious. The Christian understanding of creation would assert that we are one human family, and hence the idea of a shared species repository of common experience is not incredible. Also, the doctrine of creation would make it possible to believe that God made us to think about our lives in certain ways (i.e., archetypes). Just as Kant asserted that causality is a structure that we impose upon experience, similarly there may indeed be universal mental structures like what Jung claimed to have discovered that undergird our most important psychological realities. If they do exist and if Christianity is true, it makes sense that those structures would give us some access to religious truth. This is neither a point for or against Jungian psychology. It is an acknowledgment that he may be right here, and that Christians cannot prematurely declare him wrong.

Jungian thought is also popular in religious circles because it prizes the mystical. Disenchantment with the tyranny of propositional logic and purely dogmatic understandings of religious faith appears to be increasing in many Christian circles,[4] as is the desire to see our lives as stories that are gradually unfolding (e.g., Buechner, 1982, 1983). In an age when scientific understanding is prominent, "Jung was one of the

---

[4]See Hurding (1985, pp. 334-360) for an informed discussion of some dimensions of the more experiential dimensions of Christian faith and a careful analysis of the pros and cons of Jungian thought in understanding each.

first in a long line of twentieth century intellectuals who championed a 'meliorative sense of myth'—myth as a source of wisdom, vitality, and renewal" (Browning, 1987, p. 164; cf. Taylor, 1987). As a leader in this movement, Jung is thus warmly received by many persons of faith. There is much to be said for the Jungian appreciation of our "transrational" aesthetic, symbolic, mystical and story-telling natures.

But we share Vitz's (1987) concern that with too much emphasis on the mystical, the Jungian perspective can become a kind of intellectual gnosticism where the chief aim of life is to "know thyself" rather than the workings of the Creator-God in the larger universe (see also Hurding, 1985). The self-awareness or self-knowledge so deeply prized in this tradition can too easily become a kind of substitute form of "self-salvation," with a limited (or nonexistent) understanding of the vital importance of the incarnation and resurrection, or the crucial need for the *external* manifestations of confession, redemption and reconciliation. The great cosmic mysteries of the faith are rendered mere intrapsychic events that have their origins in the collective unconscious—not historical events anchored in the larger march of salvation history.

There is a low view of authority and external validation within the Jungian tradition. Ultimately, the authentic, healthy person is the one who trusts the meaning of the symbols that emerge from the collective unconscious. This highly subjective and experiential understanding of truth can certainly lead to a low view of the authority of the core teachings of the Christian Scriptures and of the crucial importance of the discerning role of the larger community of faith. If we are to assume that we best understand external reality from the truths that emerge from within, what prevents us from lapsing into an extreme tolerance of relativism? Is our theology ultimately a personal "psycho-theology" only? Is the "hermeneutic of self-understanding" the authoritative means for discovering biblical truth?

Knowing *truth* becomes a matter of individual discernment for the Jungian. The Jungian tradition seems to trust completely the guidance of the unconscious, but doesn't address the limitations of this awareness, including our capacities for self-serving bias, self-deception and superficiality. Christians rightly hunger for an approach that prizes other ways of knowing and other aspects of human faith and experience beyond the rational and the dogmatic, but Jungian psychology goes too far in its relativistic embrace of myth and its subjective epistemology.

We also share Vitz's fear that the Jungian perspective leads to an exaggerated individualism. For the Jungian, growth toward health is an "inner journey" (as Hurding has labeled it, 1985, pp. 334-360), a journey within oneself to the exclusion of real horizontal or vertical contact outside of oneself. A more fully developed appreciation for the vital importance of the community, family and society is needed in this tradition, as well as our ultimate dependence on the Creator-God, rather than an almost exclusive focus on the isolated, autonomous individual (Vitz, 1987). We are not faulting self-awareness per se—indeed, that is often vitally needed in our Christian communities (cf. Crabb, 1987). But when that is done at the expense of at least an equally strong desire to relate to God through the spiritual disciplines and worship, or to other persons through acts of charity, there is reason to be alarmed. Christianity is ultimately an other-directed faith that is not oriented exclusively toward self-realization and individuation.

Model of Personality

Beyond those issues covered in the last section, we find the Jungian work on psychological classification useful in elucidating aspects of human nature. This typology, as epitomized by the MBTI, is sufficiently researched and validated to be responsibly adapted for clinical application, assuming that it is sensitively and accurately interpreted. But the reduction of persons to their "types," as is often done in church applications of the MBTI, is inconsistent with the broader Jungian understanding of personality. Jung saw personality as much more fluid and multiply determined than one would suppose from the lay literature or misapplications of the MBTI.

The essentially unmeasurable nature of the linchpin of Jungian theorizing, the collective unconscious, is disturbing. As MacIntyre (1967, p. 296) has observed:

> That the existence of the collective unconscious is intended as a hypothesis is clear from the fact that it is avowedly introduced to explain why the same symbols keep recurring in dreams, mythologies, and works of art. However, there are no predictions that we can deduce from this hypothesis other than the vague generalization that such symbols do and will recur—and this, after all, is what the hypothesis was originally intended to explain.

MacIntyre may have been asking for a type of direct proof incompatible with a concept like the collective unconscious. But his criticism can at least serve to remind us that such a slippery concept should be held with a good deal more tentativeness than the convinced Jungians tend to manifest.

On the other hand, to state categorically that there is no reality beyond that which we can "see" seems equally foolish. As McLemore (1982) has observed, all too many conservative Christians have developed "an irrational bias against the nonrational." Many Christians would benefit from a healthy expansion of their spiritual consciousness, one perhaps that will foster understanding and awareness of the mystical and transcendent so deeply valued by Jungians. But such a "spiritual consciousness-raising" should protect against the quagmires of an obsession with the mysterious and mystical as an end in and of itself (McLemore, 1982, p. 128).

On a more positive note, Jungians have a high view of the worth of the individual. They are far less deterministic and mechanistic than the strict Freudians; they view human action as potentially more proactive than reactive. Our behavior makes sense in the larger context of a quest for meaning and purpose in life; it is teleological. Although affect and feeling are strongly emphasized, there is an appropriate respect for the importance of cognition and behavior in Jungian thought.

Model of Health

Jungian notions of health and wellness are certainly in the spirit of the humanistic tradition in psychology. This is problematic, because it is an incomplete understanding of wholeness. Like Gestalt and person-centered therapies (chapters twelve and ten), analytic psychology asserts that we have an infallible guide in the pursuit of wholeness, which in this system is the collective unconscious. For Jung, affirmation and self-actualization are virtues, but accountability and obedience to authority are viewed with suspicion. Any focus on the content of religious beliefs and world views would be viewed as an obstacle in the process of authentic self-realization.

Browning (1987, pp. 177ff.) astutely points out a fundamental ambiguity in Jungian thought. In some contexts, Jung speaks as if one passively follows the dictates of the unconscious in order to become whole. There appear to be no real choices to be made in this process other than to become what we were meant to become. In other contexts, Jung speaks as if we must make responsible choices about which archetypes to actualize at different points in life, and that we thus choose who we are becoming. This renders the growth process more of a reflective enterprise and underscores its fundamentally moral nature. The beliefs that shape our choices would then become highly relevant, even determinative, of the direction of our growth. Thus, Jung's theory, like all personality theories, is in Browning's analysis a moral theory: "It is a theory of what humans want, quest after, and need in order to be human. . . . It does indeed boil down to an ethics of self-actualization" (pp. 179-180).

Browning argues (successfully, we think) that Jung's ethic is not wholly incompatible with Christian thought, but does need careful correction for it to be compatible with Christian ethics.

A related concern with reference to the Jungian understanding of health and wholeness has to do with its obvious egocentric tendencies, especially in conceiving of growth only as a journey inward. We do not want to disparage appropriate and responsible self-realization. Indeed, this can be conceived as a matter of good stewardship and integrity for the committed Christian. What we fear is a lack of vision of our need for a love relationship with our Creator-God, attainable only through the forgiveness offered through the death and resurrection of Jesus Christ. A full understanding of Christian maturity is deeply informed by the confession of Jesus Christ as Lord of one's life, the cultivation and expression of the Christian virtues, and the deep love for the brothers and sisters. A biblically informed notion of costly discipleship is simply not part of the message of health and wholeness in the Jungian tradition.

Jungian thought is certainly to be commended for its willingness to address the problem of pain. Indeed, for Jung, neurosis is always based in the "avoidance of legitimate suffering." Unlike the more naively optimistic proponents in the humanistic tradition who advocate a "culture of joy" (Browning, 1987, pp. 176-177), Jungians advocate a vision for life that suggests that there can be meaning to suffering. Individuation is not the inevitable result of self-awareness alone; it may also require conscious and deliberate effort sustained throughout the life span.

The notion of a God that is absolute and beyond all human experience would be alien to Jung. For him, God had to be experienced first and foremost in the soul. Logically, then, religious beliefs are important only to the extent which they are experienced as psychic phenomena (Hempelmann, 1986). His "theology" was based on a view of wholeness that comes from the depths of our psychic nature. It was not theocentric at any level, but anthropocentric (p. 162). Wholeness does not have anything directly to do with a creed or membership in a local church. We grow through our responses to the psychic symbols which point the way toward greater personal integration.

Reason and rationality, then, are viewed with suspicion by Jungians. Through history, Jung asserted, the enduring truths of Christianity gradually lost some of their meaning as religious symbols deteriorated into mere signs or into dogmas. He felt that Christianity was too one-sided, with reason enthroned and the emotional side of the faith impoverished. For Jung, symbolic language, not propositional truth, should be at the heart of the faith. The wellspring of faith can be found, for example, in the deeper meanings of the sacraments. Effective preaching and teaching must bridge the gap between the world of the unconscious and the conscious, through symbols that relate the human to the infinite, transcendent God.

For many Christians, there is no more powerful reconciling symbol than the cross. Consider the perceptive insights of Hempelmann (1986, p. 165):

> In the cross . . . we have a symbol that (through the story in which it participates) holds together the two opposites: sinful man, who has denied God, and the loving God, who forgives them and takes them back. This is how I understand the symbol system to function in helping the individual be healed. In Christ alone is there salvation (and) healing.

But Jung would never go so far as to embrace the "alone" nature of Christianity. Further, in Christianity the symbols are not merely means of access into the realm of the collective unconscious. They also summarize historic external realities that are also at least partially understandable propositionally. Jung would seem to hold back from giving this sort of meaning to the symbols of faith.

Model of Abnormality

Perhaps the most important concern we want to raise about the Jungian understanding of the etiology and maintenance of "problems in living" has to do with the understanding of evil implicit within that perspective. As Hempelmann (1986, p. 162) has noted:

> Orthodox Christians believe that sin and the devil are real. While it is true that many Christians have not given the devil his due, thinking and speaking as though sin was only a mistake or error, but not the essential evil that 'dwells in me,' as St. Paul taught, Christianity has never gone so far as to deny the reality of evil. . . .
> In orthodox Christianity the problem of evil is central. It is the

victory over evil that comes from the cross, the symbol that points directly to the reality of evil. It also points to the power of love in God to conquer all evil—the resurrection.

In contrast, Jung was ambivalent about evil (Browning, 1987). He did not fully appreciate the power of sin and evil at either the individual or institutional level. At times, he seemed to trivialize evil by psychologizing it as the archetype of the shadow, a kind of "culturally despised and suppressed side of unused human potentiality. Here evil is simply that part of human potentiality that the prejudices of particular historical epochs teach us to disparage" (Browning, 1987, p. 169). On the other hand, Jung sometimes assumes a quasi-Gnostic position of the simultaneous existence of good and evil in both the divine and human levels.

There are problems with both options. In the former case, evil is psychologized and is primarily within, and thus the power to overcome it must come from within by making "good choices" through the raised human consciousness. In this vein, Jungians often talk about "embracing the shadow," that part of ourselves that we have cast off. There is no clearly articulated external force that has the power to overcome all evil; there is no conception of the importance of the hope of the resurrection. Indeed, the very notion of evil has been sanitized or trivialized if it has been converted to something we can embrace; it is no longer "substantially evil" (Browning, 1987, p. 194). At a rather informal theological level, it could be said that Jung essentially posits a kind of "works righteousness" approach to personal redemption. We become our own redeemers. Certainly this is a major liability in Jungian thought.

The latter case of conceiving of evil as substantial, coexistent and indeed coequal in God and humanity is equally troubling. An intriguing exchange in the *Journal of Psychology and Theology* (Griffin, 1986a, 1986b; Haule, 1986; Kelsey, 1986) addressed this theme. For Griffin (1986a, p. 276), the accurate understanding of human evil should be at the heart of the integrative dialog. He powerfully asserted that Jung had inserted a "new" tradition, a psychology of modernity, to replace the essential and enduring truths of Christian faith and experience, and that the new cosmology does not do justice to the understanding of the depths of our deceptive and evil tendencies (cf. Homans, 1978). Evident in this exchange is the Jungian tendency to view evil merely as an aspect of the good, a stance that is common in certain Eastern and "new age" religions but antithetical to orthodox Christian faith. Jung actually suggested making the Trinity into a quaternity to allow for the inclusion of Satan in the Godhead (Browning, 1987, p. 193). God is not, however, equal parts of good and evil, a melange of *Star Wars'* "good Force and bad Force."

For Christians, evil is real and has no part in the Godhead. Evil ought never to be trivialized. Jungian thought needs fully to appreciate the power of sin and evil. It needs to acknowledge the reality of an external transcendent realm that can influence day-to-day human functioning. And it must honestly confront the "powers" and "principalities" from without and not just from within.

Jung had little patience with classification of abnormality beyond the differentiation between functional and organic conditions. He had little interest in the biological bases of behavior or what we understand today as some of the sociocultural variables involved in the etiology and maintenance of psychopathology. Six decades later, that is a dangerously irresponsible position to take. Our understanding of the etiology and maintenance of psychopathology has broadened considerably to include the biological as well as sociocultural realms. Indeed, most responsible clinicians today see clearly how "problems in living" are multiply determined, so it is probably best to adopt a position of "epistemic humility" with reference to causation. Jungian explanatory schemes are too grand and overconfident. The stance of most clinicians today is considerably more modest and cautious.

Model of Psychotherapy

One does not need to embrace the Jungian view of the transpersonal unconscious to derive considerable gain from its rather broad and synthesizing perspective on life. Indeed, such an outlook, when combined with a warm and supportive counseling relationship, is likely to result in some movement toward greater wholeness. On the other hand, the tendency in Jungian therapy to avoid the specific details of an individual's life is potentially a dangerous way to approach the resolution of emotional conflicts (Kovel, 1976). Mystifying the mundane and material explanations of psychopathology runs the risk of abandoning the overt for the covert, or the observable for the transcendent.

Certain aspects of the Jungian model of change and psychotherapy offer rich insights to the Christian tradition. Although we find the lack of insistence on a specific treatment methodology frustrating, we do appreciate the profound respect that Jungians have for the self-healing that can occur within the client in the context of good therapy. We find the willingness to explore both the internal and external realities illuminating. The keen attention given to the projective tendencies of clients merits further study, as does the deep and abiding concern to assist clients in discovering the personal meanings of their inner lives—the exploration of what Jungians call archetypes and symbols may be a legitimate part of such a process. Spiritual matters are deemed highly appropriate matters to explore in Jungian therapy.

We appreciate the mentor-type role that Jungian analysts often adopt in their work with clients, not unlike that of a spiritual director (cf. Foster, 1978). In addition, perhaps no tradition of spiritual or psychological helping takes dreams more seriously than does the Jungian approach. As Sanford (1985, p. 618) observed, "Jung's emphasis on the importance of dreams . . . finds ample support in the view of the Bible and early church, where dreams were universally regarded as an important way in which God spoke to people." It certainly would be fair to assert that most contemporary approaches to people-helping that are informed by Christian distinctives have relatively little to say about the importance of dreams, or, for that matter, the importance of an active imagination, of the symbolic, or the "as if" language of the parables of Jesus. Perhaps we have something to learn here.

We agree with Griffin (1986a, pp. 274-275) that the fundamental constructs of Jungian psychology need to be more rigorously argued or demonstrated to be truly intellectually compelling. There is little or no data addressing the efficacy of Jungian therapy per se. Jung himself (1946, p. 7) was less than receptive to the call by experimentalists for quantification:

> Theories in psychology are the very devil. It is true that we need certain points of view for their orienting and heuristic value; but they should always be regarded as mere auxiliary concepts that can be laid aside at any time. We still know so very little about the psyche that it is positively grotesque to think we are far enough advanced to frame general theories. We have not even established the empirical extent of the psyche's phenomenology; how then can we dream of general theories? No doubt theory is the best cloak for lack of experience and ignorance but the consequences are depressing: bigotedness, superficiality, and scientific sectarianism.

Unfortunately, Jung set up an "either-or" choice that is not helpful. Van Leeuwen (1985) and others have called for a "post-modern" philosophy of science that takes phenomenological experience seriously, but which also makes a conscious and deliberate effort to be more explicit about theory and terminology, and a commitment to produce data of some kind. There certainly needs to be more of a "both-and" dialog between those who favor Jung's narrative method of research and the more traditional distinctives of controlled experimentation. What the Jungian movement really needs is more persons like Carlson (1980) and Helson (1982) who see the need to derive meaningful and significant hypotheses from Jungian thought that can be tested against objective criteria. The impact of Jungian concepts would be even more widespread with further serious scientific investigation.

Conclusion

C. G. Jung was a prolific and creative thinker with few equals in this century. His impact on modern thought is quite remarkable. Even his harshest critics have to admit that his thinking was "original and audacious" (Hall and Lindzey, 1985). We appreciate his willingness to raise concerns about "the soul of man," and to do so at a depth and intensity that has been seldom matched by even our most respected and articulate theological or psychological spokespersons today. It would be foolish to ignore the issues he addressed as we struggle in our attempts to become increasingly mature in Christ.

But while the issues he raised and questions he asked are vital, the answers Jung generated are of deep concern. When he grappled with Christianity, Jung seemed to have focused solely on its experiential aspects which he reinterpreted within his own system of thought. Consequently, his thought appeals more to those of a meditative, or perhaps mystical, bent. In contrast, those with a more intellectual or activistic bent have seldom been impressed (Hurding, 1985, p. 81). Perhaps the enduring value of Jungian thought for Christians will be that it raised our awareness of the great Christian mystical tradition in terms of devotional practice and godliness in life (Hurding, 1985, p. 357). The Jungian perspective may teach us that our Creator-God is not only concerned about the events of everyday living but also the deepest depths of our personalities as well.

Still, reaching in to pursue the inner journey is not without some risks, especially for persons who are already unstable, too willing to withdraw from others, or looking for a kind of spurious spirituality that will substitute for authentic Christian confession, character and commitment (cf. Boyer, 1988). And the psychology of Jung, with its deeply flawed understanding of our religious nature and the most fundamental religious truths, would be a poor guide on that inner journey.

For Further Reading

Campbell, J. (Ed.). (1971). *The portable Jung.* New York: Viking Press.
Along with Storr listed below, one of the best primers on Jungian thought.

Hempelmann, L. (1986). Is the Jungian approach Christian? An analysis. *Concordia Journal, 12,* 161-166.
A brief but insightful critique of analytic psychology.

Homans, P. (1978). *Jung in context: Modernity and the making of psychology.* Chicago: University of Chicago Press.
A scholarly and thoughtful analysis of Jungian thought in the larger socio-cultural context.

Jung, C. (1964). *Man and his symbols.* New York: Dell.

Jung, C. (1961). *Memories, dreams, and reflections.* New York: Random House.
Interesting initial readings in Jungian psychology.

O'Connor, P. (1985). *Understanding Jung, understanding yourself.* New York: Paulist Press.
A useful discussion of the relationship between spirituality and analytic psychology from a broad Catholic perspective.

Stein, M. (1985). *Jung's treatment of Christianity.* Wilmette, IL: Chiron.
Another good treatment of the relationship between spirituality and analytic psychology from a broad Catholic perspective.

Storr, A. (1983). *The essential Jung.* Princeton, NJ: Princeton University Press.
Along with Campbell listed above, one of the best primers on Jungian thought.

References

American Educational Research Association, American Psychological Association, National Council on Measurement in Education (1986). *Standards for educational and psychological testing.* Washington, DC: American Psychological Association.

Boyer, E. (1988). *Finding God at home.* New York: Harper & Row.

Browning, D. (1987). *Religious thought and the modern psychologies.* Philadelphia, PA: Fortress.

Bryant, C. (1983). *Jung and the Christian way.* London: Darton, Longman and Todd.

Buechner, F. (1982). *The sacred journey.* New York: Harper & Row.

Buechner, F. (1983). *Now and then.* New York: Harper & Row.

Buros, O. K. (Ed.). (1978). *The eighth mental measurements yearbook* (2 Vols.). Highland Park, NJ: Gryphon Press.

Campbell, J., and Moyers, B. (1988). *The power of myth.* New York: Doubleday.

Carlson, R. (1980). Studies in Jungian typology I: Memory, social perception and social action. *Journal of Personality, 38,* 801-810.

Corey, G. (1982). *Theory and practice of counseling and psychotherapy* (2d ed.). Monterey, CA: Brooks/Cole.

Crabb, L. (1987). *Inside out.* Colorado Springs, CO: NavPress.

Foster, R. (1978). *Celebration of discipline.* New York: Harper & Row.

Griffin, E. (1986a). Analytical psychology and the dynamics of human evil: A problematic case in the integration of psychology and theology. *Journal of Psychology and Theology, 14,* 269-277.

Griffin, E. (1986b). Neither/nor: A response to Haule and Kelsey. *Journal of Psychology and Theology, 14,* 285-287.

Hall, C., and Lindzey, G. (1985). *Introduction to theories of personality.* New York: John Wiley and Sons.

Haule, J. (1986). Integrating psychology and theology with bricolage: A response to Griffin. *Journal of Psychology and Theology, 14,* 278-281.

Helson, R. (1982). Critics and their texts: An approach to Jung's theory of cognition and personality. *Journal of Personality and Social Psychology, 43,* 409-418.

Hempelmann, L. (1986). Is the Jungian approach Christian? An analysis. *Concordia Journal, 12,* 161-166.

Homans, P. (1978). *Jung in context: Modernity and the making of psychology.* Chicago: University of Chicago Press.

Hughs, J. (1987). *Reshaping the psychological domain.* Berkeley, CA: University of California Press.

Hurding, R. (1985). *Roots and shoots.* London: Hodder and Stoughton.

Johnson, P. (1985). *We: Understanding the psychology of romantic love.* New York: Harper & Row.

Johnson, P. (1989). *He: Understanding masculine psychology* (rev. ed.). New York: Harper & Row.

Johnson, P. (1989). *She: Understanding feminine psychology* (rev. ed.). New York: Harper & Row.

Jung, C. (1934). A review of the complex theory. In *The structure and dynamics of the psyche,* Collected Works (Vol. 8). Princeton, NJ: Princeton University Press, 1960. (First German edition, 1934).

Jung, C. (1946). *Two essays on analytic psychology.* New York: Meridian.

Jung, C. (1953-1978). Collected works (20 Vols). (J. Read, M. Fordham, and G. Adler, Eds.). Princeton, NJ: Princeton University Press.

Jung, C. (1964). *Man and his symbols.* New York: Dell.

Jung, C. (1961). *Memories, dreams, and reflections.* New York: Random House.

Kaplan, R., and Saccuzzo, D. (1989). *Psychological testing* (2d ed.). Pacific Grove, CA: Brooks/Cole.

Kaufmann, Y. (1984). Analytical psychotherapy. In R. Corsini (Ed.), *Current psychotherapies* (3d ed.) (pp. 108-141). Itasca, IL: F. E. Peacock.

Keirsey, D., and Bates, M. (1984). *Please understand me: Character and temperament types.* Delmar, CA: Prometheus Nemesis.

Kelsey, M. (1968). *Christo-psychology.* New York: Crossroads.

Kelsey, M. (1977). *The other side of silence.* London: SPCK.

Kelsey, M. (1986). Reply to analytic psychology and human evil. *Journal of Psychology and Theology, 14,* 282-284.

Kovel, J. (1976). *A complete guide to therapy*. New York: Pantheon.

MacIntyre, A. (1967). Jung, Carl Gustav. In P. Edwards (Ed.), *The encyclopedia of philosophy* (Vols. 3-4) (pp. 294-296). New York: Macmillan.

McLemore, C. (1982). *The scandal of psychotherapy*. Wheaton, IL: Tyndale.

Moore, R. (Ed.) (1988). *Carl Jung and Christian spirituality*. New York: Paulist Press.

Munroe, R. (1955). *Schools of psychoanalytic thought*. New York: Holt, Rinehart and Winston.

O'Connor, P. (1985). *Understanding Jung, understanding yourself.* New York: Paulist Press.

Rychlak, J. (1973). *Introduction to personality and psychotherapy*. Boston: Houghton Mifflin.

Ryckman, R. (1985). *Theories of personality* (3d ed.). Monterey, CA: Brooks/Cole.

Sanford, J. (1980). *The invisible partners*. New York: Paulist Press.

Sanford, J. (1982). *Between people: Communicating one to one*. New York: Paulist Press.

Sanford, J. (1985). Jungian analysis. In D. G. Benner (Ed.), *Baker encyclopedia of psychology* (pp. 615-618). Grand Rapids, MI: Baker.

Sanford, J. (1987). *The kingdom within: The inner meaning of Jesus' sayings*. New York: Harper & Row.

Sanford, J. (1989). *Dreams: God's forgotten language*. New York: Harper & Row.

Stein, M. (1985). *Jung's treatment of Christianity*. Wilmette, IL: Chirion.

Taylor, D. (1987). *The myth of certainty*. Waco, TX: Word.

Van Leeuwen, M. S. (1985). *The person in psychology: A contemporary Christian appraisal*. Grand Rapids, MI: Eerdmans.

Van Leeuwen, M. S. (1990). *Gender and grace*. Downers Grove, IL: InterVarsity.

Vitz, P. C. (1987). Secular personality theories: A critical analysis. In T. J. Burke (Ed.), *Man and mind: A Christian theory of personality* (pp. 65-94). Hillsdale, MI: Hillsdale College Press.

THE BEHAVIORAL
PSYCHOLOGIES

6

BEHAVIOR THERAPY

✥

*B*ehavior therapy has been described as having "a long past but a short history" (O'Leary and Wilson, 1987, p. 1), meaning that although many of the techniques of this approach have been used before in human history, the systematized field has had only a short history dating back about 40 years (see Kazdin, 1982; or Masters, Burish, Hollon and Rimm, 1987, chap. 1). Since the 1950s, however, behavior therapy (especially cognitive-behavior therapy in the last decade) has aggressively stepped to center stage in the mental-health field, emerging as one of the four major paradigms in the field (along with psychodynamic, humanistic and family-system psychologies). Academic clinical psychology seems to be particularly dominated by this approach, if the typical contents of the leading journal, the *Journal of Consulting and Clinical Psychology,* is any indication. The best explanation of this popularity is probably that behavior-therapy researchers have been so very successful at generating empirical studies.

We have chosen to present the general field of behavior therapy in two separate chapters. In most Christian analyses, it is treated as one unified whole, and unfortunately the writings of B. F. Skinner are often all that are considered. This even though Skinner has had little direct effect on contemporary behavior therapy, except as a historical and perhaps "inspirational" figure.

Within the field of behavior therapy itself, distinctions between a number of subgroups are usually made (e.g., O'Leary and Wilson, 1987). We will consider the two most stringently behavioristic of the subgroups in this chapter, *behavior modification* (also known as *applied behavior* analysis) and what is called *behavior therapy* proper. We will refer to these together as behavior therapy. We will then deal with the less dogmatically behavioristic, more "cognitive" approaches of social-cognitive theory, cognitive-behavior therapy and cognitive therapy in chapter eight.

Descriptive Survey

Philosophical Assumptions

Behavior therapy was and is an outgrowth of *behaviorism*, which in turn was a product of two factors: a view of metaphysics, specifically that of *naturalism;* and a view of science, first that of *inductive empiricism* and later that of *logical positivism* (see Van Leeuwen, 1979a, among others, for an expanded discussion of these matters). Naturalism assumes that the universe is composed exclusively of matter and energy, and hence there are no such things as *super*natural entities such as gods or spirits. The human qualities that supposedly distinguish us from the rest of the universe (especially "mind"), and which are commonly assumed to transcend nature, are in this view presumed either not to exist or to be understandable by the same physical laws that explain the rest of existence. Human beings are not special in the sense of transcending these laws of the universe.

Behaviorism took shape under the influence of a particular view of science, that of logical positivism and its predecessor, inductive empiricism. According to logical positivism, all meaningful assertions must be either analytic (statements that are true by definition, such as $2 + 2 = 4$) or be *empirically verifiable* or *falsifiable*. Statements such as "God exists" are, in this view, not merely false; they are meaningless because they are not analytic and are not verifiable by empirical means. In this view, empirical sense data become the highest court of meaning and hence determine truth. Contemporary philosophers of science have convincingly documented the problems with this out-moded view of science and have begun to sketch the outlines for a better understanding of the process of human knowing (see Evans, 1977, 1989; and Van Leeuwen, 1982, for specifically Christian analyses; and Brown, 1977, for a more standard treatment of this issue from the perspective of the philosophy of science).

If the material universe, understandable only as matter and energy operating according to universal laws, is all that is, then human beings are material beings only and hence explainable by natural laws. Be-cause mental phenomena were not accessible to empirical study, be-haviorism eschewed all "mentalism." Philosophical behaviorism was first given clear articulation by the famous John B. Watson. In the 1920s he directly challenged the notion that mind or consciousness ("psy-che") was the proper subject matter of psychology, because it could not be empirically examined. For Watson, the road to progress in psychol-ogy was to follow after the natural sciences in dealing only with empirically verifiable constructs (i.e., behavior); thus behavior was understood through its material and causal relationships to other behaviors and environmental events. The specific formula for under-standing behavior was supplied later by the learning theories of Pavlov, Thorndike, Skinner and others.

Behaviorism's embrace of naturalism gave rise to what has been called _reductionism_, the principle of breaking down more complex phenomena into simpler, more elemental ones. Thus human language became understood as "verbal behavior," operating by the same prin-ciples as all overt behavior and reflexes. Thought in turn became "subvocal verbal behavior." These complex phenomena were in turn believed to be understandable in terms of the most elemental processes of learning. In this view, what we call "mental events" (such as thoughts and beliefs) become dispositions to engage in behavior and do not hold much interest apart from their direct ties to overt behavior. Everything was reduced to elemental processes.

Another implication of naturalism was _environmentalism_, not in the ecological sense but in the sense that all behaviors are caused by factors outside of or external to themselves. All human and animal behavior is viewed as caused by events in the environment. The typing behavior that created the words on this page is seen by a behaviorist as having been generated by the stimuli of the books and articles lying cluttered

about the desk, by the contingencies of others expecting a promptly
delivered book manuscript and so forth. Authors write not because they
want to, will to or because of some ill-defined creative urges or libidinal
impulses for procreation, but because outside stimuli impinging on
them compel the writing behavior.

The word *compel* above signals that we must deal with the concept
of *determinism* as well. Generally speaking, behaviorists accept the
notion that all behaviors are the inevitable results of the causally
relevant conditions that preceded them (Erwin, 1978). Skinner (1976,
p. 185) has said, "A person is not an originating agent; he is a locus, a
point at which many genetic and environmental conditions come
together in a joint effect."

If the behaviors of human beings are merely part of the stream of
natural material events occurring in a mechanistic cosmos, then it
surely follows that all our actions, including even what we call our
decisions and choices, are caused in such a way that, as Wolpe (1978,
p. 444) put it, "We always do what we must do." Human choice is
ultimately illusory; our actions are the inevitable results of the causal
forces impinging on us.

Model of Personality

Behaviorism is unique in that writers in this tradition typically make
statements about their view of persons only indirectly. The real focus
of the model is on the principles of behavior that apply to all behaving
organisms, both animal and human. Since there is really nothing special about human beings, to understand persons you only have to
understand the laws of learning. Behavioral understandings of the
person are generally that the person is a bundle of behavior patterns,
reflexes, perceptions and impressions. The self is nothing more, in this
view, than the aggregation of the person's empirical characteristics.

In contemporary texts on behavioral assessment (e.g., Hersen and
Bellack, 1981), it is not persons or their personalities that are assessed,
but rather it is behaviors and their controlling variables. Some take this
position to its logical conclusion, such as Bellack and Hersen (1977, p.
12), who say bluntly that "personality is not a real thing." Behavioral
views of the person are clearly *atomistic;* persons are best understood
by looking at the "atoms" of their behavior patterns and how these
atoms are arranged and related. These atoms are not seen as being
held together by, or emanating from, any comprehensive core of the
person which we might call a self.

The committed behaviorist asserts that *classical* and *operant learning* processes explain all behavior. So it is to these processes we now briefly turn, though the reader should be forewarned that these topics are immensely complex and have spawned an enormous literature; thus any brief summary is bound to be misleading due to oversimplification and selective attention.

Operant learning. Operant learning is also called instrumental learning. It refers to the modification of freely emitted behavior; that is, behavior which is free in the sense of being nonreflexive and non-coerced, not free in the philosophical sense. Operant learning is the process by which this emitted behavior is modified over time by the *consequences* that follow contingently upon the responses and by the *stimuli* that form the context under which the behavior occurs. The classic example is, of course, the rat in the Skinner box. Lever pressing or other forms of emitted rat behavior are modifiable by the consequences arranged to follow the behavior. Responses followed by such events as presentation of food or drink, or by the removal of unpleasant noise or shock are likely to increase the frequency of the behavior *(reinforcement)* . Responses followed by consequences such as a spray of ice water or shock, or by the removal of food or drink are likely to decrease the frequency of the behavior *(punishment)*. Rats can attend to and learn to respond to stimuli such as lights which signal that reinforcement is available (lever pressing leads to food when the green light is on) or is unavailable (lever pressing is ineffective when the red light is on).

Whereas classical conditioning (below) does not create new behavior, operant learning can lead to new and very complex behavior. First, new behaviors never before emitted by the organism can be taught through the process of *shaping*. Shaping involves reinforcing closer and closer approximations to a goal response. For example, a chicken can be taught to peck a piano key by reinforcing the behavior of being nearer and nearer the piano, then the behavior of touching the piano closer and closer to the keyboard, until a peck on the keys can be reinforced. New complex patterns of behavior can be created by *chaining,* wherein more and more "links" (specific behaviors) are required to occur together for reinforcement to be delivered, until an entire "chain" of behavior occurs before the final reinforcement (the chicken now raises a curtain, moves a stool and then plays the piano).

Those who practice behavior modification claim that human behavior is largely the result of these operant processes. Human problems in living occur when: (1) people learn maladaptive or inappropriate responses; (2) people fail to learn effective or appropriate responses due to their previous learning environments; or (3) people respond to the wrong environmental contingencies. Often the cause is described as the combination of all three factors. The negative behavior of the hyperactive child in the home and classroom may be the result of failure to learn proper skills of paying attention for sustained periods and appropriate ways of expressing boredom and anger. It may also involve having previously learned inappropriate responses of tantruming, whining and manipulating. Finally, the hyperactive behavior may be reinforced by peers, parents and teachers who, perhaps unwittingly, pay attention to the child when misbehavior is occurring and do not reinforce good behavior.

The therapeutic techniques that emerge out of this model are powerful methods for teaching new behaviors and for arranging environments to make desired behavior "pay off" and undesired behavior go unreinforced or punished. Several examples will illustrate these principles.

One of the dramatic successes of behavior modification has been in the treatment of autistic children, whose bizarre behavior and unresponsiveness to normal human interaction have puzzled professionals for decades. While the causes of this problem are still obscure, the application of operant procedures has yielded the most effective (though not perfect) treatment for this disorder (Lovaas, 1987). In Lovaas's model, autistic children are given intensive training for hours every day. They are first rewarded with food for appropriate behavior at whatever elemental level they can begin with, and new forms of behavior are slowly developed through shaping and chaining. Extremely dangerous behavior such as self-injurious head-banging may have to be directly punished, but as much negative behavior as possible is simply ignored in hopes that it will be displaced with positive responses as the child improves. Progressing from very fundamental behaviors such as language sounds and paying attention, the program reinforces increasingly more complex and socially important behaviors. As Lovaas (1987) has reported, this treatment program produced the astonishing outcome that fully half of the autistic children in the program were indistinguishable from normal children by late elementary school age, and most of the others were improved.

Another classic example of operant behavior modification is the token economy in the classroom. Skinner and others have argued for years that the best way to manage behavior is to use positive reinforcement, but this has proved difficult in the classroom, where misbehavior so often wins an inordinate amount of attention from the teacher as well as from peers. Additionally, it would be practically impossible to implement a program of immediate food reinforcers for good behavior in elementary school children; after all, a teacher only has so many hands and kids can only eat so many M&Ms! The creative solution to the problems of direct reinforcement came through creating an economic system in the classroom where children can earn tokens which count as points toward obtaining some desired reward (everything from candy to school supplies to tutoring time with older children to field trips, parties or longer recesses). Because each reward is "broken down" into points in this system, teachers can specify desired behavior and reinforce the child frequently with tokens. Such programs have been shown effective in increasing positive social behavior, academic performance and have even been used to teach children greater self-control.

One final example of behavior modification based on operant psychology is assertiveness training. Many individuals who report interpersonal difficulties lack critical relationship skills. Treatment then becomes a process of teaching clients the social skills necessary to interface more effectively with their social world. Clients will need reinforcing support and careful guidance from the therapist during the initial stages of development of new social skills, especially to prevent them from accidentally getting into failure situations where their skills are inadequate. The therapist may try to help the person take a stronger stand with regard to her personal wishes, help the person communicate more forcefully her positive feelings such as love and respect, or may try to develop fundamental communication abilities such as how to make polite initial conversation or how to express that she would like to spend more time with someone.

Classical conditioning. Classical conditioning is the process by which an involuntary response becomes reflexively associated with new eliciting stimuli. All human beings exhibit reflexive responses that are unlearned (or unconditioned) to stimuli that elicit these responses from us, as when the smell of food elicits salivation, a puff of air elicits eye blinking, a burn elicits pain, a noxious odor elicits nausea and so forth. These reactions do not demonstrate learning; we exhibit these responses without prior training. Pavlov showed that these reactions could be associated with new stimuli which themselves had previously not elicited these responses; this is learning.

The classic example of this is Pavlov's dogs, who learned to salivate at the sound of a bell because of the repeated association of the bell with the presentation of food. In this case the food was the *unconditioned stimulus* which elicited an *unconditioned response* of salivation. After conditioning trials, the previously irrelevant bell became a *conditioned stimulus* (i.e., it became a relevant stimulus only through conditioning trials) which could elicit a *conditioned response* of salivation even when no food was presented.

The procedures of Wolpe's behavior therapy are based on these principles. For Wolpe, a central feature of most adult psychopathology is anxiety, and anxiety can be rather handily conceptualized in terms of classical conditioning. For example, an intense emotional reaction, such as fear, to a "legitimate" or understandable stimulus, such as being bitten by a dog, can become associated through the process of classical conditioning with previously emotionally neutral stimuli such as going out of one's house. A person unfortunate enough to make the associations just described might well become an agoraphobic (a person generally fearful of being away from home and/or in situations where escape would be difficult), especially if he further conditioned himself by constantly reliving the dog bite in his thought life (including the pain and fear he felt). If in trying to leave his home and overcome his anxiety he gave in to the anxiety and did not leave, thus experiencing a powerful relief from his anxiety by avoiding what he feared, he would be further reinforcing the agoraphobia.

This analysis of the dynamics of the establishment of debilitating fears also leads to some fruitful hypotheses about fear reduction. Pavlov demonstrated early in the century that most conditioned responses could be changed or "wiped out" by either conditioning a new response to the conditioned stimulus, one that was incompatible to the previous conditioned response, or by *extinguishing* the conditioned response by presenting the conditioned stimulus without again pairing it with the unconditioned stimulus.

Wolpe pioneered the technique called *systematic desensitization* based on the former process of pairing a new response with the old stimulus. Wolpe understood the phenomenon of anxiety largely in terms of its physical, observable manifestations and thus reasoned that the response most antithetical to anxiety was muscular relaxation. Desensitization was developed to provide a way for relaxation to become associated with what had previously been an anxiety-evoking stimulus. He first teaches anxious clients physical relaxation and then has them slowly and gradually imagine closer and closer approaches to the anxiety-provoking stimulus while the client maintains a relaxed state. After the clients are able to maintain physical relaxation while imagining an approach to the previously feared stimulus, Wolpe then guides them to closer real-life approaches to the feared stimulus. Using this procedure, one of the authors assisted his very first client in graduate school to go from having a long-standing and severe spider phobia that was undermining her school performance and social relationships (due to constant debilitating fear) to comfortably having a spider collection (live, of course) in her apartment and being totally free from her previous fears.

Other behavior therapists have preferred to utilize Pavlov's notion of extinguishing the unwanted response. Extinction for Pavlov's dogs occurred simply by presenting the bell, which had previously been associated with food, over and over again without any presentation of the food. In this way the salivation response to the bell eventually died out.

Similarly, Marks (1981) has argued that many forms of anxiety are best extinguished by exposing the client to the feared stimulus or stimuli without the feared outcome occurring. Exposure to a feared stimulus can be gradual or massed (all at once). For example, Marks reported the case of a woman with a long-standing obsessive-compulsive problem which had previously not responded to either drugs or several forms of psychotherapy, including psychoanalysis. He worked with the formulation that the fears of germs, sickness, death and so forth were generating avoidance behaviors such as compulsive cleaning rituals and avoidance of social contacts. These avoidance behaviors in turn reduced the anxiety, which reinforced the avoidance. Therapy then consisted of exposing the patient to the feared stimuli, which Marks did in an intensive inpatient treatment program. Marks had the woman touch "contaminated" objects such as dirt, shoes, used (but not contagious) bandages, toilet seats, floors and used eating utensils, all while refraining from cleansing herself; she even was asked to put her fingers in her mouth and to rub her clothes before putting them on and to rub her own eating utensils before using them. Within days, since there was no trauma to keep the conditioned fear alive (the feared disease and death did not occur), the obsessive-compulsive neurosis and the anxiety causing it slowly diminished to a manageable level (extinguished). At follow-up, she maintained her therapeutic gains.

Model of Psychotherapy

Based on the notion that behavior is caused by its environment, behavior therapy begins with a careful *assessment* of the "controlling" conditions influencing the occurrence of the problematic behavior patterns, the factors that seem to exert some sort of influence on the problematic behavior. Note that it is not persons that are assessed, but behaviors. This is called conducting a *functional analysis* of the problem behavior. For instance, the temper-tantruming behavior of a five-year-old may be seen by the parent as being caused by low self-esteem, but the behavior modifier looks for reliable predictors of the tantrums and for the consequences that reinforce it (e.g., that the behavior occurs only when mother is present and father isn't, that the mother usually tries to "reassure" the child with attention and affection when this behavior occurs, etc.). Therapy does not begin until a clear conceptualization is obtained.

Behavior modification conducted on an outpatient basis then proceeds to foster a collaborative relationship with the client by sharing as much of the conceptualization with the client as is feasible, modifying the conceptualization as needed and enlisting the client as a collaborator in the therapy process. When behavior modification is conducted with persons with whom informed consent is not possible due to either inability to comprehend the problem (psychotics or the retarded) or the persons would not consent voluntarily to the treatment (such as prison inmates or hospitalized antisocial adolescents), permission to proceed is obtained from the custodians legally in charge of the person's welfare.

At this point the intervention has begun. Because of their commitment to the scientific method, behavior modifiers emphasize continuing assessment both throughout and after the intervention period to verify that change is occurring as expected. In inpatient settings, professionals are usually the persons directly managing the intervention process, as when psychiatric hospital staff manage a token economy on a hospital ward. In outpatient settings, the modification process is usually managed by the clients themselves or through the agency of intermediaries, such as parents implementing prescribed procedures for their child or teachers implementing procedures in the classroom.

Christian Critique

Philosophical Assumptions

The first philosophical presupposition we mentioned in regard to behavior therapy was that of naturalism. Obviously, naturalism is at odds with the Christian faith: God exists and is above nature since he is the maker of nature, and therefore dogmatic naturalism is false. There are such supernatural entities as God, angels, the devil and demons. But this quick dismissal of doctrinaire naturalism is not an endorsement of the opposite belief—that human beings are purely supernatural beings.

Authors such as Boivin (1985) have argued that while Christians must reject a behavioristic world view that denies the reality of the supernatural, it may be biblical to assert that while there are supernatural entities that interact with the created order, the created order itself (including humanity) is purely naturalistic. Compare the words of Watson (1930, p. v), "Man is an animal different from other animals only in the types of behavior he displays," with the words of Boivin (1985, p. 83), "Only our relationship and responsibility to God makes us qualitatively different from animals." Boivin asserts that a Christian understanding of the person does not need to posit more than a natural existence for humanity. He supports this view by pointing to the Hebraic notion of the unity of human existence, to the doctrines of embodied life, and to the confusion of traditional Christian anthropology about soul and spirit. He suggests, in short, that naturalism is true with reference to human beings.

We agree that there has been at times a misplaced emphasis on doctrines of disembodied souls in the Christian tradition. Nonetheless, the Christian faith seems to require viewing persons as partially immaterial beings. The naturalism of behaviorism does, however, remind us that humans have pridefully underestimated the extent to which our embodied existence conditions, shapes and even determines some aspects of our experience. But in emphasizing only bodily existence, the behaviorist misses a key aspect of human nature, that being the interplay of body and soul-spirit and the distinctively transcendent aspects of our natures (see chapter two).

The behavioristic rejection of "mentalism" and its view of the mind is also problematic. If thought is merely a behavioral disposition or a by-product of physical brain events, then humans cannot transcend the physical order of things. This provides a conceptual grounding for the doctrine of determinism. As we shall see in the paragraphs to come, such determinism is not acceptable. As one of us has argued previously (Jones, 1985), Christian belief does not lead to an easy resolution to the brain-mind issue, though it does set up certain parameters within which to choose proper resolutions to the matter. One of these parameters, though, must be some notion that thought is more than just an "epiphenomenon" as behaviorists propose. Christians cannot accept a notion that belief and thought are not effectual causes of behavior.

We have already delineated how behaviorists accept determinism. Even so, it is common to read of "freely emitted behavior" and even "freedom" in behavioral writings. How can this be? Zuriff (1985) is helpful here in noting that the language of freedom or action is used by behaviorists to designate behaviors which are not reflexively elicited or coerced. In this view, a certain action (for example, raising a hand) is free if the behavior coincides with one's desires (as when waving bye-bye to a child) but is not free when it is against one's desires (as when one raises both hands during a robbery or in response to stimulation of the motor cortex of the brain during neurosurgery). Note, though, that the actions in all three examples would be regarded by the behaviorist as causally determined; the first two by the "laws of learning" and the last one by neurological stimulation.

What makes the first instance of waving bye-bye "free" for the behaviorist is not that one could have acted otherwise under the same circumstances; in the behavioral analysis one could not have done so given one's learning history and the current environment. It was "free," in the view of Skinner and others, because the enacting of that behavior was not unpleasant for the actor and it was in accord with the person's causally predetermined desires at the moment. In other words, the actor had the subjective experience of choice, but the choice and the desires that motivated it were really predetermined by learning history. All behavior is regarded as inevitable; we can never do other than what we do. As Zuriff (1985, p. 199) says, behavioristic psychology "is not . . . compatible with the notion of a free-willed self-initiating agent."

In critiquing this view, we must first note that not all psychologists who study even animal behavior use mechanistic forms of analysis that are characteristic of the strict behaviorist. Domjam (1987), for instance, argues that theoretical perspectives that emphasize "choice" and that emphasize how patterns of reward and punishment restrict the "freedom of action" (p. 562) of animals are more fruitful than old-style stimulus-response models. But this view probably cannot be taken as a belief in animal freedom in the sense that Christians mean by that term.

We argued in chapter two that Christian belief requires a rejection of determinism—the view that every human event is the inevitable outcome of preceding events—and requires belief in limited freedom.

Though some Christian psychologists (e.g., Bufford, 1981) and some Christian groups embrace such a strong view of God's sovereignty that they could be labeled theological determinists, such a position has not been typical of historic, orthodox Christianity. John Calvin is commonly believed to have denied the freedom of persons, but along with Muller and Vande Kemp (1985), we would argue that his belief in God's sovereignty, divine election, predestination and the depravity of the human will cannot be equated with philosophical determinism as accepted by most behaviorists. Human freedom is even defended in the Calvinistic tradition, as stated in the Westminster Confession of Faith (Leith, 1973): "God hath endued the will of man with that natural liberty, that [it] is neither forced nor by any absolute necessity of nature determined to good or evil."

In most segments of the Christian tradition, human beings are regarded as responsible, as morally culpable. Responsibility for our actions seems to require the capacity to have acted other than we did in a given situation. Thus, from a Christian perspective total determinism is unacceptable and limited freedom is an essential belief (Evans, 1977). Plantinga (1983) nicely summarized the essence of a Christian position by defining the concept of "agent causation: the notion of a person as an ultimate source of action" (p. 23). The Christian must believe that a person's choices are sometimes the ultimate and deciding factor in the occurrence of an action in order to believe that we are truly responsible beings who can be held accountable for our actions before God.

But note that causes do not have to be exclusive. To argue that in a particular instance the person was an ultimate cause does not rule out that other causes also affected the behavioral outcome. Even though we make real choices, we do so as persons with experiences and constraints that exert an effect. Accepting the notion of agent causation does not mean denying the assertion that some or even much of our behavior is determined, or that the true choices of a free agent are shaped by constitutional or environmental factors.

The Christian concept of limited freedom is not the same as freedom from regularity, freedom from influences on behavior or freedom from finitude. It simply means that the final choices that create behavior were not the result of impersonal forces and the chooser was not merely a "locus" of influences coming together. Rather, the person decided among real options, influenced by his or her history and constitution. This position has been excellently delineated by Browning (1987, p. 113):

> The doctrine of the freedom, transcendence, and responsibility of
> humans does not mean that we are totally free and completely
> unconditioned by either internal impulse or external reinforce-
> ments. In fact, it means just the opposite. It means that in spite of
> our massive conditionedness by these forces, there is still a sufficient
> modicum of transcendence over them to make it possible for us to
> alter, however slightly, the course of our lives.

It would seem that we are stuck with incompatible perspectives on this
topic; determinism and limited freedom do not in fact appear to be
reconcilable.

Positively, we can learn from the behavior modifier that our behavior is influenced and shaped by many factors of which we are often
unaware. In denying determinism, Christians are often in danger of
embracing a prideful claim that their choices and actions are totally
free and unconditioned by their material existence. We are dangerously close to a self-deifying view that denies the finitude and dependency in which we exist. It also seems true that human beings are a
composite of lower and higher capacities, and that again out of pride
we want to deny the real part conditioning influences play in our basic
psychological make-up.

Model of Personality

We introduced earlier the atomistic view of the person imbedded in
behavioristic psychology. In this view there are no necessary interrelationships between discrete components of the person's behavior. If
interrelationships exist between clusters of behaviors, as when a person
tends to lie and to steal, they are there by the accident of conditioned
association or some such process. There is no necessary grounding of
any particular behavior or behavior pattern in a self.

Thus a concept of general human responsibility is impossible, since
each behavioral pattern has its own specific controlling conditions
which bears no necessary relationship to the person as a whole. There
is no "person" to hold responsible for the behavior exhibited. This is
why Skinner (1971) can call for the abolition of our criminal jurispru-
dence system as it exists today—there really are no *persons* to be
punished but only response patterns to be modified, and thus behavior
modification should replace judicial punishment. For the behavior
modifier, one negative behavior pattern (such as repeated lying)
doesn't make the person a bad person; rather, the lying is a behavior

pattern that needs to be modified. That pattern is unrelated to the "person," as the person does not exist.

There is a certain clinical wisdom and utility to such an approach, in that the spurious overidentification by a client (as a person) with a particular negative aspect of her or his behavior is genuinely problematic. We have known sincere Christians who ignore many positive areas of discipline and maturity in their lives to focus on one negative pattern ("I've not been able to kick my fingernail-biting habit; how dare I say that God is active in my life when I have no self-control!"). Thus this insight is of central value for the religious thinker: Not every behavior pattern is a true index of the state of the self. One person's rudeness in a situation may be an accurate index of their arrogance, pride and self-deification. The exact same act by another person may be an anomaly related to being inattentive to social cues at that moment because of a deep inner struggle of some sort. And perhaps even behavior patterns that are good indices of the condition of the heart will have to be changed deliberately after the heart changes. Old, sinful habit patterns don't automatically change when the heart changes, as many a new convert has discovered.

In chapter two we discussed the need for Christians to view the person as a substantive agent or self. Christian thought requires the identification of specific behaviors in some significant manner with the unified person, because a person who commits specific behavioral acts which are sins must be capable of validly being labeled a sinner. In a powerful way, a person's behavioral acts often are diagnostic of the inner condition of the "heart" or unified core of the person. As Christ said, "By their fruit you will recognize them" (Mt 7:16). So behaviors are not atoms unconnected with the heart; they are often (but not always) evidence of what lies in the heart. If we deny that persons are unified beings, then there is no one to hold responsible for sin, no unified person to be redeemed and sanctified or punished, and sins are just behaviors which occur in a person's body or in his or her actions but are unconnected with the person per se. Atomism is thus unacceptable, though instructive, to the Christian.

Every theory of personality has a view of human motivation, though we have dealt only implicitly with it in behavior therapy so far. The behavioral view is actually very simple and very complex. It is simple in proposing that human survival is the driving, evolutionarily based motivation behind our behavior.

As Browning (1987) and others have pointed out, there are remarkable parallels between Skinner's environmental reinforcement and Darwin's concept of natural selection. For the Darwinian evolutionist, nature "selects" species that successfully adapt to their environmental niche. For the behaviorist, the environment "selects" behaviors by reinforcing those responses that aid survival and adaptation to the organism's niche in life.

Looking only at rat behavior in Skinner boxes, we often mistakenly imagine reinforcement to be something that others intentionally do because they deliberately want the behavior of the subject (rat or child) to change. But in the "real world," reinforcement and punishment occur naturally depending on how good of a match the organism's behavior is to the demands of the environment. For example, a particular type of hunting behavior may be reinforced by a greater kill at the end of the hunt because the hunting response meshed well with nature. To Skinner, individual adaptation to the environment, and hence greater chance of survival, is the motivation for human behavior. And one of the distinctives of behaviorism is that it proposes only a small list of inherent motivations or instincts that are themselves critical to survival, including such drives as for food, drink and sex (Herrnstein, 1977).

But the behavioral view of motivation is also exquisitely complex, because Skinner and others believe that almost anything can become a reinforcer through its association with the limited number of more primary or basic reinforcers. Things like money or verbal praise come to be reinforcers through constant association with primary reinforcers such as food, warmth and sexual outlet. In this way we can be led to value (and hence be motivated by) a diversity of stimuli, including financial reward, the praise of our parents and peers, or by interpersonal recognition. Further, response patterns like academic excellence, artistic creativity, physical brutality and psychopathic manipulation can become vehicles for obtaining primary reinforcers and hence the response patterns can come to have a positive value in their own right. So in the behavioristic analysis there is no one core human motivation that is easily appealed to in order to understand human behavior. Rather, human motivation is idiosyncratically organized; each person's motivations may be different from those of his or her neighbors.

Christians may applaud the motivational diversity of behavior therapy, but be rightly troubled by its assumption that all effective motivations ultimately depend on basal drives shared with animals. Christians must claim that human beings are capable of acting out of higher motives, such as the desire to serve God, and that such higher motives do not always reduce to the drive for tangible reinforcers.

A Christian judgment that human motivations can and ought to be more noble and higher than they are may be valid; at the same time, appeals to "higher motives" may be ineffective incentives to change a person's behavior. For instance, Christians often object to token economies for their problem children on the grounds that the children "ought" to obey their parents and do their chores because "it is the right thing to do," not to earn points to purchase video games. But when a disruptive child is motivated only by the avoidance of punishment and the acquisition of toys, those appetites may be the best avenue for modification of the child's behavior. Such an initial change may establish the very possibility of the child being motivated by other things. Having children obey their parents, improve their school performance and attend church to earn tokens to buy toys may be the best way to expose them to activities which they "ought" to value more, and thus increase the likelihood that they will come to prefer them. Just because Christianity teaches that people ought to value more than material things does not mean they, in fact, do, and there is no psychotherapy system more humble and realistic about the depth to which human motivation can sink than behavior modification.

The approach also suggests a technology for the alteration of human values and motives through the acquisition of skills and association of events. As Clouse (1985, p. 94) put it, "God created us as beings who respond to reinforcers and punishers in our environment." Perhaps it is human pride more than anything that makes us prone to believe that we supersede all environmental influence. The deliberate structuring of our environments to build up helpful and righteous behavior seems a helpful lesson to learn from behavior modification. The New Testament epistles often give instructions not for individual effort and growth but to the creation of powerful fellowship contexts, which can be effective mechanisms for the modification of individual behavior. Sometimes the best path to personal change is the immersion of the individual into the community, with the person thus being subject to the contingencies of the personal consequences of that community. The behavioral analysis of this influence is, on an ultimate level, unsatisfactory, but it points us to an aspect of personal reality that we might not otherwise attend to.

We can also mention in passing the behavioral view of good and evil (see Cosgrove, 1982; or Browning, 1987). For the behaviorist, good and evil as such do not exist because there are no values that exist outside of human conditioning patterns. Moral codes, to Skinner, are believed to embody codified instructions about how to obtain reinforcement (this is the "good") and avoid punishment (the things to avoid are the "bad"). A moral absolute such as "Thou shalt not steal" is behaviorally understood as expressing the normative pattern in a particular culture by which persons can generally expect rewards for honesty, diligence and thrift and punishment for theft and cheating. Browning (1987) has convincingly argued that a close examination of Skinner's work, especially of his famous utopian novel about a behavioristic community, *Walden Two,* shows that beneath Skinner's apparently purely evolutionary ethic lies a commitment to a radical egalitarian justice ethic that places special emphasis on the "primary goods of liberty and opportunity" (p. 109). But because this detailed examination of Skinnerian ethics is more relevant to Skinner's utopian aspirations and is not so relevant to behavior modification as a therapy system, we refer the reader to Browning for further information.

One of the most frequent criticisms of behavior modification is that its views of the person are simplistic. But it not the case that behaviorists think human behavior is simple. They acknowledge that we are capable of exquisitely complex behavior. They attribute this complexity to the human capacity for enacting complex chains of behavior, for making fine discriminations between stimuli so that our complex behavior is well tailored to our exact circumstances, and for being guided by symbolic rules. They are forced to regard these rules as mere compound stimuli that shape our behavior rather than concepts that we "understand," because they must stay away from any mentalistic concepts. They contend the basic processes governing behavior are simple, but that just as simple brushstrokes of color may grow into paintings of the most exquisite sorts, similarly simple learning processes can yield behavioral patterns of true complexity.

The core of our complaint then must not be that behavior therapy sees complex humanity as simple, but rather that it does irrevocable harm to our view of persons for complex human processes to be reduced to instances of basic learning phenomena. This is *reductionism.* The danger is that at some point in reductionistic arguments what is essential for maintaining a full sense of what it means to be human will be lost. At the point where the human as a self, as a person, disappears and is replaced by conditioned response patterns, reductionism has gone too far.

On the other hand, we must remember that to intervene, or to have science at all, some level of reductionism is necessary. No human being can ever fully understand another in all one's complexity and richness. All of our judgments about others are "reductions" of some sort. All pithy sayings, proverbs and common wisdoms simplify situations by ignoring some aspects of human uniqueness; this seems to be the cost of choosing actions. If counselors had to understand clients in all their unique and incredible complexity before intervening, no counseling would ever get done.

The issue is whether in the process of simplification too much gets lost. We would argue that this is indeed the case in behaviorism. Even though basic learning processes can yield startling complexity, it still demeans humanity to regard all behavior as resulting from basic learning processes shared with animals. (It is not demeaning, however, to suggest that some or even much of our behavior may be shaped by such processes.) This is the fundamental and irrevocable weakness of behavior modification; that in the process of reducing complexity to fundamental processes, all that is recognizably and distinctly human disappears.

This leads us to examine the concepts of *consequence, habit* and *competence.* Remember from chapter two that a Christian view of persons asserts that we were created to exercise purposeful dominion over the earth. We might conclude from this that we are intrinsically goal-oriented beings whose actions are meant to produce tangible outcomes in our world. Hence, it is not nonsense from a Christian point of view to expect human beings to be influenced by the consequences of their actions. Scripture is full, if you will, of direct appeals to act in our own welfare, as C. S. Lewis (1980) pointed out so well in his sermon "The Weight of Glory." God through his revealed Word promises us unimaginable and eternal rewards both now and in the hereafter if we will but become his followers, and unimaginable punishment if we do not (see Piper, 1977). As Bufford (1981) effectively argues, one of the primary ways in which God deals with humanity is through consequences for our actions, and it would be foolish to deny that human behavior is profoundly shaped by the contingencies we interact with and perceive. Behaviorists have something to remind us of here.

But we cannot simplemindedly say that behaviorism is true because the Bible talks about rewards. First, behaviorists talk about reinforcement, not rewards, and use the concept in a technical sense that implies much more about human behavior and nature than Christians can accept. The concept of reward, in the Christian view, often implies moral worthiness to receive the reward, not just manipulation by consequences. Second, any psychological theory can make sense of human beings responding to material incentives; so behaviorists are merely unique in their emphasis on this dynamic, rather than being the only ones who recognize it. Nevertheless, it seems true that by emphasizing this human tendency to respond to incentives, they have come up with unique and effective means of intervening, especially with populations, such as the retarded and children, where verbal methods are less likely to effect change.

Christian thought is also hospitable to the notion of habit. In fact, the Christian counseling method of Jay Adams is actually built in part around the notion that both sinful and righteous behaviors can and do become habits. Adams (1979, chap. 14) argues that the core of a Christian counseling approach is contained in Ephesians 4:22-24, where we are instructed to lay aside the old self and put on the new self. Adams argues that these terms of self refer essentially to habit patterns formed out of the choices one has accommodated one's self to. Thus, for Adams, laying aside the old self is "dehabituation" and putting on the new self is "rehabituation" (p. 237). Habit is said to be "a great blessing of God that has been misused by sinners" (p. 161). The capacity to respond automatically is misused by it being adapted to perform sinful acts out of habit, as when we train our hearts in greed (2 Pet 2:14; see also Jer 13:23). But Adams argues that the believer can also develop godly habits with the help of the Holy Spirit (Heb 5:14), and that these habits can be undermined by, for example, bad company (1 Cor 15:33). A Christian view of persons will recognize the place of habit in human life, and behavior modification certainly does this. Adams would distinguish his approach from behavior modification on many points, but especially in his assertion that real change only happens with the indwelling of the Holy Spirit, and not through unaided human effort alone.

Behavior modification suggests indirectly that optimal human well-being is correlated with the development of competencies; the more varied capacities individuals have for interacting productively with their world, the better. With the notion of dominion in the biblical framework, competence does seem an important concept in human life.

Christianity is sometimes mistakenly identified as a religion that

requires persons to devalue themselves and view themselves as worth-
less and incompetent, and there are biblical passages that give this
impression—such as the injunction to believe that "all have sinned and
fall short of the glory of God" (Rom 3:23). But recognition of moral
bankruptcy is not equivalent to incompetence. Christianity is not
chained to perceptions of incompetence.

Jesus Christ and Moses were the only two figures in the Bible that
were described as *meek;* the best understanding of meekness biblically
is not weakness, as is commonly supposed, but "power under control."
The Greek word for meekness was actually used to describe powerful,
aggressive, but well-controlled war horses. Similarly, we have argued
previously (Jones, 1984) that through the process of assertiveness
training, a Christian client can acquire options in behaving strongly in
difficult situations; she can make more responsible choices of when to
be strong and when to be mild, thus allowing the person to more
effectively answer God's call for how to act in diverse situations, rather
than having to always act unassertively because one hasn't the capacity
to act otherwise. Such an expansion of competencies allows the person
greater responsiveness to the possible breadth of God's call to action
than a person might have been able to muster otherwise.

Model of Psychotherapy

Applied behaviorism has often been criticized with reference to how it
might be applied in a utopian attempt to shape all of humanity. For
instance, many regard C. S. Lewis's famous science fiction novel *That
Hideous Strength* to have been an early antibehavioristic tract (and a
thought-provoking one it is!).

More directly, Van Leeuwen (1979b, 1979c) and Browning (1987)
spend a great deal of time critiquing and drawing implications from
Walden Two, Skinner's behavioristic utopian novel. It is a recurrent
theme among critics of Skinner that in spite of his deterministic
assumptions, he often makes messianic pronouncements of how we
should or must implement behavioral control technology on a societally wide basis if we are to see "what man can make from man"
(Skinner, 1971, p. 206).

His critics point out the contradiction of saying on the one hand
that "all behavior is determined, everything happens as it must," while
at the same time saying, "we must seize the opportunity now to reform
and reshape humanity to save our race and better our plight." Yet there
is no contradiction in this for Skinner, as he can argue that it is

reinforcing for him to say such things and that he has come to the place through his reinforcement history where he believes these things (i.e., these verbalizations are established response patterns), and he would thus predict that society as a whole would receive a greater sum total of reinforcement from following his advice. Browning is right in judging Skinner to be endorsing something like societal husbandry to cultivate the types of behavior patterns among the populace that the elite behavior-control experts would judge as being for the common good of our species. Such a system would of necessity be elitist and totalitarian. It is on the basis of these tendencies that many dismiss behavior modification out of hand. But we will not interact further with how behaviorism *might* be implemented as social policy and grapple instead with how it is used clinically.

Let us first take what are for many the most troublesome cases: those where the recipients of therapy are not able or willing to agree to the change process. What of behavior modification with the developmentally disabled (mentally retarded) or as applied on inpatient child, adolescent and adult psychiatric wards where patients are detained against their will? There are some legitimate similarities between behavior modification applied in these situations and the more speculative accounts of how they might be applied in a totalitarian system. First, we must acknowledge that the interventions in these situations are applied with the consent of the parent, legal guardian or custodian of the persons because the clients are judged by their guardians to be in the client's best welfare. This particular dilemma is one faced by all coercive applications of therapy methods.

Further, behavior modifiers typically view what they are doing as building necessary behavior changes into clients to equip them to acquire greater freedom and choice in life. Rebellious adolescents, it would be argued, are actually experiencing diminished freedom because their behaviors are largely being shaped by deviant social cues and reinforcers. Coercive intervention may be necessary, in this analysis, to alter established behavior patterns, as when adolescents previously "addicted" to Satanic practices must conform to a token-economy system. Hopefully in the process the new "normal" behavior acquires greater value and the deviant behavior fades with disuse. Even highly aversive treatment (such as punishment by shock or physical restraint) may be necessary to disrupt highly destructive behavior such as self-abuse.

We can see some legitimacy to the behaviorist's argument that coercive treatment is sometimes valid when the suffering person is failing to act in self-enhancing fashions. What compassionate person will accept the strident demands of a twelve-year-old that only her peer group should tell her how to behave? What person will withhold shock punishment from a retardate with a ten-year history of horrible head-banging, when this treatment promises to eliminate that behavior in two days?

But what legitimately frightens skeptical nonbehaviorists is the lack of any sharp and clear delineation in the theory of how practitioners distinguish between incompetent and competent persons and between adaptive and maladaptive behavior patterns, especially since in the behavioristic view, everyone's actions are determined anyway. Behavior modification is trumpeted as a tool that can be applied to change any behavior. What then will stop abuses such as the application of "behavioral principles" in prisoner-of-war camps where human beings were deprived of sufficient food to make them more responsive to food as a reinforcer for compliance and hard work? The potential for such abuses is frightening.

In the outpatient situation, however, behavior-modification practice is less controversial. Two reviewers of behavior-therapy practice even referred to the "amorality" of behavior therapy (Woolfolk and Richardson, 1984). They argued that while behavior modification has values built into its system, as a therapy model it has a much less well-developed notion of human health or perfection than the classic psychoanalytic or person-centered models. Its supporters argue that a less defined ideal allows for greater flexibility of direction and less intrusive influence of the therapy's embedded values. This may be somewhat true, but our concern would be that such amorality would simply relocate the influence from a relatively public therapeutic model to a more elusive and idiosyncratic locus; i.e., the personal opinions and values of the therapist. In other words, the informed consumer of gestalt therapy services knows the values of the gestalt therapist with some accuracy before beginning therapy, but this is less true with the behavior therapies. Hence, its techniques can be pointed in many directions, as its abuses show. Without a built-in explicit model of healthy humanness, behavior modification becomes almost a collection of techniques in search of an application, as Tan (1987) has noted.

The fact that behavior modification has developed a diversity of techniques is both a strength and a weakness. On the surface, students of behavior therapy often feel they are studying a loosely woven collage of intervention strategies. None of the other therapies rival behavior therapy in the degree to which treatment for different persons can be truly individualized because of the many techniques found in the model, and this is a strength. Further, its supporters argue that it is not a set of techniques but a framework for analysis and modification. And yet the most frequent complaint against behavior therapy is its superficiality, and the appearance of superficiality is certainly strengthened by the chaotic explosion of technologies available. This apparent superficiality is more than mere appearance; it may reflect the more profound lack of a central organizing understanding of personhood at the center of the model.

Another reason that behavior modification is judged superficial is that its view of persons is ahistorical; the important determinants of human action (and hence of personality) are almost exclusively in the present. While operant psychologists use concepts such as learning history, their emphasis is on the current determinants of behavior. The origins of the self-defeating habit pattern are of little intrinsic interest to the therapist; the factors that cue the behavior and currently reinforce it are pre-eminent.

The issue here is the cause of distress, and the behavior therapists do have a point worth considering, that of how an event from the past can have any causal impact upon us now. They argue that past events must be made current in some form to affect us in the present. So if a person is troubled by memories of a traumatic event from the past, it is the determinants of their current memories that must be examined rather than the event in the past. Some Christians might see this present focus a strength, in that it facilitates accountability and action for growth. Others would see it as a negative in that it trivializes a person's sense of history and hence sense of self.

Of all the models, the person of the therapist is least important in behavior modification and therapy (Tan, 1987). Behavior therapists have been forced by empirical research to admit of late that the quality of the therapist-client relationship is a powerful determinant of therapeutic outcome. But this finding has been brought into the model after the fact. To the orthodox behavior therapist, the efficacy of therapy lies in the techniques applied to client problems. The relationship is merely the vehicle by which the intervention was delivered rather than an influential variable in and of itself.

With relationship variables emerging as the strongest empirical predictor of therapy outcome, behavior therapists have evolved, describing the relationship as an important medium through which reinforcement and modeling occur and a source of motivation for the client. But regardless how you cut it, there is an impersonal feel to the description of how the therapist influences the client, even though in empirical studies behavior therapists have been regarded as more empathic and positive than even "humanistic" therapists (O'Leary and Wilson, 1987, pp. 383-388). In behavior therapy, the relationship of client to therapist is never regarded as a curative factor in itself, unlike such approaches as person-centered therapy or psychoanalysis.

Behavior therapy corresponds well to the Christian concept of stewardship. Stewardship would dictate that Christian counselors be committed to documenting the effectiveness of their efforts. It is easy for counselors to get a warm feeling that they are helping people, but if hard research would show that the people who talk to those counselors were, three years after the end of therapy, no better off than before entering therapy, then all the warm feelings in the world would not justify the time and expense invested in the counseling.

Behavior therapists are typically more committed than many other types of practitioners to outcome evaluation, which is actually one of the defining principles that shapes the field. They seek hard documentation for the outcomes they strive for. In spite of this, behavior therapy has not proven more effective than traditional psychotherapy when applied to general populations (Parloff, London and Wolfe, 1986; Smith, Glass and Miller, 1980). Behavior therapists have questioned these findings, however, arguing in part that they have never claimed global effectiveness, but only to have proven superiority in specific areas. For instance, behavior modification has emerged as the most effective model that has been thoroughly tested with children and adolescents (Weisz, Weiss, Alicke and Klotz, 1987). These grand effectiveness studies have also been questioned on methodological grounds (Rachman and Wilson, 1980). Regardless of the status of the effectiveness debate, we would applaud the emphasis on outcome evaluation of psychotherapy in this model. If counseling were not a profession established on the presumption of effectiveness, this might not matter. But it is built upon that presumption, and efforts should be directed at establishing such accountability.

Conclusion

The fundamental vision of humanity embedded in the behavioristic

tradition is one of humans as temporal beings only, motivated by survival and the drive to adapt to a challenging environment successfully.
Our capacities for learning, which so often serve us well, can go awry,
with the result that we learn conditioned responses and operant
behaviors that interfere with our capacity to deal adaptively with the
challenges life throws our way. Despite being determined by our
learning histories, human beings can change through their efforts and
their interactions with those about them. Through the creative application of techniques based on research in the basic psychology of
learning, human problems can be ameliorated.

From a Christian perspective, the behavioristic claims of materialism and determinism are easily rejected. Yet the model serves to remind
us of our createdness and temporality. While we are transcendent
beings, we are not only transcendent. In our temporality and creatureliness, the reality of habit, the power of consequences and of our
environments, and the very "conditionedness" of our existence must
be more thoroughly understood and accepted by Christian counselors.
While persons may not be understood as only loose collections of
action patterns and potentials, we are beings whose behavior has
different degrees of relatedness to the conditions of our hearts. Behavior modification is one of the few approaches to counseling that gives
us effective procedures for dealing with children and others for whom
verbal discussion is an ineffective impetus for change. It also has
produced techniques for many problems which have been documented to be effective. Nevertheless, though behavior therapy may give
us a useful account of our creatureliness, it falls far short in appreciat-
ing our higher human capacities.

For Further Reading

Bufford, R. (1981). *The human reflex: Behavioral psychology in biblical perspective.*
    San Francisco: Harper & Row.
    A sympathetic apology for behaviorism by a "Christian behaviorist."
Erwin, E. (1978). *Behavior therapy: Scientific, philosophical and moral foundations.*
    New York: Cambridge University Press.
    A ground-breaking study of what the true foundations for behavior therapy
    really are.
Woolfolk, R., and Richardson, F. (1984). Behavior therapy and the ideology
    of modernity. *American Psychologist, 39*(7), 777-786.
    A penetrating analysis of how behavior therapy reflects aspects of our
    Western cultural milieu.
Zuriff, G. (1985). *Behaviorism: A conceptual reconstruction.* New York: Columbia

University Press.
A recent philosophically sophisticated attempt to make behaviorism palatable again.

References

Adams, J. (1979). *More than redemption: A theology of Christian counseling.* Phillipsburg, NJ: Presbyterian and Reformed.

Bellack, A., and Hersen, M. (1977). *Behavior modification: An introductory textbook.* New York: Oxford.

Boivin, M. (1985). Behavioral psychology: What does it have to offer the Christian church? *Journal of the American Scientific Affiliation, 37,* 79-85.

Brown, H. (1977). *Perception, theory and commitment: The new philosophy of science.* Chicago: University of Chicago Press.

Browning, D. (1987). *Religious thought and the modern psychologies.* Philadelphia: Fortress.

Bufford, R. (1981). *The human reflex: Behavioral psychology in biblical perspective.* San Francisco: Harper & Row.

Clouse, B. (1985). Moral reasoning and Christian faith. *Journal of Psychology and Theology, 13,* 190-198.

Cosgrove, M. (1982). *B. F. Skinner's behaviorism.* Grand Rapids: Zondervan.

Domjam, M. (1987). Animal learning comes of age. *American Psychologist, 42,* 556-564.

Erwin, E. (1978). *Behavior therapy: Scientific, philosophical and moral foundations.* New York: Cambridge University Press.

Evans, C. (1977). *Preserving the person: A look at the human sciences.* Grand Rapids, MI: Baker.

Evans, C. (1989). *Wisdom and humanness in psychology.* Grand Rapids, MI: Baker.

Herrnstein, R. (1977). The evolution of behaviorism. *American Psychologist, 32,* 593-603.

Hersen, M., and Bellack, A. (1981). *Behavioral assessment: A practical handbook* (2d ed.). Elmsford, NY: Pergamon.

Jones, S. (1984). Assertiveness training in Christian perspective. *Journal of Psychology and Theology, 12,* 91-99.

Jones, S. (1985). Mind-brain relationship. In D. Benner (Ed.), *Baker encyclopedia of psychology* (pp. 712-715). Grand Rapids, MI: Baker.

Kazdin, A. (1982). History of behavior modification. In A. Bellack, M. Hersen, and A. Kazdin (Eds.), *International handbook of behavior modification and behavior therapy.* New York: Plenum.

Leith, J. (Ed.) (1973). *Creeds of the churches: A reader in Christian doctrine, from the Bible to the present.* Atlanta: John Knox Press.

Lewis, C. S. (1980). *The weight of glory and other addresses.* New York: Macmillan. (Ed. by W. Hooper; originally published 1949).

Lovaas, O. (1987). Behavioral treatment and normal educational and intellectual functioning in young autistic children. *Journal of Consulting and Clinical Psychology, 55*(1), 3-9.

Marks, I. (1981). *Cure and care of neuroses.* New York: John Wiley.

Masters, J.; Burish, T.; Hollon, S.; and Rimm, D. (1987). *Behavior therapy: Techniques and empirical findings* (3d ed.). Orlando, FL: Harcourt Brace Jovanovich.

Muller, R., and Vande Kemp, H. (1985). On psychologists' uses of "Calvinism." *American Psychologist, 40,* 466-468.

O'Leary, K., and Wilson, G. (1987). *Behavior therapy: Application and outcome* (2d ed.). Englewood Cliffs, NJ: Prentice-Hall.

Parloff, M.; London, P.; and Wolfe, B. (1986). Individual psychotherapy and behavior change. *Annual Review of Psychology, 37,* 321-349.

Piper, J. (1977, March). How I became a Christian hedonist. *His,* pp. 1, 4-5.

Plantinga, A. (1983). Advice to Christian philosophers. (A paper available from the author, Department of Philosophy, University of Notre Dame, South Bend, IN).

Rachman, S., and Wilson, G. (1980). *The effects of psychological therapy.* Oxford: Pergamon.

Skinner, B. (1971). *Beyond freedom and dignity.* New York: Bantam.

Skinner, B. (1976). *About behaviorism.* New York: Vintage Books.

Smith, M.; Glass, G.; and Miller, T. (1980). *The benefits of psychotherapy.* Baltimore: Johns Hopkins University Press.

Tan, S. Y. (1987). Cognitive-behavioral therapy: A biblical approach and critique. *Journal of Psychology and Theology, 15,* 103-112.

Van Leeuwen, M. (1979a). The behavioristic bandwagon and the body of Christ (Part 1): What is behaviorism? *Journal of the American Scientific Affiliation, 31,* 3-8.

Van Leeuwen, M. (1979b). The behavioristic bandwagon and the body of Christ (Part 2): A critique of ontological behaviorism from a Christian perspective. *Journal of the American Scientific Affiliation, 31,* 88-91.

Van Leeuwen, M. (1979c). The behavioristic bandwagon and the body of Christ (Part 3): A Christian examination of applied behaviorism. *Journal of the American Scientific Affiliation, 31,* 129-138.

Van Leeuwen, M. (1982). *The sorcerer's apprentice: A Christian looks at the changing face of psychology.* Downers Grove, IL: InterVarsity Press.

Watson, J. (1930). *Behaviorism* (3d ed.). Chicago: University of Chicago Press.

Weisz, J.; Weiss, B.; Alicke, M.; and Klotz, M. (1987). Effectiveness of psychotherapy with children and adolescents: A meta-analysis for clinicians. *Journal of Consulting and Clinical Psychology, 55*(4), 542-549.

Wolpe, J. (1978). Cognition and causation in human behavior. *American Psychologist, 33,* 437-446.

Woolfolk, R., and Richardson, F. (1984). Behavior therapy and the ideology of modernity. *American Psychologist, 39*(7), 777-786.

Zuriff, G. (1985). *Behaviorism: A conceptual reconstruction.* New York: Columbia University Press.

7

RATIONAL
EMOTIVE THERAPY

❖

*T*he founder and moving force behind rational emotive therapy (RET), Albert Ellis, traces the origins of RET back to
ancient Greece. Epictetus, a Greek Stoic philosopher (c.
A.D. 50-130) said, "Men are disturbed not by things, but by the views
which they take of them" (quoted from Ellis, 1978). This pithy saying
captures a major theme in Stoic thought and also expresses the core
idea of RET: changing people's beliefs, the view they take of something,
will reduce or eliminate psychological disturbance.

As Ellis himself tells it (Ellis and Bernard, 1985, p. 2), though his
clinical training in graduate school was in the psychoanalytic tradition,
he "became increasingly disillusioned with its theory and its efficacy."
He naturally gravitated to rational and active behavioral methods to
resolve his own personal struggles and gave up psychoanalysis entirely
after several years in order to form his own model of therapy. He

subsequently went on to originate rational therapy (later RET) based on his personal experience and his wide reading in philosophy. He has built his professional life around his RET model, publishing an amazing number of articles and books on the topic. The books and articles by Ellis are, frankly, repetitive and self-promoting. One only needs to read a few of his works to gain a generally accurate understanding of his approach.

Descriptive Survey

Philosophical Assumptions

The philosophical presuppositions of RET are quite explicit, since the approach is said to be drawn from philosophical sources. RET does not, according to Ellis and Bernard (1985, p. 5), "pretend to be entirely objective and value free." This is a bit unusual as psychotherapy systems go, so the assumptions behind RET merit close examination.

First, "Ellis is an unabashed hedonist, humanist and atheist" (Walen, DiGiuseppe and Wessler, 1980, p. 12). Atheism is Ellis's personal position on the existence of God, and his atheistic beliefs dramatically shape some of the other positions he takes. For instance, Ellis (1978, p. 42) says, "Our behaving during our lifetime *as if* we were going to be immortal doesn't make very good sense when the overwhelming probability is that we will not." Ellis does allow for the possibility that persons with some religious faith in God can be emotionally healthy as long as they don't go overboard with their religion. RET hypothesizes that "devout belief . . . tends to foster human dependency and increase emotional disturbance" (Ellis and Bernard, 1985, p. 22), and hence, too much religion is necessarily bad. Atheism is not, however, an essential premise of the RET approach.

Ellis explicitly assumes that all human beings are "basically hedonistic" (1978, p. 39)—that is, we are happiness-seeking beings who try to maximize the fulfillment of our chosen goals. This point permeates RET. Though people are presumed to be hedonistic, Ellis does not claim that most people are impulsively driven to gratify their short-term desires. Rather, people have the capacity to make choices to delay gratification of an immediate desire in order to maximize opportunities to receive the greatest amount of happiness in the long-term.

Some casually dismiss hedonism as not fitting the real behavior of persons who, for instance, delay gratification to attend college and then graduate school or seminary. Ellis, however, would say that such behavior is still hedonistic in the sense of maximizing reward in a longer span of time; in other words, it is "long-term" hedonism. Even earthly asceticism can be considered an example of long-term hedonism since such persons deny themselves short-term pleasure for the purpose of maximizing long-term (or heavenly) rewards.

Given the flexibility of Ellis's description of hedonism, it might actually make more sense to describe his position on basic human motivation as egoism rather than hedonism. The term *hedonism* usually carries with it the implication of short-term pleasure-seeking. *Egoism* is a term that more precisely refers to persons acting out of their own personal self-interest, without the more narrow assumption that this implies exclusive interest in shorter-term pleasures. We will, however, continue to use Ellis's preferred term of *long-range hedonism* here.

"In humanism, the reasoning individual is the source of wisdom, not the almighty God. . . . God is not needed to explain the creation of things (that is the job of science), nor is He needed to create an ethical code (for that can be done by clear thinking)" (Walen et al., 1980, p. 11). According to Ellis himself, "People had better define their own freedom, cultivate a good measure of individuality, live in dialogue with others . . . and learn to accept their own human limitations and the fact that they will eventually die" (Ellis, 1978, p. 47). Clearly, in RET people are the only real measure of people; God is irrelevant to the human outlook. As a part of his humanistic outlook, Ellis asserts that we have the freedom to pursue rational or irrational ways of thinking. Though people seem to have innate tendencies to behave and think irrationally, we have the freedom to choose rationality.

Ellis (1978) has denied that RET authoritatively or rigidly prescribes a particular set of values for every client. Nevertheless, he enthusiastically concludes from his long-range hedonistic assumptions that people "had usually better strive to acquire and internalize the following values, many of which can be thought of as rational attitudes" (Ellis and Bernard, 1985, p. 7): self-interest, social interest, self-direction, high frustration tolerance, flexibility, acceptance of uncertainty, commitment to creative pursuits, scientific thinking, self-acceptance, risk-taking, long-range hedonism, non-utopianism and responsibility for our own emotional disturbance. By a change of terminology from *values* to *rational attitudes,* Ellis in many of his writings slips into a value-prescription mode, contradicting his stated reluctance to prescribe values.

As accurately described by Sharkey (1981), Ellis views the self as merely a collection of empirical characteristics, and in this way he is very much like the traditional behaviorists. In other words, there really isn't a self (in the sense of a responsible agent) that is at the core of a person. Rather, our feeling of selfhood is what we sense from the coincidental co-occurrence of our behavior, traits, performances, thoughts, memories and so forth. Thus Ellis often writes that while we might judge or evaluate a specific performance, action or trait, we can never judge or evaluate our *selves*, any more than one could judge the quality of the whole group of objects (the barrel of apples) by the quality of one element (the rotten apple). Why? Because those elements were gathered together by pure chance. Thus Ellis's ultimate answer to the self-esteem question is not to evaluate our selves at all. But recognizing the pernicious and irrational human tendency to evaluate their whole selves globally ("I'm a sinner; look at what I did"), Ellis concedes that at times it may be more efficient to globally and arbitrarily evaluate our whole selves, declare ourselves acceptable and be done with it. He would rather that we not grade ourselves at all, but if we are going to grade ourselves anyway, then let everyone assign themselves A+'s and be happy.

Model of Personality

RET does not have a comprehensive theory of personality per se, but focuses more on a view of emotional disturbance and health. The core assertion of RET is that a person's *thoughts* are central to understanding that person. Ellis formulates this relationship in an *A-B-C* format in all of his writings. People often come for therapy because of a *consequence* (C), an emotional or behavioral consequence which is disturbing them (e.g., "I'm horribly depressed"). It is common for people to attribute their emotional or behavioral consequence to *activating experiences or events* (A), as if there were some necessary and invariant causal relationship between A and C (e.g., "I keep having troubling thoughts about immoral behavior; that's why I'm depressed"). The A can be an external event (e.g., death of a family member, a financial setback, a fight with a girlfriend) or it can be a person's own thought or behavior. But according to Ellis (and Epictetus before him), people are not disturbed by events themselves, but by the *beliefs* (B) they hold about those events. So in order for immoral thoughts to result in depression, Ellis would postulate that an intermediate belief must be brought into play. For example, "I *shouldn't* have such thoughts, and I'm a *horrible, awful* human being who deserves to go to *hell* for having such thoughts."

The A-B-Cs of RET are the core of its approach to personality. As mentioned earlier, a full-fledged theory of personality usually attempts to predict and explain behavior in all or most areas of life. Ellis's A-B-C theory could be pressed to do so, but this would most likely result in weak, ambiguous explanations or predictions such as "her thinking and beliefs led her to act that way." Such loose explanations are largely useless in the scientific study of personality, and so RET has spawned no serious scientific hypotheses or research regarding the broader aspects of human personality. But for clinical purposes, where the focus is less on predicting or explaining behavior generally and more on the focal explanation and modification of distress, the simplicity of RET is regarded by its proponents as a virtue, in that that simplicity increases the utility of the theory.

Model of Abnormality

The RET theory of pathology is quite simple. Irrational beliefs result in undesirable emotional consequences, while rational beliefs result in appropriate emotional consequences. What is an irrational belief and how is it different from a rational belief? In large part, the two are to be differentiated by their quite different emotional consequences. (Defining the rationality of a belief by its effect is a critical point in evaluating the theory, so further discussion of this will be postponed until later.)

From time to time, Ellis has developed specific lists of commonly occurring irrational beliefs, but such lists have tended to change over time. Ellis has yet to take a stand on one finished list of major irrational beliefs. Table 1 contains his eleven major irrational beliefs as formulated in an earlier work (Ellis, 1962). More recently, Ellis and Bernard (1985, pp. 10-11) stated there were three main irrational beliefs which people hold:

a. I must do well and win approval, or else I rate as a rotten person.

b. Others must treat me considerately and kindly in precisely the way I want them to treat me; if they don't, society and the universe should severely blame, damn, and punish them for their inconsiderateness.

c. Conditions under which I live must be arranged so that I get practically all I want comfortably, quickly and easily, and get virtually nothing that I don't want.

Eleven Common Irrational Beliefs

IRRATIONAL IDEA NO. 1:
The idea that it is a dire necessity for an adult human being to be loved or approved by virtually every significant person in his community.

IRRATIONAL IDEA NO. 2:
The idea that one should be thoroughly competent, adequate and achieving in all possible respects if one is to consider oneself worthwhile.

IRRATIONAL IDEA NO. 3:
The idea that certain people are bad, wicked or villainous and that they should be severely blamed and punished for their villainy.

IRRATIONAL IDEA NO. 4:
The idea that it is awful and catastrophic when things are not the way one would very much like them to be.

IRRATIONAL IDEA NO. 5:
The idea that human unhappiness is externally caused and that people have little or no ability to control their sorrows and disturbances.

IRRATIONAL IDEA NO. 6:
The idea that if something is or may be dangerous or fearsome one should be terribly concerned about it and should keep dwelling on the possibility of its occurring.

IRRATIONAL IDEA NO. 7:
The idea that it is easier to avoid than to face certain life difficulties and self-responsibilities.

IRRATIONAL IDEA NO. 8:
The idea that one should be dependent on others and needs someone stronger than oneself on whom to rely.

IRRATIONAL IDEA NO. 9:
The idea that one's past history is an all-important determiner of one's present behavior and that because something once strongly affected one's life, it should definitely have a similar effect.

IRRATIONAL IDEA NO. 10:
The idea that one should become quite upset over other people's problems and disturbances.

IRRATIONAL IDEA NO. 11:
The idea that there is invariably a right, precise and perfect solution to human problems and that it is catastrophic if this perfect solution is not found.

Figure 7.1 *From Ellis, A.,* Reason and emotion in psychotherapy. *New York: Lyle Stuart, 1962.*

Model of Psychotherapy

Therapy begins with the detection of irrational beliefs by the therapist and the client. If the theory of personality proposes an A-B-C sequence, we might not be surprised that the core of therapy is a D; that is, *disputation* of irrational beliefs. There are many possible methods available for disputing irrational beliefs. Ellis personally uses a great deal of Socratic questioning and challenging of clients to produce scientific evidence for their irrational beliefs (with the obvious supposition that they will come up empty-handed from such a search) or to examine the practical emotional impact of those beliefs ("Why would you choose to believe something that causes you pain?"). Some therapists who practice RET use a lot of didactic teaching about the theory of RET with their clients. All RET practitioners try to enable their clients to engage in *self*-disputation of their own irrational beliefs, since therapy will presumably be maximally effective when clients are enabled to move themselves toward health and wholeness. In addition to activities focusing on changes in belief, the therapist also commonly uses many of the active change strategies of the behavior and cognitive-behavior therapists, as well as some techniques designed to be emotionally evocative such as imagery exercises and role-playing.

In Ellis and Harper (1975), the authors distinguished between two forms of RET. *Inelegant* RET is focused on changing the particular irrational beliefs that are causing the particular undesirable consequences that brought the client to therapy. *Elegant* RET, on the other hand, has the much grander goal of not only curing the person's focal disturbance but also, for the sake of the prevention of future disturbance, "converting" the person to embrace a rational life philosophy; that is, RET as a religion and way of life.

Christian Critique

We should note that RET has replaced transactional analysis as the secular therapy model most adapted for Christian consumption. Whether in the form of Crabb's biblical counseling (in its early form, 1975, 1977), Backus's misbelief therapy (Backus and Chapian, 1980; Backus, 1985), Thurman's *Lies We Believe* (1989), or others (e.g., Schmidt, 1983), RET ideas have been widely adapted for Christian consumption.

It seems unlikely that Christians will dispute the importance of thought and belief in emotional life, or the viability of direct change of these aspects of life to produce helpful change. In a remarkably clear parallel to Epictetus, Martin Luther has said, "For the Holy Spirit knows that a thing has only such meaning and value for a man as he assigns to it in his thoughts" (cited in Clebsch and Jaekle, 1975, p. 213). Nevertheless, there are some real concerns to grapple with in RET, as we will develop below.

Philosophical Assumptions

The major presuppositions of RET about humanism and hedonism are incompatible with Christian assumptions. Human beings are not the final authority in the universe, nor are they capable of total autonomy and self-perfection. Although human beings are certainly drawn toward pleasure and self-gratification, especially in our unregenerate condition, we are motivated by more than just the narrow gratification of our own desires. (The problems of hedonism as a motivational base are more thoroughly dealt with in chapters six and eight.)

Regarding valuing and values, we first note, as pointed out by Hauck (1985), that RET and Christianity share a perspective on human experience that says that what humans value is vital to their welfare and psychological functioning. RET contends to be a philosophically, and to some extent theologically, sensitive approach to psychotherapy that does not pretend to be value neutral. For the Christian reading in the field of psychotherapy, it is a breath of fresh air to encounter a major theoretician who forthrightly declares his presuppositions and values. According to Hauck (1985, p. 238), "this emphasis on the profound beliefs and values held by clients makes it a comfortable medium for the pastoral counselor and religious client." But while RET is an avowedly and openly philosophical and value-laden system, are its values and goals compatible with Christian values and goals?

Ellis (1980) once wrote a response to Bergin, a Mormon and thus a theist, who espoused theistic values as a foundation for an approach to psychotherapy. Bergin (1980) asserted that "values are an inevitable and pervasive part of psychotherapy" (p. 97), and Ellis agreed with this. Ellis took issue with Bergin's description of humanistic values, and proposed his own list of atheistic values. The values that Ellis proposed contrasted with theistic values in asserting that there is no one supreme being in the universe, that personal identity is temporal and ephemeral, that self-acceptance does not depend on the existence of a deity, that self-satisfaction is central to personal growth, that the structure of family life and sexual morality is a personal choice, that personal responsibility can exist without guilt, and that we determine our own meanings in life based on our personal desires and reason. Ellis himself declared that there are many points of contrast between his "clinical-humanistic-atheistic" values and those of the theist. The Christian reader will immediately see many points at which Ellis must be judged wrong by Christian standards. Clearly, Hauck is wrong that value explicitness alone makes this approach suitable for pastoral counseling!

Further, we can look at the respective goals of RET and Christianity. Ellis is clear about the goals of RET, which are to "help people think more rationally; . . . to feel more appropriately; and to act more functionally . . . in order to achieve their goals of living longer and more happily " (Ellis and Bernard, 1985, p. 5). Hauck declares that "the welfare of each person, indeed, the good of society, are the goals of both religion and RET" (1985, p. 239). Lawrence and Huber (1982, p. 211), after summarizing the goals of RET in much the fashion which we have, declared "similar goals are found in the Bible."

Are the goals of Christianity equivalent to those of Ellis, as Hauck, Lawrence and Huber claim? The Westminster Confession of Faith, in answering the question "What is the chief end of man?" says, "Man's chief end is to glorify God and enjoy him forever." Glorifying God is not synonymous with human happiness; a person whose human happiness is fulfilled in sexual promiscuity is hardly contributing to God's glory. Indeed, human sacrifice in the form of costly obedience (Bonhoeffer, 1959) is what God most desires from us ("Does the LORD delight in burnt offerings and sacrifices as much as in obeying the voice of the LORD?" 1 Sam 15:22). Kreeft (1986) has developed this idea further, arguing that what God desires in his people is goodness, which is not synonymous with maximized longevity or happiness. While goodness and happiness are surely not opposites nor incompatible, they are not equivalent. The vision of God's goal for humanity that permeates the Scriptures is that of human beings bringing glory to the Father through their obedient manifestation of Christ's presence in their lives through word and deed (see also Tan, 1987; and Craigie and Tan, 1989a).

Model of Personality

We have already criticized RET as not having a true, fully developed theory of personality. We will further consider two principal aspects of this incomplete approach to personality; its views of rationality and of emotion.

Christianity is a religion that emphasizes belief. What we believe matters profoundly. People are urged to change their beliefs ("Come now, let us reason together," Is 1:18), to learn Scripture (2 Tim 3:15), to think on certain things (Phil 4:8), to "have the mind of Christ" (1 Cor 2:16) and to attend to sound doctrine (1 Tim 4:1-6). One of the most often-cited verses by Christians favorable to RET is Proverbs 23:7, "as he thinketh in his heart, so is he" (KJV).

Rationality is so prized by Christians that it is described by some theologians as one of the core human characteristics that comprise the image of God in humanity (e.g., Berkhof, 1939). On this point, as we have pointed out in other chapters, Christians often detect real deficiencies in other approaches to psychotherapy that de-emphasize rationality or explain it in such a way as to leave rationality an empty shell (e.g., gestalt, psychoanalysis). RET does not commit this error, placing human rationality in an appropriately prominent place among human capabilities. RET assumes that people can ascertain truth.

This leads to the related point that this emphasis on rationality in therapy is possible precisely because human belief is conceived of as directly changeable by argumentation, evidence, logic and human determination. In a sense, RET looks at human beliefs as mental habits that can be influenced in the same way behavioral habits can be changed. This is an optimistic view of the human mind, and Christians can generally concur with this portrait. For instance, Paul in Romans 12:2 and Ephesians 4:23 calls for a renewing of the mind which seems to be a process whereby we actively participate in a radical change of understanding that results in a revolution of our spiritual lives. Such a call would be impossible without a presumption of rationality similar to RET's.

Though this valuing of human rationality is a virtue of RET, we must note that it is the extremely high prizing and estimation of rationality that is the foundation for the arrogant humanistic atheism of Ellis, who seems to ask, "Why do we need God when we have our brains?" Human reason is best understood not as the premier human characteristic of the image of God in us, but as one of quite an array of such ways in which we "image" the Lord (see chapter two). Further, it is vital to note again that human reason is as prone to the influence of sin as any other aspect of our being. For example, the fruits of the flesh in Galatians 5:19-20 contain as many sins of the mind as that of any other category. Ellis would agree that our rational capacities can cause us problems, but views rationality as our means of "salvation." Christians, however, would not trust rationality to such an extent because it is as contaminated by sin as the rest of us.

Further, we must inquire carefully about the RET understanding of the nature of belief as cognitive habit. If beliefs are cognitive habits, then simple diligence and skill will result in a change of belief. This could undergird a belief that human beings are ultimately perfectible by human effort alone. But while there are portions of Scripture that seem to support such a view (as cited earlier), there are several very significant passages that do not. In Romans 1:18-32, Paul caustically describes the sorry plight of those to whom God has revealed himself (v. 20), who respond to this revelation by not humbling themselves before the truth but rather refusing to honor God (v. 21). Proclaiming themselves wise (v. 22), they exchange the truth of God for a lie (v. 25), and refuse to even acknowledge God's existence (v. 28). Note that this response on the part of people whom Paul calls "fools" (and Ellis must fall in this category) is *not out of mere ignorance* (a bad mental habit); it is rather a culpable and deliberate rejection of God in the face of the truth. This type of response cannot be explained by a view of belief as mere mental habit.

Christian supporters of RET often cite Mark 7:20-23: "What comes out of a man is what makes him 'unclean.' For from within, out of men's hearts, come evil thoughts, sexual immorality, theft [many other sins are listed]. All these evils come from inside and make a man 'unclean.' " But this verse cannot be made to fit the RET formula. This verse has been interpreted (e.g., Sterner, 1977) as saying that it is the evil thoughts that lead to the sinful behaviors, but that is not what Christ said. Rather, he stated that evil thoughts and the specific sins of commission both proceed out of the heart; thus, the heart is surely not synonymous with a thought pattern, because the heart *precedes* the thought pattern. Thus a Christianized RET cannot simply look on the heart as a belief system; the heart must be more. This casts doubt on the most fundamental aspects of the RET understanding of rationality.

Let us turn to Ellis's view of emotion. Ellis contends that beliefs lead to or cause emotions. Roberts (1982, 1988) has developed a more formal and sophisticated view of emotion, which was formulated specifically to be compatible with a Christian understanding of persons and their emotions. His view has some broad compatibility with an RET view of emotions. In brief, Roberts argues that all emotions are "founded upon concerns" (1982, p. 14); that is, emotions are predicated on the individual caring about or having some significant interest in something. We do not have emotions in areas where we have no concerns (for instance, one may have no emotional response at all to hearing professional hockey scores on the radio if hockey was not an object of concern). But a concern is not an emotion; rather, "An emotion is a *construal* of one's circumstances in a manner relevant to some such concern" (1982, p. 15). In other words, an emotion is an interpretation about a concern or object of value in light of one's circumstances. For example, the emotion of jealousy is founded in one's passionate love for another and that emotion occurs with the interpretation (accurate or not) that one's relationship with the loved one is threatened.

It should be noted that among Roberts's concerns in formulating his theory of emotion was the fact that certain distinctively Christian emotions are described in the Scriptures and Christians are *commanded* to exhibit or develop certain emotions (e.g., hope, gratitude, kindness). If emotions are reflexive involuntary phenomena, then the teachings of Scripture are erroneous or misleading. "The fact that emotions are construals goes a long way toward explaining how we have control over them. . . . To succeed in bringing myself into a certain emotional state is to succeed in coming to see my situation in certain terms" (1982, pp. 21-22)—specifically to come to see the situation in Christian terms or from God's point of view. When we come to think and believe deeply in a Christian way, we will come to feel Christian emotions. Note that for Roberts, this is not just a matter of merely changing cognitions (as it is for Ellis), as construals are more than beliefs and emotions are founded upon concerns. So to change an emotion, I may have to change my concerns. We can conclude positively that Ellis has a view of emotion that attributes some appropriate responsibility for what we experience emotionally and has some good beginning ideas about how we can change at least some emotions. The view of Roberts, though, is more finely nuanced than that of Ellis.

On the negative side, the complexity of what we call the human *heart,* as we have just discussed, raises questions about a monolithic view of emotions flowing from or being constituted of beliefs or construals. Eschenroeder (1982), Zajonc (1980) and others have championed the cause of what we might call a "limited primacy of affect"; that is, they espouse the view that while cognition might often shape and determine emotional experience, it is credible to suggest that the reverse is often the case; that as client-centered and dynamic models of personality propose, affect can come before and shape cognition. These highly complex matters cannot be resolved here. We raise the debate to suggest that Ellis and other cognitively oriented theorists have not totally carried the day in terms of understanding the nature of human emotions.

Model of Health

Reflected in the values of RET (as in other psychotherapy systems) is a particular vision of what the optimally functioning or truly healthy human being looks like. Ellis's picture of ideal humanity is transparently reflected in the list of valued characteristics we described earlier. It is impossible in this limited space to critique every aspect of Ellis's vision, but let us briefly examine two aspects.

First, Hauck, a staunch devotee of Ellis and RET, says regarding human destiny, "We were meant to live with dignity and pride in our awesome talents. To espouse a program [i.e., a religious doctrine] that robs human giants of their stature is foolish" (1985, p. 251). From our Christian perspective, Hauck has a point, in that human beings are created in God's image (Gen 1:27) and are amazing creatures (Ps 8). But the essence of sin is the aspiration to be gods ourselves, and inordinate pride is perhaps the quickest route to that outcome. We are not giants; rather, we are what we are—human beings, created in God's image and fallen into sin and rebellion against our Creator, created of the dust (and thus part of creation) and yet made into living souls (Gen 2:7). We are the pinnacle of earthly creation, but we are not the pinnacle of existence; that rank belongs to God alone.

As a second example of a related conception of ideal humanity we can look at the RET virtue of *equanimity*. Roberts (1987) carefully analyzes a number of themes in RET and suggests that a fundamental characteristic Ellis is trying to develop in his clients is equanimity (a term which Ellis himself never uses), which Roberts describes as being "emotionally flexible and adaptable, relatively content regardless of what happens" (1987, p. 196). This is interesting in light of Ellis's tying of RET to ancient Stoic philosophy. It is commonly argued that Stoicism was a "defeatist" philosophy of life. The Greeks, experiencing a cultural decline and repeated brutal invasions and military defeats, developed a philosophy that sought to control the inner world of the mind and so be unaffected by the outer world, which was unpredictable and out of control. The virtue Ellis espouses is Stoic in nature.

Roberts suggests that there is a Christian virtue corresponding to Ellis's principal virtue, which might also be called *equanimity*—a composite of gratitude in all circumstances (1 Thess 5:18), contentment (Phil 4:11-12), perseverance (2 Cor 4:8-9, 16-18) and courage (2 Cor

5:6). What Roberts goes on to show, though, is that despite the superficial compatibility of the two virtues, they are really constituted in quite different ways because they come out of radically different mindsets. The RET virtue of equanimity carries with it the belief that when we are the recipient of disappointment or suffering that "nothing is ultimately appalling . . . nothing is of ultimate value" (Roberts, 1987, p. 197) and therefore there is nothing to be upset about ever. Only your own happiness is of high value. The Christian response of equanimity to such occurrences, however, is based on having our priorities in place and dealing with earthly disappointments "by getting them into a perspective where, by comparison with what is truly momentous, they are seen as relatively unmomentous" (p. 197). For Ellis, nothing is momentous, and so he can be described as having a trivial view of pain and suffering. For the mature Christian, the things pertaining to the kingdom of God are momentous, while other events can be highly significant but not parallel to the centrality of eternity (Rom 8:18: "I consider that our present sufferings are not worth comparing with the glory that will be revealed in us"). The source and character of equanimity is thus quite different in the two systems. And we must also remember that equanimity is not the only virtue in the Christian scheme.

By examining the notion of "self-acceptance" in RET, we will grapple with the RET view of the *self*. The essence of Ellis's position on self-acceptance is that we must not evaluate ourselves, either positively or negatively, based on either the molecular or general nature of our behaviors, performances and so forth. Sharkey (1981, p. 152) has argued that the essence of a "liberal Christian" view of God is that God's prime activity in human life is the absolute and unconditional acceptance of a fallible self. Even conservative Christians, who would add that God's acceptance of us occurs only through the atoning death of Christ, would agree that our acceptance by God is not contingent on any particular merit in our actions or character, but is absolute because it is based on Christ and not upon us at all. So with Ellis, all Christians would agree that a legalistic mindset that bases our value and acceptance on meeting the standards of God's law or our own idiosyncratic standards is antithetical to Christian faith.

As we noted earlier, the RET conception of the self is basically an atomistic one, following the long tradition of Hume and other philosophers. While this view does have some merits, it basically robs people person of seeing themselves as a self-as-agent, a substantial self, a view that we as human beings are responsible moral agents with a continuous identity through life.

Ellis uses this atomistic view of the self consistently in his writings as the answer to self-acceptance issues. He urges us never to let any particular aspect of our behavior or character become the standard by which the acceptance of the whole person is judged, because there is no whole person, no substantive self, to be judged. We should evaluate each part of our persons (the "atoms" of our being) in isolation from the whole. Lazarus (1977) expressed this well as the gap between *me* as a whole cluster of little *is* (with each *i* standing for a different aspect of the person's behavior) versus *me* as one capital *I*. Lazarus and Ellis prefer to look at a person as a cluster of *is*.

Grieger and Boyd (1980, pp. 255-256) exhibit the practical import of this approach with an extended transcript of a counseling session with a woman struggling with guilt over an abortion she had. The therapist, rather than dealing with her guilt and remorse through forgiveness or other means, deals with the abortion as an isolated behavior with no *serious implications* for evaluating the woman as a whole being. "Well, let's say you did make a mistake, how does that make you a rotten person?" asks the therapist. After some discussion, the therapist clearly states the conclusion toward which he is drawing the client, saying the abortion may have been "a big mistake, but it's still only a mistake, . . . one action of the thousands you commit in your life." The implication is clear; the isolated action of the abortion has no implications for judgment of the person as a whole.

Clearly, as we argued in the last chapter, this view has the advantage of prohibiting clients from spuriously or tragically passing judgment on their selves based on some quite inconsequential or superficial aspect of their behavior ("I failed my first history test! I'm a total miserable wretch of a human being"). But this view carries with it quite a disadvantage from a Christian perspective. It contradicts and undermines a Christian understanding of sin, depravity, forgiveness and redemption. Hauck (1985, p. 242) demonstrates this clearly by saying that "there are no bad people in the world, only bad behavior and . . . people who commit sins . . . should not be treated harshly or regarded as evil. . . . If rating of behavior and rating of people are separated, then it is wrong to judge people by their actions and total forgiveness is logically allowed; one need never damn others or oneself, and it is wrong to feel guilt at any time over any act." He actually presents this as the Christian view consistent with RET.

Hauck is wrong, however, to state that this is the Christian view. We are each persons who sin (rebel against and hence disobey God's moral law), and the fact that we sin is both caused by our being sinners and at the same time proof of our sinful natures. This is why one who violates one aspect of the Law is guilty of the whole Law; any single violation testifies to our whole natures being corrupted or polluted by sinfulness (this is the meaning of depravity). Because we are sinners as whole persons, Christ had to die for us as sinners rather than merely overlook the bad behavior of otherwise acceptable fallible human beings. Hauck calls for pastors and other Christians to revise their religious beliefs on these matters to accommodate the truths of RET; we are afraid that it is Hauck, Ellis and other secular RET therapists that need to have their view modified on these matters.

Model of Abnormality

The heart of Ellis's explanation for the occurrence of psychological problems is the concept of *irrational beliefs*. Some have actually seen Ellis's understanding of the specific irrational beliefs that trouble humanity as being compatible with a Christian perspective. Ellis's notion of the human error of absolutizing and demanding might be viewed by the Christian as the essence of a sinful, prideful, self-aggrandizing way of thinking (Sterner, 1977). Ellis even declared that a person who is disturbed by absolutizing can be characterized as a "whiney little tin god" (cited in Wessler, 1984). Christians agree that self-deification goes hand-in-hand with demanding and insisting on life fitting our preferences rather than the will of God. Craigie and Tan (1989b), for example, have sensitively explored the dysfunctional implications of our cultural mindset of "entitlement," the idea that we are "owed" or deserve things in this life. They argue that such a mindset is antithetical to biblical faith.

Lawrence and Huber (1982) went further, declaring that Ellis's (1962) eleven irrational beliefs (see Table 1) were each compatible with biblical revelation and that the Christian therapist could aid the process of using RET as a pastoral counseling approach by using scriptural references as *disputational aids* with the Christian client.[1]

---

[1]Lawrence and Huber provided the following scriptural references which they recommended for use in refuting the first five of Ellis's Bs (Table 1). We will neither quote the Bs nor the verses, but we urge you to compare the Bible passages along with other themes in Scripture with the specific Bs as listed in the table: (B1) Ps 118:6, 8; (B2) Is 45:24; 64:6; (B3) Rom 13:9; Mt 7:1; (B4) Phil 4:11; Jn 16:33; (B5) Prov 23:7; Gen 1:28

They suggest that "when the Bible is included in the disputation procedure with these individuals, the approach becomes far more therapeutically effective than when based on secular reasoning alone" (Lawrence and Huber, 1982, p. 211).While there are some substantial and many superficial compatibilities between RET judgments of irrational belief and Christian teaching, there are also many areas of contradiction.

At the level of specific belief, we might first note that many of Ellis's irrational beliefs are easily seen as irrational from a Christian perspective as well. But some of them are quite problematic. For example, irrational belief eight in Table 1 specifically declares that dependency on another is irrational. Yet isn't it precisely this human characteristic of dependency that is the foundation upon which a living faith in God is built? Human beings seem to need something or someone beyond themselves. We might judge the motive for listing this belief as irrational to be the secular assertion of human autonomy and rejection of authority. The Christian faith, on the other hand, seems to suggest that human beings are needy people designed to live in utter dependence on God and in a healthy interdependence on one another, and that a healthy dependence on a spiritual authority (pastor, elder, priest) may be an essential part of spiritual maturation.

From a broader perspective, we would note that the RET rejection of absolutistic thinking is itself absolute. According to Ellis, there are no absolutes precisely because there is no supreme authority to proclaim such universals (Wessler, 1984). Ellis rejects the use of any "should" or "must," declaring any such use to be "musturbating." We can agree that we often hide our choices of what we choose to do behind "shoulds," and thus hide from taking responsibility for our choices. There are also many Christians who are enslaved to shoulds that do not come from God but rather from social convention or social pressure. These supposed absolutes come from the warped and irrational thinking of themselves and others. But RET is wrong in denying that shoulds exist and that we have an obligation to obey them. Sterner is absolutely right in saying that "a rational Christian therapy, therefore, would encourage the client to accept the shoulds of God, while discarding the shoulds of man" (1977, p. 7). To deny any legitimate shoulds would be to undermine the importance of God's will in our daily lives.

Perhaps the most important question in thinking through the issue of RET's understanding of psychopathology is that of the standards by which it judges rationality and irrationality are judged by RET. A dis-concerting aspect of critiquing RET is Ellis's propensity for saying different (often conflicting) things in the same or different articles. Ellis (1978, p. 40) states clearly that "RET posits no absolutistic or invariant criteria of rationality. . . . The term *rational,* as used in RET, refers to peoples' (1) setting up or choosing for themselves basic values, purposes, goals, or ideals and then (2) using efficient, flexible, scientific, logico-empirical ways of attempting to achieve such values and goals." Yet clause two specifies a particular style of goal attainment (e.g., efficient, etc.) that is characteristic of RET rationality, so the open definition of *rationality* which Ellis proclaims must be in clause one, which describes openness and acceptance in RET to any values or goals that the client might embrace. So RET is open to different definitions of rationality because it is open to different value commitments. But paradoxically, Ellis (1978, p. 55) ends his article with a list of *particular* values and goals that people, if they want to obtain happiness and minimize emotional disturbance, "need to seek." In other words, after proclaiming value openness, he lists values that clients need to be taught. So much for the broad acceptance of any values by the RET therapist!

Further, Ellis and Bernard (1985, pp. 5-6) contradict Ellis (1978) by specifically arguing that "rational thoughts . . . are defined in RET as those thoughts that help people to live longer and happier, particularly by . . . choosing for themselves certain . . . happiness-producing values, purposes, goals" and then using the methods as described in clause two above to achieve these goals.

Clearly, Ellis has a specific idea (or set of ideas) about what is rational and what is not. Eschenroeder (1982) correctly identifies Ellis as postulating two primary criteria of rationality, which Eschenroeder called the *truth criterion* (called the empirical or scientific standard by Evans, 1988a) and the *pragmatic criterion* (called the evolutionary standard by Evans, 1988a); we shall here use the terms *empirical standard* and *pragmatic standard.* Following Eschenroeder and Evans, the empirical standard suggests that a belief is irrational if it is not based on clear facts or if it contradicts clear facts. Ellis often urges people to adopt scientific thinking or the scientific method, and he challenges what he judges to be the client's Bs (beliefs) by asking them to produce evidence in support of them.

The pragmatic standard is perhaps Ellis's most used standard. It is that a belief is irrational if it does not assist the individual in obtaining maximal longevity and happiness. Evans calls this the evolutionary standard because in some of his writings, Ellis talks of survival rather than longevity, thus appealing to a Darwinian evolutionary concept of survival value. The pragmatic standard says that rationality is not really judged by the truth content of the assertion, but rather by the pragmatic or functional impact of that belief. If a belief helps you, it is true.

Eschenroeder points out that the pragmatic standard, as Ellis formulates it, involves a bit of circular reasoning. Judging by the effect of the belief, a belief is irrational if it produces an irrational or inappropriate effect. But how does one recognize an inappropriate effect except by the irrationality of the belief that produced it? If one has a catastrophic depressive reaction to a belief that "My wife has been unfaithful to me, and that is awful," an RET therapist cannot judge that reaction as excessive except by having an a priori notion of exactly how upset one can legitimately be in such circumstances. Ellis and Bernard (1985, p. 6) have attempted to overcome this problem by concretely defining an inappropriate emotional response as one that impedes rather than helps persons overcome the obstacle that is causing their distress. While he saw the pragmatic standard as having problems, Eschenroeder (1982) accepted the empirical standard.

Evans (1988a) pointed out that neither the pragmatic standard nor the empirical standard is self-evident and that they actually can conflict with one another. The pragmatic standard is troublesome because *happiness* is hard to define. What is good for happiness and survival separately may not always be the same, and given our limited capacity for foresight we may not always know what beliefs are helpful for either happiness or longevity. For example, Ellis might well dismiss a Christian's feeling that he has disappointed God by saying that that reaction is interfering with enjoying life now. But on what basis is pleasing God as a source of happiness being dismissed?

The empirical standard, on the other hand, is troublesome for the same reason that logical positivism (chapter six) was troublesome; that is, it is internally contradictory or what philosophers call self-stultifying. Logical positivism said that for an assertion to be meaningful, it must be empirically verifiable. Unfortunately, the definition of logical positivism itself was not empirically verifiable and thus by its own standard was meaningless. The assertion that a belief is irrational if it is not based on facts or contradicts facts is not itself a matter of fact and therefore is irrational.

Even if we accept both of Ellis's standards, it is conceivable that a belief based on facts (empirical standard) will not be particularly helpful for survival and vice versa. For instance, believing in God may be seen as necessary for happiness for some but is not perfectly amenable to empirical proof; on the other hand, a person living in Germany in 1939 may have been empirically convinced that the Jews were not children of Satan and yet their survival would have been threatened if that belief were publicized. Ellis (1988), in response to Evans, suggested that Evans has interpreted him as being too absolutistic and suggested that happiness isn't all that hard to understand and that the two standards usually cooperate nicely. Evans (1988b) closed the interchange by noting that looking across cultures and history (and we would add religious faiths), one often finds stark differences in how people define *happiness.*

We would also note that there is no one clear standard of rationality from a Christian perspective, though Christian faith does involve a reliance on the Scriptures as an infallible source of truth. Unfortunately, the infallible Scriptures must always be interpreted by fallible human beings living and working in fallible societal and community contexts. The interested reader might want to consult Holmes's (1977) helpful book *All Truth Is God's Truth* to reflect further on standards of rationality (see also Echeverria, 1986).

Model of Psychotherapy

The highly rational and didactic nature of RET as a counseling method fits with the instincts of many conservative Christian believers who tend to be comfortable with rational discourse about belief and are primed to believe that belief has a formative impact on behavior and quality of life. We think that this is behind the recent explosion of works that "Christianize" RET. And yet this also points up a weakness in the approach for Christians—namely, that many conservative Christians who come for counseling have already exhausted the avenues of cognitive change. They have been down that road. There are no indications as yet that RET is ineffective with religious believers, however.

The bombastic style of Ellis can become too intertwined with our understanding of the process of doing RET. This can "turn off" the interested student of RET. But a broad reading in the field reveals that there are many styles of doing rational therapy, and that there are gentle, respectful ways to aid the process of cognitive change. It is vital in studying RET to separate the ideas of Ellis from his manner with clients.

When we evaluate RET for the breadth of methods it proposes, we can see that it is one of the narrower approaches. The combination of RET with the active methods of behavior therapy (see next chapter) helps to diminish the centrality of this problem.

Conclusion

Perhaps the greatest value of RET for the Christian therapist can be derived from looking at RET through a wide-angle lens rather than through a microscope. In the broad view, one sees in RET a therapy that is openly value-oriented, prizes rationality and is balanced in its attempt to deal with the thoughts, behavior and feelings of the client from a rational perspective. As a comprehensive approach to understanding personality, RET is extremely limited. On close examination, many troublesome tensions appear between RET and Christian systems of thought. Principal among these are the highly humanistic definitions of *rationality*, an individualistic, rationalistic and hedonistic vision of human health and troublesome understandings of rationality and emotion.

For Further Reading

Crabb, L. (1975). *Basic principles of biblical counseling.* Grand Rapids, MI: Zondervan.

A representative "Christianized" version of RET.

Ellis, A., and Bernard, M. (Eds.). (1985). *Clinical applications of rational-emotive therapy.* New York: Plenum.

A good introduction to RET.

Ellis, A., and Harper, R. (1975). *A new guide to rational living.* Hollywood: Wilshire. A good sample of Ellis's RET.

Thurman, C. (1989). *The lies we believe.* Nashville: Thomas Nelson.

A representative "Christianized" version of RET.

Walen, S.; DiGiuseppe, R.; and Wessler, R. (1980). *A practitioner's guide to rational-emotive therapy.* New York: Oxford.

A fine guidebook to RET for the practitioner.

References

Backus, W. (1985). *Telling the truth to troubled people.* Minneapolis: Bethany.

Backus, W., and Chapian, M. (1980). *Telling yourself the truth.* Minneapolis: Bethany.

Bergin, A. (1980). Psychotherapy and religious values. *Journal of Consulting and Clinical Psychology, 48,* 95-105.

Berkhof, L. (1939). *Systematic theology.* Grand Rapids, MI: Eerdmans.

Bonhoeffer, D. (1959). *The cost of discipleship.* (R. H. Fuller, Trans.). New York: Macmillan. (Originally published, 1937.)

Clebsch, W., and Jaekle, C. (1975). *Pastoral care in historical perspective.* New York: Jason Aronson.

Crabb, L. (1975). *Basic principles of biblical counseling.* Grand Rapids, MI: Zondervan.

Crabb, L. (1977). *Effective biblical counseling.* Grand Rapids, MI: Zondervan.

Craigie, F., and Tan, S. (1989a). Changing resistant assumptions in Christian cognitive-behavioral therapy. *Journal of Psychology and Theology, 17,* 93-100.

Craigie, F., and Tan, S. (1989b). Entitlement. *Journal of Psychology and Christianity, 8,* 57-68.

Echeverria, E. (1986). Rationality and the theory of rationality. *Christian Scholar's Review, 15,* 372-387.

Ellis, A. (1962). *Reason and emotion in psychotherapy.* New York: Lyle Stuart.

Ellis, A. (1978). The theory of rational-emotive therapy. In A. Ellis and J. Whitely (Eds.), *Theoretical and empirical foundations of rational-emotive therapy* (pp. 33-60). Monterey, CA: Brooks/Cole.

Ellis, A. (1980). Psychotherapy and atheistic values. *Journal of Consulting and Clinical Psychology, 48,* 635-639.

Ellis, A. (1988). Yes, how reasonable is rational-emotive therapy? *Review of Existential Psychology and Psychiatry, 19,* 135-140.

Ellis, A., and Bernard, M. (1985). What is rational-emotive therapy? In A. Ellis and M. Bernard (Eds.), *Clinical applications of rational-emotive therapy* (pp. 1-30), New York: Plenum.

Ellis, A., and Harper, R. (1975). *A new guide to rational living.* Hollywood: Wilshire.

Eschenroeder, C. (1982). How rational is rational-emotive therapy? *Cognitive Therapy and Research, 6,* 381-392.

Evans, C. (1988a). Albert Ellis' conception of rationality: How reasonable is RET? *Review of Existential Psychology and Psychiatry, 19,* 129-134.

Evans, C. (1988b). A rejoinder to Ellis. *Review of Existential Psychology and Psychiatry, 19,* 141-142.

Grieger, R., and Boyd, J. (1980). *Rational-emotive therapy: A skill-based approach.* New York: Van Nostrand Reinhold.

Hauck, P. (1985). Religion and RET: Friends or foes? In A. Ellis and M. Bernard (Eds.), *Clinical applications of rational-emotive therapy* (pp. 237-256), New York: Plenum.

Holmes, A. (1977). *All truth is God's truth.* Grand Rapids, MI: Eerdmans.

Kreeft, P. (1986). *Making sense out of suffering.* Ann Arbor, MI: Servant.

Lawrence, C., and Huber, C. (1982). Strange bedfellows? Rational-emotive therapy and pastoral counseling. *The Personnel and Guidance Journal, 61,* 210-212.

Lazarus, A. (1977). Toward an egoless state of being. In A. Ellis and R. Grieger (Eds.), *Handbook of rational-emotive therapy* (pp. 113-118), New York: Springer.

Roberts, R. (1982). *Spirituality and human emotion.* Grand Rapids, MI: Eerdmans.

Roberts, R. (1987). Psychotherapeutic virtues and the grammar of faith. *Journal of Psychology and Theology, 15,* 191-204.

Roberts, R. (1988). What an emotion is: A sketch. *Philosophical Review, 47,* 183-209.

Schmidt, J. (1983). *Do you hear what you're thinking?* Wheaton, IL: Victor.

Sharkey, P. (1981). Something irrational about rational emotive psychology. *Psychotherapy: Theory, Research and Practice, 18,* 150-154.

Sterner, J. (1977). Is rational-emotive therapy suitable for pastoral counseling? *CAPS Bulletin, 3,* 6-8.

Tan, S. (1987). Cognitive-behavior therapy: A biblical approach and critique. *Journal of Psychology and Theology, 15,* 103-112.

Thurman, C. (1989). *The lies we believe.* Nashville: Thomas Nelson.

Walen, S.; DiGiuseppe, R.; and Wessler, R. (1980). *A practitioner's guide to rational-emotive therapy.* New York: Oxford.

Wessler, R. (1984). A bridge too far: Incompatibilities of rational-emotive therapy and pastoral counseling. *The Personnel and Guidance Journal, 63,* 264-265.

Zajonc, R. (1980). Feeling and thinking: Preferences need no inferences. *American Psychologist, 35,* 151-162.

8

COGNITIVE-
BEHAVIORAL
THERAPY

❖

*I*n chapter six we distinguished between the more "behavioristic" variants of behavior modification and behavior therapy, on the one hand, and cognitive-behavioral therapy on
the other, and focused on the former. In chapter seven, we explored
RET, which was a forerunner to cognitive-behavioral therapy. In
this chapter, we want to understand and critique cognitive-behavioral therapy, an interesting, recent, and highly influential de-
scendant of behavior therapy and RET.

Descriptive Survey

There are many variations of this model. Unlike most schools of
psychology, cognitive-behavioral therapy does not have one founding

theorist to give it cohesion. We shall examine the three most representative groups: The first is the social-cognitive approach to human personality of Bandura (1986) and Mischel (1973), which constitutes the most aggressive attempt to understand human personality from a behavioral and cognitive perspective—though it has not developed a corresponding school of therapy. We will also examine the cognitive-behavior therapy of Meichenbaum (1977, 1985) and the cognitive therapy of Beck (e.g., Beck, Rush, Hollon and Shaw, 1979). Collectively, we will call these approaches cognitive-behavioral therapy.[1]

The work of Bandura, Meichenbaum and others evolved out of traditional behaviorism. Beck, however, was trained psychoanalytically, but developed a rationally oriented approach to therapy in much the way that Ellis did, though Beck was always more open to the infusion of other therapy techniques than was Ellis. Beck emphasized scientific evaluation of effectiveness, was clinically pragmatic rather than theoretically speculative, and emphasized the direct and focused treatment of the client's presenting problems. This led to the incorporation of Beck's approach into cognitive-behavioral therapy.

As a group, all the therapies in this chapter differ from more traditionally behavioristic approaches in two central ways. First, cognitive-behavioral practitioners believe that some human behavior is caused by internal or mental events. For the true behaviorist, all the ultimate causes of behavior are external to the person. Internal events are real but ineffectual epiphenomena, mere temporary conduits for environmental forces. In cognitive-behavioral therapy, internal events are seen as real, powerful in their own right, and not *ultimately reducible* to environmental events. In sum, thought is judged to be real and to be important.

The second major difference is that the behaviorist believes that the same laws of learning—namely, operant and classical conditioning—explain all behavior, overt *and* internal or mental. But cognitive-behavioral therapy asserts that the internal behaving of humans (i.e., thoughts and feelings) may operate by different principles than the

---

[1]These approaches have not received the level of attention from Christian thinkers that many other approaches have. Edwards (1976), Tan (1987), Propst (1988) and Jones (1988) have been among the few to interact with cognitive-behavioral therapy as a system from a Christian perspective. A number of Christian counseling approaches have drawn from this model as well, as we shall illustrate later. This relative lack of attention by Christians seems due to Christian repugnance to the behaviorism of Skinner (and this model's guilt by association), the model's recency and its lack of cohesiveness which makes it hard to summarize and digest.

simple two learning processes used to explain animal behavior.[2] These approaches differ from RET in being more well integrated into the overall discipline of psychology, more scientific in their formulation, less dogmatic and more well researched.

If there is one thing that characterizes *academic* clinical psychology today, it is the relative neglect of grand personality theories in favor of what might be called "microtheories" of specific phenomena (Briggs, 1987). Researchers today tend to be eclectic about the grand theories they draw inspiration from, being strongly wedded to none of them. Their goal is to develop well-articulated smaller-scale theories about specific phenomena (such as altruism, panic, depression or social skills), *not* about persons as whole beings. The hope is thus to make these theories more accurate than the "grand" theories by making the universe of phenomena they attempt to explain smaller. For example, cognitive therapy began as an attempt to understand and treat depression and then broadened to an approach for dealing with all "affective disorders," bringing under its umbrella anxiety as well. It is more directly a theory about pathological emotions and a proposal for effective change methods for altering maladaptive emotional reactions. It is important to note, however, that even microtheories must make general assumptions about human beings that exhibit the phenomenon of study, and thus these approaches are necessarily embedded in grand theories of human personality, though they are often less explicit about those assumptions. This complicates the evaluation of their approaches.

Philosophical Assumptions
The presuppositions of this group of approaches are not as conspicuous as those of more doctrinaire behaviorism. Cognitive-behavioral therapy is built upon the foundations of behaviorism, and thus the basic presuppositions are consistent with that perspective. Materialism, naturalism and atomism seem to be embraced by proponents of cognitive- behavioral therapy. As stated in chapter six, these are unacceptable to Christians, though there are important positive points to consider with each. While materialism denies the existence of the spiritual realm, it serves to remind us of the physicalness and finitude

---

[2]For a general treatment of the shift of the field of psychology away from strict behavioral conceptions and toward cognitive stances, see Dobson and Block (1988); for a Christian view, see Hodges (1976) or Van Leeuwen (1985).

of our existence and the way this conditions all aspects of our being.

Atomism, as embraced by cognitive-behavioral theorists, suggests that each person is a loose collection of behavioral and cognitive habits and predispositions. While this undermines notions of personal responsibility (since there is no "person" behind the behavior), atomism does help us not to overidentify with our actions.

Reductionism is also present, though the steps of "reducing" a phenomenon do not seem to go so far in the direction of basic processes as with behavior modification. Instead of reducing all events to operant learning human phenomena are understood in terms of expectancies, self-statements and so forth. Still, this is not a "holistic" view of persons such as is found in Adlerian or existential approaches to therapy.

Finally, cognitive-behavioral therapy embraces a view of science akin to that of behavior modification, though "covert events," such as thought, are not dismissed perfunctorily as nonscientific phenomena.

The antimentalism of behavior modification is altered in an interesting way in cognitive-behavioral therapy. The view that thoughts are noncausal epiphenomena gives way to the notion of thought patterns being powerful determinants of behavior. At the same time, thoughts are also regarded as being the result of naturalistic processes. Since these thought patterns are not presumed to operate by the rules of operant and classical learning, cognitive-behaviorists can remain materialists who do not believe in mentalism (in the sense of believing in an immaterial mind or soul), but at the same time can believe that human thought is a complex and causally efficacious phenomenon that is not a simple result of reinforcement. For the behavior modifier, the thought "I should write some more on my book today" is presumed to be a mere byproduct of the external reinforcement contingencies that produce chapter-writing behavior (such as calls from an editor, the past history of payment and praise for writing, etc.). In cognitive-behavioral therapy, such a thought is seen as an important contributor to writing behavior occurring; it is a causal force in its own right. That is why cognitive- behaviorists are often called "mentalists" by behavior modifiers; this is perhaps the highest insult the behavior modifier can inflict.

Determinism is also modified substantially in this model. Remember that the classic behaviorist believes that events outside the person, operating through the laws of learning, totally determine all behavior. We cannot do other than what we do. Cognitive-behaviorists sometimes take similar stances, as when Marlatt (1982, p. 333), speaking about responsibility in the development of an addiction problem, states, "The fact is that an individual who acquires a maladaptive habit pattern on the basis of past conditioning and the effects of reinforcement is no more 'responsible' for his behavior than one of Pavlov's dogs would be held responsible for salivating at the sound of a ringing bell."

Most cognitive-behaviorists, though, take a different stance toward determinism. Bandura has taken this issue on in-depth, and other cognitive-behaviorists have typically endorsed his formulation of this matter enthusiastically. He developed the notion of reciprocal determinism (1978) (also the related concept of person-environment interactionism), which asserts that while we are determined by our environments, we are also the determiners of what our environments are (to a limited degree). For example, we may be affected by what we watch on TV, but we choose what to watch, creating our "video environment" when we turn the tube on and set the dial. We may be affected by how others behave toward us at work, but we can choose (within limits) where we work, and we can be part of determining how others treat us by treating them in certain ways. We reciprocally determine and are determined by our environments. In Bandura's words (1978, p. 357),

> It is within the framework of reciprocal determinism that the concept of freedom assumes meaning. . . . Because people's conceptions, their behavior, and their environments are reciprocal determinants of each other, individuals are neither powerless objects controlled by environmental forces nor entirely free agents who can do whatever they choose. People can be considered partially free insofar as they shape future conditions by influencing their courses of action.

Thus Bandura combines a belief in freedom with a recognition of the limitations and constraints on that freedom.

Model of Personality
In the cognitive-behavioral camp, only Mischel (1973) has proposed anything approaching a grand theory of personality. He has suggested that rather than understanding personality from the perspective of universal dispositions or traits, people are better suited to "idiographic analysis" where each person is analyzed individually without reducing individual differences to measurements of universal traits (such as dominance, extroversion, sensation-seeking, etc.). Each person's per-

sonality is unique and must be understood as such.

Mischel's Five Person Variables. Mischel organizes his idiographic approach to understanding persons around *five person variables.* These are not traits or psychological structures (such as the id, ego, superego of psychoanalysis), but are categories of processes that can develop differently in different persons. There is a strong similarity between this approach and the behavioristic explanation of all personality according to the laws of learning, though here the list of processes is longer and more complex. These five person variables are:

1. *Cognitive encoding strategies.* All persons sort the raw data of their sensations of the world in different ways. It is our encoding strategies that transform a perception of a mouth movement of another into either a warm, accepting smile or a judgmental grimace of condescension; that categorize a three-sentence statement by a work supervisor into a vicious attack or a helpful exhortation. Some Christians might look at others in the church and categorize a small group as "real believers" and all others as "hypocrites," while another person may sort persons according to maturity judged by how gracious and loving they seem to be. At a broad level, the way we sort the complex world we confront "channels" our personalities and can make us different people. Persons with sophisticated, broad, adaptable ways of sorting or encoding their experiences will be more adjusted and adaptable than persons with simplistic, rigid and narrow encoding strategies.

2. *Cognitive and behavioral construction competencies.* In response to the raw data we take in through our senses and our encoded perceptions, we must "figure out" our world by constructing a cognitive model of it and then go on to construct actions for responding to it. Once we have given a label to experience, we put bits of experience together in a way that seems to make sense. These models may vary from highly accurate and productive (such as the insightful understanding of the politically astute employee in an organization) to highly inaccurate and destructive (such as the paranoid delusions of the psychotic). On the basis of that model and utilizing the skills available, the person then acts. People differ widely in the actions they are capable of exhibiting. For example, husbands differ widely in their capacity to be emotionally sensitive and responsive to their wives. We all differ in terms of the ways we make sense of our world and the capacities we possess for acting in response to it.

3. *Subjective stimulus values.* Another dimension on which persons differ is what they value and hence what motivates them. According to

Mischel, people build up from the few basic motivations that Skinner allowed (need for food, warmth, water, pleasure, etc.) to almost an infinite array of valued stimuli, which then become incentives for behavior or a focus for motivation. People can then differ immensely on what are motivations for them because of their very different learning histories.

4. *Operant and classical conditioning.* Though he has moved beyond traditional behaviorism, Mischel believes that basic learning processes are still influential in human behavior. He does not understand these in the mechanistic manner of a Skinnerian, but believes them to be operative at a cognitive level. For instance, operant learning (changes in behavior based on reinforcement patterns) is understood not as the mechanistic conditioning of operant behavior but as the influencing of choice behavior by the alteration of expectations of reward.

5. *Self-regulatory systems and plans.* One of the major contributions of Bandura (1978) and Kanfer (1979) in moving beyond traditional behavioral conceptions of persons was the proposal that persons typically internalize control of their behavior as they develop. Skinner may believe that our environment controls all, but these theorists argued that through memory, expectancy and language we take our environment inside us, and thus the thoughts we engage in become as powerful determinants of our actions as the external environment. While the study behavior of a student may be partially due to external contingencies, such as social praise from dorm associates, availability of other activities and so forth, the student can also create alternative forces that influence behavior through, for example, self-statements such as "I must study now or I will flunk out of school," or "Imagine how my boyfriend will be impressed when I get an A in this course!" The image of the boyfriend conjured up at will can be as powerful a determinant of behavior as the real person. People then differ in their capabilities to regulate their own behavior. People differ according to what behavior they pay attention to in themselves, how they judge that behavior (e.g., stringent versus generous standards of judgment) and how effectively they give overt consequences ("No TV for me tonight; I didn't do my housework!") or covert consequences (self-statements such as "I did a great job!" or "I'm a hopeless case!") to themselves.

Mischel's understanding of personality has not resulted in a formal therapy approach per se, but his model provides the best integrative framework for understanding all of cognitive-behavioral therapy, in that each intervention can be seen as targeting one or more of his person variables.

Bandura's Social-Cognitive Theory. Bandura, a prolific researcher in this field, has contributed many important concepts to cognitive-behavioral therapy. First, he focused on the phenomenon of modeling—the capacity of humans to learn not just by direct experience but by watching the behavior or hearing the thoughts of others. Modeling has become an important component of cognitive-behavioral psychotherapy. Further, Bandura developed the concepts of self-regulation and reciprocal determinism, which we have already discussed.

Finally, Bandura developed the concept of *self-efficacy*, which has become central in cognitive-behavioral practice today. This is the concept that it is not just past consequences of an action that determine its occurrence (as Skinner might argue) or even the expectation of a future consequence (a cognitive event which Skinner would deny the importance of), but it is also our *evaluation of our own competency* or effectiveness in behaving that determines action.

For example, a Skinnerian would say a shy person's reluctance to interact with others is a function of having not been rewarded for such activities in the past and of receiving ongoing rewards for shy behavior. As treatment, the Skinnerian would implement a learning strategy that would positively reinforce outgoing behavior. To this Bandura would add that the shy person must not only expect reinforcement for outgoing behavior, but she must also manifest a sense of personal efficacy for those types of behaviors, a sense that she can effectively interact with others.

The point here is that people do not attempt things just because there are rewards; we also consider our expectancy that we can be effective at the behavior it takes to obtain the rewards. This is important in cognitive-behavioral therapy where one is trying to establish new behavior. The therapist cannot simply create a reward, but must also create a sense of personal effectiveness to get the fearful person to act in courageous ways, or the lonely and depressed person to attempt new social interactions.

Meichenbaum's Cognitive Behavior Therapy. Meichenbaum's (1977) vision was to develop a method for understanding the impact of cognitions (thoughts) on behavior and emotion, and a method for changing the nature of that impact. He proposed a three-stage process for effective change. First, a person must become aware of thoughts relevant to the problem being experienced. Next, therapist and client must determine alternative thoughts (self-statements) that can believably replace thoughts that are causing the person trouble. Finally, the person must implement thought changes and begin to enjoy the benefits of nondestructive cognition.

For example, some of Meichenbaum's work has been with impulsive, hyperactive children. In this population it is assumed that the problems are due in part to a failure to establish the cognitive skills that normal children have to manage their own behavior. Thus impulsive children might be taught initially to define their task and continually remind themselves what to do ("I'm in class and my job here is listening to the teacher"), to use thoughts to cope with distractions or less than optimal performance ("Oops. My mind wandered! Back on track; just pick up where you left off") and to use positive thoughts to reward good performance and perhaps negative thoughts to punish unwanted performance ("Great! I'm doing better. I paid attention for ten minutes in a row!"). Meichenbaum's methods have been applied to such populations as children, schizophrenics, adults with anxiety disorders or chronic pain, and those with explosive tempers (see Meichenbaum, 1985).

Beck's Cognitive Therapy. Beck's work has been similar to, though independent from, Meichenbaum's. Working with depressives (Beck et al., 1979), those with anxiety disorders (Beck and Emery, 1985), and most recently couples with marital problems (1988), Beck has been a productive clinician and researcher. His work differs from RET in more fully utilizing cognitive *and behavioral* methods, in being less doctrinaire in what he regards as rational and irrational (using instead the labels "adaptive" and "maladaptive" beliefs) and most importantly in encouraging a therapeutic style less combative and rigid than Ellis's in favor of a gentler though direct Socratic questioning style.

Beck proposes that pathological levels of depression and anxiety are the result of "distorted cognitions." It is commonly noted that depressed and anxious people report thoughts that are clearly inaccurate. A depressed man says, "Everything I've ever done has been a failure"; yet friends who know him well reveal that he has done and still is doing many things satisfactorily. An anxious woman says, "There is no way I can handle that situation; it will destroy me"; yet family members disclose that she has in fact handled situations like what she is afraid of in the past and that what she fears cannot destroy her. Other approaches to counseling view these thoughts as symptomatic of other problems (low self-esteem, projection of unacceptable impulses) and thus see no benefit in directly changing the thoughts. In Beck's mind, the distorted thinking is not the symptom of the problem, it is the cause of the problem.

Cognitive therapy typically proceeds in three stages: first, the presentation of the therapeutic rationale; second, the development of awareness of dysfunctional thoughts on the part of the client; finally, the actual alteration of the dysfunctional thoughts and the substitution of more functional thinking. In a direct fashion, most clearly reflective of the Socratic philosophical tradition, Beck uses persistent but gentle logic and persuasion to alter the person's thinking. He might use such techniques as involving the client in collecting evidence to support or undermine beliefs ("Please gather all your employee reviews for the last five years; if you really are a complete failure, there shouldn't be a single positive statement on them") or suggesting new thoughts to focus on ("Please collect a list of your positive traits from your friends, list those you feel are most true, and think on these five times each day"). Not all cognitions are judged to be verbal in form. Some of the most powerful can be visual images (everyone in the neighborhood staring), auditory (the sound of people laughing at you) and so forth.

There is a danger that cognitive change can be construed in a very superficial manner. Beck and others emphasize the need to get down to the "core beliefs" of the client, and a major portion of the therapeutic effort is devoted to developing a self-awareness of what the core issues are. Often the therapist must help the client by utilizing creative modes of self-assessment or even interpret the actions and statements of the client from an objective standpoint. Changes that are not relevant to the presenting problem because they are superficial will not be that helpful. A client who complains of doubting herself, but whom the therapist suspects is deeply afraid of the rejection of her husband who makes periodic threats of leaving her, must come to grips with the real cognitive events that are shaping her responses.

Beck also uses traditional behavior-therapy techniques as well. For example, a person depressed over his unemployment may be paralyzed and miserable in part because of the catastrophic things he is telling himself, but that person may also be disorganized (and thus able to benefit from some behavioral self-management training) and interpersonally awkward, especially in job-interview situations (and thus able to benefit from assertiveness training). Beck would utilize a treatment package of all of these methods.

Models of Health and Abnormality
One of the most curious things about this approach to therapy is that

due to its emphasis on microtheories of disorders rather than broad understanding of persons, these approaches are sketchy about defining normalcy and abnormality. They assume that these are defined by society and by a person's own assessment of his or her level of distress and functioning.

Thus cognitive-behavioral therapy is characterized by what Woolfolk and Richardson (1984) call "amorality," a tendency to go along with the individual's definitions of normalcy and abnormality. If a client comes into a clinic complaining that a pattern is a problem, then for that person it is a problem. This usually meshes well with common sense; no one is going to disagree that agoraphobia or suicidal depression is abnormal. But it leaves open to the individual decision of the therapist and client the normalcy or abnormality of border cases.

A perhaps extreme example is Lazarus's (1980) work with a woman who reported having married her husband only for the financial rewards he gave her. She had had numerous sexual affairs. She came to therapy because of a developing aversion to sexual relations with her husband. Lazarus's response was not to confront the obvious narcissism of the client or to urge her to work on the marriage. Rather he deemed her aversion to sex in a loveless and pragmatic marriage a worthwhile target for therapy and taught her cognitive techniques to allow her to "turn herself off emotionally" so that she could continue to tolerate sex with her husband while continuing to enjoy her adulterous affairs. While this is an extreme example, it points up the risks of an obscure definition of normalcy.

Model of Psychotherapy

Cognitive-behavioral therapy in clinical practice tends to be characterized by shorter-term interventions targeted at specifically defined problems. These problems are attacked as directly as possible, in a manner some belittle as mere "symptom reduction." Cognitive-behavioral therapy emphasizes empirical documentation of effectiveness, so it is no coincidence that cognitive-behavioral-therapy techniques have been mostly developed for the treatment of problems which are easier to measure directly, such as depression, stress, anxiety or academic underachievement. Problems characterized by more vague complaints tend to be ignored by this approach.

The therapist-client relationship in cognitive-behavioral therapy is conceived of in a less personal way than in many approaches. For example, Kendall and Bemis (1983, p. 566) state, "The task of the cognitive-behavioral therapist is to act as diagnostician, educator, and technical consultant who assesses maladaptive cognitive processes and works with the client to design learning experiences that may remediate these dysfunctional cognitions." This is hardly a description that warms the soul! Nevertheless, as we showed in chapter six, research has actually shown that practitioners of behavior therapy and cognitive-behavioral therapy are typically perceived as very warm and caring by clients.

All of these cognitive-behavioral theorists make use of the assortment of methods of behavior modification and behavior therapy, but additionally target thought patterns and cognitive habits of the client, using methods that are not common to behavior modification, such as modeling, verbal instruction, rehearsal of thoughts and so forth. Dobson and Block (1988) suggest that there are three major types of cognitive- behavioral-therapy interventions: *coping skills training*, where the client is assisted in developing behavioral and cognitive skills for dealing with challenging situations; *cognitive restructuring*, where the focus is on some direct form of modification of maladaptive thought patterns; and *problem-solving training*, where the person expands his or her general capacity for understanding and facing challenging problems.

Christian Critique

Philosophical Assumptions
As stated in chapter six, the behavioristic presuppositions of materialism, naturalism, atomism, reductionism and scientism are unacceptable for Christians because they exclude God and supernatural activity and they strip humanity of its God-given rationality and dignity. Let us then turn to the matter of determinism.

As Christians, we must believe in limited freedom, as developed in chapter two. And we must reject the kind of materialistic determinism espoused by Skinner. But is *reciprocal determinism*, as developed by Bandura, adequate as an understanding of limited freedom?

Bandura (1989, p. 1182) says explicitly that "freedom . . . is defined positively in terms of the exercise of self-influence. . . . Self-generated influences operate deterministically on behavior the same way as external sources of influence do. . . . The self is thus partly fashioned through the continued exercise of self-influence." Note several things about this statement. First, Bandura defines freedom "positively" rather than "negatively," presumably meaning that freedom does not mean the absence of causes. Second, it is clear that Bandura conceives of the working of the self in a mechanical way, suggesting that it develops by universal laws of behavior and is "activated" by external influences that impinge on the person. For Bandura, human beings are free in the sense that their behavior has an impact on their environment and hence on the changing of their own behavior (which he calls the development of the self). Further, these self-systems are not mere way stations for environmental influence but contribute something to behavior beyond the influence of environment.

Bandura's view can best be understood in terms of the distinction between hard and soft determinism (as we discussed in chapter four; Evans, 1989). Both forms of determinism share the belief that behavior is determined and thus could not have occurred otherwise. Where the two views differ is that the hard determinist (e.g., Skinner) explicitly acknowledges that his view is incompatible with freedom while the soft determinist redefines freedom in such a way as to make it compatible with determinism, thus creating the illusion of freedom. Bandura engaged in just such a redefining move in the reference above by defining freedom not as the capacity to have acted other than the causal forces dictated but as the exercise of self-influence *even when the exercise of self-influence is itself causally determined to occur!* In other words, we have freedom whenever the self exercises its influence, even though the self-system operates by determined rules and thus could not have behaved otherwise. Bandura is clearly a soft determinist.

In Bandura's view, we are not free in the sense of having any choices over which we exercise ultimate control as responsible agents. Bandura himself stated that there is no "psychic agent that controls behavior" (1978, p. 348). For example, according to Bandura honesty may be described as an ability to resist external temptations to steal or lie, but that personality disposition is itself caused by *something other than the decision of the person.* At a descriptive level, Bandura would agree that the person has the sense of making decisions to be honest. But ultimately the development of the characteristic of honesty is caused by factors over which the person has "no control." The person learned to define honest and dishonest behavior, to value honesty and to regulate his or her own behavior, to be able to resist external temptation by the standard laws of learning. Moral choice becomes just another behavior that is acquired the way all behaviors are acquired. This is why Wren (1982) described the social-learning understanding of persons as "paramechanical." The person never escapes the closed circle of determined acts.

In none of the behavioristic conceptions of the person do we have true limited freedom. All of these models are thus "dangerous" in that they propose a view of human persons in which we are mechanisms of some sort or another, beings which always do what they must do. This is as true for Bandura's conception of the person as for Skinner's or Wolpe's. In the latter, we are noncognitive machines; in the former, we are thinking machines. Such views demean our true nature and undermine our sense (which reflects reality) of our responsibility for our actions.

Yet of all the various psychotherapies it is perhaps Bandura's view, faulty as it is, that comes closest to a Christian view of freedom. It avoids the radical suggestion of autonomous freedom embraced by the humanistic psychologies (chapters ten to thirteen) and attempts to avoid the suffocating determinism of classical psychoanalysis (chapter four) and behavior modification (chapter six). It fails because only a theistic view of persons that asserts that we are created for moral accountability has an adequate grounding for a full conception of limited freedom.

Even though at the metatheoretical level all behavior therapists embrace determinism, cognitive-behavioral therapy practitioners are distinctive among the psychotherapy approaches for being open with clients about the change process and trying to enlist the client as a "collaborator," a concept which carries with it a high view of the client's powers of choice and freedom. Compared to psychoanalysis, person-centered therapy and family-systems approaches, which seem to have a low view of the person's capacity for meaningful change apart from expert intervention, cognitive-behavioral therapy has a high view of the person's capacity for change through "self-control" and related processes.

Let us now move from the assumption of determinism to the cognitive-behavioral view of mind. There is no one cognitive-behavioral theory of mind. The general approach to the mind-brain problem in cognitive-behavioral therapy is consistent with that of behaviorism in embracing an implicitly materialistic theory, viewing thought as a naturalistic process rooted in our neurology and governed by causal laws.

But there are options in thinking about the mind-brain distinction that take the physical bases of thought seriously but do not leave us trapped in a deterministic framework. In particular, we can look at the emergentist view of Nobel Prize winner Roger Sperry.

Sperry's (1980) view of mind-brain interaction, in much too brief summary, is that human thought is founded on *but transcends in limited ways* physical determination. He suggests that human thought, characterized by limited freedom, emerges from the complex neurological building blocks of brain processes, which are fundamentally dependent on their physical substrates yet capable of transcending that physical programming. One of the analogies he uses is that of a rubber tire. By being formed into a tire shape, the rubber molecules behave in ways not predictable from knowledge of just their physical properties. Rolling freely is a property of wheels, not of rubber. Similarly, Sperry argues that thought emerges from—and has properties based on but not completely predictable from—the physical functioning of the brain. This view is intriguing, in that it proposes real freedom (a transcendent property), but not a freedom that ignores or is independent from the physical realities of our created natures.

Cognitive-behavioral therapy does not embrace an emergentist view of mind, but it moves in that direction in suggesting that the rules governing the behavior of cognition are not the same rules of learning that govern lower-order animal behavior. Our argument here is that if cognitive-behavioral therapists were to take the step of embracing emergentism, their view could be more acceptable to Christians as an integrating view of persons. We would no longer be forced to choose between operant learning at one extreme and existential choice at the other. Rather, the focus would be on understanding the gamut of processes that are at play in human experience, from the naturalistic to the transcendent.

Sperry's view suggests that the more distinctly human characteristics are built upon *but not wholly reducible* to the more basic processes we share with animals. A complicated human phenomenon such as religious conversion can involve basic processes, such as operant and classical conditioning; middle-level phenomena, such as expectancies, encoding strategies and stimulus values; and highest-level processes, such as human responsibility and existential authenticity.

Problems, too, can occur at different levels of functioning. One person may have an existential crisis (a problem at the highest level of transcendence), which is manifested as anxiety, while another can have a biologically mediated anxiety problem (perhaps as a bad reaction to a prescription medication, a "purely" chemical problem). But most human concerns are *multiple-level problems*. An example would be a person with a phobia who is biologically predisposed to emotional overreactivity and who is unfortunately exposed to some powerful classical-conditioning experiences with phobic objects and develops distorted thinking patterns and expectancies based on past experience and finally responds to these proclivities in an existentially inauthentic manner (cf. Evans, 1986). This view suggests that we can validly learn from the behavioral and cognitive-behavioral-therapy approaches in spite of their reductionism, as they give some perspicacious understandings of more primitive aspects of human psychological functioning.

Models of Personality, Health and Abnormality

Because of the propensity of practitioners in this school of psychology to focus on microtheories of the specific pathologies, there is little we can comment on from a Christian perspective regarding the discipline's overall approach to defining personality, health and abnormality. There are no grand postulates about ultimate human ideals or about motivations.

As we pointed out in the chapter on RET, there is some compatibility between Christianity and any system that places a high premium on human rationality. Cognitive therapy would say that what we believe has tremendous implications for our personal well-being. This certainly resonates with biblical themes, such as the words of Paul in Philippians 4:8-9: "Whatever is true, whatever is noble, whatever is right, whatever is pure, whatever is lovely, . . . think about such things. . . . And the God of peace will be with you."

According to cognitive-behavioral therapy and the Bible, our thoughts *are* actions over which we have control, and these thoughts have implications for the quality of our lives. A failure to believe the right things can lead to spiritual impoverishment, as we fail to appropriate God's resources.

We see this especially in the area of suffering. When we view our temporal lives as primary and have as our highest goals comfort and prosperity, then suffering will be a misery-producing and faith-undermining experience. But if suffering is viewed as an opportunity for testimony for the gospel, as a means for fellowship with Christ in his sufferings, as preparation for eternal glory through learning to loosen our ties to this life, and as an opportunity to learn to better comfort others, suffering can be transformed into a meaningful path that one treads for the sake of God's love (Kreeft, 1986).

As an example of the favorable reaction to cognitive-behavioral therapy's prizing of rationality, Pecheur (1978, p. 251) suggested "that the process of change which takes place in sanctification is the same as the process of change which occurs with cognitive therapy." According to Pecheur, Scripture teaches that what we think upon is a powerful determinant of our spiritual nature; for example, Romans 8:5 reads, "Those who live according to the sinful nature have their minds set on what that nature desires; but those who live in accordance with the Spirit have their minds set on what the Spirit desires."

Pecheur argues the Scriptures generally encourage the same sort of self-awareness of cognitions as cognitive-behavioral therapy ("Search me, O God, and know my heart; test me and know my anxious thoughts. ... And lead me in the way everlasting," Ps 139:23-24). We are to forsake unrighteous thoughts (Is 55:7) and seek a renewing of the mind (Eph 4:22-25; Rom 12:1-2) by replacing unrighteous with righteous thinking that is based on biblical standards. Thus cognitive change is believed to lead to growth. Edwards (1976, p. 99) argues similarly that "it is the positive, Christ-centered thought-life that counteracts anxiety and leads to peace with God." The major difference noted by Pecheur between Christian sanctification and cognitive-behavioral therapy is God's active participation in the process of sanctification.

This view of sanctification is one that fits well with many of the directive messages of Scripture that tend to be cognitive-behavioral in character; that is, they urge a dual emphasis on cognitive and behavioral change (as Pecheur ably points out). Further, this view meshes well with the methods advocated to promote spiritual growth by many conservative Christian groups, such as rigorous Bible study, Bible memorization, disciplined prayer and attention to good deeds.

We would agree that the processes and means for accomplishing sanctification are perhaps the most powerful parallel in the Scriptures to the therapeutic process of growth. We would not, however, assert a fundamental identity between sanctification and therapy generally or cognitive-behavioral therapy particularly. Cognitive-behavioral change does not mesh well with the more charismatic understandings of spiritual growth, which emphasize direct experiences of God's grace, nor with the more socially oriented Anabaptist traditions, which emphasize corporate life and the dynamics of life together as the route to growth (Foster, 1978; Propst, 1988).

Further, the emphasis on cognitive-behavioral change does not thoroughly comport with a relational understanding of spirituality, wherein spiritual growth is more a function of an alive relationship with the personal God than anything else. As Tan (1987, p. 106) says, "Cognitive- behavioral therapy may overemphasize the rational thinking dimension of human functioning and undermine the experiential, and even mystical aspects of the Christian life and faith." (Tan cites 1 Cor 1:18-31; 2 Cor 2:12-16; 5:7 to support his contention.) One example of the type of overemphasis Tan is criticizing might come from Edwards (1976, p. 104), who says that he would "postulate that most of God's supernatural influence on His people is through cognitions inspired by the Holy Spirit." While the cognitive-behavioral therapy emphasis on rationality is a positive, it cannot be made an absolute.

Perhaps the greatest danger in cognitive therapy is one shared with RET, that of using a distorted standard of rationality. Since the goal of therapy is the eradication of pathological emotional reactions, the beliefs or cognitions of the client tend to be judged by their *utility* rather than by their truthfulness. (We called this the *pragmatic criterion* for rationality in the last chapter.) For example, suppose that the continual recurrence of the thought "I am a sinner whose righteousness is as filthy rags before the Lord; I am wholly without merit before him" brought substantial distress to its thinker, including loss of sleep and loss of enjoyment of worldly success. With only a pragmatic standard to guide the therapist, the most expeditious course would be to attempt to undermine the belief by whatever means available with the goal of either eradicating or modifying the client's thought. Questions such as "What evidence is there that God exists or that God cares about your behavior at all?" might be pursued. The goal would be to eradicate the thought because it bothers the client. The religious counselor, on the other hand, might judge the negative emotional reaction appropriate because of the validity of the thoughts themselves. A time of true repentance and grieving over our sinfulness is a healthy part of the Christian life.

But it is also true that it does not seem to be God's wish that we all be paralyzed by our grief over our sin, and there should come a time where believers come to see their sinfulness in the context of the marvelous provision of salvation from God, and where our remorse becomes secondary to our love for this marvelous redeeming God who desires us to worship him and serve him. So in the case of a protracted and overly severe preoccupation with one's own sinfulness, the Christian cognitive-behavioral therapist would regard the thoughts as true but perhaps not in their proper context among other Christian beliefs, and hence might see the emotional response as problematic. Thus the Christian counselor would not be using the pragmatic standard for judging beliefs. The therapist's method would not be to undermine the belief, but to put it in proper perspective among other beliefs.

It is a strength of cognitive-behavioral therapy that it has a high view of rationality. But as Woolfolk and Richardson (1984) point out, in cognitive-behavioral therapy *emotion* is often treated as an add-on, a nuisance variable that must be controlled, modified or explained. Emotion is not conceived as a human capacity that enriches life or as a source of knowledge and growth. Just as in many evangelical circles, emotion in cognitive-behavioral therapy is treated as a nuisance: "Get your beliefs and your actions straight, and the emotions will just fall in line." This is a demeaning view of emotion, and is perhaps the result of a logical fallacy. Presumably the logic is that because cognition can in some cases modify or produce emotion (as when thinking "I'm a failure" leads to depression), all emotion is cognitively caused and hence incidental, which is simply not the case. Cognitive-behavioral therapy shares this weakness with RET.

Next we will consider the cognitive-behavioral notion that a person's behavior is the joint product of personal and environmental influences. This concept is called *person-environment interactionism* by some. Though we earlier rejected the deterministic residual in Bandura's reciprocal determinism, interactionism seems consistent with the Christian view that we are not radically autonomous from our environment. We are substantially affected by our surroundings. The Christian ideal is not one of rugged individualism and radical insensitivity to our impersonal and interpersonal environments. Rather, we live necessarily in mutual interdependence with other persons and are creatures of the earth affected by our material universe.

Cognitive-behavioral therapy is thus a positive balance between the radical individualism of the humanistic psychologies (chapters ten to thirteen) and the collectivism of family systems (chapter fifteen). Bufford (1977) discusses with some forcefulness how the biblical directives to exercise discernment take seriously the influence social surroundings have on us; for example, we are instructed to avoid angry persons (Prov 22:24-25), sexual tempters (Prov 5) and fools (Prov 13:20). Also, since parents form the personal environment for their children, modeling is thus an important element in teaching our children. Deuteronomy 6:4-9 would urge us to engage in behavior that will be a positive model for our children, thus drawing them closer to God.

Nevertheless, while cognitive-behavioral therapy pays attention to the interpersonal environment, it manages to do so in an impersonal way. Other persons are seen as "stimuli" in an environment; they are only sources of reinforcement, punishment or modeling. The more human and "warm" concepts such as love, wisdom and compassion are missing in cognitive-behavioral therapy. Thus, while cognitive-behavioral therapy achieves a creative balance between individualism and environmentalism, it loses the personal dimension of our interaction with others in the process.

Another issue worth addressing is that of fundamental motivations. Unlike some other approaches that explicitly label one or two core motivations, cognitive-behavioral therapy embraces motivational diversity (Mischel's "subjective stimulus values") just as behavior therapy does. Nevertheless, the underlying assumption seems to be that humans are fundamentally motivated to enhance their own welfare. For example, most cognitive-behavioral considerations of interpersonal behavior use the organizing conception of *competency* to evaluate interpersonal action. This concept suggests that human behavior is primarily directed at obtaining desired goods from the personal and impersonal environment. Competent responses are most often defined as those that are "effective" or "competent" at getting what we want or at accomplishing a specific "task" (see McFall, 1982). Behavioral theories and concepts direct our attention inexorably to the *functional value* of any human behavior; that is, *what it does for the organism.* This seems to be a holdover from the Skinnerian understanding that sees all significant behavior as operant—designed to operate on the environment to produce a desired outcome.

This orientation manifests itself in the cognitive-behavioral understanding of love and altruism. Cognitive-behavioral therapists have been active in developing clinical models of marital therapy. The fundamental premise they use in analyzing marriage is that individuals tend to pattern their behavior to maximize reinforcement for themselves (see Jacobson and Margolin, 1979, chap. 1). Stuart (1980, p. 370) calls this "the best bargain principle: The behaviors that all parties in relationships display at any given moment represent the best means that each person believes he or she has available for obtaining desired satisfactions."

So even in the most giving of human relationships, marriage, persons are assumed to be attempting to maximize their own receipt of personal satisfactions. This is also true of cognitive-behavioral therapy's view of altruism (doing good for another for no apparent reason). Kanfer (1979), for example, suggested that altruism is a form of behavior where one delays personal and immediate reinforcement for the sake of long-term outcomes: "[The] task, as in self-control, is to train persons to act for the benefits of another because it is in their own self-interest" (p. 237). They take for granted that people are basically out for themselves. People are seen as having their own welfare as their only ultimate concern.

In some ways Christian theology is similarly pessimistic about humanity. Seeing self-enhancement as a core motivation should not be a surprise for persons who believe in human depravity. But we are not just depraved, selfish beings; we are also all created in the image of God, the God of all love, the giving and self-sacrificing God. Thus it would seem that all humans have some capacity for transcending their human egocentrism and that Christians should have a special capacity for self-transcendence through God's grace, for compassion and self-sacrificing love. The love described in 1 Corinthians 13 is definitely not a self-interested love devoid of personal sacrifice. Love is a foundational human capacity created in us from the beginning, as when the first humans in the creation story were told to cleave to one another and that the two would become one flesh. Descriptively, the Christian Scriptures and tradition seem to take human selfishness into account, appealing, for example, to the rewards we will personally receive in heaven to motivate good behavior here on earth. But the Scriptures never stop at that point, going on to call persons to a life wherein our desires come to conform evermore to God's purposes without regard for our own welfare. With God's help, we are capable of such a transition.

Just as with behavior modification, cognitive-behavioral therapists often emphasize competence and the pursuit of consequences. Whereas behavior modification might emphasize the narrow pursuit of material reinforcers (paralleling the sentiment expressed by the memorable bumper sticker "Whoever Dies with the Most Toys Wins"), cognitive-behavioral therapy has a broader orientation focusing on diffuse skills for mastering life's tasks, using such concepts as self-efficacy, cognitive and behavioral construction competencies, and competence.

If we believe that the task of dominion is consistent with a biblical understanding of persons and that we are each to be about some dimension of a dominion work, then competence seems an important concept in human life. If self-efficacy (the idea that we are motivated by our beliefs in our own effectiveness) is equated with human pride, it will be viewed negatively by Christians, but it should not be viewed as such. Rather, our actions seem to have been meant by God to matter, to be effective. We are beings designed for meaningful work and effective interactions with our world. Christianity is not wedded to prescribing that each of us feel or perceive ourselves to be incompetent, as if the feeling of helplessness were a virtue. Propst (1988) correctly reminds us that Christianity is not merely a religion of the afterlife, but one which endorses a certain spirituality of everyday life. As we submit our day-to-day lives to God, he redeems them and allows us to live to his glory. But we continue to live in this world and must have effective and righteous ways of dealing with it.

Thus, it would seem that helping clients achieve meaningful mastery over their lives is a goal compatible with Christian faith. As Tan (1987) suggested, though, an overemphasis on self-efficacy can lead to pride. In our effectiveness, we seem to have been meant to live in a dynamic tension of delight in our competencies and realization of our utter dependence on God. Perhaps the best summary of this dynamic is the statement of Paul in Philippians 4:13: "I can do everything through him who gives me strength."

A Christian view of will and self-control also has some broad compatibilities with the view expressed by cognitive-behavioral therapy. The Christian view of will is that it is a capacity that can be developed, as opposed to it being an all-or-nothing, static personality trait. Hebrews 12, for instance, discusses at length the notion of discipline from God, noting that we are disciplined for our good (v. 10; note the appeal to personally desirable consequences) and that discipline is often unpleasant. Verses 12-13 ("Strengthen your feeble arms and weak knees. Make level paths for your feet") are especially interesting, in that they provide a practical agenda for the strengthening of weak spots in our personal discipline. The injunction to "make level paths for your feet" clearly means to choose a course that puts minimal stress on an area of personal weakness, as when a person consumed with envy of others might refrain from obtaining any knowledge about the performance and possessions of others in order not to open a window of opportunity for sin to occur. A voluntary refraining from opportunity for sin may give time for growth in strength to withstand sin.

Compare this view to that of cognitive-behavioral therapy's view of self-regulation (as did Bufford, 1977). Self-regulation involves developing awareness of the external factors that are powerful determinants of one's behavior and altering them deliberately to produce desired change (for instance, avoiding temptation situations and surrounding oneself with encouraging, strengthening influences), and also developing effective internal or cognitive control capacities through more effective self-observation and administration of consequences to the self (e.g., naming God's commandments, instructing and exhorting oneself). In this view, will is developed as a skill, and thus growth in self-control is possible, rather than being an unalterable personality trait caused by toilet-training practices, as in classical psychoanalysis. In this area there are meaningful compatibilities between cognitive-behavioral therapy and the biblical view of persons.

As with all the secular therapies, there is a danger in cognitive-behavioral therapy that the therapist will focus only on psychological change without any spiritual emphasis at all. The focus of cognitive-behavioral therapy is limited only to temporal aspects of personhood. Spiritual and religious matters have no intrinsic or integral part in the model. Reading a standard cognitive-behavioral therapy work, one would think that religion only existed as one rather unusual category of belief which occasionally crops up with a client, or as a nuisance variable that affects what a client values. Humans are not viewed as intrinsically religious or spiritual beings in this approach.

One final positive attribute of this approach is its idiographic emphasis. Cognitive-behavioral therapy embodies a high view of human uniqueness. Persons are not regarded as reducible to ten scales on a personality inventory. This idiographic method allows for some understanding of persons developmentally, but it makes no use of common schemes for understanding human development, such as the psychosocial scheme of Erikson. This is perhaps a good example of how the idiographic tendencies can be a curse as well as a blessing. The extreme embracing of uniqueness can mean that no two person's experience is comparable and that their development cannot be understood in common terms. This conclusion clearly seems too extreme.

Model of Psychotherapy
Perhaps no other therapy approach so closely mirrors a biblical balance of cognitive and action orientation as cognitive-behavioral therapy. Even a superficial reading of the pastoral exhortations of the New

Testament epistles yields a clear theme of obedience in actions and in thoughts as the way to maturity. If one looks at Philippians 3—4 or Ephesians 4, one sees clearly an exhortation to think new thoughts and engage in new deeds to germinate the seed of faith into full spiritual maturity. Perhaps the reason why Adams's (1973) nouthetic counseling and Crabb's (1977) biblical counseling are two of the more popular Christian counseling approaches is that both embody a combined behavioral and cognitive emphasis that parallels the theme of direct change expressed in Scripture. The real issue is whether this is the exclusive and/or dominant theme of Scripture. In any case, cognitive-behavioral therapy shares this focus.

Propst (1988) provocatively names one of her chapters "Spirituality of Action: Necessary Living Skills." In the chapter she develops some of the cognitive-behavioral strategies for returning a sense of control and effectiveness to clients in their daily lives. To the extent that this represents a God-honoring development of the capacity to exercise better stewardship over the portion of creation God has placed us in, this can certainly be a worthwhile set of procedures for Christians to embrace. To live effectively, we must be able to order the practical challenges of daily life by managing time and setting goals as well as knowing how to pray, how to communicate our feelings to our spouses and so on. The cognitive-behavioral approach assumes that many people experiencing problems of living lack one or more of these basic living skills and that directive therapy can correct these deficits.

But just as we discussed with behavior modification, the *amorality* of cognitive-behavioral therapy is problematic. "Amorality . . . refers to the modern separation of fact and value. . . . The goals of traditional psychotherapy were provided in large measure by theories of personality that supplied some definition of what people ought to be and a picture of optimal human functioning. . . . [Behavior therapy] is neutral with respect to what would constitute a personal ideal or ideal person" (Woolfolk and Richardson, 1984, pp. 780-781).

Thus, according to Woolfolk and Richardson, cognitive-behavioral therapists seem content to have their clients' values dictate the course of therapy, as we noted earlier. Because cognitive-behavioral therapy has a less well-developed notion of the ideal human state than such theories as person-centered therapy (chapter ten), it is difficult for cognitive-behavioral therapy to be a "growth" psychotherapy because there is no built-in compass pointing out the direction of growth. To read some cognitive-behavioral literature, one would get the constricted impression that growth means the absence of anxiety, depression and the major forms of discomfort; hence, to be fully human is to be without pain. This is a superficial and anemic view of human maturity. Cognitive-behavioral therapists, consequently, seem proficient at eliminating suffering (about which clients have focused goals) but less capable at producing growth. But this raises the provocative question of whether psychotherapy should be properly limited to healing or problem solving, leaving promotion of growth to such traditional resources as the church.

This amorality also has the problem of opening the door to relativism in terms of the values foisted on clients by therapists (Tan, 1987). At least with some therapies (e.g., person-centered therapy, chapter ten) one largely knows the values of the therapist by knowing her orientation. With cognitive-behavioral therapy, the therapist's orientation has little to do with values. The techniques can thus be pointed in many directions, as its abuses show. The example cited earlier of Lazarus (1980) teaching an adulterous woman to tolerate sex with her unloved husband is a classic example of the results of this deficit.

From a Christian perspective, the lack of prescriptive focus of cognitive-behavioral therapy actually can allow for a more comfortable utilization of the system by the Christian than some other systems. Some of the humanistic systems, it seems fair to say, have their humanistic values embedded deeply in the therapeutic process itself. For example, Gestalt therapy (chapter twelve) is procedurally a clear "incarnation" of humanistic values. The techniques of cognitive-behavioral therapy seem less value-encrusted and thus the system might be more effectively adapted for use by the religious therapist, as Propst has argued. Craigie and Tan (1989) provide a good example of cognitive-behavioral therapy well adapted to Christian use.

Propst's (1988) work raises some interesting issues regarding how the lack of a clear ideal can be troublesome even in religious counseling. Propst rightly points out that often the cognitions troubling a client are not in verbal propositional form (such as a wrong doctrinal belief) but are better described as troublesome images, such as a sexually abused woman experiencing fragmentary memories of her childhood abuse as she interacts with men. In her chapter "Image Transformations" Propst urges the explicit incorporation of religious imagery for religious women, specifically images of Christ. (This procedure is quite similar to the healing-of-memories approaches discussed briefly in chapter four.) She discusses different imagery interventions, such as the use of the image of surrendering our thoughts, emotions and experiences to Christ. This example would seem acceptable to almost all Christians, in that such surrendering seems an implication of the concept of the lordship of Christ.

Propst then moves on to examples that may be more troublesome to some Christians, examples that involve the person imaging Christ doing or saying things judged to be "therapeutic" but which may or may not fit his real character. The imagery examples that Propst shares include the image of Christ telling a woman that it is okay to be scared of breast cancer, of Christ rescuing and comforting a client when as a child she was being abused, and of Christ expressing acceptance and encouraging a woman who had experienced gang rape to touch him. The problem here is that we are making the Christ of our image do what we want or expect him to do in situations where his response may or may not be clear.

We have talked with clients who on their own have used even more troubling images for comfort in situations where some Christians would believe that Christ would speak rebuke. For example, a man who had just left his wife because of his agony due to being in a marriage with no love imagined Christ lovingly saying, "I understand. I have experienced unbearable agony too." In other words, he imagined Christ supporting his decision to desert his wife. Some would argue that in that situation Christ would really say, "Take up your cross and go back to your wife; follow me in obedience and I will sustain you." We risk twisting God into the shape we desire when we imagine specific responses on his part. At the same time, perhaps in many circumstances we can understand his character, his grace and his Law sufficiently to know with confidence what he would do. It will require real spiritual maturity and wisdom to understand when we are on firm ground in projecting the nature of his responses to us, and perhaps will require accountability to the church as well.

Some authors have suggested that the modeling emphasis in cognitive-behavioral therapy has its important parallels in Christian discipleship. Edwards (1976) compared Paul's exhortations for others to follow his example to the therapist's role as a positive model for the client. While cognitive-behavioral therapy embraces a more formal emphasis on modeling than other approaches, it would seem wrong to oversell this point. In fact, apart from modeling, the cognitive-behavioral approach actually pays less attention to the personhood of the therapist than most other models. If one construes the modeling impact of the therapist narrowly (such as the therapist showing the client how to behave and think in an assertiveness situation), cognitive-behavioral therapy emphasizes it more than other approaches. But if one considers the personal influence of the therapist more broadly, other approaches such as existential, person-centered and psychoanalytic therapies put more emphasis on the person of the therapist having a direct impact on the client.

Conclusion

Cognitive-behavioral therapy has at least the following strengths when evaluated from a Christian perspective: It posits limited freedom for the person, though the formal understanding of that freedom is incompatible with a Christian understanding of human responsibility. Cognitive-behavioral therapy appreciates the embodied, human aspect of our existence and has a well-articulated understanding of at least some of the person variables and processes which seem foundational to human action. The atomism of cognitive-behavioral therapy goes too far in dissolving the self, but it can help us see what is tangential and what is central to self. The ideographic style of behavioral assessment seems respectful of human uniqueness. An appreciation of the influence of the environment on behavior (though not environmental determinism) seems appropriate from a Christian perspective. The humbling and broad understanding of human motivation as basically selfish but complex is a strength. Cognitive-behavioral therapy's high view of rationality is a plus, though the standards of rationality must be modified for the Christian. The view of the centrality of habits of thought and action to making life adjustments seems realistic. The relatively less intrusive place of values, as reflected in its amorality and lack of a vision of maturity, makes it a somewhat more accessible tool for the Christian therapist than, say, Gestalt therapy. Finally, cognitive-behavioral therapy emphasizes empirical accountability in all aspects of its practice, and, for Christians, this accords well with a commitment to good stewardship of time and energies, and with a commitment to honesty.

In spite of all these positives, one is left with a clear sense that there is much more to human beings than cognitive-behavioral therapy would lead us to believe. Where is transcendence and spirituality? How do we understand self-deception or evil? Does this view really plumb the profound depths of relationships and the terrific impact we have on one another? Isn't emotion more than the output of cognitive habits? What about conflict within the person; isn't this inevitable and indeed helpful to us understanding what it means to be truly human? How are we to grow? Are there any important regularities to the way we develop as human beings? Cognitive-behavioral therapy's silence on each of these questions is disconcerting.

It seems likely that we are what cognitive-behavioral therapy depicts us as being: thinking and acting creatures of habit who act upon and are acted upon by our environments for the purpose of obtaining that which we value. But it also seems clear to the Christian that we are more than this. Nevertheless, given its many strengths, cognitive-behavioral therapy is likely to be one of the more fruitful models for Christians to explore for its integrative potentials.

For further reading

Dobson, K. (Ed.). (1988). *Handbook of cognitive-behavioral therapies*. New York: Guilford.

An informative professional handbook for this approach.

Meichenbaum, D. (1977). *Cognitive-behavior modification*. New York: Plenum.

One of the original ground-breaking proposals for moving beyond traditional behavior modification.

Propst, R. (1988). *Psychotherapy in a religious framework: Spirituality in the emotional healing process.* New York: Human Sciences Press.

Perhaps the most fully developed religious approach to counseling based on cognitive-behavioral therapy.

Tan, S. (1987). Cognitive-behavior therapy: A biblical approach and critique. *Journal of Psychology and Theology, 15,* 103-112.

A helpful article.

References

Adams, J. (1973). *The Christian counselor's manual.* Grand Rapids, MI: Baker.

Bandura, A. (1978). The self system in reciprocal determinism. *American Psychologist, 33,* 344-358.

Bandura, A. (1986). *Social foundations of thought and action.* Englewood Cliffs, NJ: Prentice-Hall.

Bandura, A. (1989). Human agency in social cognitive theory. *American Psychologist, 44,* 1175-1184.

Beck, A. (1988). *Love is never enough.* New York: Harper & Row.

Beck, A., and Emery, G. (1985). *Anxiety disorders and phobias.* New York: Basic Books.

Beck, A.; Rush, A.; Hollon, S.; and Shaw, B. (1979). *Cognitive therapy of depression.* New York: Guilford.

Bufford, R. (1977). *The human reflex: Behavioral psychology in biblical perspective.*

San Francisco: Harper & Row.

Crabb, L. (1977). *Effective biblical counseling.* Grand Rapids, MI: Zondervan.

Craigie, F., and Tan, S. (1989). Changing resistant assumptions in Christian cognitive-behavioral therapy. *Journal of Psychology and Theology, 17,* 93-100.

Dobson, K., and Block, L. (1988). Historical and philosophical bases of the cognitive-behavioral therapies. In K. Dobson (Ed.), *Handbook of cognitive-behavioral therapies* (pp. 3-38). New York: Guilford.

Edwards, K. (1976). Effective counseling and psychotherapy: An integrative review of the research. *Journal of Psychology and Theology, 5,* 94-107.

Evans, C. (1986, January 17). The blessings of mental anguish. *Christianity Today,* pp. 26-30.

Evans, C. (1989). *Wisdom and humanness in psychology.* Grand Rapids, MI: Baker.

Foster, R. (1978). *Celebration of discipline.* San Francisco: Harper & Row.

Hodges, B. (1976). Toward a model of psychological man and his science. *Christian Scholar's Review, 6,* 3-19.

Jacobson, N., and Margolin, G. (1979). *Marital therapy.* New York: Brunner/Mazel.

Jones, S. (1988). A religious critique of behavior therapy. In W. Miller and J. Martin (Eds.), *Behavior therapy and religion* (pp. 139-170). Newbury Park, CA: Sage.

Kanfer, F. (1979). Personal control, social control, and altruism: Can society survive the age of individualism? *American Psychologist, 34,* 231-239.

Kendall, P., and Bemis, K. (1983). Thought and action in psychotherapy: The cognitive-behavioral approaches. In M. Hersen, A. Kazdin, and A. Bellack (Eds.), *The clinical psychology handbook* (pp. 565-592). New York: Pergamon.

Kreeft, P. (1986). *Making sense out of suffering.* Ann Arbor, MI: Servant.

Lazarus, A. (1980). Treatment of dyspareunia. In S. Leiblum and L. Pervin (Eds.), *Principles and practice of sex therapy* (pp. 147-166). New York: Guilford.

Marlatt, G. (1982). Relapse prevention: A self-control program for the treatment of addictive behaviors. In R. Stuart (Ed.). *Adherence, compliance and generalization in behavioral medicine* (pp. 329-378). New York: Brunner/Mazel.

McFall, R. (1982). A review and reformulation of the concept of social skills. *Behavioral Assessment, 4,* 1-33.

Meichenbaum, D. (1977). *Cognitive-behavior modification.* New York: Plenum.

Meichenbaum, D. (1985). *Stress inoculation training.* New York: Pergamon.

Mischel, W. (1973). Toward a cognitive social learning reconceptualization of personality. *Psychological Review, 80,* 252-285.

Pecheur, D. (1978). Cognitive theory/therapy and sanctification. *Journal of Psychology and Theology, 6,* 239-253.

Propst, R. (1988). *Psychotherapy in a religious framework: Spirituality in the emotional healing process.* New York: Human Sciences Press.

Sperry, R. (1980). Mind-brain interactionism: Mentalism, yes; dualism, no. *Neuroscience, 5,* 195-206.

Stuart, R. (1980). *Helping couples change.* New York: Guilford.

Tan, S. (1987). Cognitive-behavior therapy: A biblical approach and critique. *Journal of Psychology and Theology, 15,* 103-112.

Van Leeuwen, M. (1985). *The person in psychology.* Grand Rapids, MI: Eerdmans.

Woolfolk, R., and Richardson, F. (1984). Behavior therapy and the ideology of modernity. *American Psychologist, 39,* 777-786.

Wren, T. (1982). Social learning theory, self-regulation, and morality. *Ethics, 92,* 409-424.

9

ADLERIAN AND REALITY THERAPIES

❖

*T*he work of Alfred Adler has been very influential in the secular counseling field. As we shall see below, it is in many ways one of the most adaptable systems for religious counselors. Despite this, it has received little attention. Adler's ideas are widely used professionally but seldom attributed to the original theoretician.

The work of Adler is not easily categorized. It is sometimes listed among the psychodynamic psychologies, sometimes among the humanistic, and sometimes among the cognitive-behavioral. We are following the latter approach because of Adler's emphasis on cognition, choice and shorter-term directive counseling.

Adler was a sickly child who overcame physical difficulties (including rickets) and an unimpressive start in school (a teacher urged his father to place him in training to become a cobbler) to attend medical school. Adler moved from ophthalmology to general practice, neurology and finally to psychiatry. He was, for a time, a colleague and collaborator with Freud. Conflict ensued when Adler began to advocate views of his own which, in Freud's eyes, underestimated the importance of sexual drives and psychic determinism. Adler resigned as president of the Vienna Psychoanalytic Society and a permanent split developed with Freud, who openly expressed contempt for the work of his former colleague.

In the remaining twenty-six years of his life, Adler was a tireless speaker, author and innovator in America and Europe. He did not narrowly focus on therapy, but was also interested in what are now called preventative community psychology interventions and indeed social change as a means of promoting human welfare. Uytman (1967) characterized Adler as more of a preacher than a scientist toward the end of his career, in that he offered little scientific proof for his ideas or documentation of the effectiveness of his work. He tended to use the same case examples over and over in his writings, and it is unclear how many clients he saw in a sustained fashion given his demanding travels and frequent relocations.

Despite Adler's vigor, the decimation of war-torn Europe and the ascendency of behaviorism and psychoanalysis in America restricted the success of the Adlerian system. The model continued to be promulgated after his death by a few devoted followers, and it is safe to say that the system is probably enjoying more popularity now than ever in its history. It is commonly suggested that the greatest sign of the influence of Adlerian ideas is that they find their way into other models, whether explicitly noted or not. For example, one of the first major disagreements between Freud and Adler was the latter's early postulation of an aggression drive; Freud initially dismissed Adler's hypothesis, but over fifteen years later incorporated such a drive into his theories (long after Adler had rejected his own hypothesis). It is commonly noted that Adler has influenced the thought of the ego psychologies, rational-emotive therapy, family therapy and many other systems (e.g., Corey, 1986, pp. 66-67).

Descriptive Survey

Philosophical Assumptions
Brink (1985b) has described five major "sources" or inspirations for Adler's thought. From Janet, Adler took the general idea of the

significance of inferiority feelings. From Nietzsche, he adapted the notion of striving for superiority. From Vaihinger, he took the idea of the "guiding fiction," the "as if" relativism of a subjective understanding of the person. From Marx, he absorbed the ideal of service to the social order which came to be expressed as the concern for "social interest." And from Freud, he took a general dynamic orientation, including the emphasis on early childhood experience and the purposefulness of neurotic symptoms.

It seems significant that Adler was an adult convert from Judaism to "liberal protestantism" (Brink, 1977) and was a socialist by political conviction (Brink, 1985a). The European Christian church was in a period of decline during the first three decades of this century; "classic liberalism" was at its zenith, and more purely social understandings of the gospel were in ascendancy. We will further develop this relationship later.

One of the most important influences on Adler was a variant of idealism, Vaihinger's "as if" philosophy, the notion that the "guiding fictions" that persons lived by were the major determinants of choice and action. These ideas were to be judged by their functional impact rather than their truth per se. Vaihinger actually described truth as "merely the most expedient error" (in Ansbacher and Ansbacher, 1956, p. 83), meaning that truth is the myth that happens to work best. To understand persons, then, one need not understand the reality they live in but must understand the world as they perceive it, the myths they live by.

This is clearly a relativistic and subjective understanding of the person. For example, Mosak (1984, p. 60) has said, "Life has no intrinsic meaning. We give meaning to life, each of us in his own fashion." Guiding fictions are thus more important than reality, and there are doubts that reality can really be known at all.

Adler believed that the ultimate causes of behavior were the final goals that a person embraced; these goals were considered *myths*. The notion of ultimate causation is Aristotelian in origin. Adler dubbed his own position "fictional finalism." His view was a teleological one wherein a person chooses actions in order to attain the goals to which he or she is committed. As Erikson (1984, p. 131) stated, Adler saw "the person as holistically pursuing self-selected goals." Thus for Adler the cause of a person's depression would be the person's goal of minimizing risk, rather than the childhood events that shaped the goal.

Adler rejected the hard determinism of Freud in favor of a notion of human freedom bounded by the subjective world of the person; we make real choices, but do so in the context of a subjective world that channels or shapes the actions.

Adler also rejected the biological scientific approach to persons that typified Freud in favor of what is today termed a "human science" (Evans, 1977) approach that does not attempt to reduce the distinctively human to universal laws formulated in a narrowly scientific fashion. Related to this, Adler insisted on a holistic approach to persons. To dissect a person into parts (such as Freud's id, ego and superego) was to risk reducing the person to an impersonal system. Thus persons were to be regarded as "indivisible." (This is why Adler's system is also known as *individual psychology*. This phrase is based on the Latin word *individium* for indivisible or holistic.)

Model of Personality

Adler argued that the fundamental ground out of which persons grew was a perception of *inferiority*; as he frequently said, "to live is to feel inferior." This was unquestionably true for Adler personally as he struggled against the burdens of physical frailty and academic underachievement in childhood. All children, according to Adler, by virtue of their size and lesser capabilities, feel inferior. It is out of experience that the drive to feel *significant* emerges. We crave a sense of mastery, purposefulness and meaning, and this becomes the prime motivator of adult life.

In the context of family, persons begin a battle to cope with their feelings of inferiority. Family has a potent impact on growing children in shaping the fictions that they live by. Adler was a major figure in drawing attention to birth order and the *psychological* position of the child in the family as a prime determinant of personality. Family interactions impart an understanding of life and the child's place in it. *[margin note: Birth order]*

Out of the raw material imparted by family, the developing person forms the *lifestyle*, a psychological map of self and world that becomes our guide for action as we strive to overcome feelings of inferiority. Mosak (1984) has understood the lifestyle to be composed of four elements: the *self-concept*, or view of the self "as is"; the *self-ideal*, or self as one ought to be; the *picture of the world*, one's model or "myth" about why things work as they do outside of oneself; and one's *ethical convictions*. This map determines who we each are, as it determines the choices we make.

Adler also proposed that we each have common life tasks to be worked out in the course of normal living; these were the tasks of living in the *society* of others, the task of *work* or occupation, and the task of sex or marriage. To these three, Mosak and Dreikurs (see Mosak, 1984) added the *religious* task of determining one's relationship to the ultimate and the task of *coping with one's self*. We approach meeting these tasks quite differently depending on the lifestyles we have developed.

Model of Health

Adler believed that it is normal to have problems to cope with; in fact, life tasks are ongoing problems that every person must continually cope with, as no problem is ever solved perfectly. The healthy person is likely to have grown up in a family where the parents modeled how to choose attainable goals and effective and flexible ways of understanding and solving problems. These people are likely to have a functional, or productive, lifestyle that guides them well in dealing with life's puzzles and problems. Most significant problems are with persons, not with the impersonal world, which is why Adler always emphasized the social dimension of life.

When persons are functioning well, they will naturally embrace what Adler viewed as the highest value, *social interest*. This is a concern for the welfare of others (in both broad and narrow senses), or "a sense of identification and empathy with others" (Corey, 1986, p. 49). The person who is solving problems well but is ultimately only out for himself is actually a troubled person who has what Adlerians call "faulty values."

Health, for the Adlerian, is not being "omnicompetent" or above life's difficulties. Adler said that to live well we must have the "courage to be imperfect." Healthy persons have the courage to do their best to accomplish the tasks of life as they understand them, to take risks and be content to do "good enough" rather than perfectly, and thus to face life squarely without evasion or excuse. Part of living is falling short and being imperfect. The healthy person continues to grow and cope with life with courage and concern for others.

Model of Abnormality

We all face life's tasks with an imperfect lifestyle, but people vary in terms of how the tasks are understood by virtue of differences in the lifestyle, what kinds of attempts at resolution are indicated by the lifestyle, and different ways of coping with the feelings of inferiority we have each inevitably experienced.

The heart of the Adlerian view of abnormality is the concept of *discouragement.* When people lose courage for directly facing life's demands and achieving significance, they may move from having inferiority feelings to having an *inferiority complex* (a concept which originated with Adler).

In this discouraged state where people are unconsciously convinced of inferiority, they engage in face-saving maneuvers to divert their own attention from the troubling feelings. The classic example of this is the development of neurotic symptomatology, which benefits the person by serving as an excuse for why he or she cannot meet life's demands: "How could anyone do well at their work when someone is as depressed as I am?" The neurotic symptoms protect people from having to struggle with their discouragement, as they can passively wait for the problems to dissipate or search for someone to cure them. They can protect their fragile self-esteem by not demanding much of themselves while they are thus indisposed.

Model of Psychotherapy

Therapy becomes a process of encouragement and change of the life-style for Adlerians. It is conceived to progress through four phases (Dinkmeyer, Pew and Dinkmeyer, 1979). The first phase is that of the *establishment of a cooperative relationship* with the client. This is facilitated by trust, respect, encouragement and a clear understanding of therapeutic goals. Next follows the phase of *analysis and assessment* of the lifestyle, in which interview techniques are used to understand how clients see themselves and their world and what their goals are. A frequently used technique is that of "early recollections." It is assumed that our earliest memory or memories give vital information about our fundamental view of ourselves. The third phase is that of *interpretation resulting in insight,* wherein the therapist begins to broaden the understanding of the client regarding the way that the person's lifestyle shapes his or her experience. Finally, "in the *reorientation* phase, counselor and counselee work together to consider alternative attitudes, beliefs, and actions" (Dinkmeyer, Pew and Dinkmeyer, 1979, p. 98). Adlerian counselors attempt to intervene cognitively and behaviorally to facilitate change.

Christian Critique

The Adlerian approach appears easily compatible with the "liberal Christianity" of Europe in Adler's day. Adler participated in a church that asserted that God exists and has revealed himself as the one who loves and desires faithful union with each person, that Christ was a man (and not the only one) through whom God manifested himself to humanity, that Christ showed us through his life and death that we are to strive to actualize the Godlikeness within us and to love one another, that what we ultimately need is courage to trust in our Godlikeness, that the mythic spiritual reality of Christ's resurrection is our inspiration to live in the face of what seems like difficulty and defeat, and finally that the specifics of theological dogma do not matter as much as whether what one believes inspires one to faithfulness and actualization of the God within. The "cash value" of such a faith can be measured, it was sometimes said, by how one treats one's fellow persons.

The Adlerian notion of religion is somewhat akin to the view we just sketched. Adler regarded the idea of God as "a concretization of the idea of perfection, greatness, and superiority" (quoted in Ansbacher and Ansbacher, 1956, p. 460). God, then, is seen as a projection of our own psyche (which was the same view as Freud's). Adler seems to have regarded the idea of God as a *psychological* concretization of an idea or impulse, and thus a projection, rather than as a particularization of a Platonic ideal as may have been typical for the liberal Christianity of his day. For orthodox Christians, God is certainly the fulfillment of perfection; the issue is whether he exists as the Creator-King who is perfect, or is a projection of our psyches because we need a concrete image of the perfect.

According to Brink (1977, p. 147), Adlerians today typically believe that "religion is health promoting insofar as it alleviates an individual's own self-bounded concern with his demise and encourages him to contribute to the welfare of the ongoing social order," and it is on this basis that so many Adlerians feel an easy kinship with the pastoral community, believing that therapists and pastors are all after the same goals (see also Baruth and Manning, 1987). Since this is presumed to be the goal and function of religion, it is clear that religious faith per se becomes a mere primitive transitional step toward the triumph of social interest based more directly on "intellectual clarification" and secularized "religious feeling" (Adler quoted in Ansbacher and Ansbacher, 1956, p. 462). Gibson (1985) rightly reported that Adler saw no serious conflict between his psychology and Christianity. Gibson seems to concur with Adler's view, but we would argue that the conflicts have been minimized by Adler's "demythologized" understanding of Christianity. Similarly, many of the enthusiastic articles compiled by

Huber (1987) on commonalities between pastoral and Adlerian counseling are based on subtle or obvious demythologizations of the Christian message. Christianity, stripped of its distinctive doctrines and transcendent realities, is rather easily melded with Adlerian psychology.

In his work of integration, Brink (1977) did not evaluate Adlerian psychology in light of Christian faith, but rather tried to see if the gospel could be satisfactorily translated into Adlerian terms. This made Adlerian thought, not Christian doctrine, the measure of truth. Brink's application provides some interesting and helpful interpretations, however, such as an understanding of the ups and downs of the Hebrews' obedience to God in the Old Testament as a paradigmatic example of the fruits of neurotic avoidance of a courageous and obedient life with God. In Brink's Adlerian perspective, the tension between law and grace is illuminated; law is fruitless, as one either succeeds and becomes arrogant or fails and feels inferior, while grace provides the solution of encouraging us, through God's acceptance, to live a courageous, responsive life of obedience.

But Brink's analysis significantly distorts orthodox Christianity at crucial points. Sin becomes "the improper attitude one has about his defects" (1977, p. 148). The Fall then must become "the realization of inferiority feeling" (1985b, p. 572), and therefore salvation is a purely psychological phenomenon and faith a therapy rather than the basis for a relationship with God. Brink (1977, p. 148) says, "Faith is faith in oneself as a child of God and serves to break the power of inferiority feeling." The metaphysical richness of the Christian understanding of our situation thus is reduced to mere psychological perceptions.

Brink claims individual psychology is more compatible with Christian doctrine than classic psychoanalysis, but establishes this only by reinterpreting the gospel in Adlerian terms. For the orthodox believer, sin, salvation and so forth may have some of the characteristics described by Brink, but they are certainly much more than what he claims. In the dialog between a therapy theory and Christianity, it can be fruitful to do such a translation, as our understanding of Christian doctrine and experience can be expanded, but we must be careful that distortion not be introduced in the process.

Philosophical Assumptions

Using Christian belief as our benchmark, we can first applaud Adler's embracing of a "humanized" understanding of the role of science in understanding humanity. Human beings are not purely naturalistic phenomena that can be understood reductionistically in terms of chemical hormone reactions and neuronal firings. It does seem, however, that Adler overreacted against the scientific attitudes of Freud and did not properly appreciate the appropriate place for empirical scientific study in understanding humanity. Evans (1989) presents a balanced picture of the relationship between these two understandings of science, and Christians interested in Adler's approach would do well to strive for such a balance.

Adler's resolution of the issue of causality is one Christians may well desire to embrace. He rejects hard determinism in favor of a limited libertarianism. Choice and human responsibility are emphasized, but always with an appreciation for the formative impact of family and the person's lifestyle (Anderson, 1970). Erikson (1984, p. 134) calls Adler's resolution of this problem brilliant, noting that "by making a distinction between 'purposeful' and 'on purpose,' as it were, he succeeds in investing the individual with responsibility without at the same time moralistically blaming him for his actions." In this fashion, we can look at an adult characterized by narcissistic preoccupation and see that she holds some responsibility for the decisions that brought her to her current condition, in that she was acting purposefully in creating her symptoms. Yet we are not forced to pretend that she made a deliberate decision to become what she is. Adler's views are indeed a welcome balance between the determinism of behaviorism and the radical freedom of the humanistic psychologies.

It may well be that a fully developed Christian psychology would place greater emphasis than Adlerians on human finitude, evil and the powerful influences from outside ourselves that Adler seemed to minimize. His is definitely an optimistic psychology, a precursor of the humanistic psychologies, and is another example of belief in the powerful individual who can transform one's life by changing how one thinks about it. Such a view can risk "blaming the victim" at times, imputing responsibility to a person when the person actually was powerless in the face of overwhelming external forces.

Adlerian psychology is ultimately a relativistic psychology. Everyone, it is argued, has a guiding fiction, and the relative merits of each fiction are only to be judged by how they aid the pursuit of social interest. As Hester (1987) has correctly pointed out, our religion would suggest that we are beings who live by stories; if this were not so, why would so much of the Scriptures be parables and life stories? But a Christian psychology, while it can and must appreciate the subjective side of our lives, cannot be relativistic. Christianity presumes objective commonalities among all people and a truth that transcends human existence, with the result that values and beliefs must be measured by ultimate standards.

This firm stance must be balanced by a humble recognition that while truth exists, Christians never possess it perfectly, and that the psychological beliefs that are of concern to Adlerians are often as amenable to nonreligious analysis as to a religious one. For example, Christians and Adlerians alike can recognize that the lifestyle belief "you have to step on people to get to the top because that is all that matters" is wrong, but they would probably diverge on why it is wrong and what to replace that belief with.

With their understanding of causation, Adlerians view humans as fundamentally teleological, goal-directed, and this certainly fits with a Christian view of persons. At a descriptive level, humans seem characterized in Scripture as goal-oriented, whether the goals being pursued are the gratification of our own appetites or the glorification of the Father. Adlerians suggest that a major part of growth is the choosing of the correct goals (which for them always involve social interest); Christians can certainly agree that health is intertwined with pursuit of the right ends.

Individual psychology is a value psychology, and this is a plus for the approach. According to Adlerians, social interest is the highest intrinsic value. Christians can applaud this value, especially when it is contrasted to the purely humanistic psychology values of RET and person-centered therapy that boil down to self-gratification.

Charity, which parallels social interest, is among the premier Christian values, and no Christian can think of social interest without reflecting on "loving our neighbor as ourselves". (Anderson, 1970; this is a recurrent theme in Huber, 1987, as well). But the soils for the two values are vastly different; for Adler, social interest is the pinnacle value because humans are "the center of the world" (Adler quoted in Ansbacher and Ansbacher, 1956, p. 461) and hence are to be worshiped, in a sense. For Christians, charity is rooted in humans being created in God's image. They are thus not to be worshiped. Rather, we serve God in some profound way through our service to persons (e.g., the parable of the sheep and goats, Mt 25:31-46). And charity at a horizontal level, directed only at other human beings, is not the premier human value; it only achieves that place when it is directed at God first and then others.

Finally, holism is a vital philosophic commitment of individual psychology and a characteristic of the Christian view of persons as well. Van Leeuwen (1987) cites theologian Berkouwer's conclusion that Scripture consistently maintains a holistic emphasis in its understanding of persons, and in this way the Adlerian approach is similar to that of Scripture.

But Scripture does not forbid a more atomistic focus, it simply focuses at a more general level because the main purpose of scriptural revelation is redemptive, not psychological. To pursue salvation, a person must understand how God views him or her as a whole. Yet a more atomistic understanding may be essential for personal change as opposed to salvation. So the focus of Scripture on the unity of persons cannot be seen as forbidding a more atomistic analysis. As with all holistic theories, this approach can be frustrating in its lack of specificity for why things occur as they do. One must raise the question of whether holism is a cop-out for lack of explanatory power, on the one hand, or a strategically maintained distinctive on the other.

Models of Personality and Health

There is an obvious parallel between the two primary Adlerian drives of superiority and social interest and the two motives we abstracted from the Christian creation story in chapter two, namely the dominion and relational motives. Human beings, in a Christian perspective, are designed for purposeful work, accrue self-esteem from that pursuit and gain affirmation and acceptance from interacting productively in a relational context. Note also that Adler's three original life tasks were the occupational task (a parallel to the dominion task), the task of marriage (a clear parallel to the relational task) and the task of relating in society. The last can unquestionably be regarded as an extension of the relational task, in that we must relate productively outside of marriage to our families and our society.

Adler's theory is unique in describing not just psychological structures, drives and processes, but tasks as well, and this comports well with the Christian understanding of persons having tasks to fulfill. The two tasks added by later Adlerians, those of religious belief and commitment and of coping with oneself, are positive additions. It is commonly noted that the Fall fractured our relationships with every part of our existence; with God, other persons, the material universe and with ourselves. The last two tasks address the repair of two of these fractures (cf. Baruth and Manning, 1987).

Adlerian psychology has been termed a common-sense psychology; this could be taken as a compliment, but is it too much so? In other words, if it makes great intuitive sense, is this an indication that it is too superficial? All complaints about superficiality are actually concealed theoretical complaints; your theory does not illuminate what my theory says should be illuminated, and therefore your theory is too superficial. The standard Adlerian reply to complaints of superficiality is to suggest that those who complain of superficiality have not mined the depths of the approach for its richness. And this approach is certainly more oriented toward understanding the childhood/historical roots of human problems than many approaches, and thus it is still generally regarded as a "depth psychology."

We will bring up one specific concern of superficiality. Adler's theory is what Maddi (in Van Leeuwen, 1987) would call a fulfill-ment theory of personality. It is an approach that suggests that humans have only one motive, one which can be "purified" by directing it toward serving or manifesting the ideal virtues that a person must embody in order to grow into health. The motive of striving for significance can be thwarted or distorted in the un-healthy person, but in the healthy person it is channeled in the direction of service to others (social interest). Christianity, it would seem, would be oriented toward viewing humans as necessarily in conflict, as experiencing the pain of ever-present choice between conflicting motives. We are pulled God-ward, but run from God at the same time. This is a more pessimistic view of the person, one which views conflict as unending and endemic.

For Adler, persons must ultimately be understood in social con-text; it is in relationships that humans have their meaning. Erikson (1984) correctly suggests that this is a strong point of contact with Christianity. Erikson criticizes the "Christian individualism" (p. 132) that so characterizes conservatives, and notes that humans properly understood in biblical perspective are always "humans-in-community." This is a point stressed by McDonald (1981, pp. 43-44) when he wrote that in Hebrew thought, "the individual was summed up, as it were, in the community. . . . Yet [at] no time was the individual quite lost." Psychological theories tend to be either individualistic (especially the humanistic theories) or collectivistic (family therapy)—in the former, community disappears; in the latter, the individual disappears. Adler's views, on the other hand, are a healthy balance of the individual rooted in relationships.

The key to normalcy for Adler is the virtue of courage. Mosak (1984, p. 59) noted that for the Adlerian, "Courage refers to the willingness to engage in risk-taking behavior when one either does not know the consequences or when the consequences might be adverse." Haavik (1986) argued that while courage per se is not a clear Christian virtue, a comparable Christian virtue would be a willingness to hear and obey God's law and Word. Such a willing obedience for the Christian would seem to flow from a clear perception of our creaturely status, of God's status as the rightful lawgiver and beneficent Father who is disciplining his children, and from a perception of the obstacles to obedience as inconsequential compared to the rewards for faithful service to God (e.g., Rom 8:12-25).

There are some direct parallels to the Adlerian notion of courage as well. As Christians, we are called to live as imperfect persons in an imperfect world, to have the courage to do the best we are capable of right now and to commit ourselves to our life tasks without evasion or excuse, serving others courageously and sacrificially. We walk a delicate balance of striving for the highest calling of perfect life in Christ, but realize that we will never achieve this perfection and must continually find acceptance from God not through our worthiness but through God's forgiveness. (This closely parallels the understanding of Christian existentialism we have developed in chapter eleven.) Haavik also notes that Adlerian courage appears to be largely an individual virtue, while for Christians, encouragement is truly to be a corporate function (1 Thess 5:14).

Many have suggested that Adler was an early cognitive-behavioral theorist. As Dowd and Kelly (1980) have noted, there are many parallels between Adlerian psychology and cognitive-behavioral therapy. The core similarities between the two include that both are future-oriented in their view of the sources of human motivation; both are cognitive psychologies which emphasize the subjectivity of the person's view of the world; both are idiographic, preferring an individual focus in the understanding of the person; both emphasize the social/interactional nature of existence; and both share some striking similarities in how they conceive of and structure the therapy process. The cognitive- behavioral approach is more well developed in terms of scientific articulation of its hypothesized personality processes and in terms of intervention techniques, while the Adlerian approach has the advantages of a more articulated view of developmental processes in the family context and shows an existential perspective that is sorely lacking in cognitive-behavioral therapy.

Model of Abnormality

Both Adlerian psychology and Christianity recognize the human propensity for self-deception. Is it understood the same way? Adlerian self-deception occurs as an attempt to preserve self-esteem; we are consumed with fear of inferiority, and shy away from a forthright confrontation of our own limitations. Christians could accept this explanation as part of the motivation for our self-deception, but would go beyond this to more sinister motives. We are not just struggling with our finitude, but we are also in rebellion against God. We justify ourselves and rationalize our disobedience by the lies we speak to ourselves. Ours is a culpable self-deception worthy of judgment (Rom 1:18—2:2). Persons in the Adlerian view are merely discouraged persons needing encouragement; in the Christian view we are this, but are pre-eminently fallen beings deserving judgment. Thus self-deception assumes an uglier, more profound meaning in the Christian understanding.

Self-deception, for the Adlerian, is a result of discouragement. Discouragement as the source of pathology may be too bland and benign a concept by itself. It is assumed that people possess all the resources they really need to make themselves well, but they are discouraged and hence not utilizing their resources. This view suggests that people do not really become enslaved to real problems, that there are not really problems that exhaust a person's capabilities. In short, this denies some of the real difficulty of change.

This emphasis on neurosis as discouragement rather than sickness does have a positive side for Christians: It restores a modicum of responsibility to the person, as we expressed earlier. Discouragement is a vital part of psychological struggle, but it must be complemented by a more profound grasp of our finitude and need for help from resources outside ourselves.

A case study of Adler's treatment of guilt may flesh these concepts out. As Erikson (1984) has argued, Adler believed that we shape our own emotional experience by our lifestyle assumptions. Adler did not often address the "normal" experience of guilt feelings, but found pathological guilt a fascinating emotion. Most mature believers have known individuals consumed with guilt, immobilized by self-reproach. Adler's interpretation of this phenomenon (in Ansbacher and Ansbacher, 1956) was that guilt can be a tool used to control others through the pity or confusion engendered by their reactions. It can also be a ploy to counter inferiority feelings by striving to feel one's guilt in a way superior to others, or it can be an excuse to push away others that are threatening. Most generally, guilt is a diversion that allows one to be preoccupied with "the useless side of life" (quoted in Ansbacher and Ansbacher, 1956, p. 272) and thus to be excused from meaningful action in service of social interest (Erikson, 1984). The person consumed with unending guilt cannot be reproached and can be excused from moving onward. Adler also saw a positive function of legitimate guilt, that being the encouragement of "active contrition" (quoted in Ansbacher and Ansbacher, 1956, p. 307). This is certainly one facet of godly repentance in the Christian tradition. These are insightful possibilities for explaining prolonged and inappropriate guilt.

But throughout his discussions, Adler never viewed guilt as the justifiable or right reaction to the violation of a moral absolute. One could say that this is an omission due to his focus on pathologically sustained or intense reactions, but his lack of belief in a transcendent lawgiver or moral code (beyond the outline of social interest) would suggest that this dimension of the phenomenon of guilt is not just a casual omission.

It is commonplace today to attribute almost all psychological disturbance to inferiority feelings or low self-esteem, and in this context, Adler's view has strong appeal. Yet Myers (1981) has suggested that an overinflation of our view of ourselves, pride, is a more pervasive problem in our contemporary society than feelings of inferiority. Perhaps today's pervasive complaint of low self-esteem is a manifestation of our desire to think extremely highly of ourselves, to even deify ourselves, resulting in a general discontent that we cannot be perfectly content with ourselves and feel consistently superior, significant and respected.

Many Christians seem perilously close to reinterpreting the core of the gospel into a prescription for self-acceptance rather than one of forgiveness for sin. Adler's approach can be faulted for not targeting pride as prominently as it does inferiority. And yet Adler does grapple with inflated views of the self, regarding them as poor attempts to compensate with inferiority feelings. Adler may be correct that feelings of inferiority developmentally predate pride, but analytic theorists would insist that infantile narcissism predates feelings of inferiority. At these early ages, it is unlikely that infantile narcissism can be equated with adult pride.

Model of Psychotherapy

We are most powerfully struck by the compatibility of Adlerian thought with Christianity when we examine its model of psychotherapy. The volume edited by Huber (1987) is full of interesting examples of such applications. We will look at the person and role of the therapist, the understanding of the change process and the modalities of change.

Mosak (1984, p. 73) describes "the Christian virtues of faith, hope, and love" as necessary ingredients of a good therapy relationship. There could hardly be a more ideal or a more challenging group of characteristics for a therapist to embody. But to Mosak, faith is "faith in the therapeutic process," hope is anticipation of change and love is merely the feeling that the therapist cares. The Christian virtues of faith, hope and love (1 Cor 13) are much more than this and would indeed provide an ideal foundation for change to occur. (We will develop our own ideas for the ideal character of the therapist in chapter sixteen.) Arnold (1987) describes well some of the parallels between the Christian and Adlerian understandings of the impact of respect and acceptance on psychological functioning.

This approach is very much in line with the biblical balance between cognitive/verbal intervention, on the one hand, and the importance of action on the other (cf. Huber, 1986). All Adlerians suggest that cognitive change must yield practical fruit of behavioral change, and if this is not forthcoming spontaneously, it must be deliberately programmed.

Ephesians 4:17-32 contains, in the opinion of Christian counselor Jay E. Adams, the crucial formula for change in biblical perspective. Verses 23-24 explain that we are "to be made new in the attitude of your minds; and to put on the new self, created to be like God in true righteousness and holiness." The former clause clearly refers to significant cognitive change, and the latter we would judge to be interpreted correctly by Adams (1979) as calling for the adoption of a new righteous behavior pattern. Both the cognitive and behavioral change must, in the view of Adams, be grounded in the active work of the Holy Spirit. Any secularized approach to therapy cannot claim this as an operative factor.

The basic procedures of Adlerian counseling are, when closely examined, skeletal at best. They involve interpretation and direct confrontation to produce cognitive change, and task-setting and securing commitments to act on therapeutic plans to change behavior. Adlerians have developed a number of interesting specific techniques, such as "spitting in the client's soup" by revealing the real purpose of his symptomatic behavior and thus making it no longer serve its hidden purpose, but these specific techniques do not provide the level of structure for the overall therapy process that one finds in, say, cognitive-behavioral therapy.

Adlerians regard people with problems as undersocialized and in need of having their beliefs brought in line with the average person and then being infused with courage to act rightly in social interest. At its worst, this can reduce to a formula familiar to some superficial approaches to Christian counseling; "Do two good deeds and you'll feel better in the morning."

In their analysis of clients' lifestyles, Adlerians look for cognitive errors that are ostensibly judged in functional terms, but this judgment process appears actually to come from an absolute point of view. Mosak, for example, discusses "faulty values" and "basic mistakes" (1984; see also Dinkmeyer, Pew and Dinkmeyer, 1979, p. 93); note that the mistakes are always mistakes and not just beliefs that sometimes do not work for some people. This parallels the value-committed nature of RET and other therapies. Christians would certainly agree that there are faulty values, but we would contend that we must have a sure basis for judgment about such matters. A Christian basis for such would be the message of Scripture, aided by the spiritual gift of discernment.

Regarding modalities of change, we would argue that an understanding of human change processes limited to face-to-face verbal modalities is too limited, and Adlerians would heartily agree. Adler was one of the first to implement prevention work in establishing child-guidance centers and was an ardent promoter of parent education to enhance parental effectiveness and child welfare. Adler even evidenced a sensitivity to cultural factors influencing mental health, especially in his outspoken support of equal rights for women. A Christian understanding of persons would necessarily appreciate the impact of culture on human welfare and be oriented toward being a change-agent of culture, as we have previously argued (Jones, 1986). Adler's approach is one of the few that takes one out of the therapy room and into the homes, schools, neighborhoods and even legislatures of society. It thus reflects the balance in intervention modality that Christians should feel called to, ranging from one-to-one therapeutic work to the pursuit of social justice at a political level. Growth can flow narrowly from a therapeutic relationship or broadly from common interactions with healthy others in one's community.

Conclusion

We agree with Brink's (1977) conclusion, mentioned earlier, that there is more compatibility between Christianity and Adlerian conceptions than with classical psychoanalysis or indeed with most of the other systems of psychotherapy, but we reached this conclusion in substantially different ways than Brink did. In Adler, we find an approach that respects human responsibility, rationality, individuality, social interconnectedness and capacities for change. It is a view that has received scant attention from religious counselors over the years, and may bear further investigation in the future.

Reality Therapy

William Glasser, as he tells the story himself (1984b), developed the system of *reality therapy,* based on practical experience, common sense, some basic ideas from the cognitive neurosciences and perceptual psychology, and some indirect influence from existential thought through his mentor and fellow psychiatrist, G. L. Harrington (Kahoe, 1985). He acknowledges broad similarities to Adlerian psychology and rational-emotive therapy, but denies that these systems had any formative impact on his thinking—though others have suggested that Adler's model is a direct ancestor to reality therapy (Rozsnafszky, 1974; Whitehouse, 1984). In fact, much of what we said in regard to a Christian critique of Adlerian thought will apply as well to reality therapy, and so we will not spend as much time with this approach as we have with most of the other theoretical orientations.

While reality therapy has had little impact on the professional psychotherapeutic community at large, it is very popular among teachers and youth guidance counselors, substance-abuse treatment counselors (Glasser, 1984b) and rehabilitation counselors (Corey, 1986). As Kahoe (1985) points out, one reason why reality therapy is not more widely practiced than it is may be that Glasser maintains tight control of all "certified" reality-therapy training, having several franchised reality-therapy training centers. This insures quality of training but prevents proliferation into established counseling training centers in university settings.

Descriptive Survey

Philosophical Assumptions and Model of Personality

Reality therapy is based on the fundamental notion that persons are responsible for the actions they take. Glasser explicitly rejects determinism. He defines a responsible action as "one that satisfies one's needs and does not prevent others from satisfying theirs" (1984b, p. 320).

Glasser really does not have a formal theory of personality; rather, he works within the framework of what he calls a *control theory* of brain functioning. He argues that all persons and all organisms, act to control their environment to achieve survival and other needs.

Human beings are not passive, determined responders, but actors pursuing desired ends. The brain creates an inner image of external reality and then acts in accord with that inner image to meet needs (compare this to Adler's lifestyle). Thus the factors that shape behavior are primarily the nature of the inner image, the action capabilities the person has available and expectations based on the past track record for how the various behavioral options have worked. "Our personality is best described as the characteristic way in which we engage, act upon, or attempt to control the world to satisfy the pictures of what we desire" (1984b, p. 329).

What are the needs which are presumed to shape behavior? Glasser (1965) originally proposed two fundamental needs: (1) to belong, to love and be loved; and (2) to define or establish one's sense of personal worth, power and purpose (in striking parallel to Adler). The former is to be established in relationship, the latter through achievement of some sort. In his latest writings, Glasser broadens the list by also including biological survival (a base level need which is usually of little relevance to psychological problems) and the needs for fun and freedom (which do not seem to figure prominently in his work).

In Glasser's earliest writings, the successful meeting of needs was believed to aid in the establishment of what he called a *success identity*, which was the composite perception of one's acceptability and meaningfulness; the alternative was a *failure identity*, which was the source of ineffectual behavior. He placed the formation of identity as the highest level need, comprised of two subdrives: belonging and worth. His latest writings have focused more on control theory than identity.

Humans are teleological and phenomenological beings who work to meet their needs as they perceive them. Glasser suggests that our brain systems compare their pictures of our needs with their pictures of available behavioral responses, thus selecting out ways of dealing with perceived reality. "We both choose the world we want [i.e., our goals] and choose the behavior that is our attempt to move the real world closer to the in-the-head world we want" (Glasser, 1981, p. 238).

Actions, thoughts and even emotions are seen as actively chosen ways of responding to the perceived world, and hence we are responsible for all aspects of our personal reality. Even destructive emotions are chosen behaviors. Thus, Glasser (1984a) never says someone is depressed (a passive description), but that they are depressing (as in "depressing themselves as a way to control"). We can never control others, but we are accountable for our own actions of all kinds.

Models of Health and Abnormality

For Glasser, human psychopathology is ineffective behaviors, which are poor attempts to meet needs. Depression, anxiety, schizophrenia and all other problems in living are unsuccessful or marginally successful attempts to control one's environment to meet needs.

These ineffective behaviors may be chosen with or without awareness, but they are chosen responsibly for such purposes as controlling other more dangerous responses we might engage in, coercing the help of others, or to excuse ourselves from doing something difficult (Glasser, 1984a). Glasser rejects completely the traditional medical-model categorizations of "mental illness" with its implicit determinism. All presenting complaints, from the most trivial to the most extreme, have the same cause: They are all nonproductive attempts to meet needs. Reality therapy is claimed to be universally applicable to all human problems in living.

Psychological health is defined rather scantily as the result of responsibly and effectively meeting one's needs. Glasser's assumption seems to be that if persons act responsibly and in accord with reality, they will be able to meet all of their basic needs to some degree. This will enable them to achieve survival and thereby experience a modicum of a sense of belonging, self-worth, fun and freedom. He does not define the normative traits of the healthy person.

Glasser deals only tangentially with religion in his writings. He suggests that religious circles are consistent sources of excessive criticism that undermine people's sense of effectiveness (1981, p. 149) and that religion is primarily an arena in which satisfaction of the more basic needs of belonging and power is attempted (1984a, pp. 16-17). His approach has no seeming appreciation for the transcendent in human experience.

Model of Psychotherapy

There are eight major steps in conducting reality therapy (Glasser, 1984b); with brief commentary, they are:

1. "Make friends and ask clients what they want." The therapist is to establish a caring rapport within the context of a professional helping relationship, be positive and emphasize client strengths. The therapist then proceeds to find out what it is that the client really wants (what need the person is trying ineffectually to meet) and whether the "want" is possible.

2. "Ask, what are you doing *now*?" The current behavior of the client is presumed to be an attempt at some form of control, a means to satisfy a want or need. The therapist attempts to get the client to own up to what he or she is doing now and to deal with evasions and abstractions by focusing on behavior.

3. "Is what clients choose to do getting them what they want?" It is essential for the therapist to help the client realize that what he or she is currently doing is ineffectual. This is not to be seen as a callous judgment of the client by the therapist.

4. "Make a plan to do better." Next the therapist helps the client to devise a plan to more effectively control that part of life that is the area of concern. While being a solution resource person and concrete planner, one never solves anything for the clients; that is their work.

5. "Get a commitment to follow the plan worked out in step 4." Those with failure identities are particularly reluctant to commit to change.

6. "No excuses." Excuses are always part of the ineffectual patterns of the past. Reality therapists are interested in the future. "If you didn't do it this week, when will you do it?" The reasons for failure can rightly be grounds for altering future plans for change, but can never be excuses for inaction.

7. "No punishment." Punishment usually involves another person controlling the client's life. Therefore, the only possible punishments available to the therapist are those that are temporary and are naturally

and logically tied to an infraction. A teenager may lose privileges until she behaves in an appropriate fashion.

8. "Never give up." To give up is to be controlled by the client's ineffectual behavior, so the therapist must always look toward the possibility of change.

It is commonly noted that while the steps of reality therapy are straightforward, the actual application of reality therapy requires substantial skill and insight. One does not become a reality therapist from a quick reading of Glasser's books. Reality therapy is practiced as both an individual and a group therapy. It is taught didactically in public education settings; and is applied in educational and organizational settings. The volumes edited by Bassin, Bratter and Rachin (1976) and Glasser (1980) contain many diverse examples of the application of reality therapy.

Corey (1986) notes that Glasser has increasingly emphasized the need for support and affirmation as a balance to his historic emphasis on responsibility and action. Once largely viewed as a confrontational therapy, reality therapy has softened somewhat with the growing recognition that clients need support and encouragement as much as confrontation and problem-solving.

Christian Critique

Philosophical Assumptions
Young (1982) wrote an article in the form of an open letter to conservative Christian parents who had objected to the use of reality therapy in public schools on the basis that it "was teaching secular behaviors and thoughts" (p. 8). Young argued that reality therapy is in harmony with "basic Judeo-Christian religious beliefs" (p. 8). He listed five major principles of reality therapy and offered proof texts for their compatibility with Christian belief: (1) "Reality therapy stresses that everyone is responsible for his or her own actions" (Rom 2:5-8; 1 Cor 3:8; Ezek 18:20; Gal 6:7); (2) "In order to be responsible, a person must have rules or principles to obey and the opportunity to choose to obey" (Gen 2:15-17; Josh 24:14-15); (3) "All actions are followed by consequences" (Jn 5:28-16; Deut 24:16); (4) "People are capable of changing their behavior" (Ezek 18:30; 33:15; Acts 26:20); and (5) "Involvement is important in changing people" (Jn 15:12, Eph 5:32).

Responses to Young's argument hinge on whether one is looking at reality therapy "expansively" as a metaphysical system in actual or potential competition with Christianity, or "narrowly" as a practical system for school discipline.

At the expansive level, Young's argument is clearly flawed; it could be compared to equating Islam and Christianity because they assert the existence of one God and of heaven, the importance of morality and so forth. Even some of his specific principles are not clear compatibilities; in his fourth principle, Young equates godly repentance with mere behavior change, as if an adulterer's decision to stop his affairs out of fear of AIDS were equivalent to true repentance.

At a narrow level, however, Young is quite right that at some fundamental points—those of human responsibility, consequences for actions and the capacity for human change—reality therapy and Christianity are in agreement. And for the limited purposes of a school-discipline program, this may be enough compatibility to placate Christian parents. It would not be enough, however, if reality therapy was the main course in a required class in "Rational Religion for Today."

Like Adlerian psychology, reality therapy comports well with Christian belief in the following areas: Its emphasis on human responsibility and limited freedom is a definite plus. Both systems see persons as teleological beings rather than as driven inexorably by their past. Both posit that the most central needs of persons are for belonging and purpose or worth; these compare well to the relational and dominion motives found in the creation story. Both are holistic and do not reduce the person to interacting parts. Both, like Christianity, call for persons to live courageously as best they can as imperfect persons in an imperfect world. Each therapy system is a balance between cognitive and behavioral aspects, consistent with the most clear passages in Scripture regarding personal change. (It should be noted that the cognitive dimensions of reality therapy are underdeveloped compared to those of Adler.) Both approaches have attempted to go beyond the one-to-one counseling room to change society for the better, and this is a plus from a Christian perspective, in that any Christian approach to counseling should do the same.

In terms of dissimilarities with Christian belief, reality therapy, like Adlerian psychology, has a limited and overly optimistic understanding of human evil and fallenness. Both are "superficial" in seeing persons as having no necessary conflict built into their very being. Both are relativistic psychologies at the core; Glasser's increasing emphasis on internal pictures is akin to Adler's concept of the lifestyle and has some of the same limitations. It is not the subjectivity of each person's lifestyle or internal pictures that is the problem, but rather the supposition that all we can ever know are these internally constructed fictions. That is what makes both systems inherently relativistic.

Both systems see pathology as the purposeful evasion of life tasks to preserve self-esteem and maintain the best control possible of one's world; Christianity doesn't have a normative view of pathology, but would probably not necessarily contradict this view.

All of the issues summarized in the above few paragraphs were more fully developed before in discussing Adler's system. Now let us develop several points peculiar to reality therapy. First, we would want to emphasize that unlike Adler, who views religion as an ally, there is no concept of transcendent reality built into reality therapy. Human beings apparently can achieve no sense of belonging and probably no sense of worth from their relationship with the Deity in Glasser's view.

Second, Glasser, more than Adler, specifically steps into the moral and ethical domains in his proclamations of what responsible behavior is. It is affirming for a secular system to acknowledge the need for more rather than less emphasis on doing what is right (Lapsley, 1972). But Glasser essentially urges us to "do what is loving and satisfies your needs as long as you don't interfere with the needs of others." This is a human-centered morality system that is an inadequate guide for human life. Satan would seem to be an example of a being who is taking overt responsibility for his behavior and who sees himself as right in his own eyes, yet he is destined for eternal destruction and probably should not be held up as a model of psychological health.

Passages such as Romans 1:18-32 offer further examples that responsible human-centered action by itself falls far short of God's intended norm for humanity. Human beings are responsible for many of their actions and are capable of substantial change, as Glasser posits. But the Scriptures teach that neither obedience to human law nor even to the divine law of God is sufficient for salvation or even for fulfillment of our intended humanness. Glasser's system is all law and no grace, and further it is law without a lawgiver, a law where right is judged primarily in terms of how actions impact human needs and not in the relations of those actions to divine will.

Model of Psychotherapy

As a moral system, reality therapy can perhaps too easily become a moralistic system. It runs the risk of being abused in the hands of an authoritarian counselor, the "expert" counselor who is furiously straightening everyone else out. This is the same danger that similar forms of authoritative "biblical" counseling run. It can be too easy and too seductive to pour out the right answers to others whose struggles we barely understand.

We thus regard it as progress that Glasser's approach has been "softening" in recent years. A Christian therapy would necessarily emphasize responsibility like reality therapy does, but how would patience ever be needed if all that is needed is brute assumption of responsibility? First Thessalonians 5:14 speaks of such patience, as well as help for the weak and encouragement for the dispirited. Second Corinthians 1 speaks of comfort offered by God through us to others. Such concepts had little place in Glasser's original system, though there is more room for them now.

Consideration of Glasser's reality therapy leads us to ask if all human concerns are problems to be solved and the result of irresponsibility. Undoubtedly, Glasser is right that many are. But both of us have had occasion to work with persons who are the epitome of Christian discipline and responsibility but who nonetheless suffered problems. One in particular, a person of sure faith, devoted to almost heroic levels of prayer, Scripture memorization, church service, family devotion and vocational achievement, nevertheless experienced vague disquiet and ever growing emotional pain. Exploration indicated horrendous rejection inflicted on the person in his earliest years of life by alcoholic parents. This growing pain could only be addressed by looking to the past; emphasizing responsible behavior in the present was a dead-end for him.

Conclusion

In summary, reality therapy affirms human accountability and appreciates the pragmatic side of life as well. It attempts to be of concrete value to persons struggling with problems. But a fully developed theory would have more place for the transcendent, for the influence of the past (without lapsing into a deterministic fatalism), and for the emotive, nonrational side of life.

For Further Reading

Ansbacher, H., and Ansbacher, R. (Eds.). (1956). *The individual psychology of Alfred Adler.* New York: Basic Books.
    A good sampler of original writings by Adler.
Bassin, A.; Bratter, T.; and Rachin, R. (Eds.). (1976). *The reality therapy reader.*

New York: Harper & Row.

This contains many diverse examples of the application of reality therapy.

Dinkmeyer, D.; Pew, W.; and Dinkmeyer, D. (1979). *Adlerian counseling and psychotherapy*. Belmont, CA: Wadsworth.

An excellent basic text in Adlerian methods.

Glasser, W. (1981). *Stations of the mind: New directions for reality therapy*. New York: Harper & Row.

Glasser's most recent comprehensive work, of a more formal theoretical nature.

Huber, R. (Ed.). (1987). *Individual Psychology, 43*(4).

Special issue on "Pastoral counseling and the Adlerian perspective."

References

Adams, J. (1979). *More than redemption: A theology of Christian counseling*. Phillipsburg, NJ: Presbyterian and Reformed.

Anderson, H. (1970). Alfred Adler's individual psychology and pastoral care. *Pastoral Psychology, 21*, 15-26.

Arnold, J. (1987). The chemically dependent family. *Individual Psychology, 43*, 468-478.

Ansbacher, H., and Ansbacher, R. (Eds.). (1956). *The individual psychology of Alfred Adler*. New York: Basic Books.

Baruth, L., and Manning, M. (1987). God, religion, and the life tasks. *Individual Psychology, 43*, 429-436.

Bassin, A.; Bratter, T.; and Rachin, R. (Eds.). (1976). *The reality therapy reader*. New York: Harper & Row.

Brink, T. (1977). Adlerian theory and pastoral counseling. *Journal of Psychology and Theology, 5*, 143-149.

Brink, T. (1985a). Adler, Alfred. In D. Benner (Ed.), *Baker encyclopedia of psychology* (pp. 22-23). Grand Rapids, MI: Baker.

Brink, T. (1985b). Individual psychology. In D. Benner (Ed.), *Baker encyclopedia of psychology* (pp. 568-573). Grand Rapids, MI: Baker.

Corey, G. (1986). *Theory and practice of counseling and psychotherapy* (3d ed.). Monterey, CA: Brooks/Cole.

Dinkmeyer, D.; Pew, W.; and Dinkmeyer, D. (1979). *Adlerian counseling and psychotherapy*. Belmont, CA: Wadsworth.

Dowd, E., and Kelly, F. (1980). Adlerian psychology and cognitive-behavior therapy: Convergences. *Journal of Individual Psychology, 36*, 119-135.

Erikson, R. (1984). Social interest: Relating Adlerian psychology to Christian theology. *Pastoral Psychology, 32*, 131-140.

Evans, C. (1977). *Preserving the person*. Grand Rapids, MI: Baker.

Evans, C. (1989). *Wisdom and humanness in psychology*. Grand Rapids, MI: Baker.

Gibson, B. (1985). Adlerian psychotherapy. In D. Benner (Ed.), *Baker encyclopedia of psychology* (pp. 23-25). Grand Rapids, MI: Baker.

Glasser, N. (1980). *What are you doing? How people are helped by reality therapy*. New York: Harper & Row.

Glasser, W. (1965). *Reality therapy*. New York: Harper & Row.

Glasser, W. (1981). *Stations of the mind: New directions for reality therapy.* New York: Harper & Row.

Glasser, W. (1984a). *Control theory: A new explanation for how we control our lives.* New York: Harper & Row. (A hardback version of this book appeared under the title *Take effective control of your life,* also in 1984.)

Glasser, W. (1984b). Reality therapy. In R. Corsini (Ed.), *Current psychotherapies* (3d ed.), (pp. 320-353). Itasca, IL: F. E. Peacock.

Haavik, C. (1986). Adlerian psychotherapy: The neurotic symptom. Unpublished paper, Wheaton College Graduate School.

Hester, R. (1987). Memory, myth, parable, and the therapeutic process. *Individual Psychology, 43,* 444-450.

Huber, R. (1986). Adler and the Trinity: Reflections on a residency in pastoral counseling. *Individual Psychology, 42,* 413-419.

Huber, R. (Ed.). (1987). Individual Psychology, 43(4).

Jones, S. (1986). Community psychology. In S. Jones (Ed.), *Psychology and the Christian faith* (pp. 240-258). Grand Rapids, MI: Baker.

Kahoe, R. (1985). Reality therapy. In D. Benner (Ed.). *Baker encyclopedia of psychology* (pp. 978-981). Grand Rapids, MI: Baker.

Lapsley, J. (1972). Reality therapy revisited. *Pastoral Psychology, 23,* 3-4.

McDonald, M. (1981). *The Christian view of man.* Westchester, IL: Crossway.

Mosak, H. (1984). Adlerian psychotherapy. In R. Corsini (Ed.), *Current psychotherapies* (3d ed.) (pp. 56-107). Itasca, IL: F. E. Peacock.

Myers, D. (1981). *The inflated self.* New York: Seabury.

Rozsnafszky, J. (1974). The impact of Alfred Adler on three "free-will" therapies of the 1960's. *Journal of Individual Psychology, 30,* 65-80.

Uytman, J. (1967). Adler, Alfred. In P. Edwards (Ed.), Encyclopedia of philosophy (pp. 15-17). New York: Macmillan.

Van Leeuwen, M. (1987). Personality theorizing within a Christian world view. In T. Burke (Ed.), *Man and mind: A Christian theory of personality* (pp. 171-198). Hillsdale, MI: Hillsdale College Press.

Whitehouse, D. (1984). Adlerian antecedents to reality therapy and control theory. *Journal of Reality Therapy, 3,* 10-14.

Young, J. (1982). The morality of reality therapy. *Journal of Reality Therapy, 1,* 8-11.

THE HUMANISTIC
PSYCHOLOGIES

10

PERSON-CENTERED THERAPY

✛

*I*t is especially difficult to get beyond mere intuitive and emotional appeal when evaluating person-centered therapy. As McLemore (1982, p. 142) has noted, when it is thoroughly described, person-centered therapy sounds "much like the skillful administration of grace—not easy-to-roll-off-the-tongue grace, but deeply meaningful interpersonal acceptance and communion." Indeed, a counselor in this tradition would strike many as a good model of what it means to be a wise and patient friend, a person with an enormous capacity to listen attentively and respectfully. In a culture like ours where interpersonal contact and intimacy can be lost to absorption in the tasks of everyday living, few would find these qualities unattractive. Perhaps one reason why Carl Rogers's theory and technique has been so warmly embraced within significant portions of the religious community is that it appears to give us valuable clues and guidance on how to respond to those in misery and distress, or how to concretely "love the brothers and sisters."

Descriptive Survey

Philosophical Assumptions

Probably no theory of counseling and psychotherapy more fully manifests the humanistic spirit in contemporary psychology than does person-centered therapy, and perhaps no single individual better embodied its essence than its founder, Carl Rogers. An ever-evolving approach since the early 1940s, person-centered therapy has experienced a noticeable renewal of late (Boy and Pine, 1982). It boldly asserts that the client, not the therapist, should be at the heart of psychotherapy (and hence, it is person-centered) since only the client has the resources by which to become more aware of and remove his or her obstacles to personal growth. It is significant that Rogers, recently deceased, grew up in a fundamentalist Christian home and rejected the faith of his parents during college in favor of "liberalistic humanism" (Van Belle, 1985b, p. 1016). He appeared not to deviate from this position for the rest of his life.

It is quite clear that person-centered therapy is a reaction against what Rogers perceived as the dogmatism of "prescriptive" religion and the elitist and rationalistic tendencies of classical psychoanalysis. In stark contrast to the strongly biological and deterministic assumptions of the early Freudian model (chapter three), Rogers stressed a highly personal, phenomenological and positive view of human experience. Person-centered therapy is often said to embody the permissive and pragmatic mindset of the contemporary North American milieu (Van Belle, 1980). Person-centered therapy emphasizes the primacy of the individual and is often criticized for contributing to modern narcissism and the erosion of any shared sense of meaning or value in contemporary society (Vitz, 1977).

Consistent with other humanistic approaches to counseling and psychotherapy, person-centered therapy warmly embraces a number of key values (adapted from Korchin, 1976, pp. 353ff.): (1) Persons should not be "atomized" or broken down into their component parts, but rather should be studied as whole and unique beings; (2) What persons tell us through self-report of their experience is to be more highly valued than what we can observe directly or objectively; (3) Since we are coparticipants in the process of self-actualization, we must be

willing to enter into the consciousness and experiential field of others
(as well as our own); (4) Intuition and empathic understanding should
be viewed as extremely important means of gaining insight and understanding; (5) Knowing something about the aspirations, dreams, goals
and values of others tells us far more than does a comparable amount
of knowledge about the biological, environmental or historical determinants of their behavior; (6) Distinctive human qualities like choice,
creativity, self-actualization and valuation should be emphasized in our
study of persons, as well as health and normalcy; and (7) Persons have
the potential to act with choice, freedom and responsibility, and not
be merely reactive to events.

The heritage of person-centered therapy is rooted in applied *phenomenology* (Rychlak, 1973). Edmund Husserl, often called the "father
of phenomenology," strongly influenced this distinctive approach to
philosophy. In briefest summary, phenomenology contends that what
we are and what we do is a reflection of our subjective experience of
the world and ourselves. External reality can only be known through
the inner reality of personal experience.

As Van Belle (1985a) has observed, Rogers had a profound respect
for the client's perception of reality, since this inner reality was
ultimately the means for promoting development and growth in the
individual. Indeed, Rogers is dogmatic in asserting that experience is
the ultimate authority in life: "It is to experience that I must return
again and again; to discover a closer approximation to truth as it is in
the process of becoming in me. Neither the Bible nor the prophets—
neither Freud nor research—neither the revelations of God nor
man—can take precedence over my own direct experience" (Rogers,
1961, pp. 23-24).

Model of Personality

Perhaps the core assertion of this personality theory is that there is but
one motivational force for all humanity: the tendency toward *self-
actualization*. All persons have an inherent tendency to develop their
capacities to the fullest, in ways that will either maintain or enhance
their own well-being.

Detractors of person-centered therapy often equate self-actualization with selfishness, but this is not strictly true. Actualization is the
realization of our potential, and our potential certainly includes the
capacity to love. Thus, Rogers would believe that out of the fully
actualized, fully functioning individual would come acts of charity and

kindness that would be a free and loving expression of the person's true inner state. Profound narcissism would actually be one mark of a failure to actualize one's potential.

While this motivation produces our movement, the direction for the movement comes from the *organismic valuing process*—an inherent capacity to choose that which will enhance us and reject that which does not. The actualization drive creates in us an urge for fulfillment, and the organismic valuing process tells us what will provide that fulfillment. The organismic valuing process is presumed to be an infallible and instinctive compass or guide for choice and action.

Model of Health

What then is the ideal course for human development, according to person-centered therapy? The child, blessed with a drive toward actualization and an inerrant organismic valuing process to guide her, still needs the acceptance and positive regard of her parents. If the parents provide this positive regard *unconditionally,* the child grows up always exquisitely aware of her natural urges and awareness (her *self-experience*). As consciousness of self emerges, the person will begin to define herself (develop her *self-concept*) in accord with her own experience of herself and not in terms of how others see her or expect her to be. Further, she has no aspirations to be other than what she is, and her *ideal self,* the perception of what she should be, then perfectly matches the self-concept which in turn perfectly matches the self-experience.

As we develop and mature, it is our self-concept that increasingly shapes and directs the organismic valuing process. Thus, a self-concept unpolluted by distortions caused by other persons' judgments of us allows the organismic valuing process to continue to operate as an infallible guide. Health, then, is seen as a congruence between what one wants to become, what one perceives one's self to be and what one actually experiences or is. To quote Rogers and Rablen (cited in Meador and Rogers, 1984, p. 177):

> The [fully functioning, healthy] individual lives comfortably in the flowing process of his experiencing. New feelings are experienced with richness and immediacy, and this inner experiencing is a clear referent [guide] for behavior. Incongruence is minimal and temporary. The self is a confident awareness of this process of experiencing. The meaning of experiencing is held loosely and constantly checked and rechecked against further experiencing.

The healthy person then is one who has an intact and functioning organismic valuing process and who completely trusts the valuing process. That person is fully aware, honest, personally satisfied and spontaneous. Health reflects trust of self, openness to experiencing and existential living in the present. Ideally, person-centered therapy posits, this will lead to a new kind of freedom whereby the person chooses to direct his or her life from within rather than by the dictates of the external world. Such "centeredness" (in the sense of balance, not self-centeredness) will release enormous potential to further oneself even more. There will be no need to deny or distort the information that is received perceptually since a strong sense of self has emerged that is consistent with deeply internalized conditions of worth. The chief Rogerian virtues are to be fully alive to the moment, completely self-accepting and strongly committed to an ongoing process of personal growth.

centeredness

Model of Abnormality

Unfortunately, few of us get through childhood so unscathed. Most of us are subjected to conditions of worth, are loved conditionally; that is, we are expected to act in accord with the expectations of parents or significant others rather than by our instincts in order to receive acceptance. Christian discipline and instruction would, for Rogers, be a prime example of disrespect for the child's self-directedness. The child is confronted with the need to deny certain aspects of his experience and act according to rules or judgments of authority figures ("God wants me to honor my parents; I guess I'm not really angry at Daddy"). He then develops an ideal self, dictated by parental wishes, which does not fit who he really is ("Good boys love their parents and don't get angry with them") and develops a self-concept that is formed in part by what the child genuinely experiences of himself and partly of what the child feels he must be ("I'm a good boy who doesn't get angry at Mom and Dad"). The distorted self-concept quickly warps the organismic valuing process, resulting in impaired perceptions of himself and his world and of the choices he can make.

In person-centered therapy, "problems in living" are seen primarily in terms of incongruence between different dimensions of the self. Psychopathology results when we become more externally oriented than internally oriented, trying to manufacture feelings or behavior that others demand we exhibit before we can be acceptable. The incongruence between what we really are and what we are trying to be creates psychological pain. The distortions in the self-concept warp the functioning of the organismic valuing process, so that the person makes more bad (incongruent) choices about what would further his or her personal actualization.

The symptoms of abnormality are seen as "signs" or "symbols" of ways in which we prevent threatening experiences from becoming more accurately represented in our conscious and subjective awareness. As the symptoms become more pronounced, our informational and perceptual processes become increasingly inadequate and rigid. In short, psychopathology is a split or incongruence between self and experience.

Model of Psychotherapy

If external conditions of worth result in the distortion of the self, what can be done about this condition formally in the context of counseling and psychotherapy, or more informally in the setting of everyday interactions? Person-centered therapy suggests that positive self-regard, and thus congruence between self-concept and the person's experience, can be encouraged by relating to the individual with congruence, empathy and unconditional positive regard.

This will, according to Rogers, encourage the person to more fully trust the organismic valuing process and move toward greater self-actualization. The major task of the therapist is to provide a climate of safety and trust, one which will encourage clients to reintegrate their self-actualizing and self-valuing processes. The therapist accomplishes this through encouraging the psychotherapeutic conditions (the "therapeutic triad") of *accurate empathic understanding, congruence* or *genuineness* and *unconditional positive regard,* which are seen as the necessary and sufficient conditions for effective counseling (cf. Hammond, Hepworth and Smith, 1978).

Empathy is not sympathy; rather, it is the therapist's capacity to experience with the client and accept the client's subjective ·inner world.

Congruence or genuineness is the therapist's capacity to truthfully and accurately perceive her or his own inner experiencing in response to the client and to allow that inner experience to affect the counseling relationship in a healthy way; it is the capacity to be fully oneself while fully relating to the client.

Unconditional positive regard is an unyielding acceptance of, respect for and prizing of the client's experience, actualizing tendencies and organismic valuing process. Each of these qualities are seen by

Rogerians as being rooted in the personhood of the therapist, and not as mere techniques. They can be learned as practical skills (one can learn lists of empathic responses, genuine responses, etc.), but to be used effectively, they must take root in the very being of the counselor. Person-centered therapy never involves advice-giving, shaming, teaching, giving interpretations, manipulation or other ingenuine interactions. These, it is argued, are based on a fundamental disrespect of others; they foster dependency, and they thwart the development of any meaningful sense of autonomy.

Understandably, for the person-centered therapist, the therapeutic relationship is of utmost importance. Unlike other approaches which see therapy as the therapist "doing something to" the client, person-centered therapy is best understood by an analogy to gardening: It is the provision of the right interpersonal soil in which the client's hidden drive to grow and develop can finally be released. Only through the proper characteristics and competencies of the therapist can the client move toward greater congruence and release of his or her own innate capacities.

As coparticipants in a process of change and discovery, the client/therapist relationship is egalitarian, informal and nonauthoritarian. Formal assessment of the presenting concerns or underlying dynamics in the forms of psychological testing or psychiatric diagnosis are seen as inappropriate and unnecessary. Techniques, of which there are few in person-centered therapy, are secondary to the therapist's attitudes, sensitivities and skills. Active listening, clarification and reflection of feelings, personal presence and "coparticipation" are seen as the only necessary "tools" in the repertoire of the person-centered therapist, coupled with a profound respect for process and inner-directedness. It is assumed that the client will freely choose to translate the changes experienced in the intimate context of therapy to outside relationships with others.

Christian Critique

Philosophical Assumptions
Compared to some traditions, person-centered therapy is explicit about its philosophical presuppositions. Many aspects of these assumptions can be appreciated. The insistence on seeing people holistically and as purposeful, the appreciation of other ways of knowing beyond rationality, and the profound respect of what it means to be a person

are all positive in many ways. But for the Christian the philosophical presuppositions undergirding person-centered therapy ought to raise a number of concerns as well.

First of all, person-centered therapy assumes that we are the ultimate force and the sole masters of our own destiny; in other words, all authority is within. This is a paradigmatic *humanistic* approach to psychotherapy in the fullest sense of the word; humanity is the center.

The self assumes a position of supreme importance in Rogers's person-centered therapy, a notion that can be traced back to the philosophy of idealism and romanticism in the nineteenth century. The strongly experiential, individualistic and relativistic "core assertions" of person-centered therapy unquestionably lead to inflated notions of the self (Vitz, 1977; Myers, 1981).

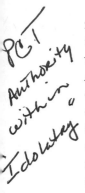

Certainly we are called as Christians to develop our identities as a matter of good stewardship, but we must also confront the realities of the created order, including the existence of evil both within us and without. Self is not all there is and should not be the center of what is. As Vitz (1977, p. 93) has said, "To worship one's self (in self-realization) or to worship all humanity is, in Christian terms, simple idolatry operating from the usual motive of unconscious egotism." In the Christian tradition, to proclaim oneself to be in control of one's own existence is the ultimate act of rebellion. C. S. Lewis (1968) once remarked that a good functional definition of hell would be the kind of place where all acted as if they were the master of their own lives.

The emphasis on self is not only a problem for ontology, but for epistemology as well. Person-centered therapy boldly states that when one's self-actualizing tendency is "in-tune" with the organismic valuing process, trustworthy self-knowledge is fully obtainable and should take precedence over all else. But to boldly assert the complete trustworthiness of self-knowledge is certainly not within the mainstream of the Christian tradition (cf. Dodgen and McMinn, 1986). The organismic valuing process is not an inerrant guide! No aspect of human nature is untouched by sin and hence inerrant.

Second, there are other ways of knowing beyond self-knowledge. Browning (1987, p. 64) noted that in theories like person-centered therapy, "the truth of life in both religion and morality is mediated through the inner subjectivity of the individual." But the Christian tradition has always had a high view of divine revelation and the authority of Scripture, as well as the role of the discerning community. Its regard for general revelation, including a deeper understanding of human nature through greater self-awareness and understanding, has been more hesitantly asserted (cf. Roberts, 1985).

Rogers takes the opposite position. He is optimistic about one's experience as the basis of determining truth, but rather pessimistic about the value of culture, dogma, traditions and systems of morality (Roberts, in press).

Person-centered therapy is also implicitly a system of ethics. In person-centered therapy, one is ultimately responsible only to oneself. Personal wholeness assumes primacy; it becomes a moral imperative (Browning, 1987), often at the expense of a proper appreciation of our responsibilities to others. Focusing only on removing our own barriers to our personal growth potential can lead to regarding ourselves too highly or to a naive optimism about the human condition.

Certainly there is a sense in which we are troubled because we don't know ourselves, but it would be inaccurate to state that we "give birth to ourselves." In conversion, we become more of a true self, but certainly not a complete self. For the Christian, it is God alone who gives us birth—not the therapist, nor the increasingly congruent person. And with that profession of faith, new opportunities and responsibilities must be assumed, including a strong commitment to becoming manifestations of God's grace in this world in word and deed. "Self-ism" runs the risk of developing into "me-ism" (Vitz, 1977).

Christians can appreciate the emphasis in person-centered therapy on individual freedom and responsibility. Individual choice and the capacity to change is affirmed in the Rogerian tradition. Initially, as Tisdale (1988) has noted, such an assessment of the human condition in the therapeutic context might seem harsh and insensitive since it centers responsibility on the client. It risks blaming clients for all their problems or regarding them as having more freedom than they actually possess. But this view has reassuring implications. People are seen as having the potential to act and make decisions despite their situations, histories or limitations, as the Scriptures frequently assert.

On the other hand, the Christian tradition describes certain limitations on our freedom; we are portrayed as in bondage to evil, self-deception and sin. Person-centered therapy recognizes none of these limitations. Still, the emphasis on responsibility in person-centered therapy is a refreshing contrast to the more pessimistic tendencies of the deterministic models and the current infatuation with "addiction" models for all human problems. There is far too much externalization and projection of responsibility going on in contemporary American society.

Browning (1987) points out a major problem with the Rogerian concept of freedom, however. Person-centered therapy reduces human growth to the process of pursuing self-actualization by following the direction of one's instinctual organismic valuing process. Rogers thus renders the intricate and complex task of moral decision-making to the merely instinctual. Browning argues that this is actually destructive of a robust view of human freedom, in that freedom "would descend to attentive listening to our biology" (p. 134). A robust view of freedom requires that we choose responsibly between real options. But in the Rogerian scheme, there is always only one real option, that of following our biologically rooted instincts. Morality then runs the risk of becoming a matter of following the instinctual compass, rather than being a rigorous and demanding response of the whole person.

Finally, person-centered therapy sees itself strongly in the human science rather than natural science tradition (Van Leeuwen, 1985). Although a number of the assertions about the philosophy of science endorsed by person-centered therapy and the broad humanistic-existential tradition have enormous appeal to many Christian students of psychology, there is reason to be concerned about some of the consequences of such thinking. Relatively little high-quality empirical research has been generated by this approach to the study of persons, although Rogers himself was a noticeable exception (Prochaska, 1984, pp. 116-120). The founder of person-centered therapy promoted an "unusual combination of phenomenological understanding of clients and empirical evaluation of psychotherapy" (p. 116). Serious proposals by Christians for more human-science strategies have been thought-provoking (e.g., Farnsworth, 1985; Van Leeuwen, 1985), but have stimulated noticeably less research than more traditional research methodologies (cf. Evans, 1989). Christian thinkers must be cautious about endorsing "either-or" options with reference to a philosophy of science. Few theoreticians or therapists have been able to emulate Rogers's example of phenomenological and empirical sophistication.

Model of Personality
There is much in the Rogerian model of personality that is initially appealing to the Christian reader. The true self, according to Rogers, is potentially in an ever-changing process of "becoming a person," and this emphasis on unending growth is attractive. The true self is not a

person who is fixed to any specific dispositions, roles or traits, and this respects our individuality.

In person-centered therapy our principal life task is conceived to be that of uncovering our true self. The self-concept and ideal self are to move into congruence with self-experience, as experience can only be what it is, while the former two can readily change. Thus people are thought only capable of change by discovering what they really are. We would agree with Rogers that most of us are not now our true selves and that growth really does mean at some significant levels becoming one's true self. We would also agree with Browning (1987) that the core notion of being born with a unique set of potentialities that we are meant to actualize is not incompatible with a Christian view of persons. We are, after all, created in God's image and each person has a unique calling from God to become the person he or she was meant to become.

The self's lack of form is troubling, for as Roberts (in press) has noted, the Rogerian self has no center or anchor, and if taken to an extreme, can turn into a formless entity defined only by its urges and sensing. According to the Christian tradition, true selves are not to be merely uncovered, but are to be formed by acting in obedience to God's call (Evans, 1990; see chapter eleven). Thus, we are not fundamentally good beings, as person-centered therapy asserts, but ones whose very selves need transformation.

Becoming a self, in the Christian view, requires a willingness to face directly one's creatureliness as well as finiteness. In our uncorrupted state, we were the crown of creation, but we became estranged from our creator. Inwardly depraved, we are incapable of returning to God apart from grace. The ultimate hope for our transformation is divine intervention as we confront our sinfulness. Christian maturity reaches its apex in terms of character formation when the Christian virtues are cultivated and expressed (Roberts, 1982). This truth, that human selves have to be transformed because we are not perfectly good, cannot be overemphasized. While the concept of self-acceptance is vitally important to a hope-filled call to passionate and compassionate living (Wagner, 1975), the Christian sees the need to balance a desire for self-fulfillment with a strong portion of self-discipline. We accept ourselves, but also yearn to become who and what God is calling us to be.

We would also argue that person-centered therapy errs in positing only one drive for human personality. Suggesting one drive, and a totally good one at that, leads to attributing all human distress to forces external to the person. If we ever experience conflict, it cannot be due to a true struggle within ourselves, but rather to a pseudostruggle between our true selves (all good) and some sort of false selves, which are presumed to have originated externally from how significant others have treated us. This is why Browning (1987, p. 62) describes the person-centered therapy view as "instinctual utopianism"; it suggests perfect inner congruence at the deepest levels for the healthy person. Christianity, on the other hand, suggests that our good impulses and our bad impulses, our love for and rebellion against God, are both representative of our true selves. Conflict is real, and goes on in the deepest dimensions of the person. Person-centered therapy has a trivial view of conflict within the person. Christianity views conflict as both internal and external, and evident at both the individual and corporate levels.

In person-centered therapy the true self is aware, through the organismic valuing process, of *internal needs,* but not necessarily of anything external like the needs and wants of others, at least until a high degree of personal congruence has been achieved. Such notions should trouble us as Christians. Person-centered therapy may appeal to our pre-existing tendencies toward being overly individualistic. The true self in the Christian tradition is in part defined in terms of relationships—with God, with neighbor, with others and with God's absolutes. Our sense of identity is meant to be shaped by both organismic needs (which certainly play a role) and by a strong sense of belonging shaped by the Christian story and our place in the Christian community (cf. Gaede, 1985). A sense of meaning and personal contentment are potentially enriched and enlivened by a strong sense of heritage, history and tradition as children of the Creator-God. The true self is the person who loves God with all of one's heart, seeks after righteousness, and loves others as oneself. A more complete understanding of the true self goes beyond self-awareness and subjective experience to a keen awareness and knowledge of others (Roberts, in press). In a very real sense, we find our identity in being and doing.

It would be fair to say that there is a dimension of self-actualizing potential in all of us. But a more traditional Christian perspective would be that this is based on a potential for a gradual, painful process of recovering the original form of the *imago dei* (image of God) that became distorted as a result of the Fall. A more balanced and theologically sensitive perspective on the forces that move us would contend that there are some less than noble drives within, and this is why we argued earlier that selves must be made and forged in the context of costly discipleship rather than merely being uncovered.

Model of Health

At first glance, there is much in these notions of health that is attractive to those who long for a more "honest Christianity" (cf. McLemore, 1984). It would be fair to state that Christians are, by and large, overly rational and often distrustful of feelings. We also put on our "happy faces" and play the roles of the conquering spiritual giants in our religious communities. It is no wonder that we feel alone in having problems among the Christians we know. If we are honest in our self-assessment, however, we are usually painfully aware of our tendencies to deny and distort reality just as Rogers would suggest. We are called often in Scripture to be more truthful in our communications, especially with our Creator-God (e.g., the frequent brutal honesty of the psalmists). Without such honesty, there can be no true repentance or confession, no true fidelity, no true reconciliation (cf. Tisdale, 1988, p. 14).

Thus one of the greatest assets of the person-centered therapy is its strong emphasis on awareness of feelings. But this is also a liability. Awareness is an end in itself in this system; awareness is health. As Van Belle (1985a) has observed, greater awareness of emotional response might lead to a sense of emotional relief, freedom, improved self-awareness, personal autonomy and interpersonal competence. But there is no guarantee that "healthier," more emotionally "in-touch" persons will anchor themselves in any abiding structure outside themselves, because as we noted the self is formless in person-centered therapy theory.

For the Christian, the inward journey of awareness may be necessary, especially as the foundation for all true repentance, but it will be insufficient by itself for forming the true self. Greater self-actualization should serve a meaningful end, namely, that we submit ourselves to God, seek after righteousness and love others as ourselves. Freedom and autonomy ought not to be ends in themselves but rather vehicles by which we more fully achieve maturity in Christ.

The person-centered therapy ideal of health is the person without a past (we are always to live in the "now"), a person without any need to submit to authority (we are our own ultimate truth), a person without real dependence on anyone else (we contain all our resources within ourselves) and a person with no firm commitment to truth (all meanings are held tentatively and revised according to changing experiences).

In contrast, Christianity paints humans as having pasts, presents and futures of fixed meanings determined by God. We are part of a community of faith that has a stable identity. We are not our own gods, but owe our submission to the rightful Lord of the universe.

There are certainly absolutes in the Christian faith, but there are relatively few in person-centered therapy. External authority is seen as potentially obtrusive and often more as a vice than a virtue. Yet we are profoundly dependent on God (Col 1:9-20) and on others (e.g., Gen 2:18, "It is not good for the man to be alone"). And we believe in a truth that is constant because it ultimately depends on a truth-speaking God who is "the same yesterday and today and forever" (Heb 13:8).

Model of Abnormality

There is a near consensus in the field of psychopathology that problems are typically "multi-causal" and "multi-maintained." A whole host of biological, psychosocial and sociocultural variables are usually involved, even in what appears to be a "simple" problem. Rogerians prefer to concentrate on their unique experiential contribution to understanding the larger causal picture. Because of this exclusive focus, person-centered therapy seems most relevant to understanding the adjustment difficulties of relatively high-functioning persons, individuals struggling with problems of "over control" or denial of their feelings.

But such an orientation runs the risk of trivializing or even ignoring the complex reality of serious psychopathology. Since careful assessment is seen as largely futile according to this model (because of the emphasis on experiencing), important clinical symptoms can be missed or minimized. Person-centered therapy runs the risk of indifference to or ignorance about the full range of human misery and suffering. Its perspective on psychopathology is at best partial and seems to have less to add to our overall understanding of human psychopathology than any other mainline approach.

A fundamental flaw in the humanistic and relativistic philosophy behind person-centered therapy is what appears to be a lack of willingness to seriously confront the fundamental depravity of persons and the reality of evil (Peck, 1983). There is so much focus on affirmation of the person that it seriously neglects those matters for which we are to be held accountable. As McLemore (1982, p. 143) has warned, there is a danger that the person-centered therapist can begin "to view evil as innocuous, effete, and generally to be dealt with by a wave of the finger and a genteel 'tsk . . . tsk.'" Using explicitly theological terms, the approach is a one-sided emphasis on "grace" and how we "image God," to the neglect of the Law and human sin (Ortberg, 1981). People need to come to grips with their own frailty, their own sinfulness and their strong propensity toward self-deception.

Perhaps person-centered therapy's one significant and enduring contribution is to examine the role of self-hate as a source of human suffering. The tradition errs, however, in univocally identifying self-hate as the source of problems. Biblically, self-love is more fundamental to our human dilemma than is self-hate. The desire to love ourselves without reference to God could be argued to be the prime cause for the Fall, and perhaps we could even argue that the root of self-hate is the motive to make more of self than we ought. We want to worship or esteem ourselves, and then we despise ourselves for not meeting up to our standards. Certainly self-love is as often a source of problems in living as is self-hate (Browning, 1987).

Model of Psychotherapy

The methods of change described in the person-centered therapy tradition—the therapeutic triad of empathy, genuineness and unconditional positive regard—have been enormously influential in contemporary psychology and the pastoral care movement. A vast literature has emerged in the past three decades that has drawn out their implications for an amazingly diverse number of settings, populations and clinical concerns.

Let us first focus on the "methods" of change which have been the focal point for much of the discussion about person-centered therapy. The role of the therapist in the person-centered therapy is seen as that of a facilitator or catalyst, not that of a guide or teacher. The nature of this catalytic method is often summarized as love. In fact, Patterson (1985) explicitly equates the therapeutic triad with *agape* love.

Positively, it is hard to say enough about the redemptive power of divine love. Thielicke (1964) briefly discussed the power of God's *agape* love which he lavishes upon us. Thielicke used the analogy of photographic development, suggesting that God's love, experienced directly from God and more indirectly through God's people, could act as the developing chemicals, sharpening and bringing into focus the masked and dormant image of God within us. To whatever extent person-centered therapy encourages a human manifestation of *agape* love, it should claim our allegiance and profound respect.

A truly Christian approach to healing and helping will surely stress the primacy of warm, empathic and genuine relationships, thoroughly grounded in an understanding of *agape* love (cf. Tan, 1987). Oden (1968), in his earlier analysis of person-centered therapy, went so far as to say that unconditional positive regard, mediated through a good psychotherapeutic relationship, was the secular translation of the Christian understanding of redemption. Ellens (1982) recognized and applauded the supreme emphasis placed on "grace" in the person-centered therapy tradition.

But it is a serious error for the Christian to equate unconditional positive regard or even the whole triad with Christian love (Oakland, 1974; Ortberg, 1981; Roberts, 1988). Christian love warmly embraces sinners, is gracious and unconditionally accepting, but does not cease to be firm and hold the self and others accountable. Certainly we need to be "fed" by deep affirmation and acceptance, but we also need to be "pruned" in the process of our growth by God's discipline and to be forgiven. Our Creator-God disciplines because he loves us (cf. Heb 12:7-10). In person-centered therapy there is no discipline, no firmness. The person-centered therapist is trained not to express disapproval or give instruction in any form or fashion (Ortberg, 1981).

We as Christians need to learn more about the importance of affirming persons deeply "as they are." Indeed, we are all too often preaching or talking when we should be attentively and respectfully listening. But divine acceptance and Christian love place certain demands and expectations on relationships. Discipline and struggle go hand in hand with accepting that we are of immense worth in the creational order. God's grace is a gift that is not merited but is given freely. It can not be earned and we should reject a works theology forthrightly. But that does not mean that there is no place for a proper understanding of discipline, moral accountability, judgment or repentance in the Christian life. And if these are present, therapy will certainly be more than the creation of a tolerant, accepting atmosphere in the counseling relationship. Unfortunately, we seem to know far more about preaching and exhorting than we do about listening and comforting. There is much we need to learn about love within limits and about caring and commitment (cf. Smedes, 1978).

Because of its one-sided embrace of love without discipline, person-centered therapy may support clients without challenging them. Client and therapist may hide behind empathic listening and reflecting without getting into the deeper issues that need to be confronted if growth and change are to occur. In all fairness, person-centered therapy has moved in the direction of "caring confrontation" (cf. Rogers, 1980), but there still seems to be an almost phobic avoidance of dealing with the inevitable differences of opinions or conflicts that occur in human relationships. In fact, descriptions and definitions of the therapeutic qualities are typically written in such a way that most confrontations that one might imagine flowing from Christian moral stances would be judged to be ingenuine, nonempathic or conditional, and hence to be avoided. Sometimes these concerns are well-taken; Christians probably engage in a fair amount of "premature orthodoxy" (i.e., jumping to conclusions). What we are concerned about, however, is a steadfast pattern of avoidance, which can only lead to a moral relativism or an ethic without any "teeth." Truth-telling is full of risks and responsibilities, but so is the alternative.

Next we will examine the motivation for love or positive regard of the counselee. For the person-centered therapist, we are to love because the other merits it and it is congruent for us to do so. For the Christian, there are a number of foundations for positive regard. First, love is rooted in the recognition of our common status as persons created in God's image; we are all part of one common family. Also, we are urged to love others because God first loved us, to love as an overflow of God's love of us (Roberts, 1988). We are urged to love as a reflection of God's character, of his presence in our lives. Finally, we are commanded to love others as ourselves because it is a deep expression of our understanding of our purpose on earth. *Agape* love is grounded in an objective reality outside the self, whereas positive regard is ultimately anchored within the individual.

What of the process by which therapy occurs, the type of experience the client is urged to have? Person-centered therapy appears to focus too much on inner subjective experience and present-centeredness. If "problems in living" are seen as rooted in aberrations in perception, then it makes sense to focus on the client's awareness of the here-and-now. Christian faith is not necessarily incompatible with a deep concern about individual inner experience, and there is a sense in which the Christian tradition values the immediacy of the present existential moment. After all, we are told to ask only for our "daily bread" and to live each moment fully "as unto the Lord."

But the Christian tradition values others as well. Even mystical contemplation is seen largely as a means to empower oneself for more focused and concentrated ministry rather than as an end in itself. And the Christian tradition is deeply rooted in a strong sense of God's working throughout redemptive history. Becoming centered "fully in the moment" runs the risk of leading to a limited sense of familial, historical, personal or spiritual identity. We need a personal and collective "story," or we will eventually have to face an overwhelming sense of emptiness (cf. Lasch, 1979; or Bellah, Madsen, Sullivan, Swindler and Tipton, 1985).

There are risks for the person-centered therapy therapist as well. It is tempting for the Rogerian therapist to mask his or her own identity and uniqueness by being constrained to relate to clients in a "person-centered" manner. The therapeutic triad of congruence, empathy and unconditional positive regard can all too easily degenerate into a bland, safe and ineffectual way of relating to persons in general. Further, these qualities should not be reduced to skills or sensitivities that can be turned on or off as the occasion demands. Indeed, this would be the epitome of incongruity.

There is a risk in person-centered therapy of the client developing an unhealthy dependency relationship with the therapist. McLemore (1982) reminds us of the almost inevitable tendency of a client to overidentify with the therapist if the therapist does not set appropriate expectations, clarify his or her role, or establish reasonable limits. Good therapy needs to help persons to learn how to deal with the reality of conditional love in the world (Strupp and Binder, 1986), but a poorly managed empathic relationship can eventually increase unhealthy dependence and regression, rather than a greater degree of autonomy and maturation. For the Christian clinician in particular, it is imperative that credit is given to the ultimate source of grace, since, in some mysterious and powerful way, we embody "Jesus Christ" for the client

Person-centered therapy has probably been the most widely adapted approach to people-helping that has ever been developed. Applications for the business, educational, familial, group, individual, marital and parental context abound in the literature (cf. Corey, 1986). Person-centered therapy is also widely appreciated for the ways in which it has been adapted for the training of lay and paraprofessional counselors. It has helped mental health professionals to "give psychology away" to the people, with all the obvious risks and benefits that entails. No doubt person-centered therapy is the dominant method used in the initial phases of counselor training (cf. Meier, 1989)—perhaps because it has built-in safety features. Even eclectic, empirically based books on psychotherapy show a tremendous indebtedness to the person-centered therapy tradition (cf. Garfield, 1980). An approach that stresses active listening, learning to respect the client's frame of reference, and minimizing advice and unsolicited interpretation has immediate and obvious appeal. Person-centered therapy may certainly move some toward greater wholeness, but it is probably "longitudinally limited" in its capacity to bring about lasting change.

Carl Rogers is to be commended for his serious commitment to clinical research. Next to the cognitive and behavioral traditions, no approach has been as willing to state its formulations in terms of testable hypotheses and to commit itself to such extensive and collaborative research endeavors. Hardly a static system, person-centered therapy has gradually evolved over the past fifty years due, in part, to its willingness to modify theory and technique in light of insights gained from research. Person-centered therapy has left an impressive legacy. After three decades of solid research, few clinicians or theoreticians would doubt that congruence, empathy and positive regard are essential "building blocks" for effective change; everyone agrees they are helpful, and in many situations they may be necessary. The debate is over whether or not they are sufficient conditions for change to occur.

Rogers has strongly influenced our understanding of the proper role and function of the therapist. Rogers is consistent with his theoretical understandings about the nature of growth in construing the most effective role of the therapist to be that of a facilitator or catalyst who must embody in word and deed the qualities of congruence, empathy and unconditional positive regard. Consequently, it is seen as counterproductive for therapists to set themselves up as "experts" or "wise old sages."

In line with our earlier argument of the need for discipline to complement love, of law to complement grace, we would question whether a Christian understanding of the role of the counselor could ever be divorced fully from seeing the counselor as a teacher or sage. Whether the particular person-centered therapy formulation of love and respect is equally true for other cultures and contexts is currently a topic of debate and discussion (cf. Wohl, 1982). The literature in cross-cultural psychology strongly suggests that differing amounts of directness and support are needed in specific sociocultural contexts.

Person-centered therapy tends to be naively and romantically optimistic. Rogers's unbridled optimism about the potential for growth from within can be less than helpful to those whose hurt and pain reflect a greater variety of biological, psychosocial or sociocultural causal factors than merely "blocks to their self-actualization." No doubt, the therapeutic conditions of acceptance, empathy and honesty are powerful medicine, but they are not necessarily sufficient to combat the diverse challenges of the human situation.

Perhaps the approach is most helpful when the client doesn't need to go very deep or very far, or where, practically speaking, the client cannot (cf. Kovel, 1976). And as Corey (1986) has argued, are we really to believe that one particular relationship, no matter how powerful it is, can reverse the effects of years (or decades) of highly conditional love? And how does an experience of person-centered therapy prepare us for a world where so few persons evidence those qualities of health that are "canonized" by Rogerian therapy (i.e., congruence, empathy and unconditional positive regard)? The greater the discrepancy between the dream and the reality, the more potential there is for despair and frustration.

Conclusion

Few models of people-helping have been as widely discussed in Christian circles as has person-centered therapy. We have already developed at length the most important criticisms of this model. As a "purist" humanistic theory, there are too many inadequacies in person-centered therapy for it ever to serve as the foundation for a thoroughly Christian approach to personal healing.

Perhaps the enduring legacy of person-centered therapy for Christians will be the respect this tradition has for persons. Rogerians have taught us much about what it means to deeply care for (and be cared for by) others. Although we must be careful to realign certain concepts so that they conform more closely to the truth of the revealed will of God, we can certainly be grateful that Rogers and his followers have deeply sensitized us to what it means to listen to someone (Jacobs, 1975).

As Bonhoeffer (1954, p. 97) perceptively observed more than a half-century before, "The first service one owes to others in the fellowship consists in listening to them. Just as love to God begins with listening to His Word, so the beginning of love for the brethren is learning to listen to them." All too often Christians are talking when we should be listening. Bonhoeffer warned, "It is little wonder that we are no longer capable of the greatest service of listening that God has committed to us, that of hearing our brother's confession, if we refuse to give ear to our brother on lesser subjects. . . . We should listen with the ears of God that we may speak the Word of God" (pp. 98-99).

For Further Reading

Egan, G. (1986). *The skilled helper* (2d ed.). Monterey, CA: Brooks/Cole.
    Uses Rogerian skills as the foundation upon which to build solid generic counseling skills. Egan is excellent at translating concepts into specific skills. The book comes with a workbook.

Ellens, J. (1982). *God's grace and human health*. Nashville: Abingdon.
    The author develops a grace theology from a progressive evangelical stance in a manner that reflects the influence of the person-centered therapy tradition.

Oden, T. (1966). *Kerygma and counseling*. Philadelphia: Westminster.
    A widely referenced and influential initial study of person-centered therapy from a mainline Protestant perspective. The work reflects the initial enthusiasm about the application of person-centered therapy to the pastoral counseling setting.

Rogers, C. (1961). *On becoming a person*. Boston: Houghton Mifflin.
    A widely read introduction to the values inherent in person-centered therapy. This is probably the most autobiographical of Rogers's many books and articles.

Van Belle, H. (1980). *Basic intent and therapeutic approach of Carl R. Rogers*. Toronto: Wedge Publishing.
    Perhaps the most comprehensive and intensive critique of person-centered therapy from a Christian perspective. Written specifically from a conservative Reformed viewpoint.

Vitz, P. (1977). *Psychology as religion: The cult of self-worship*. Grand Rapids, MI: Eerdmans.
    A strong Christian critique of the "self-psychologies."

References

Bellah, R.; Madsen, R.; Sullivan, W.; Swindler, A.; and Tipton, M. (1985). *Habits of the heart*. Berkeley, CA: University of California Press.

Bonhoeffer, D. (1954). *Life together*. New York: Harper & Row.

Boy, A., and Pine, G. (1982). *Client-centered counseling: A renewal*. Boston: Allyn and Bacon.

Browning, D. (1987). *Religious thought and the modern psychologies*. Philadelphia: Fortress.

Corey, G. (1986). *Theory and practice of counseling and psychotherapy* (3d ed.). Monterey, CA: Brooks/Cole.

Dodgen, D., and McMinn, M. (1986). Humanistic psychology and Christian thought: A comparative analysis. *Journal of Psychology and Theology, 14*,

194-202.

Ellens, J. (1982). *God's grace and human health.* Nashville: Abingdon.

Evans, C. (1989). *Wisdom and humanness in psychology.* Grand Rapids, MI: Baker.

Evans, C. (1990). *Søren Kierkegaard's Christian psychology.* Grand Rapids, MI: Zondervan.

Farnsworth, K. (1985). *Whole-hearted integration.* Grand Rapids, MI: Baker.

Gaede, S. (1985). *Belonging.* Grand Rapids, MI: Zondervan.

Garfield, S. (1980). *Psychotherapy: An eclectic approach.* New York: John Wiley.

Hammond, D.; Hepworth, D.; and Smith, V. (1978). *Improving therapeutic communication.* San Francisco: Jossey-Bass.

Jacobs, J. (1975). A Christian client considers Carl Rogers. *Journal of Psychology and Theology, 3,* 25-30.

Korchin, S. (1976). *Modern clinical psychology.* New York: Basic Books.

Kovel, J. (1976). *A complete guide to therapy.* New York: Pantheon.

Lasch, J. (1979). *The culture of narcissism.* New York: Warner Books.

Lewis, C. S. (1968). *A mind awake: An anthology of C. S. Lewis.* (C. Kilby, Ed.) New York: Harcourt, Brace and World.

McLemore, C. (1982). *The scandal of psychotherapy.* Wheaton, IL: Tyndale.

McLemore, C. (1984). *Honest Christianity.* Philadelphia: Westminster.

Meador, B., and Rogers, C. (1984). Person-centered therapy. In R. Corsini (Ed.), *Current psychotherapies* (3d ed.) (pp. 142-195). Itasca, IL: F. E. Peacock.

Meier, S. (1989). *The elements of counseling.* Pacific Grove, CA: Brooks/Cole.

Myers, D. (1981). *The inflated self.* New York: Seabury.

Oakland, J. (1974). Self-actualization and sanctification. *Journal of Psychology and Theology, 2,* 202-209.

Oden, T. (1968). *Kerygma and counseling.* Philadelphia: Westminster.

Ortberg, J. (1981). Accepting our acceptance: some limitations of a Rogerian approach to the nature of grace. *Journal of Psychology and Christianity, 1,* 45-50.

Patterson, C. (1985). *The therapeutic relationship: Foundations for an eclectic psychotherapy.* Monterey, CA: Brooks/Cole.

Peck, M. (1983). *People of the lie.* New York: Simon and Schuster.

Prochaska, J. (1984). *Systems of psychotherapy: A transtheoretical analysis* (2d ed.). Homewood, IL: Dorsey.

Roberts, R. (1982). *Spirituality and human emotions.* Grand Rapids, MI: Eerdmans.

Roberts, R. (1985). Carl Rogers and the Christian virtues. *Journal of Psychology and theology, 13,* 263-273.

Roberts, R. (1988). Unpublished class notes. Wheaton College Graduate School, Wheaton, IL.

Roberts, R. (in press). *Taking the word to heart.* Grand Rapids, MI: Eerdmans.

Rogers, C. (1961). *On becoming a person.* Boston: Houghton Mifflin.

Rogers, C. (1980). *A way of being.* Boston: Houghton Mifflin.

Rychlak, J. (1973). *Introduction to personality and psychotherapy.* Boston: Houghton Mifflin.

Smedes, L. (1978). *Love within limits.* Grand Rapids, MI: Eerdmans.

Strupp, H., and Binder, G. (1986). *Psychotherapy in a new key.* New York: Basic

Books.

Tan, S. (1987). Intrapersonal integration: The servant's spirituality. *Journal of Psychology and Christianity, 6,* 34-39.

Thielicke, H. (1964). *The ethics of sex.* (J. Doberstein, Trans.) New York: Harper & Row.

Tisdale, J. (1988, October). Humanistic psychotherapy assumptions and Christian counseling. Paper presented at the International Conference on Christian Counseling, Atlanta, Georgia.

Van Belle, H. (1980). *Basic intent and therapeutic approach of Carl R. Rogers.* Toronto: Wedge Publishing.

Van Belle, H. (1985a). Person-centered therapy. In D. Benner (Ed.), *Baker Encyclopedia of Psychology* (pp. 822-825). Grand Rapids, MI: Baker.

Van Belle, H. (1985b). Rogers, Carl Ransom. In D. Benner (Ed.), *Baker Encyclopedia of Psychology* (pp. 1016-1017). Grand Rapids, MI: Baker.

Van Leeuwen, M. (1985). *The person in psychology: A contemporary Christian appraisal.* Grand Rapids, MI: Eerdmans.

Vitz, P. (1977). *Psychology as religion: The cult of self-worship.* Grand Rapids, MI: Eerdmans.

Wagner, M. (1975). *The sensation of being somebody.* Grand Rapids, MI: Zondervan.

Wohl, J. (1982). Eclecticism and Asian counseling: Critique and application. *International Journal for the Advancement of Counselling, 5,* 215-222.

11

EXISTENTIAL THERAPY

✛

Responsibility

Freedom

*E*xistential therapy has been defined as "a dynamic approach to therapy which focuses on concerns that are rooted in the individual's existence" (Yalom, 1980, p. 5). Although only four per cent of the psychotherapists in America endorse existentialism as their primary orientation (Prochaska and Norcross, 1983), this approach has had a far greater impact than this small figure would suggest. Indeed, one Christian existential psychotherapist, John Finch, had a major influence in the founding and development of the Graduate School of Psychology at Fuller Theological Seminary (Malony, 1980).

Perhaps most accurately described as a diverse group of attitudes and philosophical approaches to psychotherapeutic practice, existential therapy is generally not seen as a separate school of psychotherapy like behaviorism or psychoanalysis. Nor does existential therapy seem to lend itself to neatly defined models of personality, psychopathology or psychotherapy. Yet the attitudes and values that undergird existential therapy have been incorporated into many systems of counseling and psychotherapy; so that existentialism has become a "strange but oddly familiar" orientation for therapists of all persuasions irrespective of their control beliefs and world views (Yalom, 1980). At the same time, in the judgment of Norcross (1987, p. 41), existential therapy "is a diffuse and declining approach plagued by a lack of consistency, coherency, and scrutiny."

Descriptive Survey

To facilitate understanding of this diffuse but important approach to understanding human difficulties and growth, we will start with a summarization of the psychological thought of Søren Kierkegaard, regarded as the father of existentialism and a controversial though increasingly appreciated figure in Christian circles. (Existential therapy is a unique system in that it counts a Christian thinker as one of its founders.) We will then briefly discuss the most popularized version of existential therapy, Viktor Frankl's logotherapy. Finally, we will proceed through our more formal presentation of the essentials of existential therapy in its broader forms and conclude with our Christian critique.

Søren Kierkegaard's existential psychology. Søren Kierkegaard[1] viewed personhood both in terms of what we are and what we should become, with the emphasis on the latter. Therefore, we both are selves and must become selves.

Kierkegaard regarded human beings as created by God and constituted of disparate elements that did not naturally synthesize. He argued that these disparate elements could only be synthesized through an effortful deciding; we must act to create our selves. In a temporal and limited sense, we are the authors of our lives. Kierkegaard regarded the fundamental incompatibilities that require continuous active wrestling to be the polarities of *infinitude and finitude, possibility and necessity,* and *eternity and temporality.*

---

[1]In presenting a sketch of the views of Kierkegaard, we relied heavily on the writings of Evans (1990) and Mullen (1981). The writings of Kierkegaard himself are difficult for the casual reader to penetrate, though by universal acclaim his *Sickness unto Death* (1980) is the one work most pivotal for understanding his thought. Following Evans, we regard Kierkegaard to have been a distinctively Christian thinker who deserves a thoughtful reading by all who read this book.

To give only one example of these polarities, Kierkegaard would say that we all struggle with the nearly infinite possibilities of our existence, all the things we might do with our lives, on the one hand, and the pathetic necessities of our existence, including our limitations, failings and creatureliness, on the other. Many of us lose our courage as we manage this tension and cop-out by living a life of dreaming or fantasy about our possibilities, while others give up their dreams to live a life of grudging slavery to the necessities of life. Both of these options are failures to be a self, because in both instances the person has surrendered and stopped living by choice, choosing instead to simply live one of the two polarities of tension.

Becoming a true self, a true person, begins with *anxiety*, which is the result of the awareness of the necessity of making choices about synthesizing elements of our being which do not naturally go together. The capacity for choice is the essence of what it means to be a spirit. The core existential paradox is that there are no pat answers to the choices we must make, no answers that "feel just right." The only way to escape from anxiety is to deny the reality of choice; and so the only humans living without anxiety are those who are less than human because they are evading choice. Thus, "anxiety is a necessary part of genuine human life" (Mullen, 1981, p. 52).

The failure to become a self was called *despair* by Kierkegaard; despair as he describes it is an objective state and not an emotion, so that a person can be in despair and yet never feel despairing. We are in despair when we stop choosing to be *selves*.

The crux of Kierkegaard's ideas comes in his assertion that to be a true self is to synthesize our opposing tendencies as we are grounded in God. Being a true self is something that does not come naturally, and which few actually achieve. In fact, Kierkegaard proposed a theory of human development of sorts. According to Evans (1990), he suggested that we all start at the *aesthetic* stage, wherein the essence of life is believed to be having one's own way. Sometimes this takes the form of rude hedonism, but most often is a more cultured and subtle selfishness that comports well with getting along or succeeding in life. Many despair of aestheticism and then progress to the *ethical* stage, wherein one commits oneself to ethical principles to guide one's life. Finally, a few go on to the *religious* stage, which is constituted by a trusting personal relationship with the transcendent God of the Christian faith.

Thus, to be a fully functioning or developed human being, a true self, is to respond to the gift of anxiety by making one's existential choices in the context of one's transparent (or totally honest) relationship to God. In the words of Kierkegaard, "the self in being itself and in willing to be itself rests transparently in God" (quoted in Evans, 1990, p. 57). For Kierkegaard, to be a true self is to be a self grounded in Self (i.e., the Creator-God). To become perfectly transparent is to be fully cognizant of our propensity toward deception and denial (i.e., not being ourselves).

It is interesting to note two additional points. First, Kierkegaard, the "father of existentialism," would almost certainly regard modern secular existentialism as a form of despair, specifically what he called the despair of defiance. He believed that the only genuine and true decisions that could be made about becoming a self had to be made transparently before and in relationship with God. The very idea of autonomously choosing what sort of self to become, with no recourse to the one in whom we have our being (the essence of secular existentialism), was anathema to the thought of Kierkegaard.

Second, because we are to make our choices of who to become in the context of our relationship with God, it is clear that there is definitely a self that I am to become, a "true self" that I am to actualize by making the "right" choices. Our personhood is not wholly "plastic," moldable to any shape, as many existential thinkers today would assert. Rather, we are to become the people that God would hold out for us to become.

Thus, we see in the thought of Kierkegaard a Christian analysis of the nature of humanity, of where we go wrong in not becoming what we should be and a prescription for how to change and grow. In this way, as Evans (1990) has declared, Kierkegaard is surely a Christian "psychologist" whom more contemporary Christian thinkers should study. While there are many other dimensions to Kierkegaard's thought, this skeletal outline will give us a sufficient base from which to interact with existential therapy.

Viktor Frankl's logotherapy. Viktor Frankl authored the widely read *Man's Search for Meaning* (1959), in which he outlined the essentials of logotherapy. In all his works (e.g., 1965, 1975), Frankl discusses the formative impact of his personal experiences in the Nazi concentration camps of World War 2, and his depictions of those experiences are profound and moving. From those experiences, he took one overriding lesson: that persons who have a purpose or meaning for what they are experiencing can endure and grow even in the most devastating of circumstances, while those without meaning will wither and languish, and, in a prison-camp setting, might actually die as a direct result of their apathy and despair.

From this, Frankl came to believe that there is a fundamental drive to have a meaning or meanings to live by, what he called the "will to meaning." He did not deny the existence of other basic drives such as sex, aggression, survival and so forth, but argued that the drive for meaning is just as fundamental as any other motives in life. Frankl asserted that human beings are fully capable and responsible for determining the direction of their own existence. He claimed that the meanings we choose are or can be different for each person because there are no set meanings to life that demand a person's allegiance. He argued that there is a universal religious impulse in all of humanity, a need for spiritual meanings, which gives rise to religion. Thus the roots for religion are within persons and not in the objective existence of a deity beyond ourselves. In this way, Frankl was clearly agnostic and very much a humanist.

Frankl believed persons to be composed of three distinct aspects of being: the *somatic* or physical domain, the *psychological* domain and the *spiritual* or meaning domain. Persons can have problems in all three domains or in combinations of the domains. Frankl distinguished between problems of living that were primarily psychological (functional neuroses) and those which were more directly related to problems of meaning. He suggested two main types of problems of meaning; one was the neurosis that is born out of a *value* or *moral conflict*, and the other was the problem of *existential vacuum* or *meaninglessness*, in which the person's problem is not conflict but the total lack of significant meanings by which to guide one's life.

Frankl did not regard logotherapy as the treatment of choice for purely psychological or neurotic problems, but argued that purely psychological interventions that ignored the spiritual side were inappropriate for problems of meaning. It is for these problems that logotherapy was meant.

Frankl added one major new technique to the general mental-health field, that of *paradoxical intention*. Because the fear of a neurotic symptom (a phobic anxiety, for example) actually contributes to its occurrence, and thus the person's whole life can become oriented about that symptom, Frankl would paradoxically invite the patient to intend to do the very thing he did not want to do, to actually continue or increase the occurrence of the symptom. Thus the phobic client might be asked to put himself in the presence of what he feared and make himself have the very panic attack he feared most. He argued that because we are responsible agents, this choosing to exhibit a symptom allows the person to experience a control he had previously denied and to thus regain control over a part of his life.

Frankl developed other techniques for dealing with problems of meaning. Having the therapist prescribe a meaning is never likely to help, though a therapist may tentatively suggest meanings for the client to "try on." Frankl argued that those without meaning may find a value for themselves by doing a meaningful deed (in order to find meaning in the doing), by experiencing a value such as love or by experiencing suffering. Frankl also used the technique of "dereflection," wherein clients choose to deflect attention from their troubling symptomatology and thereby put that attention onto the real meanings of their existence and the actions that a commitment to those meanings demands.

Frankl seems often to challenge clients to look over their life, including imagining their future, and to choose or even assert a value that is worth living by. He gives the example of a depressed survivor of the concentration camps who had lost all of his family, wife and many children to the Nazi ovens and gas chambers. This individual could find no meaning to his suffering or his life. Frankl tentatively asked if it was possible that his suffering might be meant to allow the client, through his suffering, "to become worthy of joining them [his family] in heaven" (1959, p. 190). He reported that the individual subsequently became better able to bear his suffering.

Philosophical Assumptions
Existential therapy is first and foremost a growth model of people-helping, stressing wellness rather than illness, and radical personal freedom over and against psychic or biological determinism. From the ranks of philosophers and theologians, it draws heavily on the works of Bergson, Brunner, Buber, Heidegger, Kierkegaard, Niebuhr, Nietzsche and Sartre. From the ranks of European psychiatrists, it emphasizes the work of Binswanger, Boss and Frankl (Corey, 1986; Rychlak, 1973). But in this country, a psychologist, Rollo May (1961, 1981; May and Yalom, 1984), has probably done more than anyone to explain the personal relevance of the existential attitude for both applied clinical practice and life in general. More recently, Bugental (1978, 1981) and Yalom (1980) have had a significant impact on shaping the character of the

movement through their more clinically oriented efforts.

In terms of its philosophical roots, existential therapy can best be understood as a strong reaction to what it perceives as the overly deterministic, mechanistic or reductionistic tendencies of classical behaviorism and psychoanalysis. The word *existential* comes from the Latin *ex sistre,* meaning literally "to emerge or to stand out" (Finch and Van Dragt, 1985).

Existentialism[2] emerged in European intellectual and religious circles in the last century, largely as a strong protest against the growing dominance of rationalism and empirical science across the disciplines. It was in part a response to what Maritain called Hegel's "totalitarianism of reason" (i.e., "If you can't measure it it doesn't exist"; Korchin, 1976, p. 355). In response to science and philosophy attempting to understand human beings in terms of fixed mechanisms or substances ("essences"), some argued that persons must be understood in terms of "existence." Sartre argued that "man's essence is his existence. The meaning of this sentence is that man is a being of whom no essence can be affirmed. . . . According to Sartre, man is what he acts to be" (Tillich, 1960, p. 12).

The nature of humanity is deemed to be fluid, being defined and bounded only by the choices we make. Thus existentialists seek to understand persons in their processes of becoming or emerging. They prefer to stress the uniqueness of persons, not the commonalities between persons. Existentialists stress the primacy of the "self," seeing persons as dynamic and fluid beings, rather than as fixed or static individuals.

In short, to adopt an existential attitude is to respect the primacy of the developing or emerging person. As Evans (1984) has observed, existentialism is in the purest sense autobiography: to describe one's own experience and to relate it to the experience of one's audience. Knowledge is highly personal, and the basis of authority is the *authenticity* of personal experience.

Existential therapy shares much in common with certain other humanistic approaches, especially aspects of person-centered and gestalt therapies. It shares most of the orienting values of the hu-

---

[2]To understand more fully the philosophical heritage of existentialism, the interested reader could consult Kaufman (1975) and Solomon (1974) for straightforward and appreciative presentations from a nonreligious perspective, Friedman (1973) for a critical nonreligious perspective, and Evans (1984) for a distinctively Christian appraisal.

manistic tradition, especially its holistic emphasis, the importance of the self-report of direct experience, the need for coparticipation in research and clinical work, the high respect for empathic understanding and intuition, and the emphasis on strivings for growth and health (Korchin, 1976). Existential therapy, however, as it has developed in this country, is rather distinct from its roots in European philosophy and theology and certainly reflects aspects of contemporary American culture. The core assertions of the existential outlook would include the following (May and Yalom, 1984): (1) human beings are free and have to make a choice of whether or not to be authentic—we create ourselves through our choices; (2) we must make choices in a world without fixed meanings; (3) we are deeply related to others and to the world, but ultimately we are alone in the universe; (4) existence inescapably implies nonexistence or death, which is the source of much of our anxiety; (5) we grow through encounter with the abyss, our personal and private "dark night of the soul" (Van Dragt, 1985); (6) modern man feels alienated, resulting in an "existential vacuum"; (7) psychological symptoms are symbols and signs of our despair, the meanings of which need to be explored; and (8) we tend to become dependent persons who want other persons, places and things to be "good to us on our terms" (cf. Finch, 1982).

There appeared to be little serious interest in such "philosophical" matters in many sectors of contemporary American psychology until the last decade, especially in those traditions that stressed the more explicitly "scientific" approach. Thus it is not surprising to learn that existential therapy has generally not been well received in academic and research circles. Yalom (1980, p. 14) notes that existential therapy is like "a homeless waif who was not permitted into the better academic neighborhoods."

Models of Personality and Health
The respect for persons and their unique experiences of "being in the world" are the distinctive emphases of an existential model of personality. We are all in a continual, ongoing process of "becoming," according to existential theorists, trying to discover and make sense of our existence. Though the specific questions we ask may vary according to our developmental, maturational and sociocultural context, the fundamental questions persist: "Who am I? Who have I been? Who can I become? Where am I going?" (cf. Corey, 1986). Surely these are questions that also ought to interest serious Christian thinkers as well,

and these can hardly be dismissed with well-rehearsed "answers" or simple "solutions," responses that are far too common in many Christian circles.

Although it is hard to characterize a particular personality theory as definitively and distinctly "existential," most theoreticians talk about three levels of existence. These are referred to as *umwelt, mitwelt* and *eigenwelt. Umwelt* refers to the physical or biological dimension of existence. *Mitwelt* is the relational aspect of existence. And *eigenwelt* is the personal, existential world of meaning (i.e., the reality that Kierkegaard termed *spirit,* the most important concept in an existential understanding of human nature). Because we are capable of self-awareness, we can reflect and make choices in all aspects of being, thereby increasing our possibilities for freedom.

Finding meaning *is* a struggle. We are constantly confronted with the choice of what kind of person we are becoming, a task that is never fully completed in this lifetime. We must accept the responsibility for directing our lives. Periods of emptiness, guilt, isolation, loneliness and meaninglessness are inevitable in this quest. Although basically alone, we have the opportunity with a clearer sense of identity to relate to others at deeper and more meaningful levels (cf. Tillich, 1952).

With the awareness of our responsibility for the choices available to us and of the consequences of those choices, comes *anxiety.* Anxiety, in the existential therapy tradition and in line with Kierkegaard, informs us of our freedom and responsibility. In order to fulfill our destiny, we must be a self in truth, relentlessly. To be whole, we must be deeply rooted in our being, not the being of others who are too important to us.

Like anxiety, *guilt* resulting from our failure to make authentic choices is an ally, not a foe, since it too reminds us of our refusal to be ourselves in truth. When we attempt to deny or distort the anxiety or guilt we experience, our *self* becomes strange to our *spirit,* and consequently, we become unknown to ourselves and others (cf. Finch and Van Dragt, 1985). Healthy relationships with others are built on the basis of clearly established identities, not by trying to be or become something other than who we are.

To summarize, then: Persons are essentially spirit, radically free and responsible for the quality of their existence and the choices they make. As we develop a clear sense of identity, we have an increasing ability to make conscious and deliberate choices about whether or not we will be a self in truth, or alternatively protect ourselves from real or imagined threats by becoming more inauthentic. Daily we face an uncertain world without fixed values and must confront the possibility of our nonbeing (i. e., death). The healthy adult has a clear commitment to becoming, which includes having a well-formulated philosophy of life that will guide current and future actions. These persons see themselves as increasingly capable of identifying and removing blocks that thwart the maturation process.

Model of Abnormality

Our personal response to the issues of death, freedom, isolation and meaninglessness are at the core of the existential model of psychopathology. As Yalom (1980) has noted, the core of existential psychodynamics has to do with how specifically we have avoided these challenges and how that has led to psychological disturbance.

Psychopathology arises when we refuse to live authentically and responsibly in all of the levels of existence (*umwelt, mitwelt, eigenwelt*). All too often we adopt defenses and strategies that are inauthentic and self-deceptive, in that they evade freedom and responsibility (i.e., we lie to ourselves and/or others). This is especially evident when we are afraid to stand on our own two feet and are intimidated by the possibility of self-transcendence. We tend to lose touch with our own vital center, our capacity to be a self, and thereby commit ourselves to an inadequate philosophy of life that inevitably gives rise to symptoms.

If we do not embrace both the freedom and responsibility of being a true self, we are choosing to stagnate or regress toward a more inauthentic and immature life stance. It is not surprising, considering the enormity of this task, that so many in our confused society choose to become externally directed beings only, resulting in an inward sense of emptiness and hollowness, and a lack of any clear sense of identity or worth.

All psychological symptoms, according to existential therapy, result at some level from decisions to be inauthentic. We too often prefer the illusory safety and security of superficial self-protectiveness over and against the more meaningful and significant life of the self. We make a conscious and deliberate choice to live in a "state of forgetfulness of being" (after Heidegger, 1962). We allow ourselves to become trapped in a web of self-deceit.

Living in the awareness of one's being produces authenticity, but it is also fraught with anxiety. Rather than directly confronting and dealing with the anxiety, we tend to lie to ourselves and others about the nature of our predicament and attempt to coerce or manipulate others into supporting this deception. Psychological symptoms such as depressions or anxiety attacks are then seen as means of self-protection or avoiding existential anxiety and guilt, as when a person avoids confronting fears about one's own competence, meaningfulness and adequacy by being too anxious to ask for a promotion at work.

Model of Psychotherapy

Existential therapy is difficult to describe since it is less a coherent and consistent set of theories and techniques and more of an approach or attitude about how best to help others grow. The core goals in existential therapy are to enable clients to realize that they are free to make choices about the direction of their lives and to help them make commitments that hopefully will assist them in becoming more authentic in their existence. This is done not through mechanistic techniques, but through the highly personal encounter between therapist and client.

Existential therapists are very concerned about the risk of objectifying (making objects of) clients. They see their essential tasks as understanding the world of the client, clarifying this subjective world, and challenging or confronting the client with her capacity for choice and her need to assume full responsibility for her actions, insights and relationships. In that process, the qualities of the therapist-client relationship are vitally important. To use Buber's famous phrase, the therapy relationship must be an "I-Thou" encounter. Such a deep human-to-human encounter has the potential to change both the client and therapist profoundly.

Few specific techniques flow from existential therapy. Existential therapy has been wedded to nearly all major traditions except perhaps for the classic forms of behavior therapy (Norcross, 1987). Thus most existential therapists are "existential-psychodynamic," "existential-family systems" and so forth. Typically, psychological assessment and diagnosis are seen as antithetical to understanding the client, since such methods always risk objectifying the client and are thus avoided unless deemed absolutely necessary.

Still, certain themes appear consistently across the diverse and varied approaches to existential therapy. Client awareness is cultivated in existential therapy. With awareness comes the potential for health and greater authenticity, though much anxiety and threat will be encountered in the process, because awareness creates the possibility and indeed the necessity of choice. Freedom and responsibility are stressed, and great effort is exerted in the psychotherapeutic context to help the client to risk acting freely and responsibly.

The search for meaning and significance constitutes a major focal point in therapy. Assisting clients to more fully appreciate their own identity and uniqueness is encouraged so that they can increasingly tolerate being alone as well as with others in healthy, interdependent relationships. Anxiety, guilt and awareness of the inevitability of death are seen as important dimensions of the human condition, rather than topics to be avoided in the context of the psychotherapeutic encounter. The reader can see that these are emphases and topics which might be pursued, rather than clearly specified ways of intervening; this is why existential therapy is so often wed to other approaches.

Existential therapy appears to be well suited for individuals who must confront developmental and personal crises. "Existential concerns" are widespread in our culture, and many struggle with issues like making choices, dealing with freedom and responsibility, coping with anxiety and guilt, or finding a sense of direction in life.

Christian Critique

Philosophical Assumptions and Model of Personality

One finds in existential therapy (including logotherapy) an approach to understanding human beings that is genuinely struggling with the very aspects of existence that Christians find to be most significant. Compared to the bulk of "mainline" psychology, which is preoccupied with what seem at times to be comparatively trivial slices of life, existential therapy distinguishes itself by grappling with death, aloneness, choice, meaning, growth, responsibility, guilt and so forth (Tweedie, 1961, p. 163). No approach to psychology mirrors the concerns of the faith as well as does existential therapy.

These concerns are biblical concerns as well. Haden (1987, p. 58) argues that the writer of Ecclesiastes surveys human life from the human perspective, only to confront what Haden calls "alienation. He [the writer] is unable to find significance in nature, in his achievements, with reason, or even in seeking out the plans of God." Christians at times naively assert that "Jesus is the answer" to all such concerns, offering as answers what are often no more than trite Christian bumper-sticker slogans. But the writer of Ecclesiastes is more honest than this. Like Kierkegaard, the writer of Ecclesiastes does not simply lapse into relativism either. Rather, he finds meaning in living and choosing responsibly before God. The beginning of this process is to "fear God and keep his commandments" (Eccles 12:13). The absence of easy answers may daunt us, but "meaning exists because God exists" (Haden, 1987, p. 66). God is revealed only in the ways he sovereignly chooses, so that we must affirm and embrace our creaturehood, and in spite of the "daily uncertainties of life," we must "trust in God's divine plan" (p. 66).

The fundamental problem of secular versions of existential therapy, then, is not the questions being asked, but the form that the answers are forced to take when skepticism, relativism and pluralism are favored over the writer of Ecclesiastes' and Kierkegaard's concept of the self being grounded transparently in God.

As Tweedie noted, we are meant to "ground life in the realm of objective values" (i.e., values that exist as an external reality because God exists; Tweedie, 1961, p. 165), not to simply make brute assertions to define ourselves. It seems clear that for nonreligious existential therapists, any answer that is authentic is adequate. To some extent answers that rely on God and his Word are usually judged to be inauthentic or at least incomplete because they rely on something outside the self. For the Christian, all right answers will also be authentic answers (i.e., ones for which the person stands responsible and which the person must choose), but not all authentic answers will be right. Authentic atheism may be psychologically healthy, but it can be spiritually bankrupt. Again, Kierkegaard would define the secular existentialist's way of defining self to be a form of despair.

It appears that in secular existential therapy the self is viewed as continually in process, never clearly fixed or anchored in anything external to the self. To be authentic, we must be radically open to our experience in any given moment. As Roberts (1986) observed, this appears to be what it means to be alive in existential therapy and to be a true self.

There is a serious risk in such radical openness that it will lead to a personal identity where there is no clearer agenda for living than to be fully alive, aware and authentic in any given moment. But a Christian understanding of spirit would include certain undeniable commitments, like the formation of character through the cultivation and expression of the Christian virtues and a commitment to God's kingdom and the lifestyle that this entails. Our real goal as Christians is not just to be radical experiencers of the here-and-now, but to become Christ's coworkers in the kingdom of God and to be growing in Christlikeness (Roberts, 1986).

Existential-therapy notions of personhood may serve well as a needed corrective for our tendencies to deceive ourselves and to be satisfied with trite, superficial answers to life's questions. What is lacking, though, is a more thorough understanding of character formation and the deeper goal of such maturation (i.e., a commitment to kingdom values). The notion that "we are whatever we act to be" is too fluid and ill defined to be acceptable for the committed Christian.

The most central of existential therapy's assertions, that human beings are required to make the choices to define or create their own selves, can be troublesome depending on how it is interpreted. In Kierkegaard's terms, it seems quite noncontroversial to most Christians to say that we have the responsibility to make choices in life and that through these choices we make we are in fact constructing our ultimate selves. Through dishonest, rebellious, sinful choices we create a self truly worthy of judgment from God. Through conversion unto the forgiveness available in Christ and with the empowerment of the Holy Spirit, we can create selves that ever more closely approach the "new self" that God would have us become (Col 3:9-17).

But Christians should have serious reservations about endorsing a conception of the process of creating a self that is understood only in terms of human autonomy. It is in secular existentialist circles where the answers to life's questions are seen as authentic only when they are made without reference to God. In Reformed Christian circles, the pursuit of truth is understood as the attempt to "think God's thoughts after him." It would seem that we could broaden that concept to define the formation of the self by saying that the righteous attempt to create a self will be to make decisions that are in accord with God's wishes for us.

For the committed Christian, the rejection of psychic and/or biological determinism can certainly be appreciated. Especially in the work of Viktor Frankl, there is evidenced a profound respect for the more "spiritual" dimensions of personhood. As Hurding (1985) has commented, one sees something of the glory and ruin of humankind in aspects of existential therapy. Frankl argued that even in the midst of the most dreadful conditions, the human spirit can still soar to achieve a "will to meaning," especially when that is directed to something or someone other than oneself. As Hurding noted, perhaps this is similar to the thrust of what Jesus meant in Matthew 10:39, "He who finds his life will lose it, and he who loses his life for my sake will find it" (RSV).

We appreciate the fact that existential therapy takes personal pain and suffering seriously. Especially in the more explicitly religious forms of this tradition, anxiety, deception, despair and sin are not avoided, but powerfully confronted in deep and meaningful ways (Evans, 1989). Although existential therapy approaches vary considerably in their proposed solutions, few could doubt the value of this tradition's willingness to confront the more complex and challenging dimensions of reality and the human condition.

A transcendent reality is not necessarily discarded, but it is accorded varying degrees of respect in the specific versions of the approach. Again, the personal and subjective is given great authority in existential therapy, but in a far more rigorous and "soul-searching" manner than in the more romantic and optimistic traditions of person-centered and Gestalt therapies. Existential therapy generally eschews the more hedonistic direction of the humanistic approaches, stressing the need for and deep commitment to a well-developed conscience and a high degree of personal (although not necessarily corporate) responsibility.

Christians will have significant objections to the conception of religion in logotherapy and the other existential therapies. Frankl, as best we can tell, is typical, in his universalist conceptions, of the popular view that sees religion as a common urge that is mainly directed in drawing human beings to a truer knowledge of themselves and other human beings. Frankl (cited in Tweedie, 1961, p. 6) has declared different denominations and religions to be "something like different languages," none of which can be declared true or superior. He also declares that the stronger one's faith, the less strongly one clings to dogma, with the clear implication that true faith is devoid of intelligible dogmatic content and grounded only in isolated subjective experience (rather than in a sovereign and self-revealing God as orthodox Christianity would claim). This often results in a high tolerance for religious pluralism and personal relativism. Those aiming to develop a "Christian existentialism" need to be concerned about this tendency.

The emphasis on experiencing can result in an antipathy toward the rational side of faith. If unchecked, this can result in a purely subjective understanding of faith. Sin can become only an inner event of inauthenticity of the self, and not an interaction between God and person. This can in turn lead to equating emotional wholeness or authenticity with salvation. Both views provide incomplete understanding of the natures of sin and salvation.

Proponents of existential therapy, like Kierkegaard, are certainly right in arguing that the forging of a self is an effortful and demanding enterprise. The existence of the realm of "ought," in addition to "must" and "can," in human action is an indication that our natural instincts do not always guide us rightly and that our choices may be agonizing (Tweedie, 1961, p. 164). In this way existential therapy is a refreshing contrast to the more naively optimistic Rogerian and Gestalt notions of forming the self by following one's instincts. The Christian may also find the distinction between the authentic self and the "fake self" to be quite compatible with the biblical perspective on the human condition. A Christian understanding of persons could hardly dispute the assertions that self-deception and general deception are commonplace and that despite our best efforts, our true self all too often gets through to us with the "spirit urgings" overtly expressed in symptoms of anxiety, guilt or mood disturbance.

Another problem that we have with the existential therapy understanding of human nature is the danger of "psychologizing"—the tendency to give the subjective psychological perspective on any phenomenon pre-eminence over other valid perspectives, or the tendency to assume that the psychological perspective is the most basic perspective (Vande Kemp, 1986). In existential therapy, the problem is the extreme emphasis on the subjectivity of our inner experience. By understanding the reality "out there" only through the reality "in here," we run the risk of becoming almost reductionistic ourselves. The radical openness to experience so deeply valued in existential therapy can all too easily degenerate into an almost excessive emotionalism. Since a true understanding of our self depends on a deep appreciation of a reality external to ourselves (i.e., God), we must become fully cognizant of how we limit our full awareness of the nature of personhood when we adopt an epistemological stance of extreme relativism and subjectivity. We must understand the limits of our capacities to know or to be known.

Model of Abnormality
We appreciate that in existential therapy choice and responsibility are taken seriously. The existential tradition perceptively describes how we can become "stuck" at certain stages of development and become overly dependent on others to nurture us. The Christian gospel clearly asserts that to be human is to evade responsibilities (cf. the story of Adam and Eve; Gen 3). There are striking parallels between the existential therapy account of pathology and the Romans 1 drama

depicting humans "who suppress the truth by their wickedness" (v. 18); this suppression is both the result of their failure to acknowledge the truth they know (self-deception) and a defense that allows them to sustain their self-deception.

But we are convinced that the existential understanding of psychopathology is incomplete. First, it looks at guilt only existentially as a manifestation of inauthenticity, and not as the result of moral violation (Tweedie, 1961, p. 167). Also, as with other humanistic approaches, existential therapy seems to ignore or minimize the importance of the creaturely aspects of our existence, particularly any biological or sociocultural factors that can play such an important role in the causation or maintenance of psychopathology. Its rather extreme emphasis on choice and responsibility introduces an element of hope into the change process, but runs the risk of attributing behavior to choice rather than to other causal factors. Existential therapy also runs the risk of only blaming the victim. Although personal choice and responsibility are certainly major factors in psychopathology, they are clearly not the complete picture. Indeed, 1 Thessalonians 5:14 clearly states that different responses are needed depending on whether a person is rebellious, discouraged or "weak." Certainly, there are varying degrees of choice and responsibility when dealing with the challenges of everyday living.

On the other hand, it is all too common for persons who have great capacities to change to hide behind their symptoms. Existential therapy correctly states that anxiety and guilt are all too quickly interpreted as "negative" symptoms to be eliminated, rather than signs or symbols of the specific manner in which we haven't listened to our awarenesses. Few of us do not harbor fantasies of unhealthy dependencies toward symbolic "parents" in our lives (cf. Mt 10:34-39), nor are many of us willing to "find our life" through losing it. Indeed, existential therapy seems to be a much needed corrective for those of us who become content in our current situations, unwilling to discipline ourselves to "become a self in truth, relentlessly" (cf. Malony, 1980). We are far too easily pleased and content with the preservation of homeostasis or stability in our lives, often at great expense to our personal development.

Existentialism tends to assume that there are enormous resources for choice to draw on within all individuals. Existential therapy should be appreciated for the contribution it has made to our understanding of how high-functioning persons struggle in the quest for meaning and significance in their lives. There are probably different degrees of capacities for choice and responsibility in the broad spectrum of humanity. People struggle with such a diverse range of "problems in living" that it seems likely that some are pure "choice" issues (e.g., to be authentic or inauthentic) while others may involve lesser degrees of choice (e.g., a biologically based mania or the residual struggles of a person severely abused as a child). Thus the expectations for responsibility of the existential therapy tradition are highly appropriate for many, but they could become inappropriate and/or unrealistic for others. We thus must be careful about the potential arrogance or pride of applying such an interpretation of competence in a condescending or patronizing manner.

One can only wonder whether or not these keen assertions about psychopathology are generalizable outside the context of Anglo-American psychology. Although this could be said of nearly all major psychotherapies, we often are not aware of the ways in which fundamental assumptions might be limited beyond a particular sociocultural context. While choice and the ability to shape our self through reflection would clearly seem universal human capacities, is existential therapy's way of understanding these choices peculiar to our highly individualistic and selfish culture? Do persons in more communal and less pluralistic cultures look at these choices differently? Persons in societies with less leisure time and material prosperity may not have the luxury of reflecting on issues of meaning to such a length as to cause problems in living as they might in our culture.

Model of Health

Again, there are certainly dimensions of existential therapy that can be endorsed by the Christian, but its view of health appears limited and incomplete. Existential therapy calls us to have an objective and realistic view of ourselves and others. Christianity does as well, but there are certain differences in emphasis. We are told to perceive ourselves and others from both a divine and human perspective, cognizant of our need to be new creatures in Christ (2 Cor 5:17). Ideally, this should affect how we view believers, unbelievers and the social order (cf. Carter, 1985).

Likewise, existential therapy calls us to accept ourselves (or more accurately, our authentic selves). Unfortunately, it is far less clear about the need for accepting others as well. The Christian gospel stresses both, but also stresses the consequences of the Fall (i.e., the recognition that both the self and others are sinful and fallen). True Christian acceptance of ourselves calls us to a high standard of warmth and maturity in our relationships, fully aware of our limitations and weaknesses. Existential therapy lacks any clearly articulated notions of *agape, philia* and *koinonia* love (Carter, 1985, p. 501). The assumption appears to be that the quality of our relatedness will inevitably deepen as authenticity flourishes. Consequently, there doesn't appear to be any explicitly developed ethic other than "to be a self in truth, relentlessly," clearly a more internal rather than interpersonal ethic (cf. Finch and Van Dragt, 1985). Certainly this is important, but it is also rather incomplete.

Existential therapy is to be commended for stressing the impor- tance of living fully in the present and having long-term goals. The Scriptures stress present actions and attitudes, but frame them very differently, emphasizing the cultivation and expression of Christian virtues. We are to "abide" and "grow up" in Christ. This epitomizes a balance of living in the present and making deliberate choices for the future. The key difference appears to be in the focus. Christians are to focus more on others and less on themselves, more on a commitment to kingdom values and less on "experiencing" and "growing" as an end in itself.

Existential therapy rightfully stresses the importance of having self- chosen values. We find the existential analysis painfully accurate re- garding how "our" values are all too often uncritically adopted from respected others or merged with those of others. Much of our energy in the critical years of adolescence and early adulthood ought to be spent on "choosing, owning and prizing" our values, so that they will increasingly undergird our insights, actions and relationships (Parks, 1986). Existential therapy and Christian faith converge in asserting that a commitment to our values ought to cause us to reassess and realign our identities and lifestyles. But for the Christian, this process means "being in Christ" and not just being in our own subjective valuing process (Carter, 1985, p. 502).

Existential therapy correctly observes that superficiality is the curse of our age. As Foster (1978, p. 1) has noted, the "desperate need today is not for a greater number of intelligent people, or gifted people, but for deep people." The discipline and commitment required in existen- tial therapy, when coupled with a more complete understanding of who we are and who we can become, are laudatory and can be embraced by Christians. But they need to be coupled with an understanding of the importance of the spiritual disciplines and Christian virtues, and the crucial relevance of the discerning and disciplining community of faith. The mature Christian has character and integrity shaped and formed by the mind of Christ and is a person whose attitudes and actions are both Christlike and self-congruent (Carter, 1985, p. 504).

In summary, the existential therapy picture of a healthy individual as self-defined is off target to the extent that it asserts that the content of one's decisions is irrelevant. Yet the perspective of existential therapy is a useful corrective to a Christian conformity where the correct rules and values are so simplified and conformity so overemphasized that authenticity of experience is ignored. Mature Christianity entails, in part, becoming a responsible self who is transparently grounded in God, as Kierkegaard suggested over a century ago.

Model of Psychotherapy

Evans (1990) traces the centrality of spirit throughout the work of Kierkegaard. As persons created in the image and likeness of God, we have freedom and responsibility to actualize that potential. The reality, though, is that we have obscured that potential in an elaborate network of defenses and self-protective strategies.

At one level (cf. Finch, 1982), sin can indeed be seen as both a defense against our true self and a sickness created by a predictable tendency to assert ourselves as the masters of our own souls (i.e., arrogant pride). Although there are dimensions to sin, the net result is the same: We are cut off from intimate relationship with God. In contrast to much of contemporary existential therapy, Kierkegaard and certain Christian existential therapists, like Finch and Van Dragt (1985), see Christ as the only true ground of being (i.e., a self grounded in Self). Authentic reassessment and realignment occurs best in the context of a right relationship with God and not just with ourselves.

For the more explicitly religious existential therapist, then, the core of treatment is to facilitate a person's encounter with the God-Spirit. This is done by firmly but lovingly confronting the strategies of the false self (cf. Malony, 1980). In some cases, this includes an encounter with the abyss, the very personal and private hell of our inner feelings. As Van Dragt (1985) has persuasively argued, these "dark nights of the soul," when effectively worked through, can be transformed into a remarkable peace, a peace that becomes a major integrative focus where one falls into existence rather than out of existence. Unfortunately, much of the existential-therapy tradition has abandoned the original Kierkegaardian emphasis on the ultimate reference point for the self or spirit (i.e., the Creator-God). The deepest confrontation one can thus have, in the secular versions, is with oneself; there is no God to meet one in the depths.

This does not diminish, however, the importance of the intensification of awareness in the context of psychotherapy. As McLemore (1983) has observed, it is this very deliberate kind of soul-searching that will get us beyond the ready-made explanations for the complexities that all too often confront us in life. Existential therapy can reduce our inevitable tendencies toward rationalization, intellectualization and projection by powerfully confronting us with the many ways in which we attempt to deny and distort our inner realities (Kovel, 1976). But again, what is to prevent us from wallowing in the immediacy of our own subjective experience? A keener appreciation for the importance of deep insight in existential therapy must be coupled with an equally strong commitment to truth external to the person, as well as action and healthy relationships with others. Likewise, there is a real need to recognize the importance of our history and heritage, grounded in a Spirit outside of ourselves.

Certain themes tend to emerge from the writings of clinicians about the assets and liabilities of existential therapy. Because of its lack of proven effectiveness, at least as assessed by widely accepted methods of empirical validation, some consider it an approach or an attitude with some intuitive appeal, but prefer not to view it as a theory of therapy. Existential therapy offers little specific help in terms of intervention. Without more clearly articulated working models, it is possible for existential therapy to lead to a kind of anything-goes anarchy, a concern raised by even May himself in his early writings on the subject (1961).

The philosophy of science embedded in existential therapy cannot help but lead to some degree of irrationalism or solipsism, creating a dilemma in which we have no "objective" way of measuring the relative worth of any clinician's or client's experience. Norcross (1987, p. 63) warns that "in the future, existential therapy must move towards a definition for something: that is, in a proactive or positive manner. In doing so, its identity must be firmly rooted in a coherent and useful theoretical structure. More important, existential therapists' practices must be examined with particular reference to therapy process and outcome."

Bugental (1978) sees this as a difficult but not impossible challenge. By rejecting any serious type of scientific evaluation, existential therapy leaves us in the difficult position of not knowing how best to approach the serious study of its distinctive emphases. Hard and creative work will need to be done to develop the kind of measures and instruments that get at the deeper dimensions of personhood.

More psychodynamically oriented clinicians fault existential therapy for not doing justice to the complexity of psychodynamics, especially in terms of the crucial importance of the complex relationship between client and therapist. There are certainly limitations on freedom and choice, both in terms of responsibility for symptoms at an individual level, and responsibility for social order at the community level. We ought not to be radically free for our choices, especially in choosing our rules for living—the net result could be chaos (cf. Prochaska, 1984). Some tend to criticize secular existential therapy for focusing too much on anguish, despair and death without offering much solace beyond keeping a stiff upper lip.

Certain emphases in existential therapy on the importance of the phenomenal world can be appreciated. Indeed, much of Anglo-American psychology is probably overly objective, deterministic or detached from the "subject" (Van Leeuwen, 1985). But existential therapy runs the risk of overstating the case for conscious and contemporary experience (Korchin, 1976). There is a clear ahistorical bias in existential therapy that risks ignoring the fact that who we are at any moment in our development surely reflects where we have come from. Our capacities to deal with the demands of everyday living can surely be increased by a deeper recognition of how we have coped in the past and what skills and sensitivities we need currently to adapt even more effectively.

Clearly, much work needs to be done to make the central concepts of existential therapy more readily accessible to academicians, clients, clinicians and researchers. The approach needs to be more honest about its limited applicability in terms of the diverse and varied range of mental and emotional disorders. Still, both Yalom (1980) and Bugental (1978) claim that it is a powerful paradigm whose key concepts and ideas can be readily incorporated into most psychotherapeutic traditions.

Therapists in existential therapy take on an incredibly important role. As Evans (1989) has noted, it is on the role of "midwife," or what Kierkegaard called the *maieutic ideal*. As Christian clinicians, we want to assist persons in the work of developing the kind of self-concern that will allow them to engage more fully the claims of the Christian gospel on their lives. Although it is only God who creates faith in the individual, we must learn how to become a channel in which others meet God. Correctly understood, existential therapy sees part of the problem as our constricted understanding of what our most essential task is to be as human beings—to become a self grounded in Self. A serious encounter with Christ gives us deeper insight into who we are and who we should be. When such insight and awareness is mediated through a loving and healing relationship, and coupled with a strong emphasis on action, real and lasting change can be brought about (Benner, 1988).

But this final strength has its parallel weakness or caution. Does the existential therapist take on more than is legitimate? In taking on the midwife role of bringing about authenticity in the client, have we stepped too far into the domain of the role of pastor or priest? The therapist in this tradition leaves far behind the mundane goal of repairing psychological damage and alleviating suffering, and has embarked upon the task of formation of the self in all areas, including those traditionally considered religious. Does the existential therapist have a legitimate mandate for such activity? Where does the role of therapist leave off and that of spiritual director begin?

Conclusion

The Christian psychotherapist certainly values the importance of insight, action and a loving, healing relationship. But unlike the emphasis in the classic secular versions of existential therapy, no assumption is made that the truth is already within the client. Indeed, the truth must be brought to us by the Creator-God, and clients must encounter Jesus themselves in order to be fully whole (cf. Finch and Van Dragt, 1985). Deceit, manipulation or heavy-handed pressure should never be utilized in the process of assisting the client in the "birthing process." Rather, the healing context should be the kind of setting in which we can find ourselves free to pursue our search for meaning and significance, and make choices that will truly be authentic (cf. Parks, 1986). Indeed, content is of the utmost importance, but the processing of "knowing as we are known" is often an essential prerequisite to a deeper and more intimate spirituality, both in the context of our private lives and in the context of the communities of which we are a part. Existential therapy can be of great help in better understanding the questions we are to ask and the ways in which we can help ourselves and others make more authentic choices in response to those questions.

For Further Reading
Bugental, J. (1981). *The search for authenticity: An existential-analytic approach to psychotherapy* (rev. ed.). New York: Holt, Rinehart and Winston.

A fine example of how the "existential attitude" can be combined with more traditional approaches to psychotherapy.

Evans, C. (1990). *Søren Kierkegaard's Christian psychology*. Grand Rapids, MI: Zondervan.

Excellent introduction to the specifically psychological thought of Kierkegaard.

Frankl, V. (1959). *Man's search for meaning: An introduction to logotherapy*. New York: Pocket Books.

The essential introduction to logotherapy.

Malony, H. (Ed.). (1980). *A Christian existential psychology: The contribution of John G. Finch*. Washington: University Press of America.

A survey of the thought of John Finch, an influential Christian existential psychologist.

May, R. (Ed.). (1961). *Existential psychology*. New York: Random House.

The book that is widely credited with introducing existential thought to the North American scene.

Mullen, J. (1981). *Kierkegaard's philosophy*. New York: New American Library.

Excellent introduction to the general thought of Kierkegaard.

Yalom, I. (1980). *Existential psychotherapy*. New York: Basic Books.

The definitive reference in existential psychotherapy.

References

Benner, D. (1988). *Psychotherapy and the spiritual quest*. Grand Rapids, MI: Baker.

Bugental, J. (1978). *Psychotherapy and process: The fundamentals of an existential-humanistic approach*. Reading, MA.: Addison-Wesley.

Bugental, J. (1981). *The search for authenticity: An existential-analytic approach to psychotherapy* (rev. ed.). New York: Holt, Rinehart and Winston.

Carter, J. (1985). Healthy personality. In D. Benner (Ed.), *Baker encyclopedia of psychology* (pp. 498-504). Grand Rapids, MI: Baker.

Corey, G. (1986). *Theory and practice of counseling and psychotherapy* (3d ed.). Monterey, CA: Brooks/Cole.

Evans, C. (1984). *Existentialism: The philosophy of despair and the quest for hope*. Grand Rapids, MI: Zondervan.

Evans, C. (1989). *Wisdom and humanness in psychology*. Grand Rapids, MI: Baker.

Evans, C. (1990). *Søren Kierkegaard's Christian psychology*. Grand Rapids, MI: Zondervan.

Finch, J. (1982). *Nishkamakarma*. Pasadena, CA: Integration Press.

Finch, J., and Van Dragt, B. (1985). Existential psychology and psychotherapy. In D. Benner (Ed.), *Baker encyclopedia of psychology* (pp. 372 -377). Grand Rapids, MI: Baker.

Foster, R. (1978). *Celebration of discipline*. New York: Harper & Row.

Frankl, V. (1959). *Man's search for meaning: An introduction to logotherapy*. New York: Pocket Books.

Frankl, V. (1965). *The doctor and the soul: From psychotherapy to logotherapy*. New York: Bantam.

Frankl, V. (1975). *The unconscious god*. New York: Simon and Schuster.

Friedman, M. (Ed.). (1973). *The worlds of existentialism: A critical reader.* Chicago: University of Chicago.

Haden, N. (1987). Qoheleth and the problem of alienation. *Christian Scholar's Review, 17,* 52-66.

Heidegger, M. (1962). *Being and time.* New York: Harper & Row.

Hurding, R. (1985). *Roots and shoots.* London: Hodder and Stoughton.

Kaufman, W. (Ed.). (1975). *Existentialism from Dostoevsky to Sartre.* New York: Meridian.

Kierkegaard, S. (1980). *The sickness unto death* (H. Hong and E. Hong, Trans.). Princeton: Princeton University Press.

Korchin, S. (1976). *Modern clinical psychology.* New York: Basic Books.

Kovel, J. (1976). *A complete guide to therapy.* New York: Pantheon.

Malony, H. (Ed.). (1980). *A Christian existential psychology: The contribution of John G. Finch.* Washington: University Press of America.

May, R. (Ed.). (1961). *Existential psychology.* New York: Random House.

May, R. (1981). *Freedom and destiny.* New York: Norton.

May, R., and Yalom, I. (1984). Existential psychotherapy. In R. Corsini (Ed.), *Current psychotherapies* (3d ed.) (pp. 354-391). Itasca, IL: F. E. Peacock.

McLemore, C. (1983). *Honest Christianity.* Philadelphia: Westminster.

Mullen, J. (1981). *Kierkegaard's philosophy.* New York: New American Library.

Norcross, J. (1987). A rational and empirical analysis of existential psychotherapy. *Journal of Humanistic Psychology, 27,* 41-68.

Parks, S. (1986). *The critical years.* New York: Harper & Row.

Prochaska, J. (1984). *Psychotherapy: A transtheoretical analysis* (2d ed.). Chicago: Dorsey.

Prochaska, J., and Norcross, J. (1983). Contemporary psychotherapists: Characteristics, practices, theories, and attitudes. *Psychotherapy: Theory, Research and Practice, 20,* 620-627.

Roberts, R. (1986, April). John Finch on our two selves. Unpublished paper presented at Wheaton College, Wheaton, IL.

Rychlak, J. (1973). *Introduction to personality and psychotherapy.* Boston: Houghton Mifflin.

Solomon, R. (Ed.). (1974). *Existentialism.* New York: Modern Library.

Tillich, P. (1952). *The courage to be.* New Haven, CT: Yale University Press.

Tillich, P. (1960). Existentialism, psychotherapy, and the nature of man. *Pastoral Psychology, 11,* 10-18.

Tweedie, D. (1961). *Logotherapy: An evaluation of Frankl's existential approach to psychotherapy from a Christian viewpoint.* Grand Rapids, MI: Baker.

Vande Kemp, H. (1986). The dangers of psychologism: The place of God in psychology. *Journal of Psychology and Theology, 14,* 97-109.

Van Dragt, B. (1985). A peace that passeth understanding: An existential view of the "dark night." *Journal of Psychology and Christianity, 4,* 15-18.

Van Leeuwen, M. (1985). *The person in psychology: A contemporary Christian appraisal.* Grand Rapids, MI: Eerdmans.

Yalom, I. (1980). *Existential psychotherapy.* New York: Basic Books.

12

GESTALT THERAPY

✛

*G*estalt therapy is perhaps the most phenomenological and pragmatic of the humanistic approaches to people-helping. The exclusive focus in Gestalt therapy is on the here-and-now of immediate experience and the integration of fragmented parts of the personality. Gestalt therapists agree that emphasizing the "why" of behavior (i.e., insight and explanations) or analyzing past events is far less therapeutically useful than stressing the more overt "what" and "how" of present behavior, or the specific ways in which unfinished business from the past intrudes on current functioning. Gestalt therapy appeals to those who are looking for greater depth and meaning in their intimate relationships. Members of the religious community might find it especially attractive if they want something beyond the "unhealthy, sticky, manipulative, and symbiotic togetherness" that sometimes characterizes our efforts to build and maintain community (McLemore, 1982, p. 162).

The founder of Gestalt therapy, "Fritz" Perls, trained as a psychoanalyst in Germany between the wars (as he discusses in his autobiography, 1969b). Gestalt therapy reflects certain emphases of the psychoanalytic tradition, especially the role of the defense mechanisms in the development of symptoms. The academic Gestalt psychology tradition in Europe, which researched sensation and perception, also influenced Perls. The major characteristics of perception which these researchers stressed are summarized in such maxims as "The whole is more than the sum of the parts." The prevalent existential philosophy of the time also had a substantial impact on Perls. He eventually forged Gestalt therapy as a creative merger of concepts from existential philosophy, psychoanalytic and Gestalt psychology, and techniques developed in the creative or expressive arts (e.g., psychodrama).

Before his death in 1970, Perls made considerable use of ideas from Zen Buddhism, Taoism and the human-potential movement. For years, he was a resident "guru" in workshop and retreat centers across North America. A strong and forceful personality, Perls had a devoted following in both lay and professional circles. Although the influence of Gestalt therapy has waned considerably in the past decade, it was documented in videotapes, audiotapes and therapy transcripts when it was at its apex of popularity.[1] Although few clinicians today would describe themselves as Gestalt therapy "purists" philosophically or methodologically, many of the techniques of this approach have been widely adapted to the psychotherapeutic context.

Descriptive Survey

Philosophical Assumptions and Model of Personality

The initial formulations of Gestalt therapy by Perls and his colleagues are difficult to evaluate because they are so decidedly antirational, openly disparaging intellectual precision and rigor. More recent versions of Gestalt therapy are more respectful of cognitive processes, but they share with earlier formulations a tremendous disdain for "mind games" (irrational intellectualisms or rationalizations). As such, its proponents tend not to detail the philosophical assump-

---

[1]Good summaries of its therapeutic strategies can be found in Fagan and Shepherd (1970), James and Jongeward (1971), Latner (1973), Passons (1975), Polster and Polster (1973), Simkin and Yontef (1984), Van De Riet and Korb (1980) and Zinker (1978).

tions or values on which the Gestalt therapy is based, making it more difficult to perceive its implicit convictions about human nature.

Gestalt therapy is an approach that stresses the unity of mind, body and feelings. It is a hybrid approach that draws rather freely on psychodynamic and phenomenological formulations. Gestalt places great emphasis on awareness, authenticity, confrontation, encounter, immediacy, personal responsibility and risk taking. The key assumption is that we are *fully responsible* for our own behavior and experiencing. Perhaps this is nowhere more clearly evident than in the widely quoted "Gestalt prayer": "I do my thing and you do your thing. I am not in this world to live up to your expectations and you are not in this world to live up to mine. You are you and I am I and if by chance we find each other, it's beautiful. If not, it can't be helped" (Perls, 1969a, p. 4). Easily interpreted only as a license for self-gratification or irresponsible hedonism, it more accurately reflects the extreme emphasis gestalt therapy places on personal autonomy as well as the need for individuals to more fully experience the present moment through increased awareness of what they are thinking, feeling and doing when they are interacting with others.

Perls argued that persons are essentially biological organisms with strong needs. He generally limited these to breathing, hunger, thirst, sex, shelter and survival. A major task in a given day is to get these organismic needs, or "end-goals," met. The meeting of these needs in the present situational context is the Gestalt-therapy version of a "self-actualization" drive (as opposed to the "optimization of personal potential" version of Rogerian psychology, chapter ten).

Meeting one's own current organismic needs in a constructive, creative and healthy fashion is the ultimate goal of Gestalt therapy. This could result in either greater self-integration or hedonism, depending on one's perspective. Whether this will translate into more responsible ethical and moral behavior in the larger societal context is a matter of intense debate in both lay and professional circles (e.g., Browning, 1987).

Gestalt therapy assumes that greater awareness of organismic needs and situational requirements is curative in and of itself. Persons are assumed to have the capacity *within* to support themselves in adaptive ways if they are willing to examine and perhaps change the unique and specific ways in which they see, feel, sense and interpret the realities of their personal needs and of their situational context in the present moment. In other words, accurate perception of self and surroundings will unleash the inherent capacity of the individual to meet his or her own needs.

Former students of "introductory psychology" should remember the example of the famous *figure/ground* perceptual phenomenon, most often exemplified by the "face-vase" figure. When one focuses on the vase, the faces become mere background, but when one focuses on the faces on either side of the vase figure, the vase disappears to become mere background. Perls asserted that we normally form figure/ground perceptions of our needs, but experience these as discomfort or pain when they are disrupted (called "dis-integrated" figure-ground differentiation by Gestalt therapists). Perls argued that *greater awareness* of our organismic needs and situational requirements could potentially result in *greater integration*. We try out solutions, discard those that do not work for us and assimilate those which do work for us.

As we bring completion to these end-goals, we form wholes or "Gestalts" which we can "let go of." The assumption, consistent with other humanistic approaches, is that there is an innate tendency within all of us to become more self-aware and thereby move toward a position of greater autonomy or wholeness (the term Gestalt therapy practitioners tend to use instead of *autonomy*).

Gestalt therapy places absolute confidence in our capacity to regulate ourselves from within. Authority resides *exclusively* with that awareness. External criteria apart from subjective experience are not to be trusted. "Mind games" (and often cognitive processes in general) are downplayed because they tend to be the repository of rules, laws or regulations that have been assimilated from others without personal integration. Thus these externally derived rules almost inevitably result in unhealthy forms of dependence, usually in persons relying on moralisms or "shoulds" for guidance rather than on their own perceptions.

Gestalt therapy has a rather low view of accountability to others since our wants and needs assume a position of absolute primacy. The fully functioning person is the one who is fully alive and aware, who meets biological needs in an adult and responsible fashion, and who is not dependent on others to meet these needs. Individuality tends to be glorified, and this can readily translate into a low view of relationships. In other words, we are responsible to support ourselves first and foremost and to stop depending on others to meet our needs for us. Self-sufficiency, then, is a pre-eminent virtue in Gestalt therapy.

In therapy Gestalt practitioners place great emphasis on our capacity to take care of ourselves. The assumption is that in the long run continuous perceptual feedback and integration will help us find adaptive and healthy ways to meet our needs through our proactive responding. This is certainly a pragmatic and often brutally realistic (if not pessimistic) approach to human relationships. The visible social roles we adopt, Perls argued, usually reflect the kind of dependencies we prefer over more autonomous methods of meeting our needs. Gestalt therapists are often suspicious of roles.

Model of Health
In Gestalt therapy, psychological wholeness is seen as an end in itself. Perls warmly embraced the humanistic spirit of the 1960s, contending that if you truly want to grow as a person, you must "lose your mind and come to your senses." This is generally interpreted to mean that we think too much in self-defeating ways and are not aware enough of what we are doing or experiencing, especially emotionally, in any given moment. In Gestalt therapy, the healthy person is the one who is free of façades and is not preoccupied with fixed social roles or with thinking "too much" (e.g., always making excuses). Healthy individuals are fully cognizant of their end-goals and find constructive ways to meet their biological needs. The psychologically whole person in Gestalt therapy is open and responsive to the full range of organismic experience and is fully functioning in the here-and-now. The "constraints of the past" or the "pull of the future" are generally seen as "distractions."

Healthy individuals take full responsibility for themselves but not for anyone else. They are truly self-supporting and certainly not dependent on outside sources of affirmation for their existence. In short, authentic and healthy adults trust themselves, are fully alive and aware, know their biological needs and can meet these in a nondependent and non-manipulative manner. By doing that, they facilitate their personal growth and achieve a higher degree of organismic self- regulation. Since considerably less time will be spent on manipulating the environment to meet their needs, they are a lot freer to authentically and congruently respond to the needs of others. Correctly speaking, the goal of Gestalt therapy is nonmanipulation—one's true identity will only emerge to the extent that one is ultimately "truthful" with self and others.

Model of Abnormality
Problems in living originate when one is not fully functioning (experi-

encing) in the here-and-now. This is most often due to the intrusion of "unfinished business" from the past or an unwillingness to become more fully aware. For example, as children, we may be taught not to trust ourselves but rather to obey rules forced on us ("You'll take a nap when I say you'll take a nap, young man!"), to deny and distort our own emotional reactions ("Wipe that scowl off your face and say you are sorry!"), to define ourselves in ingenuine ways ("You were quiet all afternoon; that's a nice girl!") and to prefer environmental support to self-support ("I don't care what you think; do it my way and it will come out right!").

Our needs cannot be met in adaptive and healthy ways if we are not aware of them to begin with. The "figure" (our needs) never clearly emerges from the "background" (all the competing needs) and thus we never act in accordance with our more "intuitive" instincts. When needs are unmet, they do not naturally recede into the background; this is what Gestalt therapy calls *unfinished business.* We then tend to subsequently distort the sensory-perceptual field and stimuli we receive in other contexts. Eventually, we begin to see everything incorrectly (cf. Perls, 1969a). We become increasingly preoccupied with the social roles we choose as an expression of our other-dependence; these eventually become the games we play. With repetition, these *games* become self-destructive and rigid patterns that symbolize "disowned" or "fragmented" parts of our true personality; they are only *part* of who we are, but we mistakenly believe they make up *all* of our identity. We choose to be less than we could be by not choosing to become more alive and authentic in the present moment.

Our problems or symptoms are "signs" or "symbols" of the diverse and varied ways we attempt to avoid awareness of our moment-to-moment experiencing. All problems are at some level "con games" perpetrated by the person for the purpose of running away from awareness. Consequently, our energies are misguided into the social roles we play and the symptoms we manifest, rather than into meeting our biological needs in more adaptive ways. The full range of our emotional and sensory-perceptual processes becomes constricted, and we develop increasingly fragmented views of ourselves as well as our external environments.

Perhaps the most widely recognized contribution of the Gestalt therapy model of psychopathology is its emphasis on the different layers of deceit (after Corey, 1986). The initial layer is the *phony* level where we play games in our social relations, acting out what we think others want us to be. Perls argued that we put a great deal of our psychic resources into constructing elaborate fantasy lives that do not help us to meet our needs in adaptive or healthy fashions. If we penetrate the façade, we often next encounter the *phobic* layer. Because we deny, distort or disown important parts of ourselves, we fear and avoid awareness. If we can penetrate the fear, the next layer is the *impasse* where we tend to get stuck in our own efforts to foster our maturation process. We become convinced that we cannot find the means to support ourselves except by looking elsewhere (rather than within). We play "stupid" or "crazy" or "enraged" or "religious" in a thinly disguised attempt to get others to take responsibility for us. We can spend a lifetime developing manipulative strategies of coercing others into "loving" us and "taking care" of us. Underneath the impasse layer are the *implosive-explosive* layers, where we increasingly vacillate between the experience of the deadness of the parts of ourselves that we have disowned and the potentially positive explosive energy that has been invested in maintaining a false, ingenuine "homeostasis." Only if we are willing to penetrate all these layers do we really encounter our real selves. But it is only when we confront the explosive layer that we can free up the previously unused energy that can be directed into love, anger, joy, grief or other strong and powerful experiences of being more fully human.

Another contribution of Perls is his belief that in avoiding full awareness of ourselves, including the inner contradictions that are part of normal humanness, we often develop a splitting of our awareness into polarities. These polarities function to allow us to deny part of our experience. Perhaps the most common example of this is the overly rational person who has periodic emotional outbursts, usually of sadness or anger, which are regarded as "ego-alien," or "not the real me" ("Don't mind me; I'm just a puddle of tears today.").

Polarities manifest themselves in persons who do not have a holistic sense of their experience, regardless of whether the experienced parts all "make sense." Some of the polarities which Perls discussed include *emotional versus rational, spontaneous versus deliberate, personal versus social, conscious versus unconscious* and *top dog versus underdog.*

In short, psychopathology in Gestalt therapy is the failure to take the risk of being a truly alive and responsible person. We surround our core being with multiple layers of deception. Our defense mechanisms are used extensively and rigidly to distort reality so that we lose any real sense of who we are (or could become).

Model of Psychotherapy

In a now-famous demonstration of his methods, Perls (Perls and Shostrum, 1965) began an interview with Gloria by stating that they would be talking for a brief time. Gloria responded that she was very nervous and afraid about talking with Perls, to which Fritz immediately replied, "You say you are afraid but you are smiling." He proceeded into a series of rather direct confrontations with the client about the incompatibility of fear and smiling, and never once throughout the interview asked what the client would like to talk about. He thus exemplified how Gestalt therapy pushes for awareness (and "frustrates the neurosis") in the present, with the confidence that the aware client will solve her own problems in her own time. To push for insight, conceptual formulations and so forth is not just a waste of time, but can be a reinforcement of the client's defenses against awareness.

Gestalt therapy is a highly experiential therapy that stresses "doing" more than "saying." It seems especially well suited for group rather than individual therapy. Its core assertion is that we will grow only to the extent that we come to grips with the "what" and "how" of our behavior in the here-and-now. For Perls, we less need to be affirmed for who we are (Rogers) and more need to stop playing games, summon the courage to perceive ourselves and our world accurately, and stand on our own two feet. Growth is thus not through affirmation (Rogers) as much as it is through confrontation and encounter.

Immediacy and vitality in experience are the ultimate virtues in Gestalt therapy. The "shoulds" of collective morality are seen as vices, especially when they are used as a substitute for avoiding personal responsibility or risk-taking in the interpersonal context. As Korchin (1976) has perceptively observed, Gestalt therapy's strongest appeal is perhaps to those persons who feel overburdened and oversocialized by the demands of contemporary Western societies but feel relatively powerless in their efforts to become more aware of their own needs and wants (i.e., they are "out of touch").

Gestalt therapy is certainly the most directive and confrontive approach to people-helping. If it follows from the theory that clients must discover the fragmented parts of their personality, then it follows that this can only be achieved by focusing exclusively on the direct experience of the here-and-now. Working primarily through the observable nonverbal and bodily clues, the therapist works toward the goal of assisting the client in seeking fewer environmental or external supports and toward greater integrity and personal responsibility. By focusing exclusively on the here-and-now of immediate experiencing, the client develops greater self-initiative and risk-taking. Biological needs are then met in more adaptive and constructive ways. The ultimate goals, then, of Gestalt therapy are (1) growth into self-support, (2) personal integration of the fragmented experience of self and (3) greater integrity and responsibility with reference to self.

The therapist in Gestalt therapy focuses on the "what" and "how" of the client's behavior and experience, rather than the "why" (i.e., insight and interpretation are strongly de-emphasized). Removing "blocks" to client self-awareness is seen as far more useful than direct teaching. Such immediate and existentially relevant personal experience is seen as the core of good therapy. Therapist modeling, although not unimportant, is not emphasized. As with all humanistic-existential approaches, there is a deep faith and confidence in the ability of clients to intuitively decide what is best for themselves.

The rules and games of Gestalt therapy have been influential in a variety of psychotherapeutic applications (cf. Levitsky and Perls, 1970; Smith, 1976). Gestalt therapy techniques are designed to intensify direct experiencing and to integrate conflicting feelings or polarities within the individual. Gestalt therapists insist that their clients communicate entirely in the present tense, using "I" language rather than "it" or "you" language. Asking questions is strongly discouraged, nor are clients permitted to talk about persons, only to them (i.e., "no gossiping"). They are encouraged to focus on the affective and bodily sensations of their immediate experience and to talk to the therapist or other group members as "equals" (an "I-Thou" encounter). Collectively, these are known as the rules of Gestalt therapy.

In addition, Gestalt therapy employs a rather impressive repertoire of psychotherapeutic exercises to facilitate awareness of immediate experience. First and foremost amongst these is active *role-playing,* in which participants act out different "splits" or polarities within their personalities. *Dream analysis,* in which participants are asked to act out each human and nonhuman part of the dream in the here-and-now, is also highly valued.

Gestalt therapy epitomizes the experientially oriented approach to people-helping. Its exclusive focus on the here-and-now of immediate awareness and experience is perhaps best suited for growth-oriented groups of high-functioning members, though it has been adapted for a variety of family, individual, institutional and marital settings. It appears that Gestalt therapy is best suited for persons who feel somewhat constricted in their ability to express either the depth or full range of their feelings and who are relatively free of "gross" psychopathology (e.g., psychosis, severe neurosis, organic mental disorders, developmental disabilities, etc.). While judged by many to be effective in helping those who tend to overcontrol or repress their emotional expressiveness, serious concern should be raised about whether it should be used with persons who are, comparatively speaking, undercontrolled or impulsive (e.g., antisocial or borderline).

Both clients and therapists in Gestalt therapy are actively involved in encountering and confronting unfinished business—that is, unresolved figure/background Gestalts. Treasured virtues in Gestalt therapy, developed through greater organismic self-regulation, include full acceptance of personal responsibility, living fully in the present moment and direct experiencing as opposed to talking about things. When we are truly willing to confront our "impasse," greater energy is released as we "implode" and eventually "explode" into the full recognition of our biological needs. Until then, we will only "perfect our neuroses" rather than confront them. Only when we are willing to confront the contradictions and polarities of our lives can we move toward reintegration of the "disowned" parts of our being.

Christian Critique

Philosophical Assumptions and Model of Personality
Gestalt therapy strives to be a system that optimizes human freedom and autonomy while putting thinking in its proper place. We will discuss autonomy below, but will here focus on the understanding of freedom and cognition.

First, with Browning (1987) we would note that in making self-actualization a narrowly biologically based drive for fulfillment, Gestalt therapy renders its account of human nature one which actually makes it impossible for human beings to transcend their physiological constraints. Gestalt therapy asserts that we are ultimately free only when we do what our biological urges push us to do, assuming that we act in a nonmanipulative manner. This runs the risk of being a profoundly impoverished view of freedom.

By equating being human with being physiological, humans are trapped. Perls's injunctions to follow one's biological urges may create the illusion of choice, but they actually deplete our greatest window of choice, that being our capacity to transcend, with God's help, the bounds of our own selfishness and physicalness to do what God calls us to. To be human is to be a biological being (and to rejoice in that state), but we are not merely biological beings.

The broader issue in Browning's (1987) analysis is that psychotherapy systems often take somewhat legitimate descriptions of "nonmoral goods," such as feelings, needs, awareness and so forth, and then arrange them in contrasting priority with other facets of human experience. In so doing, the psychological system becomes a moral system, because a moral system is, at least in part, a comparative ranking of the "goods" and "not goods" that we face. Gestalt therapy, for instance, takes many nonmoral goods, such as emotional awareness, and transforms them into moral imperatives when it specifies that the awareness process takes precedence over all others as one's source of answers for how to act in getting needs met. Gestalt therapy arranges needs into a quasimoral system by prizing experiencing above all else.

And yet Gestalt therapy is not a formal system of universal rules as are most ethical systems. It can only press its moral agenda by assuming that if everyone simply "does their own thing" that all of our "things" would mysteriously be in alignment, with the result that everything would be "groovy." It is for this reason that Browning describes the humanistic psychologies as examples of "instinctual utopianism" (1987, p. 62).

Gestalt therapy assumes that all human needs will ultimately harmonize, with the result that if everyone were truly doing what was best in his or her own eyes, we would all almost magically be doing what was best for everyone else. In short, Gestalt therapy is far less clear on how greater self-awareness in the present moment will translate into a responsible and well-formulated interpersonal ethic. The assumption appears to be that individual integrity and wholeness are the necessary and sufficient conditions for producing corporate change and instilling responsibility. This is an incomplete ethic at best (cf. Prov 14:12).

Further, Gestalt therapists seem strangely unconcerned with larger questions of meaning and purpose in life. Perhaps it is true that too many "why" questions, especially in the psychotherapeutic context, can be a means to avoid dealing with more important issues, but this does not erase the fact that we have a compelling need to ask such questions.

In contemporary American society it is all too easy to give up the search for meaning. Indeed, the seemingly all-pervasive American milieu of individualism and relativism strongly suggests that this is often the case (cf. Bellah, Madsen, Sullivan, Swindler and Tipton, 1985).

An undue emphasis on objectivity and detachment in science and life may contribute to some serious social and relational problems. Nonetheless, these are some of the essential qualities that will be needed (in proper perspective) if we are ever going to improve the world in which we live. Gestalt therapy's abandonment of the quest for purpose and meaning is hardly a satisfying alternative. The need to know, to properly understand, is at least as central to living a life of integrity as is the Gestalt-therapy imperative to be fully alive to the moment. Quite frankly, understanding *is* a basis for hope.

The socialization process inherent in certain versions of Gestalt therapy may run the risk of encouraging people to adopt unhealthy positions of arrogance, autonomy, irrationality or isolation. Personal freedom and the need for organismic self-expression, the values pushed in Gestalt therapy, can easily lead to a "do your own thing" approach in life. Granted, this may more accurately reflect a lack of true awareness of self, or a paucity of good feedback from others, but without any clear sense of obligation or responsibility to anyone except oneself, Gestalt therapy runs the risk of epitomizing a philosophy of irresponsible hedonism.

We would agree with Yankelovich (1982, p. 239), who in discussing some of the potential risks of the more explicitly humanistic strategies of personal growth and development commented: "By concentrating day and night on your feelings, potentials, needs, wants, and desires, and by learning to assert them more freely, you do not become a freer, more spontaneous, more creative self; you become a narrower, more self-centered, more isolated one. You do not grow, you shrink."

Such a stance is nowhere commended in Scripture. Perhaps for some who are excessively emotionally constrained or locked in martyr roles, this socialization process makes sense in a limited, temporal way. But for the majority of us, the need is to learn how to relate to others in more loving and nonmanipulative ways, with the distinct risk that certain of our needs most certainly will *not* be met. Indeed, it is this kind of commitment to caring that speaks volumes about our character as well as to those virtues we hold most dear.

The initial goal of greater self-awareness in Gestalt therapy is not necessarily incompatible with the Christian tradition. But the key issue is the type of "self-awareness" being advocated. The conformity pressures within our Christian communities and subcultures run the risk of denying and distorting personal experience (cf. McLemore, 1984). More understanding about the way we manage the inevitable differences of opinion that occur in human relationships might do much to help our Christian communities achieve a greater sense of unity of purpose. Likewise, greater candor about our efforts to create intimacy in relationships might be an important beginning point in establishing and enhancing truly interdependent relationships.

But we are concerned about the extreme emphasis in Gestalt therapy on self-awareness and self-fulfillment as critically important goals in themselves, especially when they are not translated into a broader relational context. The balanced Christian is not just self-directed but other-directed as well. Self-sufficiency is ultimately an illusion since we are created to be in relationship with God and others. While we should take seriously the need to be fully alive and aware, it is not a substitute for concentrated and focused ministry that is primarily other-directed. Personal experience should indeed be valued, but its value is limited, especially when compared to the importance of the authority of Scripture or the discerning role of the local community of believers.

To Perls and other Gestalt therapists, the willingness to conform oneself to moral rules from the Scriptures and the guidance of others would be seen as a form of dependent, ingenuine "other-regulation." The pursuit of autonomy or wholeness rules all. Gestalt therapy at its best—when it is relatively free of its irresponsible hedonistic distortions—is still an incomplete education. The awareness that is so deeply valued in Gestalt therapy is only a partial and temporal understanding of certain aspects of selves, but when this assumes a position of absolute primacy in our understanding of who we are it is most certainly a pernicious view.

Finally, we note the strong distrust of thinking in most versions of Gestalt therapy (Benner, 1985). Though it would be fair to say that we all engage in "mind games" in the course of everyday existence, the fear of irrational intellectualism and rationalizations need not—and should not—generalize to the whole domain of cognitive processes. The "go with your gut" instinct that tends to emerge from most forms of Gestalt therapy potentially leads to destructive pluralism and relativism where there is eventually little hope of achieving any clear consensus on integrating theory or, more importantly, a coherent purpose or reason for living.

Part of our difficulty in writing about Gestalt therapy is that a clearly articulated model of personality is lacking in the writings of Perls and others. Gestalt therapy is almost deliberately antiscientific or at least prescientific. Indeed, to be told that the only true way to "understand" Gestalt therapy is to "experience it" can leave the "uninitiated" with a strong sense of frustration (if not exasperation). To be fair, though, this is not unlike the dilemma that exists when the nonbeliever tries to fully comprehend Scripture. A fair statement would probably be to assert that Gestalt therapy requires a "leap of faith" in which the novice must be willing, at least temporarily, to suspend certain critical faculties in order to more fully appreciate its curative potentials.

Model of Health

Some aspects of Gestalt therapy's view of health are not incompatible with the Christian view of wholeness. For example, Gestalt therapy has enriched our understanding of what it means to be truthful. Its primary emphasis on nonverbal distortions has given us significant insights about the "layers of deceit" that all too often characterize our interpersonal relationships (cf. McLemore, 1984). Gestalt therapy teaches us about the need to place greater stress on experiencing and doing rather than merely talking about things, certainly a reasonable admonishment to those of us who care deeply about facilitating a commitment to lifelong learning and growing.

To a limited but significant degree, the emphases in Gestalt therapy on body awareness, directness, freedom, honesty, openness, responsibility and spontaneity can be appreciated. Perls correctly says that our "problems in living" are often a function of our misuse of these capacities, of our deliberate decisions to "play games" or of our losing courage. But these "means," these capacities, were meant to serve far different "ends" for the Christian. They are not directionless, but were meant to be targeted on a goal. We are told repeatedly to embrace justice and mercy, walk humbly and show compassion, not because of what they "do" for us, but because they are appropriate responses to God's grace. Clearly lacking in Gestalt therapy is any concept of holiness or spiritual maturity. Self-fulfillment in proper alignment might be good temporal stewardship of our gifts and talents, but it needs to be directed toward a much higher purpose—worshiping God and serving others because "he first loved us."

A person may embody the characteristics of health as developed in the Gestalt therapy tradition, yet be living an impoverished life in a spiritual sense. On the other hand, persons who appear (at least on the surface) to have achieved some measure of spiritual holiness could be living lives that are personally or psychologically bankrupt. To be fair, however, it should be said that it is possible for a person to embody aspects of the Gestalt therapy view of health and also be mature spiritually. Indeed, we have both interacted with colleagues who embraced certain elements of the Gestalt therapy vision of health without visibly sacrificing their Christian commitment and witness. Authentic maturity implies a high degree of congruence between the inner and outer dimensions of our lives. We fear that Gestalt therapy all too often stresses the former without seriously addressing the latter.

The enduring question that emerges is whether the more fully functioning person in the Gestalt therapy tradition is any more receptive to basic assertions of the Christian faith. Our fear is that this fulfilled person in the Gestalt therapy understanding may be an individual who is culturally, historically and personally dislocated. Indeed, the person may have an inflated sense of self, or at least a seriously incomplete understanding of her or his fundamental humanity.

Our identity as Christians is deeply rooted in a growing sense of our place in the march of redemptive history, nurtured in the context of Christian community. We feel strongly that it is a decided risk in Gestalt therapy that one can be so "fully alive to the moment" that one loses all sense of a proper respect for the past or appropriate concern about the future. The potential distrust of "right thinking" (i.e., orthodoxy) can result in such extreme detachment from external reality and transcendent absolutes that there is little engagement in the demands of everyday living beyond the personal realm. Although it may be argued that we exaggerate the risks involved, from an eternal perspective, we should not take these concerns lightly. We fear that one of the main virtues of Gestalt therapy, self-understanding, might potentially lead to the pride inherent in a growing sense of self- sufficiency rather than self-support.

Model of Abnormality

There is much in the Gestalt therapy model of psychopathology that the Christian can find useful. The description of the levels of our deception, for example, can be painfully accurate (cf. McLemore, 1984; Peck, 1983). In Christianity, these aberrations are ultimately consequences of the Fall, and more directly and immediately the result of our propensity toward sinning. In Gestalt therapy, they are first and foremost decisions to get others to take responsibility for us and meet our needs. Further, Gestalt therapy does not address the origins of such deceit in the larger societal context; psychopathology is primarily a *personal* choice to remain overly dependent, inauthentic and irresponsible. In contrast, a more complete understanding of deception in the Christian context views sin as both personal and corporate, as well as both phenomenological and historically determined. Gestalt therapy focuses only on how the broader context is individually manifested and/or experienced.

Gestalt therapy manifests a one-dimensional perspective on causation of abnormality, with little attention paid to broader physiological or sociocultural determinants. As with other humanistic therapies, there is the decided risk in Gestalt therapy of placing too much emphasis on personal responsibility, thus mistakenly attributing too much responsibility to the self, a proclivity that social psychologists have convincingly demonstrated that we are all prone to.

Still, radical personal responsibility, although initially overwhelming, carries with it the potential for change and the hope for alleviation of symptoms (i.e., if you "caused" your problems, you can with greater awareness "confront" them). Despite this obvious advantage, the one-sided emphasis on personal attribution is simply misguided in light of the overwhelming evidence for the complexity of causation. Christians would do well to be reminded that emotional and personal problems are nearly always more complex than they appear to be on the surface (i.e., they are multiply determined and multiply maintained). Unfortunately, our statements about the origins of these concerns are far too often naively simplistic, if not condescending and patronizing.

Model of Psychotherapy

Responsible clinicians generally appreciate a number of emphases in Gestalt therapy. Exploring inconsistencies between what is said and what is done is fertile material to pursue in any approach. Gestalt therapy seems unusually insightful with reference to the games we play in our interpersonal relationships. Its emphasis on "doing" rather than just "saying" introduces new dimensions of accountability into the psychotherapeutic relationship.

The methods of confronting and directly encountering "unfinished business" have enormous intuitive appeal to many clinicians who work with reasonably high-functioning clients. Focusing on the "how" and "what" of behavior and experience certainly seems to raise client awareness. Although few therapists will go as far as the Gestalt therapist does to "frustrate the neurosis," they generally agree that "control issues" are central to the process of change and healing. Perls perceptively observed that many of us would rather have "confirmation of our neuroses" than confront our inevitable tendency to deny, distort or disown parts of ourselves. Most of us can recognize dimensions of ourselves in the "layers of deceit" in the model of psychopathology in Gestalt therapy.

Gestalt therapy is decidedly critical of what it perceives to be distorted, defensive thinking, and often tends to be explicitly nonrational. Cognitive processes are distrusted as a source of insight into ourselves. This is simply inconsistent with the more holistic emphases of Scripture and the Christian tradition. The Scriptures emphasize the renewal of the mind as well as other important aspects of our humanness (e.g., the body and feelings). Correctly understood, what we really need to do is to stop engaging in so many speculations, rationalizations, explanations or manipulations (Perls's "lose your mind") and renew our whole beings.

As is increasingly being seen in the cognitive-behavioral tradition (cf. chapters seven and eight), thoughts and beliefs appear to play a significant role in the development and maintenance of psychopathology and the healing of these problems. Perhaps in part because it so questions the value of excuses and explanations, Gestalt therapy all too easily translates into a more widespread distrust of cognitive processing in general. Gestalt therapy is obviously in need of a cognitive theory that will balance its overemphasis on biological end-goals. It correctly diagnoses the potential distortions of certain cognitive processes, but it is less than satisfying in what it proposes as a viable alternative.

Another concern often raised by some contemporary clinicians has to do with the "games" or "rules" of Gestalt therapy. Few doubt that these procedures and techniques are powerful tools, but the concerns surround the possible misuse or abuse of these tools in a power game perpetrated by the therapist. It is certainly possible for the clinician to enter into an unhealthy relationship of power with the client, or to avoid dealing with his or her own countertransference problems. As with all approaches, the issue appears to be one of timing, tact and sensitivity, as well as the personal and professional competencies and qualities of the clinician (Guy, 1987). But until recently (Hedlin, 1987; Simkin and Yontef, 1984) there has been little written about how best to deal with some of the potential limitations or risks inherent in these Gestalt therapy procedures.

Gestalt therapy can be of use to us as we seek to more fully comprehend important dimensions of the human condition. Gestalt therapy has taught us something about the importance of being more fully alive to the moment. It would certainly be fair to say that for some of us, our obsessive remembering of the past, our anxious anticipation of the future or our drive to understand everything in a three-point sermon greatly interferes with our capacity to be present to one another in our fellowship. All too often in our Christian communities, what passes for "love" is more accurately an unhealthy dependence on others, masked under the guise of "togetherness" or "Christian unity" (cf. Parks, 1986).

What is truly needed in an age of cultural relativism and isolated individualism is examples of cohesive and healthy communities where commitments to one another are made, honored and maintained (cf. Smedes, 1988). That sticky and manipulative symbiotic closeness that Gestalt therapy so accurately exposes raises tough questions about the bases on which "Christian fellowship" all too often forms. As Miller and Jackson (1985) have observed, perhaps this is because we really do not know how to be fully present to one another or how to really listen to what the other person has to say. As a Gestalt therapist might respond, if we were more "aware" and took greater "responsibility" for our thoughts, feelings and actions, we might be able to become more sensitive and truly compassionate in our relationships.

One can only wonder if the attempts at community in the Gestalt therapy tradition during the past three decades have been any more successful than the Christian fellowships throughout the last two millennia. Suffice it to say that it is our position that these communities will need a much deeper commitment to shared truths, the Truth, if they are going to survive the less than attractive dimensions of our fundamental humanity.

Although the view of persons in Gestalt therapy is incomplete and the suggested strategies for remediation are inadequate for fully confronting the human condition, one can hardly fault this tradition's blunt and frank assessment of the layers of deceit that all too often surround us. Awareness of the many subtle and diverse forms of self-deception we engage in is certainly a desirable goal for the committed Christian, especially in those circles where "the truth" has been more often used as a weapon (McLemore, 1984), or as a means to bringing about conformity to the expectations of others (Peck, 1987). The resulting enmeshment of identities, or the symbiosis of relationships, often makes it exceedingly difficult to separate our authentic Christian beliefs and convictions from the cultural trends and values we all too readily incorporate into Christian faith and experience (cf. Dolby, 1968; Donovan, 1985). As McLemore (1984, p. 11) has warned, "Love must be ultimately grounded in truthfulness or it becomes little more than a murky pool of rhetoric that ends up in stagnation."

Conclusion

Gestalt therapy is one of the purer humanistic therapies, with all of the hindrances that that implies to the Christian consumer. These weaknesses have been emphasized in this chapter. But perhaps Gestalt therapy has something to teach us about what it means to love one another in truth and honesty. As McLemore (1984) has perceptively noted, because of the way that God has made us, and how this derives from his own truth-love nature, we cannot love other persons unless we are willing to be ourselves with them. Without involvement and disclosure, and awareness of our tendencies to deceive, it is not really possible to bind the wounds of others. Honest Christianity demands that we do not deny or distort our experience or value it only as an end in itself.

That this approach has appealed to both laypersons and mental-health professionals is undeniable. In its pure form, Gestalt therapy is a creative response to what many perceive as elitist and overly intellectual tendencies in some of the traditional approaches to counseling and psychotherapy. Many of the creative methods and techniques Gestalt therapy has generated have been widely accepted and adapted, although the philosophy of life it embraces has been more widely rejected in the late 1980s. It may "loosen up" constricted people and be a catalyst for change, at least initially, but its enduring contribution remains highly controversial.

For Further Reading

Fagan, J., and Shepherd, I. (Eds.). (1970). *Gestalt therapy now*. New York: Harper & Row/Colophon.

One of the classic references in the gestalt therapy literature.

James, M., and Jongeward, D. (1971). *Born to win: Transactional analysis with Gestalt experiments*. Reading, MA: Addison-Wesley.

A delightful self-help presentation of these two humanistic approaches to personal growth.

Latner, J. (1973). *The Gestalt therapy book*. New York: Bantam.

A brief summary of the major strategies and techniques utilized in Gestalt therapy.

McLemore, C. (1984). *Honest Christianity.* Philadelphia: Westminster.
  Although not directly related to Gestalt therapy, its powerful analysis of why
  it is so difficult to be truthful in the context of Christian communities is
  certainly relevant.
Perls, F. (1969). *In and out of the garbage pail.* Moab, UT: Real People Press.
  The rather entertaining autobiography of the founder of Gestalt therapy.
Polster, E., and Polster, M. (1973). *Gestalt therapy integrated: Contours of theory
  and practice.* New York: Brunner/Mazel.
  A major professional work geared toward practicing clinicians who want to
  understand and appreciate the contributions of Gestalt therapy.
Van Diert, V., and Korb, M. (1980). *Gestalt therapy: An introduction.* New York:
  Pergamon Press.
  A more recent professional discussion of the uses and benefits of gestalt
  therapy.
Zinker, J. (1978). *Creative process in Gestalt therapy.* New York: Random
  House/Vintage.
  Represents some of the more recent adaptations of Gestalt therapy for a
  variety of clinical concerns and populations.

References

Bellah, R.; Madsen, R.; Sullivan, W.; Swindler, A.; and Tipton, M. (1985). *Habits
  of the heart.* New York: Harper & Row.
Benner, D. (1985). Gestalt therapy. In D. Benner (Ed.), *Baker encyclopedia of
  psychology* (pp. 468-470). Grand Rapids, MI: Baker.
Browning, D. (1987). *Religious thought and the modern psychologies.* Philadelphia:
  Fortress.
Corey, G. (1986). *Theory and practice of counseling and psychotherapy* (3d ed).
  Monterey, CA: Brooks/Cole.
Dolby, J. (1968). *I, too, am man.* Waco, TX: Word.
Donovan, V. (1985). *Christianity rediscovered.* Maryknoll, NY: Orbis Books.
Fagan, J., and Shepherd, I. (Eds.). (1970). *Life techniques in Gestalt therapy.* New
  York: Harper & Row.
Guy, J. (1987). *The personal life of the psychotherapist.* New York: Wiley-Intersci-
  ence.
Hedlin, S. (1987). Gestalt therapy: Aspects of evolving theory and practice. *The
  Humanistic Psychologist, 15,* 184-196
James, M., and Jongeward, D. (1971). *Born to win: Transactional analysis with
  Gestalt experiments.* Reading, MA: Addison-Wesley.
Korchin, S. (1976). *Modern clinical psychology.* New York: Basic Books.
Latner, J. (1973). *The Gestalt therapy book.* New York: Bantam.
Levitsky, A., and Perls, F. (1970). The rules and games of Gestalt therapy.
  In J. Fagan and I. Shepherd (Eds.), *Gestalt therapy now* (pp. 140-149). New
  York: Harper & Row/Colophon.
McLemore, C. (1982). *The scandal of psychotherapy.* Wheaton: Tyndale.
McLemore, C. (1984). *Honest Christianity.* Philadelphia: Westminster.
Miller, W., and Jackson, K. (1985). *Practical psychology for pastors.* Englewood

Cliffs, NJ: Prentice-Hall.

Parks, S. (1986). *The critical years*. New York: Harper & Row

Passons, W. (1975). *Gestalt approaches in counseling*. New York: Holt, Rinehart and Winston.

Peck, M. (1983). *People of the lie*. New York: Simon and Schuster.

Peck, M. (1987). *The different drum*. New York: Simon and Schuster.

Perls, F. (Featured therapist), and Shostrum, E. (Producer). (1965). *Three approaches to psychotherapy: Part 2, Fredrick Perls* [Film]. Corona Del Mar, CA: Psychological and Educational Films.

Perls, F. (1969a). *Gestalt therapy verbatim*. Moab, UT: Real People Press.

Perls, F. (1969b). *In and out of the garbage pail*. Moab, UT: Real People Press.

Polster, E., and Polster, M. (1973). *Gestalt therapy integrated: Contours of theory and practice*. New York: Brunner/Mazel.

Simkin, J., and Yontef, G. (1984). Gestalt therapy. In R. Corsini (Ed.), *Contemporary psychotherapies* (3d ed.) (pp. 279-319). Itasca, IL: F. E. Peacock.

Smedes, L. (1988). *Caring and commitment*. San Francisco: Harper & Row.

Smith, E. (Ed.). (1976). *The growing edge of Gestalt therapy*. New York: Brunner/Mazel.

Van De Riet, V., and Korb, M. (1980). *Gestalt therapy: An introduction*. New York: Pergamon.

Yankelovich, D. (1982). *New rules: Searching for self-fulfillment in a world turned upside down*. New York: Bantam Books.

Zinker, J. (1978). *Creative process in Gestalt therapy*. New York: Random House/Vintage.

13

TRANSACTIONAL ANALYSIS

✛

*M*any of the psychotherapy systems have been utilized in religious and church settings, but few have ever been adopted as enthusiastically, uncritically or as widely as *transactional analysis* (frequently referred to as TA). For an extended period in the 1970s and early 1980s, TA was touted as the pastor's best tool for improving ministry, and books relating TA to the work of the church abounded. This was probably a function of a number of factors, including the packaging of TA in a way that made it understandable outside of professional psychotherapy circles, its short-term action orientation, its optimistic stance toward change and the insight it fostered regarding puzzling human interactions. As we will see, there are ways in which TA is helpful to the Christian counselor, but major problems in its being *the* approach for the church.

Descriptive Survey

Philosophical Assumptions

TA analyzes persons at four levels.[1] The *structural analysis* looks at individual personality; *transactional analysis* looks at interpersonal interactions in a molecular fashion; *racket and game analysis* looks at repetitive relational patterns that are dysfunctional; and *script analysis* looks at life patterns at the broadest thematic levels. Because each level of analysis has its own implications for the understanding of personality, health and abnormality, these will be discussed in presenting the levels. (We should also note that TA has often been creatively melded with Gestalt therapy; e.g., James and Jongeward, 1971.)

The philosophical presuppositions of TA are not explicitly stated. One quickly discerns in the approach a commitment to human responsibility within the limits of family and cultural influence; in other words, a belief in limited freedom. TA asserts that *acceptance* (OKness) and *value* are fundamental to all persons. Persons start from a position of OKness in childhood, only to have that position eroded by parents and the child's social environment. Other presuppositions will emerge in the discussion below.

Models of Personality, Health and Abnormality

Structural analysis. Berne and his followers taught that each person's personality structure is composed of three conscious or preconscious *ego states,* which are organized psychological systems of feelings, thoughts and behaviors that are usually distinct and mutually exclusive. The three are the *Parent* (P), the "tape-recorder-like" composite of the memories of how parents and significant others acted, thought and felt; the *Adult* (A), the computerlike processor of information from the other two ego states and the external world; and the *Child* (C), the urges, feelings and thoughts of the "child-within-us" that never grows up.

Students often imagine more overlap than is accurate between the TA ego states and the three Freudian psychic structures, since one could superficially see the id as childish, the ego as an information processor like Berne's Adult, and the superego as parental. But for Berne, all three structures are part of the ego, as all are conscious

---

[1]The following presentation will draw from Berne (1964); Harris (1969); James and Jongeward (1971); Woollams, Brown and Huige (1976); and Woollams and Brown (1979).

or potentially so, whereas only Freud's ego was deemed conscious. Second, to the Freudian, psychological experience is the result of the interaction of the three structures of personality, but to the TA therapist, personality is largely the function of one autonomously experienced ego state at a time. Proponents of TA emphasize the distinctness and complementarity of the ego states rather than their constant interaction in determining behavior.

Figure 13.1

Further complexity is introduced by suggesting that the Parent can be further subdivided into the *Nurturing Parent,* the composite of the loving, supportive, accepting messages we received, and the *Critical Parent,* the composite of the rejecting, controlling, judgmental messages. The Child also is subdivided into the *Adapted Child,* the child that denies or ignores its own instincts and tries desperately to please parents by conforming to their demands; and the *Natural* (or *Free*) *Child,* the spontaneous, joyous, impish, uninhibited responder to the world. Some theorists even add a third division in the Child, the *Little Professor,* which delights in learning and is the childlike parallel to the Adult ego state.

TA proposes that we are almost always in one ego state or another, and that the ego state we are functioning in can be detected straightforwardly by the content and manner of expression (especially nonverbal) of what we think, feel, say and do. The preacher proclaiming universal sinfulness is in the Critical Parent; the charismatic believer dancing before the Lord in ecstasy is in the Natural Child; the student in a Bible study on major doctrines of the church is in the Adult; the penitent saying confession before a priest is in the Adapted Child; and so forth. Healthy individuals are able to act out of each of the ego states, but will spend the majority of their experience in the Adult, Natural Child and Nurturing Parent (in that order). The influence of the Critical Parent and Adapted Child are to be minimized.

Psychopathology can occur when persons confuse their ego states, constantly slipping back and forth between them without completing transactions with others. An example might be the person who is ineffectual in making business presentations (an Adult function) because she lapses into inappropriate humor (the Child).

Problems also occur when people do not experience their ego states distinctly, but rather one state contaminates another. An example might be a racist, in whom the information-processing Adult is contaminated by the Critical Parent so that prejudicial attitudes and feelings of hate bias his capacity to see the objective equality of persons.

Pathology can also occur when one or two ego states dominate the personality and exclude the others—as when a believer is always in the Critical Parent state and thus acts moralistically, superior and judgmental at all times; or when a husband is always in the Adult and is a dispassionate information-processor (like the computers he works with), incapable of sharing any spontaneous feeling with his wife.

Humans need *strokes,* and this need is called *stimulus-hunger* in TA circles. Strokes can be physical, verbal and nonverbal. A stroke is any interpersonal event that "recognizes" the existence of another person. Obviously, some strokes are better than others, but any stroke is better than none. True intimacy is the most powerful stroke of all. Criticism and rejection are destructive, but are better than being ignored. It is in relationships that we exchange strokes, and so TA next focuses on the analysis of transactions.

Transactional analysis. At the most molecular level, because persons are usually in one of their three major ego states (Parent, Adult, Child), transactions are typically between ego states, and the way that these interactions occur determines their meaning and effect. Healthy interactions occur in *complementary* ways, meaning that the ego state communicated from and to is reciprocated: (1) "What time is it?" (A to A); "It's 10:00" (A to A); (2) "Look at my new car!" (C to C); "Awesome!" (C to C); (3) "I'll never learn Greek; I'm so discouraged" (C to P); "You can do anything you set your mind to; you're so smart!" (P to C).

Thus the arrows depicting the complementary interaction are parallel. Transactions are pathological when they are *crossed;* as when a student asks the professor for more detail regarding a lecture point (A to A), and the professor responds, "If you paid attention better, you wouldn't ask questons like that!" (P to C). Another problematic transaction is the *ulterior* transaction where there is a covert message that crosses the superficially complementary messages, as when by the fifth request for clarification, the professor begins to discern that the student is less asking for information (A to A) and more communicating, "You are a lousy lecturer and I'm going to humiliate you in front of the class" (P to C).

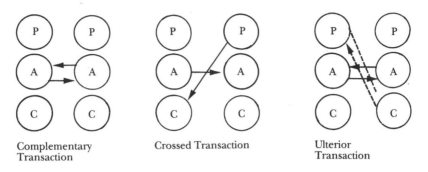

Complementary
Transaction

Crossed Transaction

Ulterior
Transaction

Figure 13.2

As people interact, we experience stimulus-hunger and the second
need, a desire for stability or structure in our transactions. This is called
structure-hunger. Berne creatively suggested that there is a continuum
of human interaction based on how stable and predictable the
interactions are and how truly rewarding it is. At the extreme of total
stability and least reward, we have *withdrawal,* where we take no risks at
all and we achieve total predictability by interacting not with real
people, but only with our fantasies of people. The person addicted to
pornography might be a withdrawn person willing only to deal with
fantasized women who do exactly what the pictures show. At the other
extreme we have true *intimacy* that is spontaneous and unpredictable,
trusting and affirming of the OKness of the other; intimacy is very risky
and yet has the potential for the greatest reward.

Between the extremes of withdrawal and intimacy, and moving up
the scale from withdrawal toward steadily less predictability and greater
reward, we have first *rituals,* which are totally predictable interactions
with real people ("How are you?" "Fine, and how about you?" "Not bad");
pastimes, which are innocuous and impersonal but less structured interactions (such as a ten-minute dialog about one's favorite football team or
the weather), *activities* where people cooperate together on external tasks
that channel their interactions in spontaneous but safe ways; and finally
games and rackets, where meaningful strokes are exchanged but the outcomes are predetermined rather than spontaneous (discussed below).
Intimacy is the most rewarding but most risky form of interaction because
it is the least structured and most unpredictable.

Racket and game analysis. Each of us assumes a *life position* regarding
our own OKness and the OKness of others. This results in the famous

four possibilities of "I'm not OK, you're not OK"; "I'm not OK, you're OK"; "I'm OK, you're not OK"; and "I'm OK, you're OK," described by Harris (1969; Berne actually discussed nine positions based on the combinations of the OKness of I, you and they).

We all have a third need, called *position-hunger,* to have our basic assumption of a life position confirmed or supported in interactions with others. Thus even though the last position, "I'm OK, you're OK," is the healthiest, we all tend to stay static in our assumed position. We generate support for an I'm-OK-you're-OK position via real, risky intimacy, and solicit support for the other three negative positions by games and rackets.

Rackets are habitual ways of feeling that persons create within themselves, such as the woman whose anger is always on slow-burn (the chip-on-the-shoulder syndrome) or the man who is in an habitual state of self-pity. These inauthentic habitual feelings, which are unrelated to reality as currently experienced, are created expressly to authenticate the person's life-position assumptions. Self-pity ("nothing ever turns out right for me; I've got to accept second-best in life because it is my lot") affirms the position I'm not OK/you're OK and justifies the person never taking risks with real intimacy or achievement. After people experience enough inauthentic feelings ("saving up stamps"), they often feel justified in engaging in self-or other destructive behavior ("trading in their stamps"), as when persons wallowing in self-pity engage in a drunken binge because of all they "have to bear in life."

Games occur when persons turn to others for confirmation of their negative "not OK" position assumption. Rather than allowing unpredictable intimacy to occur, they predetermine the outcome of the transactions by engaging in ulterior and crossed transactions to *make a predictable outcome happen.* The payoff is the confirmation of their assumption; the game works when the assumption of not-OKness is confirmed by the reaction of the other with whom the game has been played.

Berne and other TA therapists give provocative and creative names to the games they analyze. The most famous TA book, Berne's *Games People Play,* discusses Rapo, Now I've Got You You SOB, See What You Made Me Do, Harried and so forth. As one example, the game See What You Made Me Do is probably played by the person who takes the I'm not OK/you're not OK position. Due to fear of failure and inability to accept his own foibles, a man subtly looks for another to blame when he nears completion of significant tasks or interactions. Any distraction (the misbehavior of a child, an argument with the spouse, "stress" at work) becomes the handy scapegoat to hide behind, with loud protests to self and others of "Look how you made me mess up [You're not OK]! It's not my fault that it didn't turn out well [I'm not OK, but I have an excuse for that]." Some people major on one game all their lives; others have a wide repertoire of games to play.

Games and rackets are pathological, though to varying degrees. They cause us to stay anchored in a nonfunctional life position and yet provide enough payoff to prevent us from looking seriously for better strokes. Games can be particularly troublesome when two people, such as a husband and wife, parent and child, or boss and employee, begin to play games that are pathologically complementary.

One such example is when a husband plays Kick Me, a game of self-defeating mistakes that prove one's not-OKness, and the wife plays If It Weren't for You, a game of not even trying to achieve anything and blaming your failure to try on the person you are connected with. In this case, the wife has no real desire for the husband to overcome his pitiful ineptitude because it protects her from the threat of finding out who she could really be; and the husband can use the wife's moaning about how she could have done so much better in life without him as one more negative payoff for his failures, which further proves he is not OK, one more failure others can kick him for.

Script analysis. In discussing scripting, TA therapists assume that bad transactions, rackets and games do not occur at random, but are patterned toward a desired end. *Scripts* encapsulate a person's life direction, one's life themes. Scripts are set up for the person at an early age, usually by the parents. In the publications of some TA experts, scripts consist largely of grand injunctions against certain critical, healthy life developments or processes. Examples include scripts of Don't Feel, Don't Get Close, Don't Grow Up, Don't Be Childish or Don't Succeed. For others, scripts are defined temporally, such as the Always script of unyielding consistency, the Never script of total pessimism and the Almost script of never-ending near-misses. Some define scripts in terms of life-theme clichés, such as Getting Even, Being Helpful, Carrying My Cross or Looking for the Pot of Gold. Finally, some define scripts in terms of childhood mythology, with the belief that adults live out literary metaphors from childhood that have come to symbolize their lives; these would include the Cinderella script of sighing and waiting for the invitation to the ball to arrive, or the Peter Pan script of refusing to grow up.

Just as with games, scripts are especially destructive when they intersect with the script of someone close, as when an alcoholic plays a Victim script and her husband plays either the Rescuer or the Persecutor. Here the scripts of both persons provide fuel for that of the other—victims need rescuers and rescuers need victims. Some scripts can be helpful if they give the person permissions ("I can") rather than injunctions ("I can not"), but the healthiest person is one who escapes scriptedness altogether.

Model of Psychotherapy

TA therapy typically starts with a contract between client and therapist regarding the nature of the change to be attempted. In part, this contract is to structure the relationship in order that destructive games not damage it beyond repair. It also reflects the expectation that the client must exert effort to change.

TA is usually done in a group therapy format with individual counseling as an adjunct. TA is highly educational and experiential. More than in any other therapy, clients are taught the theory itself, as it is assumed that information provided to the Adult ego state forms the basis for new and different decisions about life. The therapist doesn't change the client; rather, the therapist is a catalyst for the client to do what he or she will.

Therapy proceeds in the same pattern by which we explained the approach; it starts with helping clients understand their ego states, make choices about which to experience at a given time and enable them to experience more of those states that have been blocked. Transactions are then analyzed at a molecular level, followed by education about and confrontation around the games and rackets of the client. The basic life position is examined and the client challenged to make a deliberate and Adult decision about life position. The way the client structures time is examined, with the goal being to encourage real intimacy. Finally, clients are encouraged to change their life script, at the very least to a healthier script definition, but optimally to give up scripts entirely and to live in the spontaneity of intimate living. To accomplish all this, the therapist attempts to give protection from harm to the client during the difficult process of change, permission to change by constantly affirming the client's OKness, and potency by offering good insights and effective concrete strategies for change. Therapists seek to act out of their Nurturing Parent, Natural Child and Adult ego states to empower the same states in clients.

Christian Critique

Of all the Christian publications we discovered regarding TA, only a few interacted critically with the system.[2] Most of the religious (we hesitate to apply the adjective *Christian*) publications about TA uncritically reinterpret Christian experience and truth in TA terms and/or enthusiastically apply TA as the panacea that will allow true ministry to flourish.

The cloaking of TA in religious terminology can create some especially troublesome confusions and falsehoods. Some of the excesses of this genre of literature include the reduction of God to a spiritual force within all people or "power at the bottom of the well" (James and Savary, 1974); the reduction of the doctrine of the Trinity to a projection onto the deity of our own tripartite ego structure, with God the Parent, Jesus the Adult, and the Holy Spirit the Child (Bontrager, 1974, pp. 124ff.); the reduction of Jesus to a mere man who lived in the Adult and Natural Child ego states (Haughton, 1974; Bontrager, 1974); and the reinterpretation of conversion variously as the releasing of the Natural Child (Bontrager, 1974; Greer, 1975), the release of "benevolent spiritual energies within people" (James and Savary, 1974, p. ix), the freedom of knowing our own OKness (James, 1973) or the releasing of the person from life scripts (Haughton, 1974).

One of the greatest strengths and weaknesses of TA is its creative, catchy and intuitively appealing terminology. Berne was committed to his work not becoming fodder for academic dissertations, that it be accessible to the masses. He aimed for the TA system to have practical value for the client in terms of it being able to generate productive insight for the person who will learn the system. Its appealing concepts are easily grasped and applied. Students of TA often report a sense of empowerment that flows from understanding interactions going on around them; interactions which were previously obscure and baffling. before. They often also gain insight into their own self-defeating patterns. Significantly, TA is one of the only systems that illuminates *interpersonal* (as opposed to intrapsychic) reality. Since so much of our meaningful life experience is interpersonal, this is a significant

---

[2]Oden's (1974) seminal analysis and extension of TA was very helpful, and will be referred to frequently below. Hedman and Kruus (1987) summarized and built on Oden's work. The works of Reuter (1974), Batey (1976) and Malony (1980) each provided some helpful criticisms, all of which will be developed below.

contribution of the approach.

The negative side to this accessibility is that the TA language system can be used to excess, thus creating a barrier to the outsider in much the way that religious language ("God-talk") can create a distance between the Christian and the unbeliever. In TA literature, the reader is bombarded with phrases, concepts, lists, clichés, in-group language or abbreviations that can baffle even the most devoted reader. A hearty dose of second-degree games, second-order functional analyses of structural diagrams, Parent-in-Child ego states, drama triangles, NIGYSOB and so forth can present a real challenge. In its attempt to be accessible, TA theorists have created a system more encumbered by awkward idioms than perhaps any other; it has become a subculture of its own, replete with its own "sociological passwords."

Classification or naming can often be the first step toward understanding and is often a first step in gaining insight in therapy, but true understanding is premised on correct classification. We can mistakenly believe that we have understood or explained something just because we have labeled it. Do we really understand a person's ecstatic utterance of "Hallelujah!" merely because we have labeled it as coming from the Natural Child? A system that categorizes stimuli incorrectly may obscure more than enable true understanding. Because there has been little scientific validation of TA concepts,[3] while TA jargon has become so extensively developed and seemingly precise, the TA approach risks confusing labeling and understanding. This criticism holds for many approaches to therapy, but is a special risk for TA.

Philosophical Assumptions

The philosophical assumptions behind TA are not clear. They are obscured behind an aggressive attention to popularizing the system. Berne claimed that his system was complete, "encompassing everything [a person] may feel, think, say, or do" (cited in Hedman and Kruus, 1987, p. 176). Given such a claim of total understanding of personhood and its environment, the exclusion of any spiritual reality within or outside of the person cannot be interpreted as a function

---

[3]Techniques like the "egogram" developed by Dusay (Dusay and Dusay, 1984), where the "energy" committed or cathected to each of the ego states is portrayed in a bar graph, merely create the illusion of precision for what is only a subjective judgment by the TA therapist. A similar criticism holds for research that consists only of concensual ratings of transactions or ego states.

of mere modesty, but as a denial of the spiritual or an attempt to radically reinterpret it. Thus we must approach this system cautiously as we would an alternative faith system, because in its claims of all-encompassing breadth (e.g., James, 1985) this seems to be its ambition.

The matter of human freedom has been a recurrent one in our analyses. The TA vision of human freedom is broadly compatible with the idea of limited freedom we outlined in chapter two. TA recognizes the human tendency to be shaped by our past (Oden, 1974, cites biblical examples of "intergenerational scripting," including Ezek 16:44-45 and Jer 31:29). Yet we have the capacity to transcend our "programming" by responsibly making those decisions we are consciously confronted with in the present. Lawrence (1983) correctly pointed out that the main emphasis in the biblical concept of repentance is change, making a new decision. But there are obvious differences between the TA and Christian views of freedom, repentance and redecision.

While TA superficially appears to embody a balance of optimism and pessimism, recognizing the human capacity to change but also the barriers to change, its proponents err consistently in embracing a humanistic optimism that asserts humans exercising their freedom have a boundless capacity for change. This position is certainly much more optimistic about the human condition than classic Christianity. Whereas TA seems to emphasize the romantic notion of freedom from restraints, Christianity emphasizes freedom to serve God and freedom in submission (Oden, 1974). In TA, freedom is the capacity to act autonomously, but in Christianity God is the empowering agent for all good human action. In fact, Christianity posits that a fundamental problem of humanity is our tendency to live on our own strength (Malony, 1980), and TA encourages this tendency.

To the Christian protesting that we need power from outside ourselves, TA would respond that it is an evasion and denial of our capacity for human change to make a deity the source of that capacity. Perhaps proponents of TA have a point when we confront the extent to which some Christians evade change by denying that God has empowered them to make responsible choice, choosing instead to wait for a dramatic "empowering" or "healing."

Furthermore, the TA vision of human evil is too bland. It appreciates the phenomenon of human weakness and finiteness, but does not grapple with the depth of human depravity. Oden (1974) discusses the

TA understanding of self-deception as mired in destructive scripts we are living out. Evil is psychologized into the mere result of not-OKness or the influence of the Parent ego state (e.g., Bontrager, 1974; James and Savary, 1974), and is again understood as embedded in our scripts. But note that the motivations behind scripts are always benign; they boil down to validating the not-OK assumptions we absorbed as children. Oden (1974, p. 88) states, "For Berne, it is 'the adaptation to parental influences' that spoils the natural child."

But since parents were just acting out their scripts as well, we are left, as with all humanistic therapies, with a naive view of evil where everyone is excused. Thus full-blooded hatred, human rebellion against God and the like become mere "mistakes" that flow from our psychological conditioning. The result of this is that TA lacks a compelling moral vision. Morality in the TA system means acting spontaneously out of the Natural Child as moderated by the Adult ego state. This reduces to a typical humanistic self-actualization ethic where it is presumed that all fully functioning persons will naturally act in moral accord. As Malony said, "TA does not analyze the human condition with enough seriousness, and thus it lacks the power to transform persons from scripts to freedom" (1980, p. 105).

Model of Personality

A major concern with TA is that it is guilty of overly "dichotomous" thinking at the most fundamental levels (Hedman and Kruus, 1987). Especially in comparison to the psychodynamic system, where there is tremendous appreciation for uniqueness and flexibility in conceptions, TA is prone to simplistic, crayon-stroke divisions between human characteristics: people are OK or not OK, scripted or not scripted, engaging in intimacy or not, and so forth. We also see this in TA's grappling with each person's past. We are to negate the past and our continuity with it by throwing off life scripts and old "Parent tapes" and engage in spontaneous redeciding of our identities. Hedman and Kruus (1987) point out that this means that continuity of human identity is negated; we are to throw off all *imposed* sources of identity in favor of living spontaneously in the now. We must compare this negatively to the "redemptive history" approach of Scripture, where God continually calls us to understand our identity in light of his historical dealings with us (e.g., see 1 Pet 2:9 for an example of "bestowed" identity).

This dichotomous thinking is especially clear in TA's dealing with ego states (Oden, 1974, and others). In TA, we are intrinsically and properly divided beings. It is simply incredible to believe that we consist of three distinct and separate psychological states (or five, if one further divides into Nurturing and Critical Parents, Natural and Adapted Children; six, if one adds the Little Professor). Is a person truly in a separate ego state if she takes a break from work to have a tickle fight with her children? TA would have us think so. Such a supposition suggests that we are all "garden-variety" multiple personalities who disassociate from state to state in the course of any given day.

Some approaches to contemporary psychodynamic thought might agree to some common level of dissociative experience, but would call this a mark of our unhealthiness, not a standard for normalcy. TA would call us to celebrate and enhance this psychological divisiveness. Positively, it must be said that there probably are different facets to persons, and drawing these facets in sharp contrast may aid in encouraging the manifestation of all the God-created aspects of our personhood. But this is a pragmatic argument for the use of some idea of ego states as a heuristic model, not as a serious proposal about psychological reality.

The only attention to intrapsychic integration of ego states in the TA literature is an occasional common border drawn around the three principal ego states in some TA diagrams, but even this is usually omitted. In TA, we are actually encouraged to pursue further "segregation of ego states" (Hedman and Kruus, 1987, p. 177) as we grow, rather than to integrate these disparate parts. The earliest work in the structural-analysis stage of TA therapy is that of sharpening client awareness of their ego-state status. The common sense reaction to this must be one of incredulity; the idea of people changing ego states like they might change hats, of the ideal being separation of the feeling and fun-loving part of us from the thinking part from the moral and nurturing part of us, is unacceptable.

TA's stance on ego segregation both as what is and what should be is unacceptable from a Christian perspective as well. At a rather naive level, one could argue that the Christian revelation supports personality division, what with attention given in the Bible to such "parts" as mind, spirit, soul, body, flesh, bowels, kidneys, heart and so forth. But it is always our unity that is stressed in the Scriptures.

When we are told to "love the Lord your God with all your heart and with all your soul and with all your mind" (Mt 22:37), it is clearly the intent of our Lord to command love of God by the integrated, whole person, not love by those three parts to the exclusion of other ego parts, or love by three ego states (heart/Child, soul/Parent, mind/Adult) where the three states do not interact. It also seems clear to us that the Christian eschatological vision for sanctified personhood is one where all aspects of the person are transformed at the core and integrated. Our wisdom is not that of a calculating computer free of values, but is clear thinking infused with the joy of God's presence, a reverence for his law and passion for his glory. Our joy is intertwined with our intellectual appreciation of sound doctrine and our total dependence on our Creator and Sustainer, and issues forth in a loving response of desiring to follow him in loving obedience. Such integrated and complex responses do not seem appreciated in the TA system.

In questioning the value of this part of TA, we must not lose sight of the value of calling for a redemptive appreciation of all aspects of our personhood. TA as a heuristic model can foster valuable insight into personal differences. For example, Bontrager (1974) includes a discussion of how faith might be differently experienced and expressed by persons who are predominantly "cathected" into the different ego states. His discussion actually does give us good categories for distinguishing the intellectually or doctrinally oriented believer living in the Adult from the Critical Parent judgmental believer. But we must beware of thinking that categorization equals explanation or understanding, or that there are only three or five types of believers corresponding to the ego states.

We must also beware of post hoc examinations of cases, especially biblical cases, with easy diagnoses of ego states and interaction styles. Is determination of ego states (if they exist at all) really as easy as suggested in TA books? For example, Bontrager (1974, pp. 55ff.) studies the ego states of Jesus, seeming to conclude that he was ineffectual in his early ministry because he was stuck in the Parent, preaching condemnation and repentance. But, according to Bontrager, when Jesus switched to the Child ego state, with messages spoken in parables (stories that hook the Child in all of us), when he taught childlike love and whimsically urged others to "follow me" in the style of a child's game of "Follow the Leader," then he was a success, a winner. Even the Transfiguration (Mt 17) "shows Jesus and his disciples in the dimension of the Natural Child" (1974, p. 73)!

Here we are in a dilemma; creative interpretation of Scripture and indeed of much of human experience involves adding to the raw data of Scripture our own interpretive matrix of meaning and experience.

But TA may be too easily applied, with its intuitive and simple conceptual scheme, with interpretations that too easily achieve the status of truth with no adequate reality check other than that the interpretation sounds "right." But these interpretations can also be fruitful; for example, we found Haughton's (1974, pp. 174ff.) analyses of Christ's interactions interesting and challenging.

Putting aside our complaint that OKness and not-OKness is a simplistic dichotomization of a more complex human reality, let us grapple with the ontological roots of OKness. Reuter (1974, p. 45) correctly notes that TA bluntly asserts that "man is really, ultimately OK. He only feels not-OK." We thus desperately need to bring our feelings in line with the ontological reality. The presumption in TA is that our psychological feelings must in some way mirror reality for us to be healthy and to function to our full capacity. But why are people regarded as ontologically OK? The thoughtful person needs a base for OKness. If OKness is a value, then that value could not seem to arise from an impersonal universe, but must be imputed by an "OKer" (bestower of value) through an "OKing process" of some sort. TA endorses no such OKer or OKing process.

In affirming our *ultimate* OKness, TA is offering a secular salvation. In ignoring a bestower of OKness, TA pretends that OKness exists autonomously from God and without regard to other people—it is a reality one appropriates from the universe by an individual decision. Reuter (1974) is correct that TA teaches that it is self-deception to believe that we are not OK; therefore we must engage in a process of self-discovery to arrive at the self-acceptance of realizing our fundamental OKness. But TA self-acceptance, in the Christian analysis, is another form of self-deception, in that we are not OK before God apart from Jesus Christ. Oden (1974, pp. 60ff.) correctly calls TA's conception of OKness "demythologized . . . forgiving grace" (see also Batey, 1976). Thus TA is a "different gospel" (2 Cor 11:3-4).

What is the proper Christian corrective to the problem of not-OKness if the Christian therapist is to use TA appropriately? Some have simply baptized the TA assumption of OKness, concluding that you're OK because God declares you to be so (James, 1973; Bontrager, 1974; and others). Others have attempted to draw closer to the historic Christian message, declaring that Christianity teaches "I'm not OK; you're not OK, but that's OK. This is redemption" (Malony, 1980, p. 104). But we feel that any grappling with our ultimate status, our redemptive status, in terms of OKness will necessarily result in a trivialized understanding of redemption. As Oden (1974, p. 86) said, "The OK image is flat in comparison to New Testament images of God's approach to humanity."

Salvation is simply not reducible to psychological OKness. The incomparable drama of history by which humans mired in fallenness are made to be the adopted children of the holy, righteous and loving King through the sacrificial death of his Son transcends easy summarization in terms of OKness. In fact, reducing salvation to "I'm OK!" degrades that great reality. We are neither OK nor not OK; our status before God is one of wonderful complexity.

The defender of the TA conception might well argue that all human understandings of the divine drama are simplifications, and that OKness is an acceptable simplification. For example, a favorite verse of Christian TA apologists is 2 Corinthians 1:19-20, where Jesus is described as the "yes" of God; this is interpreted as a "you're OK" message directed at us. These verses may entail the affirmation that we're OK, but this "yes" is embedded in a much more complex revelation regarding the status of believers in Jesus Christ. TA proponents seldom go beyond the overly simple level of analysis, and at some point simplification must be regarded as trivialization.

There is no atonement in TA; none is seen as needed, as humanity is OK from the start and only needs to realize and appropriate this OKness. TA proponents consistently promote their approach as answering all of life's needs for happiness (see, for example, James, 1985, who claims self-reparenting in the TA tradition provides all that is needed for happiness; religion is never mentioned in the book though James is an ordained clergyperson). We have faulted TA on this point. Yet evangelicals must catch a vision that calls for more than conversion in human life; salvation involves both conversion and growth into Christlikeness (i.e., discipleship). TA fails as an understanding of human redemption from a Christian perspective. Yet it can be helpful as a tool to aid in growth.

Models of Health and Abnormality

At one level, the TA vision of pathology is like that of orthodox Christianity. Pathology results from people failing to grasp the OKness that is theirs. The ego-state confusion, maladaptive transactions, games, rackets and scripts that result are symptoms of this fundamental failure. Similarly, in Christianity, the pathology we experience is in part the result of our failure to embrace the resources that

God holds out to us, starting with repentance and forgiveness leading to salvation, and including the spiritual resources he offers us directly such as the fellowship of the community of faith, daily forgiveness, prayer, growth through knowing his Word and so forth.

But the failure to grasp these resources is more complex than TA would propose. As we mentioned earlier in discussing evil, ours is a fallen state where we are both victims of natural and moral evil and perpetrators of moral evil. We are culpable rebels as well as victims. In TA, pathology results from failing to appropriate that which is naturally and rightfully ours; in Christianity, our pathology is a result of our fallenness, our own culpability, our victimization by a fallen world, and our failure to allow God to transform us into a "new creature" (2 Cor 5:17).

TA is a fulfillment model of personality, in that all of the natural instincts and motives of humans are regarded as fundamentally good, and thus the sources for all problems are regarded as external to the person. At the most profound level, persons are consistent, and conflict is an unnatural state for us. This conflicts with the Christian view of persons, wherein to be human is to be conflicted and torn by the internal and external conditions of our lives.

As a result of this, in TA parents are consistently the "bad guys," the source of all problems (the system hardly stands alone on this point). In the TA literature, "the parenting voice is [always] the witch, devil, ogre, or pig" (Oden, 1974, p. 87). Whether the parenting voice is that of the biological parents or of one of the parenting institutions (teachers, clergy, etc.) makes little difference. Recognition of the positive influence of biological parents is rare—of institutional parent figures, nonexistent. This may be because TA is focusing on problematic cases, but parents are left with a clear impression that the less they interfere with their children, the better off they will be. The implicit model clearly is the romantic notion of the actualizing child who is best left alone to develop naturally; outside interference can only damage the child.

In TA publications, health is consistently proposed to be a function of the Adult and Natural Child ego states. The goals of TA are the unblocking of love and the experiencing of true spontaneity, joy, excitement and solid decision-making. Healthy individuals are unscripted; they have left the confines of their parental programming and have emerged to become their own spontaneous selves. At the most fundamental level, the goal of all life is that of intimacy.

Oden has argued rightly that the fundamental values of TA are those characteristic of adolescents: "autonomy, self-direction against parental voices, ego-strength against the superego" (1974, p. 89). Virtues such as discipline, self-transcendence, generativity, self-sacrifice and love of the truth are missing from TA. Most of the avenues for satisfaction through service to a transcendent goal or even meaningful work are mere lower levels of time structuring, mere activities we keep ourselves busy with while we wait for those rare experiences of intimacy. Even the fundamental value of intimacy is conceived as "a pleasure relation, a gratification relation, often on a Child-to-Child level" (Hedman and Kruus, 1987, p. 179). As such, intimacy as presented in TA does not lead us to trust in others nor to trust in institutions, and so the basic advice is to become autonomous. To be dependent on others is a game, a script. For Christians, others are not means to the gratification of our needs, but are part of our community and rightful recipients of our care. One gets the picture in reading TA materials that healthy people live for those brief experiences of intimacy, and that all else is marking time; this is certainly a disordered value system.

The win-or-lose motif so commonly promoted in TA is an "ill chosen image of acquisitiveness" (Oden, 1974, p. 93). Why should Christians, who are to model themselves after the "man of sorrows," chase after a "gospel" of winning in life? The moral depth of TA hardly ever goes beyond an emotional hedonism; it is less crass perhaps than materialistic hedonism, but it is a problem no less. The pursuit of happiness is, in the Christian analysis, ultimately doomed to failure. As C. S. Lewis argued in his autobiography *Surprised by Joy,* for the Christian true joy is a by-product of the pursuit of God; whenever it becomes an end in itself, it becomes unattainable.

TA suggests that to be truly healthy, we must become "unscripted." TA takes its place with the other humanistic therapies in being anti-authoritarian in its rejection of institutions and traditions. Are Christians to follow scripts? We would argue that Christlikeness paradoxically involves submission to a script so that we might find our true selves. Faith calls us to become what we naturally are not, and hence we need a blueprint for what we are to become. In obedience and submission to the script of the Scriptures, we are meant to find a freedom to enact our true identities: "For whoever wants to save his life will lose it, but whoever loses his life for me will find it" (Mt 16:25).

Yet TA helpfully reminds us, as do many facets of Christian experience, that cold obedience to God's law is not an avenue to true human fulfillment. Haughton (1974, pp. 57ff.) helpfully discusses experiences like those of Pascal and Aquinas, whose prodigious doctrinal and rational efforts brought them minimal satisfaction compared to their indescribable personal emotive encounters with God. As C. S. Lewis reminds us throughout his Chronicles of Narnia series, our God is not a "tame" God who can be contained in finite human words or concepts. Even the words and concepts of his own choosing and our experiencing of him can never be predicated on obedience alone.

Evangelicals are a favorite target for scorn in religious TA books; they are portrayed as so paranoid about being right that they never experience abundance. Bontrager (1974) suggests that conservatives are often stuck in Adapted Child, desperately concerned with giving the right answer, and hence happy to create a personal vision of a God who is primarily a purveyor of rules and doctrines. Relating to him, then, becomes merely a matter of obeying the rules and knowing the doctrines. One of us had a teenage friend fond of saying "I love doctrine"; it wasn't until years later that we wondered why it wasn't the living Lord that was his object of love. Evangelicals sometimes seem less passionately in love with God and his people than they are with mechanically spitting out the answers that are perceived as right. Thus, we fear that some of the barbs from TA are well deserved and provide an often needed corrective to this imbalance.

Haughton suggested that the legalistic arrogance of the Parent ego state must die in the Christian, but that a "redeemed" Parent can serve useful functions. We would agree. The book of Galatians suggests that the law is a "tutor" or "schoolmaster" (3:24) that draws us toward God. While some TA sources present unequivocally negative views of the Parent, other sources suggest that health is to be found in purging the Parent of irrational, overly restrictive, legalistic rules and instilling in the reconstructed Parent ego state healthy, reasonable injunctions and guidelines. This is a clear parallel to the Christian balance of law and grace.

Model of Psychotherapy

The general outlines of the therapeutic experience of TA reveal a profound optimism in the client's ability to change. More than most therapies, TA attempts to empower the client both through the person of the therapist and by educating the client in the TA perspective on the process of change. Like Christianity, it is not a mystery religion where devotees are expected to blindly trust its practitioners as they wade slowly and unknowingly forward at the direction of the guide; rather, what is expected of them is acknowledged up front, and they have as much access to the theory guiding the therapist as does the therapist. The acceptance of clients offered by the therapist is meant to empower them to appropriate their own OKness. But in Christian counseling, the hope would be that the responses of the therapist would be an incarnation of God's response, so that the client would be drawn toward the source of all good, rather than to simply trust in his or her own autonomous OKness.

TA takes a no-nonsense approach to change; Berne (quoted in Malony, 1980) stated, "Get well first—we can talk about it later!" This can be viewed positively as good stewardship—the attempt for therapy to be efficient and goal-oriented. TA therapy is typically brief, intense, and highly educational. This fits well with an American evangelical orientation toward rational answers, a success orientation and efficiency.

Unfortunately, TA doesn't seem to have an appreciation for the mysterious, conflicted dimensions of human life. Hedman and Kruus (1987) complain that the TA therapy process treats clients as objects in that, rather than starting with trust, one starts with a contract, and instead of understanding the clients, one teaches the language of TA so the clients understand the therapist (and hopefully come to understand themselves). There is a sense in TA that the therapist is less interacting with beings only "a little lower than the heavenly beings" (Ps 8:5) and more teaching a system, separating ego states, rewriting scripts and so forth. This may be an inevitable repercussion of the focus in TA being less on persons than on states, transactions and scripts.

One particular approach within TA circles that merits considerable suspicion is that of *reparenting*, a natural outgrowth of the less aggressive standard therapeutic approaches of redeciding or de-scripting. In reparenting the therapist aims at a total restructuring of the client's Parent ego state by becoming a new and effective Parent. Such procedures sometimes involve the therapist-directed regression of the client to childlike states and the almost total guidance of the client's life by the therapist. We have seen several tragic examples of such work, with clients of reparenting therapists forsaking vocations, spouses and even their own children as they attempt to reconstitute their Parent ego state.

Oden (1974) recognized early the authoritarian dangers of

reparenting and the "hubris" of the extravagant claims and agendas of reparenting. People fall into parenting their own children rather naturally, but it takes a special *chutzpah* to take on the task of reparenting an adult who has been scarred by her first parents. In such a process, there is always the risk of an autocratic or arrogant imposition of the values of the therapist. Self-reparenting (James, 1985) has been proposed as a do-it-yourself version of reparenting. There is no direct parallel to such a process in Christian experience, though it is certainly true that the church is to function in a somewhat "parental" fashion in providing guidance, exhortation and even discipline in the life of the believer. In the context of church, however, such functions emerge in a community context where there is more diffused personal responsibility (and hence community accountability), on the one hand, and more explicit commitment to a public agenda (dictated by the Scriptures and church tradition), on the other. The independent therapist with accountability to no one and whose values are not always revealed clearly can be a far more powerful figure with greater potential for abuse.

Conclusion

Our most general conclusion regarding TA is that there are other much more satisfying approaches to personality. TA too often substitutes clever labeling for in-depth understanding. The problems it presents in its understanding of individual persons have been enumerated. Most prominently, TA is one of the approaches that almost becomes an alternate faith system of religious proportions.

But TA does have one unique positive contribution it can make. Few systems pay such rich dividends in understanding our important *interpersonal* realities. Natural evil, moral evil and our human finitude have broken our relationships and locked us into destructive and repetitive patterns of relating to others. It is in the interpersonal domain that we so often see our pathologies played out. Given that it is in community that we can often experience the most profound healing as well, TA may have a unique role to play in increasing our understanding about pathological interactions. Umphrey and Laird (1977), James (1973) and Bontrager (1974) all present fruitful analyses of the kinds of "games Christians play." James and Savary (1974, pp. 56ff.) present interesting hypotheses about the different textures of faith for believers in different life positions. These sorts of analyses can enlarge our understanding of interpersonal reality even if the system as a whole cannot hope to form a comprehensive foundation for the practice of counseling and psychotherapy.

For Further Reading

Berne, E. (1964). *Games people play.* New York: Grove Press.
A helpful summary of TA.

Bontrager, J. (1974). *Free the child in you.* Philadelphia: Pilgrim/United Church Press.
An example of an overexuberant application of TA to the work of the church.

Harris, T. (1969). *I'm OK, you're OK.* New York: Harper & Row.
A helpful summary of TA.

James, M. (1973). *Born to love.* Reading, MA: Addison-Wesley.
An example of an overexuberant application of TA to the work of the church.

James, M., and Jongeward, D. (1971). *Born to win.* Reading, MA: Addison-Wesley.
A helpful summary of TA.

James, M., and Savary, L. (1974). *The power at the bottom of the well.* New York: Harper & Row.
An example of an overexuberant application of TA to the work of the church.

Oden, T. (1974). *Game free.* New York: Harper & Row.
A positive but critical examination of TA and Christian faith

References

Batey R. (1976). *Thank God I'm OK: The gospel according to TA.* Nashville: Abingdon.

Berne, E. (1964). *Games people play.* New York: Grove Press.

Bontrager, J. (1974). *Free the child in you.* Philadelphia: Pilgrim/United Church Press.

Dusay, J., and Dusay, K. (1984). Transactional analysis. In R. Corsini (Ed.), *Current psychotherapies* (3d ed.) (pp. 392-446). Itasca, IL: F. E. Peacock.

Greer, A. (1975). *No grown-ups in heaven.* New York: Hawthorn.

Harris, T. (1969). *I'm OK, you're OK.* New York: Harper & Row.

Haughton, R. (1974). *The liberated heart.* New York: Seabury.

Hedman, D., and Kruus, L. (1987). An evaluation of transactional analysis as a tool and method in pastoral counseling. *Pastoral Psychology, 35,* 172-186.

James, M. (1973). *Born to love.* Reading, MA: Addison-Wesley.

James, M. (1985). *It's never too late to be happy: The psychology of self-reparenting.* Reading, MA: Addison-Wesley.

James, M., and Jongeward, D. (1971). *Born to win.* Reading, MA: Addison-Wesley.

James, M., and Savary, L. (1974). *The power at the bottom of the well.* New York: Harper & Row.

Lawrence, C. (1983). Redecision and repentance. *Transactional Analysis Journal, 13,* 158-162.

Malony, H. (1980). Transactional analysis. In G. Collins (Ed.), *Helping people grow* (pp. 99-112). Santa Ana, CA: Vision House.

Oden, T. (1974). *Game free.* New York: Harper & Row.

Reuter, A. (1974). *Who says I'm OK?* St Louis, MO: Concordia.

Umphrey, M., and Laird, R. (1977). *Why don't I feel OK?* Irvine, CA: Harvest House.

Woollams, S., and Brown, M. (1979). TA: *The total handbook of transactional analysis.* Englewood Cliffs, NJ: Prentice-Hall.

Woollams, S.; Brown, M.; and Huige, K. (1976). *Transactional analysis in brief.* Ann Arbor, MI: Huron Valley Institute.

THE FAMILY
SYSTEM
PSYCHOLOGIES

14

FAMILY THERAPY

❖

*F*amily therapy is a generic name for a rather diverse and varied group of treatment approaches that have emerged since the early 1950s. The family therapy movement developed out of the growing recognition in child guidance and outpatient clinics that often *a troubled family*, rather than just a troubled individual *in* a family, needed treatment. This was especially evident in studies of communication patterns in the families of schizophrenic patients (Korchin, 1976). Eventually, the clinical relevance of treating entire families was readily apparent, especially when there were crises that affected all members or when there was noticeable marital discord or intergenerational conflict. Just how dramatically this went against the analytic tradition of individual treatment as the only allowable option cannot be underemphasized. Proponents argued that if sufficient focus was not given to the family system, but only to the "identified patient" (the person labeled as "having a problem"), the benefits of psychotherapy would be limited.

Rather than focusing on the intrapsychic or unconscious dynamics of the individual, *or even on the individual at all,* this approach by and large examines interpersonal *relationships* within the social structure of the family. According to Hazelrigg, Cooper and Bourdin (1987), family therapy represents a major paradigmatic shift in the conceptualization and treatment of psychopathology in its move to examining families rather than individuals. These reformulations are potentially freeing and liberating, enabling clinicians creatively to focus more on communication patterns and family interactional styles rather than on just individual psychodynamics (Schreck, 1983). If "problems in living" are intimately related to these larger systemic variables, it makes a great deal of sense to explore conceptual alternatives to traditional individualistic formulations.

A core assertion in this movement is that to be a person requires relatedness in the family of origin and beyond. What a refreshing contrast, notes Roberts (in press), to the all-too-familiar encouragement of narcissism and self-centeredness that is evident in so much of the human-potential movement. Family therapy at its best encourages social virtues as well as an ethic of personal responsibility. The focus on "me" (the individual) is replaced with an emphasis on "we" (the family). And it is within this context that family therapists explore expectations, forms of communication, power structures and the roles of family members. Since membership in the family system is "fixed," it makes sense to explore how the participants will affect and influence each other throughout the life span in the context of this most basic and important social system.

Descriptive Survey

Philosophical Assumptions and Model of Personality

The nuclear family is assumed to be the basic context in which problems occur (Hazelrigg, Cooper and Bourdin, 1987). The family is seen as a rule-governed organization that has a dynamic which transcends that of its separate participants (Anderson and Guernsey, 1985). The analysis and exploration of those variables that either facilitate or retard this dynamic are the subject matter of the systems therapies. If it is our intention to really understand a particular individual, it is argued, then we must become thoroughly familiar with his or her larger social context.

Such thinking logically follows from a tradition that accepts the relevance of general systems theory in biology (von Bertalanffy, 1968) and cybernetics in computer science (Prochaska, 1984) to the people-helping context. Systemic thinkers dislike analyzing and reducing phenomena to their most basic elements (reductionism or atomism); they prefer studying the complexities of organizational structures. And they are especially curious about patterns of communication and control in troubled individuals and their extended families.

A *system* can be defined as a group of interconnected or interrelated parts which mutually interact across time (Foley, 1984). Thus, a family is a system, as is a living cell or a human body, while a group of persons in an elevator is not. A group of people who work together at an office are a system, but not as influential a one as the family. A system has as real of an existence as the parts that make it up. Just as a human is as real as the organs that make him up, so also is a family as real as the people that make it up.

Systems have distinctive properties. First, they are characterized by *wholeness;* they are made up of their parts and the relationships of the parts, and thus the system is greater than the sum of its parts in isolation. The human body, like a family, can only be understood by looking at the parts *and* the way the parts work together. Second, systems are characterized by *interrelatedness,* in that all parts influence each other; there really are no unimportant parts, as the person who stubs her little toe often finds out. Third, systems have *boundaries* that differentiate one system from another system or define their subsystems. Our bodies stop at our skin; our families must stop at some point or they cease to exist. Fourth, living systems are either *open* (ideally) or *closed;* in other words, they are either capable of change and responsiveness to a changing environment or they are rigid and fossilized. When they are flexible, open and responsive to forces within and without, they can maintain a dynamic equilibrium, or *homeostasis.* The tendency to maintain a *dynamic homeostasis* is the fifth critical characteristic of systems.

All living systems are complex in terms of their alliances, coalitions and relationships. Ideally, they are fluid rather than static, continually evolving as developmental crises and challenges are faced and dealt with in an adaptive and healthy manner (cf. Carter and McGoldrick, 1980). How family members in these systems cope with conflict and change will be reflected in their interactional styles across time (i.e., they are predictable). Perhaps the most formidable challenge facing the family system is instilling in its members a sense of belonging while at the same time modeling and teaching those competencies that are essential for members (especially children) to individuate and establish a sense of separateness within the context of belonging (Salinger, 1985). If these essential skills and sensitivities are imparted, there comes a growing sense of self-esteem and personal security. Without them, it is difficult to see how a person can develop a repertoire of adaptive life skills or establish a new identity apart from the family of origin.

The family is seen as a living social system that extends over at least three generations. The specific way it functions (e.g., establishes roles, communicates and deals with differences of opinions) has significant implications for the well-being of its individual members (Goldenberg and Goldenberg, 1985). A particular member's dysfunctional behavior reflects a family system that is in disequilibrium. Thus, the "identified patient" represents a family that is in trouble. Unless the family relationships that undergird the lack of stability can be addressed, permanent change is not likely. How those family members deal with the inevitable changes and crises of life, or the developmental tasks that face any family (cf. Carter and McGoldrick, 1980), will determine the course of development of individual family members as well as the family as a whole.

Family therapists usually speak less about notions of persons and more about functional or dysfunctional family systems. There is a sense in which the psychodynamics of any given individual disappear in the larger social context. While this may be a welcome change from the oppressive individualism of much of contemporary personality theory, it tends to blur or erode the importance of individuality (cf. Van Leeuwen, 1984). A personality theory, then, is more implicit than explicit in most system therapies, because they frankly tend to be disinterested in the functioning of individual human beings. And since several of the family approaches can be viewed as extensions or extrapolations from some of the major individual approaches to people-helping, it is not possible to summarize coherent or consistent notions of personhood.

Model of Health
Perhaps some of the most valuable contributions from the family therapy movement have to do with its characterizations of the qualities

of strong families. Many of these qualities have their clear parallels in Scripture. Both popular (e.g., Stinnett, 1979; Curran, 1983) and professional (Beavers, 1982; Kantor and Lehr, 1975; Lewis, Gossetl and Phillips, 1976; Olson, Sprenkle and Russell, 1979) treatments of the subject suggest a number of parallel themes. When coupled with a full appreciation of the normative structures and functions established by God as part of the created order, we can gain greater insight into our obligations and responsibilities as members of both biological and spiritual families from grappling with this literature.

In the family therapies perspective, strong families:

1. *Respond positively to challenges and crises.* Rather than denying or distorting reality, they draw on their individual and collective resources to develop adaptive and healthy coping strategies. When these families are unable to find the resources within, they readily admit problems and seek help elsewhere.

2. *Have a clearly articulated world view,* sometimes expressed in terms of a specific religious commitment. This undergirds their moral development, altruistic endeavors and sense of history and heritage.

3. *Communicate well.* They know how to actively listen, affirm and support, express their thoughts and feelings, and manage the inevitable differences of opinion that can occur in the family system. These families have a well-developed repertoire of conflict-management skills.

4. *Choose to spend time together in a variety of tasks,* including both planned and spontaneous activities. They can work hard together toward a common goal, and they know how to enjoy each other when they play or work.

5. *Make promises and honor commitments to one another.* The marital and familial tasks and responsibilities are taken seriously. There is a sense of belonging and respect for individual differences. The family is seen as the context for the development of a strong sense of self-esteem and personal security so as to encourage an affiliative and risk-taking attitude toward life.

6. *Know how to express their love and appreciation for one another.* Family members know and respect one another. They are caring, compassionate, respectful, tolerant and trusting.

As might be assumed from earlier comments, health and normalcy are viewed from the context of the social system rather than from a more personal perspective. Qualities that contribute to the well-being of the family of origin may not necessarily translate into personal wholeness.

Model of Abnormality

"Problems in living" are usually viewed as symptoms of a dysfunctional family system by most family therapists. In particular, the unique and specific ways in which the family faces the stresses related to the inevitable changes, challenges and crises of life will determine familial well-being. Pathological communication patterns, enmeshment or disengagement, scapegoating, family violence or substance abuse are just some of the dysfunctional ways in which these events and transitions can be mishandled by the family system. The characteristic of homeostasis, the tendency to maintain the status quo mentioned earlier, is an asset to the healthy family, but is an enemy when maladaptive patterns are occurring, as it impedes change.

Wynne, Jones and Al-Khayyal (1982) argue that healthy communication is essential if parents are going to develop adaptive behaviors in their children. *Communication deviance* occurs when two or more persons are unable to stay focused and share meaning in their interactional efforts. In dysfunctional families, the verbal content and/or nonverbal behaviors are often strikingly dissonant between family members. This is especially evident in the patterns of communication where overt content (what is said) is inconsistent with covert process (how it is said), as when a parent yells, "Of course I love you! Do you think I would put up with all your crap if I didn't?" Indeed, such dissonance and inconsistency is the most common reason family members seek professional help.

Some examples of particularly pathological communication patterns include: (a) the *double-bind,* where two messages are logically inconsistent, as when an icy, rejecting husband scolds his wife for not being more affectionate, thus communicating both "love me" and "don't love me"; (b) *mystification,* where family members befuddle, confuse or mask what is really going on, as when people deal in such generalities as "the feeling just isn't there"; (c) *symmetrical relationships or one-upmanship,* where rigid roles are the norm and power relationships emphasize rule giving and enforcing, exemplified by the rigidly authoritarian father who is afraid to relate to his children in a personal way; and (d) *complementary relationships,* where personal pathologies feed on each other, as when the alcoholic "loser" is married to the "suffering martyr." (Gurman and Kniskern [1981] is an especially helpful reference source for greater clarification of these destructive patterns.)

Every family system is seen as having rules, some of which are explicit and many of which are implicit. When family systems have rules that allow for change, there is potential for constructive adaptations to life's challenges. But if the system is too rigid, due to ineffectual rules (e.g., "a 'real man' never asks for help!") or pathological communication, tension builds up and needs to be released in order for the system to maintain equilibrium or homeostasis. Unhealthy systems tend to be static and resistant to change. They can project the tension between two members of the system (such as marital conflict) onto a third member of the system (such as the adolescent daughter who takes on an identity as the "rebellious one" or as "the bulimic") rather than dealing more directly with the issues at hand. This phenomenon of projection is called *triangulation*. More healthy systems are less rigid and able to evolve through a process of controlled change.

Enmeshment (blurred family boundaries) and *disengagement* (rigid boundaries) are other forms of pathology that threaten family stability. In healthy families, individuals are able to balance a sense of personal identity ("I-ness") with a sense of group belonging ("we-ness"). Unhealthy enmeshment occurs when certain family members are over-concerned and/or overinvolved in each other's lives, thereby thwarting the development of essential life skills. This can be seen in the family where the ultimate family "virtue" is loyalty at all costs, exemplified by the young woman who never makes the break to attend college because her family continues to "need her" and expresses their caring in meddling ways. They do not see that authentic caring respects the other's freedom.

Differentiation and individuation become extremely difficult in such families (Minuchin, 1974). If boundaries are too rigid, family members may become too independent and autonomous, without any clear sense of family commitment. Enmeshed families care too much or care in the wrong way; disengaged families don't care enough. Both extremes can produce psychopathology. Extremes of enmeshment or disengagement have been implicated as significant variables in the etiology and/or maintenance of antisocial behaviors, eating disorders, certain psychosomatic illnesses, substance abuse and problems related to inappropriate roles and expectations in the family of origin (cf. Goldenberg and Goldenberg, 1985).

We mentioned earlier that tension builds up in the family when any of these pathological tendencies is present. At some point, the tension is expressed through one or more family members. The symptomatic behavior of the family member(s) is assumed to reflect distress and dysfunction in the system, which is struggling to maintain its equilibrium and homeostasis. The symptomatic family member, whether a fearful child, anorexic adolescent or alcoholic husband, is deemed to be manifesting *system disturbance*. The shape the pathology takes and the way family members deal with it are critical clues to understanding and intervening to change the family.

Model of Psychotherapy

As Goldenberg (1983, p. 297) has summarized, the "focus of family therapy is on changing the system—the characteristic family pattern of interacting with each other, their style and manner of communication, or the structure of their relationships—so that each member experiences a sense of independence, uniqueness, and wholeness while remaining within the context and security of the family relationship."

There are probably at least seven major models of family therapy in the field today (after Balswick, 1987):

The *structural family therapy model* sees the reorganization or strengthening of family relational structures as the major goal of treatment (cf. Minuchin, 1974). A very direct and often manipulative approach, it focuses on establishing more adaptive patterns of interactions by creating clear, flexible boundaries between family members and strengthening the parental hierarchy.

The *strategic family therapy model* is a highly active and problem-focused approach to treatment (cf. Fisch, Weakland and Segal, 1982; Haley, 1976). Rather than attempting to alter family structures, it attempts to resolve the presenting problems through a variety of creative and often "paradoxical" (seemingly indirect and opposite) therapeutic directives that have no obvious bearing on the problem or existing family structures. Its practitioners assume the family will sort out new relational structures as a result of symptomatic change.

The *family systems model* of family therapy can be described as a direct but nonconfrontational approach that focuses on the individual's role in the extended family system (Bowen, 1978). Assisting family members in differentiating themselves from the "ego mass" in their family of origin (i.e., establishing independent identity) is the major task of treatment. Ideally, this differentiation improves individual cognitive functioning and emotional reactivity through modification of the family system.

The *communications model* of family therapy asserts that symptoms are nonverbal messages in reaction to dysfunctions in the interactional styles of family members (Satir, 1983). Therapists in this tradition are rather active and see themselves as role models and teachers of good communication skills and sensitivities. It is assumed that when communication becomes clear and direct, significant growth and improvement can occur for all family members.

The *behavioral social exchange model* of family therapy stresses the application of behavioral or social-learning principles (chapters six and eight) to the resolution of family concerns (Patterson, 1971, 1982). As might be expected, it stresses the need to establish concrete and observable goals, the realignment of the contingencies of social reinforcement, the modeling of appropriate behaviors and the establishment of family "contracts" that seek to develop more adaptive interactional styles. It also tends to be an active and direct approach to treatment, with the therapist often functioning as a teacher or contract negotiator.

The *psychodynamic/object-relations model* (chapter four) focuses more on the individual in the context of the family system. Unresolved conflicts and losses in the family of origin are explored so as to assess how they might be influencing current interactional patterns (Ackerman, 1966; Boszoremenyi-Nagy and Ulrich, 1981). It is assumed that in addition to individuals having intrapsychic problems, family members contaminate each other with their pathologies, with the result that only a family intervention can produce effective change. Through increased insight and awareness, unresolved issues from childhood can be processed, eventually leading to more satisfying interpersonal relationships. As might be expected, the therapist tends to adopt a more neutral stand than in the previous approaches.

Finally, the *experiential model* shares the humanistic spirit of the communications model by emphasizing increased awareness, greater authenticity and more fulfilling interaction styles in the family system (Whitaker, 1976). As might be expected, the therapist is actively involved and highly responsive (chapter twelve). The key difference is that the focus is on the self in the context of the family rather than on communication patterns per se.

Obviously, with such diverse models it is hard to make broad generalization about such a complex and ever-changing movement. It is possible, however, to differentiate models in terms of whether they are *pragmatic* or *aesthetic,* based on their goals and typical modes of action (cf. Hazelrigg, Cooper and Bourdin, 1987, pp. 428-429).

Pragmatic approaches are typically concerned with behavioral outcomes and stress activity. Hence, they focus on directly and quickly alleviating presenting concerns by disrupting unhealthy power coalitions or interactive patterns in the family system. The structural, strategic and behavioral approaches probably best fit this description.

Aesthetic approaches, in contrast, are more "process-oriented." They are less likely to focus only on presenting complaints, but more likely to see them as catalysts for growth. Therapists in this tradition tend to be less active and directive, and more willing to bypass immediate concerns for what they consider to be more important ways to promote long-term growth and healing. The family systems, communications, psychodynamic and experiential models most often fit this description.

For the remainder of this chapter, however, we will focus largely (though not exclusively) on the models which have arisen out of the systems-theory movement, namely, the structural, strategic, family systems and communications models. The behavioral, experiential and psychodynamic models are largely adaptations of more traditional individual psychotherapy techniques for the family context. Thus they each respectively share the strengths and weaknesses of their parent theories. The models most influenced by systems theory, however, are truly different ways of looking at human nature.

Initially, family therapists are concerned about how presenting symptoms are related to the interactional patterns in the family, and how particular family members may play different roles in that process. In an effort to assess these dynamics, family therapists may meet with the entire family or any of a number of the members of the system or interdependent subsystems. For instance, they may meet with children, parents and grandparents together or with the parents alone. According to Goldenberg and Goldenberg (1985, p. 262), this seems most useful when there is serious marital conflict, sibling rivalry, intergenerational conflict or other relationship difficulties. Family sessions seem contraindicated when one or more members are too destructive, violent or psychologically fragile.

Although the styles adopted by family therapists vary widely, they tend to agree on the primary goals of treatment. According to the Group for the Advancement of Psychiatry (1970), improved communication, autonomy and individuation are most important, followed by increased empathy, more flexible leadership styles, improved role agreement, reduced conflict and greater individual symptomatic and task performance improvement. Different traditions may stress individual psychodynamics over and against family processes. Across the traditions, the role of the therapist is seen variously as a role model, facilitator, teacher or change agent. The emphasis placed on assessment varies considerably, with some seeing it as an essential and useful activity, and others as potentially disruptive and distracting. Creative and novel assessment strategies have been developed by some (e.g., Haley, 1976).

A bewildering number of interventions have been described in the family therapy literature. As Beels and Ferber (1969) have described it, some family therapists could best be described as reactors who tend to be nondirective and passive, whereas others could be more accurately described as conductors who tend to be highly active and directive in all phases of treatment. Obviously, the latter have generated the bulk of the more creative and innovative techniques. Generally, the latter group "act on" the family rather than looking at family members as collaborators in the therapeutic process. The general presumption seems to be that since family systems are nonrational entities which tend to maintain the dysfunctional homeostasis, there cannot be much collaboration with the individual clients.

One of the most widely used and often controversial of the family techniques is *reframing,* which involves giving an interpretation that puts the problem symptoms in a new light. For example, a married couple may be asked to thank a fearful child for distracting them all from their unresolved arguments. Another technique is *symptom prescription,* such as asking the family to intentionally schedule its arguments late at night when they are most likely to have really destructive battles (Deschenes and Shepperson, 1983). Sympton prescription is one form of *paradoxical* intervention, which we will discuss at the end of this chapter. A third is the creative utilization of *metaphors* and *parables,* which are aimed at altering a family's understanding of its own functioning by creating new "stories" by which they define themselves (Boghosian, 1983). Finally, *family genograms* are used, where families graphically portray how they are perpetuating or recapitulating long-standing problem patterns in their current relationships (cf. Goldenberg and Goldenberg, 1985).

The family therapy movement has grown enormously in the past three decades. The majority of its practitioners came out of traditions of individual therapy and have incorporated those perspectives into their systemic theorizing and practice. It would be fair to say that the theoretical bases for family techniques have not been firmly established despite the considerable faith many family therapists have in their efficacy and efficiency (Bednar, Burlingame and Masters, 1988). Still, the notion of intervening in the family system in response to certain problems has enormous intrinsic and intuitive appeal, especially if that attraction can be coupled with examples of persons who have been able to confront their feelings about their families of origin, disentangle their lives, and communicate more clearly and directly their needs and wants (Korchin, 1976).

The growth and development of family therapy in the past four decades has been impressive to even the most seasoned observer of the trends in psychotherapeutic theory, research and practice (Gurman and Kniskern, 1981; Piercy and Sprenkle, in press). This growth is especially evident in the increasing membership in such professional organizations as the American Association of Marriage and Family Therapists (which has doubled in size since 1979), as well as in the growing number of professional books, journals (e.g., *Family Process*) and papers at most conventions of mental health professionals. In 1989, marriage and family therapy was recognized by the Department of Health and Human Services as one of the "core" mental-health disciplines, along with psychiatry, psychology, social work and nursing (Piercy and Sprenkle, in press).

As might be expected in the developing stages of a major paradigm shift, there are a large number of psychotherapeutic models flourishing (Jacobson, 1985). Unfortunately, it is uncommon in the field of family therapy to see advocates of specific models interacting with other traditions to develop a common theoretical base, a core repertoire of clinical assessment and treatment strategies, or high-quality process or outcome research. As Prochaska (1984) has observed, it is all too common for family practitioners in print or in public to argue that their methods and techniques are applicable to an incredibly diverse and varied group of problems or populations. Therefore it is essential to look at comparative research studies if we are going to introduce any reasonable degree of accountability or consensus into this growing movement.

Christian Critique

Philosophical Assumptions
We applaud the emphasis this tradition places on the family as the

primary context in which people can grow. For the Christian, the normative structure and essential functions of the family are a crucially important part of the creational order (cf. Holstege, 1982). Indeed, an important part of our identity as Christians has to do with our place in both our biological families and in the church as our new family of God. As we noted in chapter two, God seems clearly concerned with more than just individuals, and has in the biblical record dealt with his people as families, as a tribe and as a body. Through Christ we are connected by grace and by a covenant of love in which we are all brothers and sisters—a family in a very deep sense (cf. Anderson and Guernsey, 1985).

But we are concerned about the difference between studying both the family and the individual versus focusing on the family *rather than* the individual. Several (though not all) versions of family therapy seem to implicitly or explicitly embrace what might be called a "collectivist" view of persons. A collectivist view of persons is one that sees persons as largely or exclusively a product of social interaction. More specifically, it contends that our core identity is best seen as that of being part of a system, a collective of people, whether that be a class, familial or societal grouping. Individual personality is deemed trivial or insignificant. Because who we are and how we behave is a function of the interpersonal systems we exist in, what matters is the character and functioning of the system, not the person.

Our fear is that in the more extreme versions of the collectivist perspective, individuality largely disappears. With this largely exclusive focus on structured relationships in family systems, a respect for internal processes and developmental histories vanishes (cf. Prochaska, 1984). These concerns are similar to those expressed about a much more strident and extreme collectivist approach to persons, that of doctrinaire Marxism, where individuality evaporates into the collective of the social class. We want to draw some lessons from one critique of Marxism, but please note that we are not equating family therapy with Marxism, nor are we saying that family therapy is Marxist.

Pannenberg (1989, p. 217), in critiquing Marxism, states that a collectivist view of persons is "sharply opposed to Christian personalism, because in a Christian perspective the individual person is constituted by his or her immediate relation to God. Therefore in a Christian view the person cannot be considered to be thoroughly dependent on the social context." Any conception of persons that minimizes or obliterates the individual on behalf of the family runs the risk of seriously degrading a Christian understanding of personhood. A healthy family is one that fully appreciates the richness and strength of diversity and encourages individuation; it does not stress homogeneity to the neglect of heterogeneity.

Should not a healthy family therapy theory also respect appropriate individualism? To their credit, approaches such as the family-systems therapy of Bowen do support such an understanding of the individual in the family. But it is difficult to believe in an autonomous self when one asserts that an individual is defined and controlled by the system of which he or she is a part, as the more radical approaches to family therapy do (Prochaska, 1984, p. 359).

Further, in Marxism alienation from the collective, which occurs in the form of individualism in various forms, is considered to be the fundamental problem of human experience. But "in a Christian perspective, of course, it is the Marxist reductionism, the reductionism of the person to a function of social interaction, that produces the alienation of the human person from the constitutive center of his or her human life, i.e., from God" (Pannenberg, 1989, p. 217). We cannot be truly human when our understanding of ourselves and our condition uproots a fundamental sense of ourselves as individuals, though grounded in our relationships with God, family and others. Such a view would cause, not alleviate, true alienation.

Pannenberg (1989, p. 218) also argues that atheism is not accidental nor incidental to Marxism, but interwoven throughout the system. It is central to Marxism to argue that human systems create persons, while Christianity, on the other hand, argues that we are creatures of God. Thus, in the Christian view people must transcend the social context and be ultimately grounded in relationship to God to be a self. Unless we are, we run the risk of asserting that we create our own identities primarily by the way we relate to others. Consequently, we have little use for a transcendent reality like God. Family theory can, in like fashion, see the individual as purely a product of family processes and hence judge God to be irrelevant. A more balanced perspective on personhood would stress dimensions of community, family and individuality as bases for our identity, but anchor our understanding of them in the context of a personal relationship with a Creator-God. In other words, understanding personhood only in horizontal relationships in the social context is inadequate without the vertical dimension as well.

Consequently, we object to the loss of respect for individuality evident in the more strategic and structural models of family therapy. The most striking and salient characteristics of an individual are at risk of being replaced by the global and sometimes generic characteristics of family systems. It seems ironic to make this criticism, in that we have roundly criticized many other therapy systems for their rank individualism, but family therapy in some instances swings too far in the other extreme. Christians have always had a high view of the person and the family. Persons are created in the image and likeness of their Creator-God (i.e., the doctrine of the *imago dei*), and the family has certain God-ordained functions (e.g., procreation, socialization and support, mediating between the individual and society, etc.). Systemic thinking, although it is a refreshing alternative paradigm for creative working models of personality, psychopathology and psychotherapy, tends to blur those qualities that make us most distinctive (i.e., our potential to be active agents engaged in a quest for meaning and significance). Responsible persons who make choices are surely more than the sum product of external social forces.

Many of the core assumptions of systemic therapies tend to be deterministic and environmentally based, almost as much so as Skinnerian behaviorism (chapter six). Systemic language can be mechanistic (if not reductionistic) when used to describe family dynamics. At least at a covert level, the theory assumes that family members often have very limited resources to directly and responsibly confront their issues or really control their lives.

Certainly we do not want to minimize the reality of the fears and failures of many family systems, especially in a time of social upheaval and transition in contemporary American society. We do not share, however, what appears to be an underlying pessimism in much of systemic thinking. The more pragmatic family therapists, especially, assume an extreme utilitarian stance toward family dynamics, assisting members in "adjusting" to each other, but not really helping them in more fully realizing their potential as responsible agents. Family members are assumed to have the capacity to gain only limited insight into causes and cures of problems. One concrete manifestation of this is how rarely it is in strategic versions of family therapy for clients to be encouraged to understand the interventions offered by the therapist or to develop insight about the changes they have been through (more about this later). "Restructuring" is often deemed more important (or curative) than awareness and understanding. Free will and the personal dimensions of causation need to be taken more seriously in systemic thinking. Individuals and families have more potential for change than they are generally credited with by many family therapists. They should be treated responsibly, not approached with ingrained assumptions about resistance and pessimism toward change.

Finally, we are concerned about the philosophy of science inherent in systemic thinking. Models that stress emotionality appear to be in the human science tradition (cf. Van Leeuwen, 1984). Those that stress rationality and activity are more squarely in the natural sciences tradition. Although research productivity is becoming voluminous, much remains to be done (Olson, Sprenkle and Russell, 1979; Piercy and Sprenkle, in press; Zuk, 1976). There needs to be far greater commitment to assessment and evaluation of outcomes, clearer formulations of both theory and technique and less reliance on personal anecdotes and "clinical case studies." Epistemic humility ought to characterize a young and developing field.

Model of Personality

Family therapy stresses the importance of clearly defined structures and roles, including clarity about familial hierarchies. As Salinger (1985, p. 405) has noted, a strong family is rooted in a marital relationship that reflects a high degree of involvement and investment on the part of both persons, one characterized by a strong covenantal commitment and an ordered mutuality that gets beyond personal needs and wants (cf. Anderson and Guernsey, 1985). Indeed, the analogy referred to in Scripture is sobering, that our marriages ought to reflect the union of Christ and the church (Eph 5:25-30). Although there is considerable discussion and debate about the specific implications of these directives (e.g., Grunlan, 1984; Bilezikian, 1985; Van Leeuwen, 1990), one can hardly minimize the strong view of marriage in the Christian tradition where structures and roles are given serious consideration, especially since they have consequences beyond earthly existence.

Ideally, a strong marital coalition undergirds the development of the children. Guidelines for the care and nurture of children are present in the Scriptures, ones which presuppose certain skills and sensitivities on the part of both parents. As Balswick and Balswick (1987) have described it, families ought to be increasingly characterized by covenant, empowerment, grace and intimacy, essential family values which should be taught in word and deed. This is a tall order indeed for parenting, one that requires the shaping of family life in accord with clear roles for the marital dyad as well as for the various subsystems between parent(s) and child(ren). But these scriptural guidelines need to be worked out in such a way that they transcend our personal and cultural idiosyncrasies and preferences, especially as they relate to single-parent, "blended" or "child-free" families (Johnson, 1983; Van Leeuwen, 1990).

Healthy family functioning also presupposes clearly established (but not inflexible) boundaries. Family cohesion must always be balanced with the individual growth of the members. The Scriptures clearly warn about the possibility of conflict in one's family of origin as one seeks to do the will of God (cf. Mt 10:34-39). Indeed, integrity seems to demand, at times, a response that will tax our emotional resources as we seek to reconcile seemingly discrepant personal and familial priorities (cf. Salinger, 1985, p. 406). But Christian commitment demands an even more challenging responsibility—to expand our boundaries to include our brothers and sisters in the larger "family of faith" (cf. Anderson and Guernsey, 1985). Indeed, Christians are called to balance love and respect for one's immediate family with appropriate care and concern for all who love and obey God (cf. Mt 12:50). These are all "boundary issues."

Yet our understanding of these biblical imperatives will always be interpreted within the context of our personal problems, failings and inevitable distortions due to our humanness, fallenness and finiteness. All too easily our family relationships can become distorted, fixated and/or stagnated—grace can turn into law, empowerment can lead to a sense of possessive power, covenant can be replaced by contract, and personal aloofness can substitute for any real sense of intimacy (cf. Balswick and Balswick, 1987). Once again, it is imperative that we draw from the resources of our faith and the local discerning community of believers. This presupposes that we are connected in the kind of support system that is characterized by a healthy balance between affirmation and accountability and by a strong commitment to "being the church" in word and deed (Anderson and Guernsey, 1985).

In summary, then, we see much in the family therapy understanding of families that has exciting integrative possibilities for the Christian concerned about helping people grow. The importance of clearly defined roles and structures, and firm but flexible boundaries, has been consistently emphasized. Indeed, research efforts appear to support these key assertions (e.g., Lewis, Gossetl and Phillips, 1976). A key difference between much of family therapy and the Christian view appears to be the ultimate basis for such characteristics—the former based in a pragmatic and utilitarian mindset (i.e., because they work), but the latter rooted in the command to manifest these qualities as an expression of our covenantal and grace relationship with the Creator-God (i.e., we love because God first loved us).

Despite the utility and importance of the foregoing, family therapy does not give us a personality theory. This makes it difficult for the practitioner in this tradition to fully respect individual differences.

Model of Health

The purpose of the Scriptures is not to give a detailed description of the stages of family development or specific instructions for dealing with the diversity of challenges and tasks that face parents and their children (Narramore, 1979). Still, there are specific commands and promises given to parents and children in the Bible. Subjects like discipline (Prov 22:6; Prov 29:17), good communication (Eph 6:4; Col 3:21) and familial responsibilities (1 Tim 3:1, 4-5; 5:8) are certainly addressed. But it would be a mistake to look at the Scriptures as a textbook on family functioning.

As Smedes (1976, p. 24) has perceptively observed, it would be more helpful to look to the Bible as informing us about human life as a whole so we can increasingly understand and evaluate our experiences as persons in our nuclear and extended families. It is specifically this kind of wisdom and discernment we should seek as we try to understand what we are as members of the family, what we tend to make of ourselves and what we can be through grace and the covenant of love. Seeking to make sense of what it means to have God as our parent (and for us to be God's children) and how we should reflect that in our relationships with one another are good places to start. When coupled with a growing awareness of the characteristics of healthy and strong families, this gives us a perspective on what skills and sensitivities we will need to acquire and develop if we are going to be effective members of our biological and spiritual families (cf. Anderson and Guernsey, 1985).

A recent study (McKeon and Piercy, 1983) compared concepts of healthy family functioning as perceived by family therapists, Roman Catholic priests and Southern Baptist ministers. They shared similar perceptions about the importance of togetherness, individuation, leadership, order, flexibility and healthy communication. The Southern Baptist ministers, however, placed greater emphasis on structure and authority rather than individuation, and both groups of clergy rated structure and authority higher than flexibility. Obviously, these are potential areas for discussion and debate between practitioners and laypersons alike. Indeed, such interaction might enrich our understanding of what it means to be "family," whether we understand that to mean our biological families only (the historic secular emphasis) or our larger and more extended family of faith (the classic Christian understanding).

As with any approach to people-helping, family therapy approaches endorse a certain philosophy of life and world view, especially about the relative importance of individual well-being in the context of the functioning of the family. Pragmatic and utilitarian family practitioners, argued Hare-Mustin (1980), all too quickly give inappropriate priority to the good of the family as a whole when an individual's needs conflict with the whole. This could potentially thwart legitimate attempts to "differentiate" or "individuate" and perhaps even encourage a new kind of "enmeshment." Hare-Mustin, like others, also argued that family therapy typically is not conducted in a gender egalitarian way, but implicitly and thoughtlessly endorses stereotyped or traditional roles for men and women.

Possible abuse of authority and overemphasis on the needs of certain family members needs more serious discussion in the family therapy movement (cf. Piercy and Sprenkle, in press). Indeed, it is exceedingly difficult for the family therapist not to be unduly influenced by the pathological power coalitions or dysfunctional interactional styles of family systems, a reality of treatment that can lead to coercion, manipulation or pressure on the part of the therapist for the supposed "good of the family." It is to his credit that Haley (1976) recognized early the potential for abuse here, but he himself ended up advocating power for the therapist rather than to the person in the system as the answer to this conundrum. Recently, an entire special issue of *Counseling and Values* (Doherty, 1985), the official journal of the Association for Religious and Value Issues in Counseling, was devoted to consideration of values and ethics in family therapy. This hopefully indicates that we are entering a time when full and public discussions of these issues will occur.

Apart from the concerns about the potential abuse of authority and power in the context of treatment, there is growing concern about some of the assumptions made by family therapists about the nature of the "ideal family." More specifically, attention is focusing on the implicit assumptions being made about sex roles and division of responsibilities in the healthy family. All too often, these assumptions tend to support rather traditional and stereotyped divisions of labor in the family system, something that ultimately might thwart the development of the individual gifts and talents of family members (cf. Bilezikian, 1985, for a view challenging traditional Christian conceptions of roles). As Christians, we must be careful to balance a respect for the rights of individuals with a concern for the well-being of the family as a whole, but with the added responsibility of helping all to become meaningful and significant parts of the larger family of faith that has committed itself to expressing the kingdom of God (cf. Van Leeuwen, 1990).

The lesson in all of this is that it is imperative that the family therapist be explicit about his or her assumptions and values. For Hare-Mustin (1980, p. 938), this would include explaining to an individual or family client the therapist's beliefs about appropriate sex-role requirements, distribution of power and responsibilities, convictions about extended families and other support systems, as well as attitudes about nontraditional family arrangements. In her analysis and that of others, family therapists rarely do this, because of their low view of client capacity for insight or meaningful rationality. For us, it would also include sharing our understanding of what it means to be part of the extended family of faith and the specific manner in which the family reflects God's created order through grace and covenant (cf. Anderson and Guernsey, 1985).

Model of Abnormality

Family therapy is clearly a psychosocial model of psychopathology. It seems most useful when there are family crises that affect all members, marital discord that influences the equilibrium of the system or conflicts along value or generational lines (cf. Korchin, 1976, p. 381). Certainly, family models have a depth of understanding of familial dynamics, but not necessarily a broad-based understanding of psychopathology in general (Langsford, 1978). An appreciation of its assets must be balanced with its liabilities. Our concern is aroused when the family receives the exclusive or even predominant emphasis in either assessment or treatment. Holistic factors, including the biological, intrapsychic and sociocultural dimensions, are ignored. Not every problem should be construed as a systems problem. At worst, family therapy can further intensify the "blame your family" approach to dealing with our own problems. And it is not helpful for understanding problems that are more directly related to individual choice and responsibility.

Despite these reservations, we find a number of the theoretical concepts in family therapy to be enormously helpful in our efforts to understand the richness and complexities of human interactions. A therapist who can be reasonably objective about these familial dynamics can help family members who need to learn how to effectively communicate with one another. Candor and directness, as well as loving support and encouragement, seem in order as family members seek to develop skills in forming a sense of personal as well as familial identity, both in the context of the biological family and the larger family of faith (cf. McLemore, 1983). All too often, "ministry to families" in the local church has been rather superficial. We would like to see a greater respect for how religious attitudes, values and behaviors are influenced by family dynamics (and vice versa). Family concepts give us a language that does justice to the all-too-familiar but often subtle ways in which we attempt to deceive ourselves and each other in our interpersonal relationships.

Model of Psychotherapy

Family therapy correctly recognizes that symptoms often appear in a larger context (e.g., the family of origin or in a marriage). Directly confronting aberrant power coalitions and dysfunctional interaction patterns is a logical way to confront neuroses and related forms of psychopathology. This does not necessarily imply any sacred commitment on the part of practitioners to the "sanctity of hearth and home" (Kovel, 1976, p. 185). In reality, the appeal of the focus on the family system is probably related to more pragmatic and utilitarian concerns, namely, the perceived effectiveness of the methods, than to a deep moral commitment to the family. This ethos sounds dangerously close to an ends-justifying-the-means approach to clinical intervention (Prochaska, 1984).

A more generous interpretation would be that family therapy practitioners are deeply concerned about the need for greater relatedness in contemporary American society. A fair assessment would be to conclude that the individually focused approaches have taught us much about what it means to assist persons in becoming more self-aware and capable individuals who can better respond to the demands of everyday living. In contrast, the family therapy movement may be able to help individuals grow toward greater maturity in the context of their families of origin, with the secondary effect of helping families grow.

We appreciate this emphasis, since it is clear from a careful reading of Scripture that God works out his plan for humankind in families across the generations (cf. Anderson and Guernsey, 1985). Contemporary Americans often lack a strong sense of cultural, historical, familial or personal heritage. The focus on families is potentially freeing and liberating in that it can restore some sense of history in a society where interdependence is not necessarily seen as a virtue.

But the perspective of the family therapy practitioner is incomplete; awareness needs to extend beyond the family processes to the larger ecological or societal system, a reality that the Christian gospel speaks directly to (i.e., God works through persons and family systems, but also through the larger "family of faith" and societal contexts). In other words, we as Christians are called to be responsible not only to our biological families, but to close relationships with others who are committed to exemplifying the kingdom of God. In this way, the context for our caring and commitment is greatly enlarged (Roberts, in press).

But in those areas where family therapy does focus, it still appears to help individuals deal with the kind of problems that often most directly affect them, the ones that are perhaps most obvious to any sensitive observer of the family system. At its best, family therapy encourages more responsible attitudes toward other people. At its worst, individual therapy promotes selfism and selfishness. Family therapy is not without its risks due to its pragmatic and utilitarian emphases.

As Christians, we feel this emphasis is important for other reasons as well. Pragmatic and utilitarian clinicians tend to have poorly articulated values. In the worst possible scenario, such a mentality can lead to a rather mechanistic and reductionistic mentality. "Fixing things" tends to become the *modus operandi*. All too often, this can lead to viewing persons as "objects" rather than "subjects," parts of systems to be manipulated, rather than persons to be more fully understood, appreciated and valued.

Embedded in such a mentality is often a low view of rationality. Certain family interventions are introduced without rationale (or with a deceptive rationale) to the client family and are based on the premise that individual behavior is the nonrational result of systemic forces, not personal choice. Positively, we appreciate the way that family therapy has sensitized many clinicians and Christians to some of the alternatives available to direct confrontation when persons have psychological and spiritual problems. Many dysfunctional families simply do not change as a response to more direct "collaborative" interventions. As Boghosian (1983) has observed, certain "counter-rational" interventions like paradox[1] parable and metaphor can be quite helpful with persons whose dysfunctional patterns are highly resistant to change. Although there is considerable controversy about the ethics of such procedures as paradox (cf. Deschenes and Shepperson, 1983), family therapy procedures have the potential for "high voltage" responses in the family system.

One of the lasting legacies of family therapy may be the recognition of the need to consider "nonrational" alternatives to more conventional and direct interventions. The Christian understanding of the need for such interventions does not, however, rest ultimately in a low view of rationality, but rather in a sad recognition of the profound capacity for self-deceit, rebellion and bondage to sin which we all manifest. Indeed, such interventions, when used with integrity, might be the most efficacious, effective and ethically appropriate procedures available.

Conclusion

We find family therapy to be a refreshing contrast to some of the excesses associated with certain overly individualistic approaches to change. Certain emphases in this tradition bring a whole new understanding to what it means to be in the family of God as well as a member of our biological families. The approach reminds us of the need to struggle with what it means to honor first our Creator-God rather than familial relationships ("A man's enemies will be the members of his own household," Mt 10:36).

"Problems in living" more times than not have dimensions of familial involvement, and family therapy certainly illuminates this. By emphasizing certain themes like the need for a firm parental coalition and appropriate generational boundaries, family therapy has encour-

---

[1]Perhaps the biblical examples that come closest to exemplifying paradoxical interventions would be God's commanding Abraham to sacrifice his son Isaac (Gen 22) and Solomon threatening to chop a baby in two to resolve a dispute over whom the child belonged to (1 Kings 3:15-28). In neither case were the supposedly desired outcomes the real focus; God did not want Isaac dead, and Solomon did not want the baby dead. Both interventions had outcomes that neither Abraham nor the disputing women could have projected.

aged us to make explicit our notions of healthy family functioning, while reminding us of how often the "ideal" is thwarted. Perhaps few other God-ordained institutions can manifest the discrepancies between the "dream" and the "reality" of our humanness, fallenness and finiteness than our families. When characterized by grace, covenant and empowerment, family is a very beautiful thing, but when it is ruled by law, contract and possessive power, it is a very dark and painful reality (cf. Anderson and Guernsey, 1985).

This chapter was one of the hardest to write given the widely divergent models of family therapy. We wish the literature of family therapy was clearer about its basic descriptive concepts (and firmer about its commitment to meaningful process and outcome research). As a young but developing movement, family therapy models need to be synthesized, integrated and critically evaluated (cf. Piercy and Sprenkle, in press). At the present, the connection between theory and technique is often weak in this approach. There is no clear, rational basis for choosing one intervention over and against others.

Further, we would like to see a greater appreciation for the varieties of family experiences, including the religious family, in the family therapy movement. This will require a more clearly articulated set of assumptions about personhood, psychopathology and psychotherapy, as well as a broader set of theoretical conceptions. Our fear is that the family therapy movement may become a victim of its own "success," and these important concerns will be neglected. As always, there is a need for greater accountability at all levels of personal and professional involvement on the part of practitioners, especially in the areas of training, supervision and practice. Few approaches offer so many potential benefits and risks as does family therapy.

For Further Reading

Anderson, R., and Guernsey, D. (1985). *On becoming family.* Grand Rapids, MI: Eerdmans.
   A most valuable "theology of the family" from an orthodox Christian perspective.
Feiner, J., and Yost, G. (1988). *Taming monsters, slaying dragons: The revolutionary family approach to overcoming childhood fears and anxieties.* New York: Arbor House/William Morrow.
   A readable but rather self-promoting lay introduction to the field.
Goldenberg, I., and Goldenberg, H. (1985). *Family therapy: An overview* (2d ed.). Monterey, CA: Brooks/Cole.
   A useful introduction to the many diverse and varied models of family

therapy.

Haley, J. (1987). *Problem-solving therapy* (2d ed.). San Francisco: Jossey-Bass.
The most recent revision of strategic family therapy by a very creative clinician. It makes for interesting reading.

Minuchin, S., and Fishman, H. (1981). *Family therapy techniques.* Cambridge, MA: Harvard University Press.
A professional-level discussion of specific family therapy interventions from the perspective of the structural model.

Piercy, F., and Sprenkle, D. (in press). Marriage and family therapy: A decade review. *Journal of Marriage and the Family.*
A helpful discussion of the theoretical and research trends in marriage and family therapy in the past decade.

Satir, V., and Baldwin, M. (1983). *Satir step by step.* Palo Alto, CA: Science and Behavior Books.
A definitive treatment of the communications-model approach to family therapy.

Van Leeuwen, M. (1990). *Gender and grace.* Downers Grove, IL: InterVarsity Press.
A thoughtful analysis of what it means to be a man or woman of God in the contemporary Christian context.

References

Ackerman, N. (1966). *Treating the troubled family.* New York: Basic Books.

Anderson, A., and Guernsey, D. (1985). *On becoming family.* Grand Rapids, MI: Eerdmans.

Balswick, J. (1987). Unpublished class notes, Fuller Theological Seminary, Pasadena, CA.

Balswick, J., and Balswick, J. (1987). A theological basis for family relationships. *Journal of Psychology and Christianity, 6*(3), 37-49.

Beavers, W. (1982). Healthy, midrange, and severely dysfunctional families. In F. Welsh (Ed.), *Normal family processes* (pp. 45-66). New York: Guilford.

Bednar, R.; Burlingame, G.; and Masters, K. (1988). Systems of family treatment: Substance or semantics? *Annual Review of Psychology, 39,* 401-434.

Beels, C., and Ferber, A. (1969). Family therapy: A view. *Family Process, 8,* 280-332.

Bilezikian, G. (1985). *Beyond sex roles.* Grand Rapids, MI: Baker.

Boghosian, J. (1983). The biblical basis for strategic approaches in pastoral counseling. *Journal of Psychology and Theology, 11*(2), 99-107.

Boszoremenyi-Nagy, I., and Ulrich, D. (1981). Contextual family therapy. In A. Gurman and D. Kniskern (Eds.), *Handbook of family therapy* (pp. 159-186). New York: Brunner/Mazel.

Bowen, M. (1978). *Family therapy in clinical practice.* New York: Aronson.

Carter, E., and McGoldrick, M. (Eds.). (1980). *The family life cycle: A framework for family therapy.* New York: Gardner Press.

Curran, D. (1983). *Traits of a healthy family.* New York: Ballantine.

Deschenes, P., and Shepperson, V. (1983). The ethics of paradox. *Journal of*

Psychology and Theology, 11(2), 92-98.

Doherty, W. (1985). *Counseling and values, 30*(2).

Fisch, R.; Weakland, J.; and Segal, L. (1982). *The tactics of change: Doing therapy briefly.* San Francisco: Jossey-Bass.

Foley, V. (1984). Family therapy. In R. Corsini (Ed.), *Contemporary psychotherapies* (3d ed.) (pp. 447-490). Itasca, IL: F. E. Peacock.

Goldenberg, H. (1983). *Contemporary clinical psychology* (2d ed.). Monterey, CA: Brooks/Cole.

Goldenberg, I., and Goldenberg, H. (1985). *Family therapy: An overview.* Monterey, CA: Brooks/Cole.

Group for the Advancement of Psychiatry. (1970). *The field of family therapy.* (GAP Report #78). New York: GAP.

Grunlan, S. (1984). *Marriage and the family: A Christian perspective.* Grand Rapids, MI: Zondervan.

Gurman, A., and Kniskern, D. (Eds.). (1981). *Handbook of family therapy.* New York: Brunner/Mazel.

Haley, J. (1976). *Problem-solving therapy.* San Francisco: Jossey-Bass.

Hare-Mustin, R. (1980). Family therapy may be dangerous to your health. *Professional Psychology, 11*(6), 935-938.

Hazelrigg, M.; Cooper, H.; and Bourdin, C. (1987). Evaluating the effectiveness of family therapies: An integrative review and analysis. *Psychological Bulletin, 101*(3), 428-442.

Holstege, H. (1982). *The Christian family.* Grand Rapids, MI: Calvin College.

Jacobson, N. (1985). Towards a nonsectarian blueprint for the empirical study of family therapies. *Journal of Marriage and Family Therapy, 11*(2), 163-165.

Johnson, C. (1983). *The psychology of biblical interpretation.* Grand Rapids, MI: Zondervan.

Kantor, D., and Lehr, W. (1975). *Inside the family: Towards a theory of family process.* San Francisco: Jossey-Bass.

Korchin, S. (1976). *Modern clinical psychology.* New York: Basic Books.

Kovel, J. (1976). *A complete guide to therapy.* New York: Pantheon Books.

Langsford, R. (1978). Understanding the role of extrafamilial social forces in family treatment: A critique of family therapy. *Family Therapy, 5*(1), 73-79.

Lewis, J.; Gossetl, J.; and Phillips, V. (1976). *No single thread: Psychological health and family systems.* New York: Brunner/Mazel.

McKeon, D., and Piercy, F. (1983). Healthy family functioning: What family therapists, priests, and ministers say. *International Journal of Family Therapy, 5*(3), 190-202.

McLemore, C. (1983). *Honest Christianity.* Philadelphia: Westminster.

Minuchin, S. (1974). *Families and family therapy.* Cambridge, MA: Harvard University Press.

Narramore, B. (1979). *Parenting with love and limits.* Grand Rapids, MI: Zondervan.

Olson, D.; Sprenkle, D.; and Russell, C. (1979). Circumplex model of marital and family systems I: Cohesion and adaptability dimensions, family types, and clinical applications. *Family Process, 18,* 3-28.

Pannenberg, W. (1989). Christianity, Marxism, and liberation theology. *Chris-*

tian Scholar's Review, 18(3), 215-226.

Patterson, G. (1971). *Families: Applications of social learning to family life.* Champaign, IL: Research Press.

Patterson, G. (1982). *Coercive family process.* Eugene, OR: Castalia.

Piercy, F., and Sprenkle, D. (in press). Marriage and family therapy: A decade review. *Journal of Marriage and the Family.*

Prochaska, J. (1984). *Systems of psychotherapy: A transtheoretical approach.* Chicago: Dorsey Press.

Roberts, R. (in press). *Taking the word to heart.* Grand Rapids, MI: Eerdmans.

Salinger, R. (1985). Family therapy: Overview. In D. Benner, (Ed.), *Baker encyclopedia of psychology* (pp. 404-406). Grand Rapids, MI: Baker.

Satir, V. (1983). *Conjoint family therapy* (3d ed.). Palo Alto, CA: Science and Behavior Books.

Schreck, P. (1983). From sheets to systems: A perspective of theological/psychological integration. *Journal of Psychology and Christianity, 2*(2), 21-25.

Smedes, L. (1976). *Sex for Christians.* Grand Rapids, MI: Eerdmans.

Stinnett, N. (1979). *Building family strengths.* Lincoln, NE: University of Nebraska Press.

Van Leeuwen, M. (1984). *The person in psychology: A contemporary Christian appraisal.* Grand Rapids, MI: Eerdmans.

Van Leeuwen, M. (1990). *Gender and grace.* Downers Grove, IL: InterVarsity Press.

von Bertalanffy, L. (1968). *General systems theory: Foundation, development, applications.* New York: Braziller.

Whitaker, C. (1976). A family is a four-dimensional relationship. In P. Guerin, Jr. (Ed.), *Family therapy: Theory and practice* (pp. 182-191). New York: Gardner Press.

Wynne, L.; Jones, J.; and Al-Khayyal, M. (1982). Healthy family communication patterns: Observations in families "at risk" for psychopathology. In F. Walsh (Ed.), *Normal family processes* (pp. 142-165). New York: Guilford Press.

Zuk, G. (1976). Family therapy: Clinical hodgepodge or clinical science? *Journal of Marriage and Family Counseling, 2,* 299-303.

TOWARD
CHRISTIAN
PSYCHOLOGIES

15

RESPONSIBLE
ECLECTICISM

✛

*A*t the broadest possible levels, what have we claimed so far in this book? We have claimed that it is legitimate and necessary for the dedicated Christian to stand on the fundamentals of the faith. We must let those beliefs, values, attitudes and commitments have their proper sway in all that we think, do, and feel. This is what integration of faith and understanding means at the most basic level. We have argued that the Christian faith has a great deal to say about personhood, though it does not propose a specific psychology as we understand it today.

Further, we *need* a psychology, a comprehensive and explicit understanding of persons, if we are to be of optimal assistance in helping hurting people achieve healing and growth. In our analysis of the main psychotherapy theories, we hope we have documented two main points. First, that each of the models has several compatibilities with the faith, as well as many insights, strengths, uses and points of attractiveness. Second, that each model has both incompatibilities with biblical faith and other flaws, inconsistencies, weaknesses and problems. None of the theories can be rejected out of hand, but none can be wholeheartedly endorsed by the Christian counselor. Some models hold more promise than others because they are more well elaborated, have more evidence supporting their effectiveness or have more pervasive commonalities with Christian belief and practice.

We do not have *the* definitive model to propose in place of the many theories we have examined. In fact, we do not believe that a definitive model exists and think it unlikely that it will ever exist. If after two millennia Christians cannot agree about some of the most fundamental points of theology (as documented by the diversity of denominations and theological "schools"), how can we expect congruence on a "Christian" psychology?

So how can the field be put together? How can counselors achieve some order in their understanding of people so as not to be paralyzed with indecision and confusion when confronted with a hurting person? We would argue that it is reasonable at this point in history for Christian counselors to be *eclectic* or *pluralistic* in their approach, drawing first on the faith for the foundations of a view of persons and then elaborating on that view with conceptions taken from secular psychology or the writings of the Christian counselors of the past and the present. And lest the result of this be a sloppy, unsystematic hodgepodge of ideas, we will survey ways in which this eclecticism might be conducted.

As we start out, we would argue again, as we did in chapter two, that the Bible does not teach a personality theory, though it does teach us much about persons. Van Leeuwen (1987), working within the framework of personality theorist Salvatore Maddi, suggests that it is vital to distinguish between suppositions of *core* personality tendencies and characteristics (about which the Bible and the faith has much, though not everything, to say) and more the *peripheral* statements about personality types, modes of human development and the like.

For example, the concept of sin is central to the faith, but that concept, with all its meaning, does not tell us why one person sins by committing adultery while another sins with a prideful, arrogant attitude or by a lack of compassion for the poor. The faith tells us that God did not intend for us to be riddled with anxiety, but it does not tell us how to deal with a person who is phobicly afraid of social situations, nor does it tell us why some avoid feared objects while others overcompensate for their fear with an exaggerated bravado. Our faith tells us the ultimate meaning of life, but it does not tell us why so many conversions to saving faith occur in adolescence rather than in late adulthood. Only our psychologies address these complex and intricate issues.

Several authors have noted that the theoretical allegiances of counselors to different counseling approaches tend to change over time. While there is no solid empirical research to back up these claims, they are intuitively appealing. Halgin (1985) suggested that there are a number of pressures that encourage students of counseling approaches to make identifications with particular approaches even before they have received substantive training in these approaches. This may be due to student perceived congruences between a model and that student's personal life philosophy, identification with a professor or teacher who emulated a certain approach, or pressure exerted by graduate admission processes which encourage early identification of a preferred model. In the graduate training environment, student allegiances to a model are dramatically affected by training opportunities available, both in terms of courses and practicum experiences and personal experiences with therapy. Training programs often are strong in one approach to the detriment of others. Also, those educating students in therapy seem more likely to be theoretical purists than community practitioners because such theoretical purity makes classroom communication easier and may facilitate research productivity.

In practicing therapy (following Halgin, 1985; and Norcross, 1985) the clinician inevitably confronts the limits of his or her model. This may be minimized for those who work in settings where they are exposed only to a homogeneous population needing help, as in the case of the behavior modifier working only with the mildly developmentally disabled (retarded), or the existential therapist only working with high-functioning, verbal and intelligent persons experiencing milder dissatisfactions with life. For most, though, confrontations with the limits of one's model occur quite soon in practice; we run into counseling problems that either stretch our working model to the limits or clearly fall beyond the bounds of our model.

We also encounter cases where our model *should have worked* if the approach is true, and we must confront the fact that it did not work. These experiences are akin to the psychological challenges we face in personal development when our status quo is shaken and the resulting disequilibrium forces us to grow a bit more. Without such crises, we would be unlikely to ever grow.

Our reaction to such challenges may be rigidly to claim the exclusive correctness of our model and to deny its limitations (a response not in the best interest of therapist or client). Some will acknowledge the limitations but confidently believe that it is only a matter of time until the essential correctness of their approach is borne out. Some may lapse into a relativism that results in the kind of "supermarket" (Nelson-Jones, 1985) or chaotic eclecticism we will describe below. But the healthiest response is to make a commitment to growing in effectiveness through knowing the limits of our approach and understanding how other models might complement and make up for the weaknesses of our own. The options for responsible eclecticism will be our topic in the next two sections.

The Nature of Eclecticism

"What binds most eclectics together is a stated dislike for a single orientation, selection from two or more theories, and the belief that no present theory is adequate to explain or predict all of the behavior a clinician observes" (Norcross, 1985, p. 21). As Smith (1985) notes, the word *eclectic* etymologically means to "pick out from among or select from." The most frequently cited psychological definition of *eclecticism* is that of English and English (1958, p. 168), who describe it as the "selection and orderly combination of compatible features from diverse sources, sometimes from otherwise incompatible theories and systems; the effort to find valid elements in all doctrines and theories and to combine them into a harmonious whole."

As stated, this position seems to make infinite sense, especially after the analysis in this book which has been directed at showing the inadequacies in all the approaches. As Garfield and Bergin (1986, p. 7) note, "None of the traditional theories of change has succeeded in convincing the professional public that it deserves singular precedence; consequently, practitioners and researchers are exploring ways of synthesizing diverse elements into flexible multifaceted orientations."

Nevertheless, eclecticism has largely been viewed negatively in psychology up until the last decade. In the period of ascendancy of the major theories there was unbridled optimism about their accuracy and efficacy. In this context, eclecticism was often branded with labels such as "muddle-headedness," "the last refuge of mediocrity," "undisciplined subjectivity," "conceptual laziness," "clinical indecisiveness," "professional nihilism" and even "minimal brain damage" (Norcross, 1985; Rychlak, 1985; and others).

But in the last ten to fifteen years, theoretical dilettantes have been humbled by the positive but nonspectacular empirical evaluations of the effectiveness of their personally accepted approaches and the indisputable positive outcomes of other models which are quite incompatible with their own perspectives. Eclecticism is seen by many as necessary if there is no one best approach and if the literature contains documentation of effective approaches emerging from theories other than one's own (Smith, 1985).

The end result today is that between a third and a half of clinical psychologists now describe themselves as eclectic, the largest identifiable group orientation (Norcross and Prochaska, 1988). Other mental health therapists (social workers, guidance counselors) are probably even more eclectic than psychologists. Yet, as pointed out by Garfield and Bergin (1986), this identification as eclectic tells us very little about what these practitioners do. The term *eclectic* is actually more a term of negation ("I do not adhere to any one approach") than a positive description ("I do adhere to x, y and z").

In its worst manifestations, eclecticism can be aptly described by the negative terms listed earlier. We do know therapists who seem to be more influenced by the latest charismatic speaker at a professional conference or weekend seminar making unsubstantiated claims of therapeutic effectiveness than by any reasoned and deliberate multifaceted approach to understanding persons. This can result in the therapist attempting to combine mutually contradictory concepts and techniques, and approaching the client in a manner that lacks logical coherence. Patterson (1985) calls such a stance "atheoretical syncretism." We hope, by the discussion to follow, to encourage a reasoned, deliberate and Christian approach to eclecticism.

Approaches to Eclecticism

There are numerous schemes for understanding eclecticism (e.g., Nelson-Jones, 1985; Norcross, 1985; Norcross and Prochaska, 1988; Held, 1984). In the scheme we utilize below, we are combining elements of these and other authors, and adding very little that is new from us. We will describe four basic approaches to eclecticism.

Chaotic Eclecticism

Chaotic eclecticism is what we will term the negative practices we described above of unsystematically throwing together a hodgepodge, "syncretistic" approach to counseling. In an empirical survey of ways therapists approach eclecticism, Norcross and Prochaska (1988, p. 172) reported that at least one practitioner, when asked what system he used to combine contrasting theories, replied honestly, "I have none." Some practitioners will even experiment with approaches more because they are interested in the techniques than because the client needs the intervention (Norcross, 1985). Thankfully, we have no evidence that this is a widespread problem. Obviously, we regard chaotic or unsystematic eclecticism as unacceptable, even inexcusable, and to not merit further discussion. There are, however, three approaches that are worthy of discussion, though none is without its problems.

Pragmatic Eclecticism

Pragmatic eclecticism is the approach that Norcross and Prochaska (1988) found to be most commonly endorsed in their empirical study. It centers on the commitment to operate not out of theoretical preference, but out of what seems best for the client. Specifically, it means to use the methods that comparative outcome research has shown to work best with the problems manifested by the clients. Thus, a child manifesting bed-wetting would be treated with behavior modification, a depressed adult with cognitive therapy, and so forth. Arnold Lazarus (1984) has probably been the most outspoken proponent of this approach. Gary Collins's (1988) substantive *Christian Counseling: A Comprehensive Guide* in many places seems to represent the pragmatic approach to eclecticism.

Discussing pragmatic eclecticism raises the core question of just how effective psychotherapy is and which psychotherapies are best for which problems. Though this will take us on a sizable tangent, we will pause to deal with those questions here.

How effective is psychotherapy generally? On the whole, scientific studies show that participation in psychotherapy is better than no psychotherapy at all for most individuals with a wide variety of problems, and that the general effect is "significant" (Smith, Glass and Miller, 1980; Brown, 1987). The research to date has failed to show the superiority of one therapeutic approach over another for all disorders, even under controlled experimental conditions (Smith et al., 1980). Therapies within the major traditions have demonstrated a wide range of usefulness in treating a variety of psychopathologies. The few studies on specifically Christian approaches to counseling tend to be poorly designed and executed from a methodological perspective, so optimistic statements about their effectiveness should be taken with a "grain of salt." There needs to be a more serious commitment to outcome research on the part of all clinicians. In the interim, we must be cautious in our claims about clinical effectiveness and exercise some much needed humility.

Even though psychotherapy overall has been shown to be effective, we still believe that the Christian clinician needs to answer the question, "How do I know that what I do is effective?" To answer this question, the clinician needs to know about both the qualitative and quantitative options available for the *assessment of the effectiveness* of a particular theory or technique. One should view with particular caution the use of self-report by clients or therapists of judging effectiveness, because of the obvious possibilities of distortion and response bias. The "human science" methodologies mentioned earlier use a variety of self-report and interview strategies to generate "broad-range" data about human behavior and experience. These methodologies are more rigorous than uncontrolled testimonials or single-case reports and introduce a higher degree of accountability than mere subjective judgment. In conjunction with more traditional measures of evaluation (e.g., clinical observation, objective and projective tests), these strategies can be useful in promoting more of an ongoing assessment of the people-helping process (Butman, 1987).

How effective are specific therapies? There are some specific conclusions about the varying effectiveness of certain approaches or strategies with certain populations that are beginning to emerge. For example, a recent "meta-analysis" claimed to demonstrate the superiority of cognitive-behavioral interventions with most disorders of childhood and adolescence (Weisz, Weiss, Alicke and Klotz, 1987). At this stage in the research, however, extreme caution must be exercised in drawing too much from such conclusions. For example, one could argue that the Weisz et al. study was an analysis of published studies in professional journals and that those journals tend to require experimental rigor that favors behavioral studies because those therapy methods are most easily rendered into acceptable scientific form. Further, one could argue that the clients treated in these experimental studies could not represent the breadth and complexity of the kinds of child and adolescent problems seen in a community counseling clinic since those clients that do not fit the narrow definitions of the study population are screened out of experimental studies. We do not feel that these considerations should lead one to a crippling skepticism about the use of such research on comparative effectiveness. But we must be careful about impulsively jumping to conclusions before strong conclusions can be drawn from the literature.

We will briefly summarize the current state of knowledge regarding the empirical effectiveness of the major therapy approaches. First, we can generally say that the Jungian, Adlerian, reality, existential, Gestalt and transactional analysis approaches each have too few methodologically sound studies to provide even minimal evidence about effectiveness. Each literature includes a wealth of case studies, which provides some encouragement about their potential, but none of these can be regarded as finally persuasive. It must be noted that some of the approaches embrace an understanding of persons, of the change process, and of science which makes empirical study somewhat incompatible with their approach. Existential, Gestalt and Jungian therapies are perhaps notable in this regard. They would each argue that empirical research inevitably runs the risk of dehumanizing persons by treating them as "objects" in a mechanistic or reductionistic fashion. Each of these approaches reports findings in more phenomenologically oriented case studies. Such reports can further our understanding of the inner subjective experience of a limited number of clients, but they are not maximally helpful in evaluating whether or not the model achieves its stated purpose of helping people grow compared to other approaches (cf. Norcross, 1987).

With regard to person-centered therapy, Rogers combined a unique paradox of commitments in his early work to both a thoroughly humanistic and phenomenological approach and to a rigorous use of scientific methodology. The result of those commitments is a rich body of sophisticated research on this approach. Most of this research has, however, been on understanding the *process* of successful therapy with a limited population of clients. This research has fed the gradual evolution of the person-centered-therapy approach over time by highlighting the critical elements of successful Rogerian therapy. But the research has not focused on gauging the *effectiveness* of the therapy with the wide range of client populations, with the result that we cannot say forcefully how successful person-centered therapy is or with what type of problems it is most effective.

The effectiveness of classical psychoanalysis has not been adequately assessed, though there is a substantial literature in this area. Throughout much of the first half of this century, case studies which are open to many possible biases and distortions were the norm. Gradually these case studies were supplemented by survey studies that relied initially on subjective, then later more objective, outcome criteria. Only a limited number of reasonably controlled research studies have been published to date (e.g., Kernberg, 1973; Sloane, Staples, Cristol, Yorkston and Whipple, 1975). Well-designed research studies are rare in this tradition. This is a rather sad commentary on a method that Freud himself initially perceived to be more of a research tool than a clinical strategy for facilitating change. Currently, the defense of psychoanalysis tends to remain an assertion of faith as much as it is a conviction based on scientific methods. In the interim, Freudian theory and technique will most likely continue to be viewed by many as more descriptive than prescriptive.

Similar evaluative comments could be made about contemporary psychodynamic therapy approaches. The bulk of the scholarly work of psychodynamic theorists continues to be case studies and challenging conceptual refinements. As mentioned in chapter four, the recent development of empirical tests of some versions of this model, such as the study of interpersonal therapy as a treatment of depression (Elkin, Shea, Watkins, Imber et al., 1989), are producing positive results. This is a welcome and much needed development.

There have been a number of excellent integrative reviews of family therapy of late, stimulated perhaps by the many public pronouncements of the effectiveness of this approach. The earliest study was the most positive, suggesting that family therapy appeared to be as effective as individual therapy for a wide range of presenting problems (Olson, Russell and Sprenkle, 1980). Hazelrigg, Cooper and Bourdin (1987) were somewhat more cautious and sober in their assessment of the effectiveness of family therapies. They concluded that the results of their meta-analysis showed that the family therapies in their general form do have a positive effect on clients compared to no treatment, but were only slightly more effective than some alternative treatment strategies.

But the most impressive integrative effort done to date was the most humbling (Bednar, Burlingame and Masters, 1988). This review presented separate meta-analyses on the systems approaches and the behavioral approaches to family therapy. They concluded that the basic concepts of the systems approach were not defined with sufficient clarity and precision to assert that family therapy is even a unique treatment modality, much less that it is as efficacious as individual therapy (p. 417). They argued that the systems approach is in dire need of more fundamental descriptive information before it attempts to establish empirical relations among crucial variables in treatment. They were somewhat more optimistic in their assessment of the behavioral family approach, noting that the conceptual system is more clearly defined and that there is more evidence that it is a useful form of treatment. They do not view it as a major conceptual advance over existing treatment options, however. Overall, aggressive assertions about family therapy's effectiveness are premature (see also Piercy and Sprenkle, in press). Its widespread acceptance is probably as much a response to the intuitive appeal of the approach and to the reality of the disintegration of so many families in contemporary American society as to any demonstrated empirical or clinical effectiveness.

Finally, we must discuss the three more "behavioral" approaches. Behavior modification has been shown to be effective with a variety of problems, as discussed in chapter six. These methods must be seen as the treatment of choice for such problems as childhood autism, developmental disabilities (retardation), nocturnal enuresis (bed-wetting) and so forth. Further, the methods have been shown helpful in work with acting-out adolescents, psychotic populations and substance abusers. But demonstrating effectiveness with certain highly defined problems is not the same as globally establishing the approach as the best overall approach, especially as applied to adult problems. Here, behavior modification is clearly lacking.

While Ellis is prone to claiming that his rational emotive therapy has been broadly and conclusively shown to be clinically effective, and typically cites very long lists of studies to support his claims, others (such as Mahoney, 1977) have been much more modest in surveying the clinical research. Ellis tends to cite studies that are methodologically flawed or provide only the most tangential and vague support for his methods. But as with behavior modification, while there is little doubt about the utility of his methods with some populations, the RET approach falls short of being a comprehensive system.

As we have noted, behavior modification and RET have been subsumed into cognitive-behavioral therapy, making this approach one of the more broadly based and important therapies today. Because it is a recent development, an extensive literature on the effectiveness of cognitive-behavioral therapy is still developing. Reports of the utility of cognitive-behavioral therapy with selected disorders have been published. We have already cited the Weisz et al. (1987) study, which suggested the superiority of behavioral methods with children and adolescents, and the Bednar et al. (1988) study, which suggested that the behaviorally oriented family therapy approaches were the most effective among the family approaches. The methods of Beck with depressives and Barlow with panic victims actually work as well as the highly touted psychiatric medications for these disorders (Elkin et al., 1989; Barlow, 1988). Global comparisons of cognitive-behavioral therapy with other approaches to date have suggested the strengths of the theory but can only be viewed as suggestive at this time, though O'Leary and Wilson (1987, p. 378) claim that every well-done meta-analysis of treatment with a discrete patient population to date has demonstrated the "clear cut superiority of behavior therapy over other psychological approaches." Many of the studies showing the effectiveness of cognitive-behavioral therapy procedures have been plagued by lack of substantial follow-ups and by using nonclinical research subjects (e.g., studying college students who are anxious and want to do an experiment for extra class credit, as opposed to studying people who come to a clinic complaining of anxiety). We would note that there are fewer problems such as these with cognitive-behavioral therapy studies compared to other models. We agree with Tan (1987) that the overall picture of empirical effectiveness is encouraging but not yet conclusive.

Now let us return to our reflections on pragmatic eclecticism. The basic rationale for using the proven best therapy for a particular client concern seems compelling.

The main problem with the stance is that it all too often provides no direction at all for the practitioner. The decided superiority of behavior modification for bed-wetting aside, it is probably the minority of persons requesting therapy that manifest discrete enough problems that allow them to be clearly matched with existing treatment studies. This is partly due to the reality that clinical research on treatment outcomes is often done in university and medical school settings where only "pure cases" of particular problems are accepted for the studies.

For example, only forty per cent of those coming to the clinic complaining of depression might eventually be accepted in a rigorous study of depression treatment. The other sixty per cent might be excluded because they manifest other problems as well (they might be depressed and anxious), for not manifesting the right severity of problems (persons might be excluded for being too depressed, suicidal and immobilized, or for not being depressed enough), or for any number of other reasons. It would be callous and unethical for counselors to turn away people coming for counseling on the basis that research does not exist regarding which treatment approaches work best with their type of problem.

The pragmatic eclectic stance also presupposes that practitioners are committed to keeping up on the empirical treatment literature. We regard this as an ethical imperative; who would go to a medical doctor who had not read a medical journal in fifteen years? But whole approaches to therapy exist whose proponents rarely if ever bother to assess their empirical utility, as we have already discussed. This fact means that "the claim that practice is based on what works is supported only by the subjective evaluation of the practitioner" (Patterson, 1985, p. vi). And to be blunt, we must remember that the author or practitioner claiming effectiveness usually has a vested financial interest in making such a claim. Further, we would ask what a therapist is to do in those areas where empirical outcome research is inconclusive.

Finally, we would note that it is simply unrealistic to expect that most counselors can know so many theories well that they can be a cognitive therapist one hour, a behavior therapist the next, an object-relations psychotherapist the third, an experientially oriented Gestalt therapist before lunch and so forth. The only practical way this position could be worked out would be for groups of professionals of varying approaches to work together and freely refer clients to each other according to empirically determined effectiveness; this is an attractive ideal.

Metatheoretical or Transtheoretical Eclecticism

While pragmatic eclecticism is the approach most often endorsed by practitioners responding to surveys, it is our impression that it is metatheoretical or transtheoretical eclecticism that is most likely to be followed by researchers and authors. Metatheoretical eclecticism is the approach that looks for a "theory or practice behind or beyond the theory."

This approach suggests that proponents of psychotherapy may simply be wrong about how "what they do" works, and that the best chance for the advancement of the effectiveness of the profession is the empirical or phenomenological study of what differentiates effective person helpers from those who are less effective, regardless of the "theories" that they think differentiate them from others. Suppose, for example, that empirical study of effective helpers from several different orientations showed that what distinguished the effective helpers from others was not their theories or what they call their techniques, but rather that they consistently engaged in communications with their clients that were affirming and genuine (as empirically defined for the purposes of the research). Such a finding would be the starting point for a metatheoretical approach grounded on emphasizing affirmation and genuineness.

One genre of this approach has arisen from the work of Carl Rogers, the founder of person-centered therapy. Before his substantive plunge into theory, Rogers worked from the premise that the substrata of an effective counseling relationship could be empirically measured and carefully defined, and then counselors could be specifically and concretely trained in precisely those qualities that truly made one effective. While Rogers went the direction of an increasingly nuanced theory, others[1] stayed with the model of attempting the systematic training of the basic verbal and nonverbal counseling responses that are used in all of the theoretical schools (Ward, 1983).

Patterson, for example, argues that the "necessary and sufficient" conditions for effective psychotherapy have been empirically specified, and that they are composed of four *responsive dimensions* and three *action dimensions*. The responsiveness of the therapist is to be understood on the dimensions of *empathic understanding* (to experience with a client), *respect* or *warmth, facilitative genuineness* (the therapist acts in an authentic way that helps the client) and *personally relevant concreteness* (as opposed to abstractness). The actions of the therapist are most importantly *confrontation* (though not in a hostile or superior fashion), *therapist self-disclosure* for the benefit of the client and *immediacy of the relationship* (the ability to deal with the counselor's relationship with the client in the "here and now"). In Patterson's view, whether the therapist is analyzing transference, doing assertiveness training or analyzing a lifestyle hardly matters as long as *these characteristics are present*. In other words, this form of transtheoretical eclecticism is less concerned with the content of what happens in therapy than it is with the process of what happens.

Other variants of metatheoretical eclecticism attempt to determine common stages in therapy and to come up with generic understandings of processes and content. These approaches are less often built on empirical research into common determinants of effective therapy than

---

[1]Patterson (1985), Carkhuff and Anthony (1979), Egan (1986), Ivey and Authier (1978) and Kagan (1975) all probably fall in this camp.

they are a conceptual analysis of therapy processes. The approach of Prochaska and his colleagues is perhaps a good example of this (Prochaska, 1984; DiClemente, McConnaughy, Norcross and Prochaska, 1986).

In their truly inclusive model, therapy is analyzed according to what clients try to change or what problems they try to solve, where the client is in the process of change and the type of technique the therapist chooses to use. Prochaska classifies types of client problems in thirteen specific categories under the four general headings of intrapersonal conflicts, interpersonal conflicts, individual conflicts with society and the problem of life fulfillment and meaning. Where a client is in the process of change is classified according to a five-stage model (precontemplation: "I don't have any problems, so why is everyone worried about me?"; contemplation: "I've got to do something about this before I crack up!"; action: "I'm working on it but why is it so hard to change?"; and maintenance: "I've tried and tried to change but it seems I'm slipping back into the same old patterns."). Finally, DiClemente et al. (1986) list ten major therapist interventions, including conscious-raising/insight, contingency control in the spirit of operant behavioral psychology and social liberation such as joining a support group. Prochaska would argue that how a therapist or counselor intervenes is a function of what problem the client presents and where in the change process that person is.

The approach of Prochaska differs from that of Patterson in that in the latter, relationship is primary and the content of the therapy is largely secondary; whereas for Prochaska there is specification of the content of focus (client problems) and of types of interventions, so that we know that it is not just the quality of the relationship that determines the outcome.

The metatheoretical position is harder to critique than pragmatic eclecticism and has many strengths. There must be some explanation for why so many different therapies seem to work well at least some of the time. Also, since Christians believe in the centrality of relationships to human life, we should not resist placing quality of relationship at the very core of our understanding of the therapy process.

Perhaps the major weakness of the metatheoretical approach is that there is a central inconsistency imbedded in the very notion of trying to "get behind the theories," in that we can never be without a theory. There is no such thing as raw, uninterpreted reality. We are beings of meaning, of interpretation, and we are always seeing through the filters of our understanding. As such, metatheoreticians are never getting behind a theory; they are rather attempting to subsume one theory with another. In the process, they see some new information but ignore other information, much in the same way that a practitioner of one psychotherapy theory sees things differently than another.

It is significant that most of the skill-training models (Egan, 1986; Ivey and Authier, 1978; Carkhuff and Anthony, 1979) wind up being problem-clarification and solving models. As such, they have real value but definitely do not subsume all other theories; as structured, they have little compatibility with psychoanalytic understandings of the person, for example.

In summary, our main concern is that often on close analysis, metatheories wind up simply being another kind of theory or approach, and they have not yet proven themselves to be superior in any way to other approaches.

Theoretical Integrationism

Theoretical integrationism (also called pluralism by Smith, Glass and Miller [1980]) typically attempts to overcome the limitations of a single preferred theory by using it as one's foundation or "home base" while reaching out beyond that theory to one or two other models which can, by assimilation of parts of the new approaches, help to expand and enrich the foundational approach. The work of Strupp and Binder (1984) or of Garfield (1980) are good examples of attempts to work from a psychoanalytic or psychodynamic foundation to build a more inclusive approach. Norcross and Prochaska (1988) reported that the five most common combinations of two theoretical approaches self-reported by practitioners were: cognitive and behavioral, humanistic and cognitive, psychoanalytic and cognitive, behavioral and humanistic, and interpersonal and humanistic. Anyone who knows well the therapy theories will see instantly what a terrific chasm there is between many of these pairings, yet we can see how the pairings could, if achieved, ameliorate some of the glaring deficiencies of each of the models.

Perhaps the only "success story" in integrating models to date is the uniting of traditional behavior therapy with RET and cognitive therapy to form cognitive-behavioral therapy. The foundations for this successful marriage were laid through the empirical documentation of therapeutic effectiveness of each of the models in different areas: Ellis and Beck's experimentation with incorporating behavioral elements in their treatment paradigms, and the careful conceptual work of

Bandura, Mischel, Kanfer and others which was directed at broadening the behavioral understanding to include the cognitive determinants of human action. Thus when Meichenbaum's highly influential volume *Cognitive-Behavior Modification* appeared in 1977, the ground had been prepared for a tremendous surge of support for such an integration. While some voices within the Association for the Advancement of Behavior Therapy decried the incipient "mentalism" infecting their purist behavioral approach, it did not take long before the leading journals and textbooks in behavior therapy were recognizably cognitive-behavioral.

One of the most visible examples of theoretical integrationism is the growing literature of rapprochement between behavior therapy and psychoanalysis (a seemingly "odd couple" marriage if there ever was one; see the work of Goldfried, 1982; and especially Wachtel, 1977). The attempt to unite such disparate systems has a long history, going back to the historic efforts of Miller and Dollard, who decades ago attempted to translate psychoanalytic psychology into behavioral learning terms.

Several critics of the integrationist movement have suggested that the goals of the group driving toward theoretical integration would be better served by attempting the merger of systems that start off a bit closer to one another than psychoanalysis and behavior therapy. One example would be Dowd and Kelly's (1980) comparison of Adlerian psychology and cognitive-behavioral therapy. They argued that there are core similarities between the two approaches—both are future oriented in their understanding of sources of motivation; they are subjective and relativistic; they are idiographic (highly individualized in their style of analyzing client personality); they are both oriented toward a social/interactional understanding of persons (as opposed to the extreme individualism of humanistic approaches); they are cognitive and have a high view of rationality; and they propose a similar problem-focused, shorter-term therapy process. Cognitive-behavioral psychology has greater specificity of interventions than does the Adlerian approach, and is more scientific in outlook. Adlerian therapy, on the other hand, has the developmental and existential perspectives on human life and the incorporation of values that cognitive-behavioral psychology sorely lacks. Dowd and Kelly argued that merging the two would create a new approach that would have fewer weaknesses than each manifests by itself.

The strengths of the integrationist agenda are substantial. Such an approach can be sensitive and responsive to the empirical outcome literature (like the pragmatic eclecticism approach), especially as that literature serves to document an area of weakness in one model. It can recognize weaknesses in an approach and take steps to deal with those weaknesses. Perhaps most importantly, it attempts to produce *conceptual integrity* by not throwing together incompatible ideas and concepts, and *practical integrity* by providing a common, consistent core model to guide counseling, so that the practitioner is not bouncing around the psychotherapeutic landscape in dealing with different clients. Its main weakness is simply that the jury is still out as to whether separate models from different sources actually can be satisfactorily united. There are not many who regard the marriage of psychoanalysis and behavior therapy to have been satisfactorily consummated at this time.

Whether the theoretical integrationist agenda can actually be achieved remains to be seen. Suggesting this approach as a model for the individual practitioner places a tremendous challenge before that person—how is the individual practitioner, whether psychologist, pastoral counselor or social worker, to achieve a workable integration of models in the midst of demanding professional duties and other obligations when the academics who have time to think and write about such matters cannot see their way clear to achieve the final synthesis? This remains an unsolved puzzle and a continuing challenge.

Conclusion

Given the relative merits of chaotic eclecticism, pragmatic eclecticism, transtheoretical eclecticism and theoretical integrationism, we believe that theoretical integrationism is the approach of choice for the Christian counselor. We take this position because we regard the Christian faith to be one which emphasizes coherence and truthfulness of belief. The faith has a core message about human nature, as discussed in chapter two, which can serve as an organizing foundation for our approach to persons in pain. With such a cohesive core, we have a basis from which to critique theories as we have in this book, and from which to build an integrated approach to therapy.

We have described the many strengths and weaknesses of the various approaches to psychotherapy, and feel that each model has problems which need to be remedied. Probably the two models that come closest to true comprehensiveness and have the least problems are the newer and broader psychodynamic approaches (chapter four) and cognitive-behavioral therapy (chapter eight). The approaches to family therapy based on either psychodynamic or cognitive-behavioral models are useful extensions of these approaches, but do not themselves represent a comprehensive approach.

Even so, as we have shown, the recent psychodynamic and cognitive-behavioral approaches have serious drawbacks from a Christian perspective, and each needs to be fundamentally modified conceptually and in practice to be suitable for enthusiastic use by the Christian professional. At the very least, each needs to seriously confront the greater respect for that which is distinctly personal and human as understood in the existential therapy perspective (chapter eleven). And each of these models has much to learn from the strengths of the other psychotherapy approaches as well.

As a brief example, we might note that Christian counselors who have clarified their theological foundations could ably use cognitive-behavioral therapy as their predominant orienting theoretical approach. Precisely because of their commitment to a Christian understanding of persons, they would recognize many deficits in this working orientation. They would begin with the Christian foundations in resolving these deficits. They may recognize the inattention that cognitive-behavioral therapy manifests to existential issues of meaning to which Christianity speaks, and draw from existential therapy, logotherapy and Adlerian therapy to better understand this dimension of life. From the psychodynamic therapies, they could learn much about the likely influence of early relationships on emotional and personality development, and about the deeply conflictual nature of human motivation and its role in the phenomenon of human self-deception. Because Christianity speaks of the mysterious, nonrational, transcendent dimensions of our existence, they could struggle with the ideas of Jungian therapy to further expand their understandings in this area. A study of family therapy and TA could expand their understanding of the influence of family and social networks, as our faith would indicate the importance of these. Finally, the study of gestalt therapy and the emotionally cathartic therapies may yield insights about the emotional dimensions of healthy personality, as this dimension is minimized by cognitive-behavioral therapy.

Following Prochaska and Norcross (1986) and Rychlak (1985), we would note some of the following dangers in making integration of counseling theories occur successfully. First, the development of well-articulated, comprehensive Christian models will not be facilitated by the presence of divisiveness, territoriality and claims of exclusive possession of the truth ("My way is Yahweh," as a colleague has said). Humility and a commitment to community interaction and feedback are vital for progress to occur. Second, the effort must be interdisciplinary both in spirit and reality. The exclusion of certain groups from the dialog will be counterproductive. Third, the effort must emphasize a balanced commitment to conceptual integrity and rigorous research. Finally, and most importantly, those making this effort must seek to be thoroughly biblical and faithful to the historic orthodox Christian faith while being appropriately ecumenical in spirit.

Dimensions of a Comprehensive Christian Counseling Approach

What will a comprehensive approach to Christian counseling embody? Drawing from chapter two and our discussions in each of the chapters, we would suggest the following skeletal and nonexhaustive outline. A comprehensive theoretical approach to Christian counseling would embody:

A deep appreciation of the value of being human and of individual human beings;

A vision of our need for a love relationship with our Creator, attainable only through the forgiveness offered through the death of Jesus Christ;

An understanding of the essential place of the work of the Holy Spirit in ultimate healing;

An understanding of our intrinsic purposefulness and need for meaning;

An understanding of our fundamentally relational natures and need for love and acceptance, including the importance of family and community for us all;

A balance of emphasis on thinking, feeling and behaving, as each has a clear and important place in human life;

An appreciation of the power of sin and evil;

An understanding of the influence of a spiritual world on day-to-day human functioning;

A respect for human freedom and agency, yet one which recognizes limitations to human choice as well;

An appreciation of habit, skill and learning;

A balanced attention to within-the-person and external-to-the-person influences on human action;

A vision of life that suggests there can be meaning to suffering and that we are called to pursue something more than our personal gratification;

A respect for individuals that is grounded in God's love for each person, yet without a worshiping of the individual disconnected from others;

A commitment to holism in understanding the person, but with a sufficiently developed set of specific postulates about molecular processes in personality to guide actual intervention and the change processes;

A respect for our intrinsically moral natures and the value of obedience to appropriate authority, pre-eminently to God and his Word;

A respect for physical and nonphysical aspects of existence;

An appreciation but not a deification of rationality, balanced with an equally appreciative understanding of our "transrational" aesthetic, symbolic and story-telling natures;

A recognition of our need to worship and be committed to the one who transcends all that we can know or imagine; and

A love for Christ's body, the church, and a commitment to furthering the church's work in this world.

Such a well-articulated, comprehensive and integrated approach to Christian counseling does not exist today. We cannot offer the definitive model. We hope, along with our readers, to be involved in the development of such a model in the years ahead.

For Further Reading

Garfield, S. (1980). *Psychotherapy: An eclectic approach.* New York: Wiley.
   An excellent example of a "theoretical integrationist" approach to eclecticism.
Smith, M.; Glass, G.; and Miller, T. (1980). *The benefits of psychotherapy.* Baltimore: Johns Hopkins University Press.
   The first and most frequently cited general empirical analysis of the effectiveness of psychotherapy.
Strupp, H., and Binder, J. (1984). *Psychotherapy in a new key: A guide to time-limited dynamic psychotherapy.* New York: Basic Books.
   An excellent example of a "theoretical integrationist" approach to eclecticism.

References

Barlow, D. (1988). *Anxiety and its disorders: The nature and treatment of anxiety and panic.* New York: Guilford.

Bednar, R.; Burlingame, G.; and Masters, K. (1988). Systems of family treatment: Substance or semantics? *Annual Review of Psychology, 39,* 401-434.

Brown, J. (1987). A review of meta-analyses conducted on psychotherapy outcome research. *Clinical Psychology Review, 7,* 1-23.

Butman, R. (1987, April). The assessment of psychological and religious maturity. Paper presented at the annual convention of the Christian Association of Psychological Studies, Memphis, TN.

Carkhuff, R., and Anthony, W. (1979). *The skills of helping.* Amherst, MA: Human Resource Development Press.

Collins, G. (1988). *Christian counseling: a comprehensive guide* (rev. ed.). Waco, TX: Word.

DiClemente, C.; McConnaughy, E.; Norcross, J.; and Prochaska, J. (1986). Integrative dimensions for psychotherapy. *International Journal of Eclectic Psychotherapy, 5,* 256-274.

Dowd, E., and Kelly, F. (1980). Adlerian psychology and cognitive-behavior therapy: Convergences. *Journal of Individual Psychology, 36,* 119-135.

Egan, G. (1986). *The skilled helper* (3d ed.). Monterey, CA: Brooks/Cole.

Elkin, I.; Shea, T.; Watkins, J.; Imber, S.; et al. (1989). National Institute of Mental Health treatment of depression collaborative research program. *Archives of General Psychiatry, 46,* 971-982.

English, H., and English, A. (1958). *A comprehensive dictionary of psychological and psychoanalytic terms.* New York: Longmans, Green.

Garfield, S. (1980). *Psychotherapy: An eclectic approach.* New York: Wiley.

Garfield, S., and Bergin, A. (1986). Introduction and historical overview. In S. Garfield and A. Bergin (Eds.), *Handbook of psychotherapy and behavior change* (pp. 3-22). New York: Wiley.

Goldfried, M. (Ed.). (1982). *Converging themes in psychotherapy.* New York: Springer.

Halgin, R. (1985). Teaching integration of psychotherapy models to beginning therapists. *Psychotherapy, 22,* 555-563.

Hazelrigg, M.; Cooper, H.; and Bourdin, C. (1987). Evaluating the effectiveness of family therapies: An integrative review and analysis. *Psychological Bulletin, 101*(3), 428-442.

Held, B. (1984). Toward a strategic eclecticism: A proposal. *Psychotherapy, 21,* 232-241.

Ivey, A., and Authier, J. (1978). *Microcounseling: Innovations in interviewing, counseling, psychotherapy, and psychoeducation* (2d ed.). Springfield, IL: Charles C. Thomas.

Kagan, N. (1975). *Influencing human interaction.* Washington, DC: American Personnel and Guidance Association.

Kernberg, O. (1973). Summary and conclusions of "Psychotherapy and psychoanalysis: Final report of the Menninger Foundation psychotherapy research project." *International Journal of Psychiatry, 11,* 62-77.

Lazarus, A. (1984). The specificity factor in psychotherapy. *Psychotherapy in Private Practice, 2*(1), 43-48.

Mahoney, M.. (1977). A critical analysis of rational-emotive theory and therapy. *Counseling Psychologist, 7,* 44-46.

Meichenbaum, D. (1977). *Cognitive-behavior modification.* New York: Plenum.

Nelson-Jones, R. (1985). Eclecticism, integration and comprehensiveness in counseling theory and practice. *British Journal of Counseling and Guidance, 13,* 129-138.

Norcross, J. (1985). Eclecticism: Definitions, manifestations, and practitioners. *International Journal of Eclectic Psychotherapy, 4,* 19-32.

Norcross, J. (1987). A rational and empirical analysis of existential psychotherapy. *Journal of Humanistic Psychology, 27*(1), 41-68.

Norcross, J., and Prochaska, J. (1988). A study of eclectic (and integrative) views re-visited. *Professional Psychology: Research and Practice, 19,* 170-174.

O'Leary, K., and Wilson, G. (1987). *Behavior therapy: Application and outcome* (2d ed.). Englewood Cliffs, NJ: Prentice-Hall.

Olson, D.; Russell, C.; and Sprenkle, D. (1980). Marital and family therapy: A decade review. *Journal of Marriage and the Family, 11,* 973-989.

Patterson, C. (1985). *The therapeutic relationship: Foundations for an eclectic psychotherapy.* Monterey, CA: Brooks/Cole.

Piercy, F., and Sprenkle, D. (in press). Marriage and family therapy: A decade review. *Journal of Marriage and the Family.*

Prochaska, J. (1984). *Systems of psychotherapy: A transtheoretical analysis.* Chicago: Dorsey.

Prochaska, J., and Norcross, J. (1986). Exploring paths toward integration: Ten ways not to get there. *International Journal of Eclectic Psychotherapy, 5,* 136-139.

Rychlak, J. (1985). Eclecticism in psychological theorizing: Good and bad. *The Personnel and Guidance Journal, 63,* 351-353.

Sloan, R.; Staples, F.; Cristol, A.; Yorkston, N.; and Whipple, K. (1975). *Psychotherapy versus behavior therapy.* Cambridge, MA: Harvard University Press.

Smith, D. (1985). Eclecticism in psychotherapy. In D. Benner (Ed.), *Baker encyclopedia of psychology* (pp. 337-339). Grand Rapids, MI: Baker.

Smith, M.; Glass, G.; and Miller, T. (1980). *The benefits of psychotherapy.* Baltimore: Johns Hopkins University Press.

Strupp, H., and Binder, J. (1984). *Psychotherapy in a new key: A guide to time-limited dynamic psychotherapy.* New York: Basic Books.

Tan, S. (1987). Cognitive-behavior therapy: A biblical approach and critique. *Journal of Psychology and Theology, 15,* 103-112.

Van Leeuwen, M. (1987). Personality theorizing within a Christian world view. In T. Burke (Ed.), *Man and mind: A Christian theory of personality* (pp. 171-198). Hillsdale, MI: Hillsdale College Press.

Wachtel, P. (1977). *Psychoanalysis and behavior therapy: Toward an integration.* New York: Basic Books.

Ward, D. (1983). The trend toward eclecticism and the development of comprehensive models to guide counseling and psychotherapy. *The Personnel and Guidance Journal, 62,* 154-157.

Weisz, J.; Weiss, B.; Alicke, M.; and Klotz, M. (1987). Effectiveness of psychotherapy with children and adolescents: A meta-analysis for clinicians. *Journal of Consulting and Clinical Psychology, 55*(4), 542-549.

16

CHRISTIAN
PSYCHOTHERAPY

✛

*I*n the last chapter, we elaborated on options in theoretical
eclecticism. In a sense, that chapter culminated our discussion
of *theories* of psychotherapy and counseling by suggesting how
we might move toward a Christian theory of counseling. A Christian
psychotherapist may use any one or number of therapy approaches,
when such approaches are suitably criticized and modified to deal with
the central incompatibilities with Christian faith.

A counselor is not Christian merely by virtue of being anti-Freudian
or anti-behavioral, but we would also argue that a counselor is not
thoroughly Christian merely by virtue of throwing around a few Bible
verses. None of the existing counseling theories, religious or nonreligious, adequately plumb the depths of the complexity of human character and of the change process. So there are many theoretical options
open to counselors who desire to be distinctively Christian in what they

do. Christian counselors may operate very differently from each other.

But we would argue that there will be or *should be* certain common-alities across all therapists who are attempting to be distinctly Christian. It is these commonalities we wish to develop in this chapter.

The basis for these commonalities is the special claim the gospel has on the counseling process compared to work in other vocations, such as medicine, accounting or construction. We agree with Christian critics of psychology such as Jay Adams who say that the counseling processes are of such a nature that they must be thoroughly reconcep-tualized from a biblical foundation to lay claim to the adjective "Chris-tian."

This assumes that there is something special about the field of psychology specifically, and the mental health professions generally, that demands that we put unusual efforts into making our work an extension of the Christian faith and of God's redemptive activities in the world. We would argue that the theoretical appraisal process, of which this book is an example, is only part of the process of adjusting the nature of the counseling process in a way to allow it to be honoring to God. This chapter is about other aspects of that task.

The Counseling Vocation

Persons who hold to rigid sacred/secular distinctions and claim that *real* Christians go into the ministry while people of lesser faith go into secular work are quite wrong. They are also wrong to think that God has different values for different types of work, such that the work of a farmer or engineer is less honoring to God than that of a minister of the gospel. Christ redeems all of life and gives everything honor and goodness and meaning, whether it be plowing a field, counseling a suicidal person or administering the sacraments. All work is to be done under the lordship of Christ, as unto him (Col 3:23), and this lordship commitment means different things in different vocations. We must work creatively and diligently to effectively discharge this lordship responsibility.

While almost all careers are good potential options for Christians (we might rule out prostitute, drug dealer, assassin and so forth), and God honors all righteous vocational commitments, nevertheless the claims of the gospel on different vocations vary in kind and extent. The claims of the gospel over our vocational lives express themselves both in the area of *character and concerns* (including our ethical standards) and in the area of the *structure and content of the work.*

We can take farming as one example. Christian farmers are called to be patient, honest, just, compassionate and generous. They are called to farm in accord with kingdom ethics, looking on what they do as an exercise of stewardship over the earth. Thus they might think carefully about the ecological implications of their planting, watering, fertilizing and pest control procedures. But with regard to structure and content, the gospel does not have very much to say, except perhaps at the very broadest level of seeing the earth as God's creation and so forth. The faith simply does not dictate the way farmers are to plow a field, fertilize, harvest and so forth. The gospel does not change their understanding of what they work with—corn is still corn and a pig is still a pig. The gospel exerts its claims almost exclusively over their character and concerns, but has less to say of the structure of their work.

At the other extreme, we might take the gospel ministry. Here, as with farming, the claims of the gospel over the character of ministers are clear and total, demanding that they exhibit the same virtues that God desires in Christian farmers. But the gospel also directly dictates much, but not all, of the structure and content of the work of ministers. The gospel dictates the general form of worship, of the sacraments, of pastoral ministry, of doctrine and hence the content of Christian education. The faith prescribes the core of how we understand salvation and sanctification, and how we understand the people that are to be saved and growing. The gospel does not dictate all ministers do; they can profitably learn from social science studies of church growth or small group dynamics, from recent studies of innovative educational methods or from administrative studies of office management. But ministers' work, if it is honoring to God, should clearly bear the mark of God's revelation in his Word in its very structure and content.

We would argue that the work of counseling and psychotherapy is much more like that of the ministry than farming. It is a clear example of a group of vocations that are just one step back from the professional ministry in terms of the demand for transformation of our work by the gospel. And we share many of the same risks and responsibilities of those in the professional ministries.

The claims of Christian truth should fundamentally transform, at a basic and profound level, the ways we conceptualize and understand our human subject matter, as well as our problems, our goals and the processes of change. That is what the bulk of this book has been about—how Christians can interact thoughtfully with secular psycho-therapeutic theory and transform these approaches to conform with Christian revelation. We would argue that it does not stop there. It is not just our theories, our understanding of our subject matter, that needs to be transformed, *but our very understanding of the contours of the profession as well.*

Why is this so? The reason is because of the undeniable relevance of God's revelation for the work of mental health professionals, and because Christian marriage and family therapists, clinical social work-ers, psychologists, psychiatrists and pastoral counselors are doing part of the work of the church. The mental health field mirrors in some striking ways the redemptive work of the church when it strives to foster the salvation of its members.

Salvation is biblically more than a one-shot harvesting of the ephemeral souls of the believers in one instantaneous conversion. Biblically, *salvation* refers to the healing and restoration of wholeness to the entire lives of believers, though especially in their relationship with God (White, 1984). Mental health workers, then, whose work is so often seen in our society as facilitating growth toward wholeness, are mirroring and partaking in the redemptive or salvific work of the church whether we like to think so or not. As Ray Anderson says, "The cure of souls . . . is a ministry and service of the Christian community" (1982, p. 202).

Even though many mental health professionals do not style them-selves evangelists or pastors, the truth is that our work often penetrates to the personal core of the life of our clients. In that core, there is often very little distinction between the religious/spiritual component and the personal/emotional/psychological component. Because our work so closely intersects with kingdom concerns, we must be about the task of structuring our work deliberately and thoroughly in ways that are honoring to the kingdom and which are compatible with God's own efforts on behalf of his people (Anderson, 1987). If we don't make this a premier concern, we run the risk of contributing to a system compet-ing with the church of Christ for servicing the welfare of God's people. We ought to supplement or complement the work of the church, not offer an alternative to it.

When we work to bring healing and wholeness to the hurting, Christ is present in a unique way. He is present in the one seeking help, for he promised that anyone ministering to the suffering was minister-ing to him (Mt 25:31-46). And he is present in the one ministering and attempting to heal, for he is the source of all growth and healing and comfort (2 Cor 1:3-5). Some have even called psychotherapy an incarnational ministry (Benner, 1983). If in the healing encounter, then, both persons are partaking of the presence of Christ, how can we argue that there is nothing special that distinguishes the therapeutic vocation from many other professions?

Imaging God in Therapy

In chapter two we discussed the centrality of the concept of the *imago dei* and its implications for our personality theories. Understanding the nature of the *imago dei* has been an important concern of theology off and on throughout the last two millennia. Theological anthropology usually looks at the image as our common denominator or denominators, the image as shared necessarily by all persons, asking what it is that we all share that makes us individually and corporately imagers of the Most High. We are all responsible moral agents; we are all rational beings; we are all gender differentiated and thus intrinsically social beings and so forth. We might call this the *descriptive* or *de facto* dimension of the image, because these things and more are true of us all as a matter of our existing as humans because we are made in God's image. We exert no special efforts to manifest this aspect of the image. In fact, no matter how we run from it, we are always imagers of God in these fashions. We cannot not image him in these ways.

But there is another side of the imaging reality that is captured in numerous biblical verses: "Be imitators of God, therefore, as dearly loved children" (Eph 5:1); "Put on the new self, which is being renewed in knowledge in the image of its Creator" (Col 3:10). From this perspective, we are to be continually striving to actualize the image we have been entrusted with in an ever more conspicuous and pure fashion, to work diligently and deliberately to image our Maker. As Dallas Willard said (1990, p. 29), in an article entitled "Looking like Jesus." "As disciples (literally *students*) of Jesus, our goal is to learn to be like him."

The image of God in us, from this perspective, goes quite beyond the more passive "common denominator" approach we often take when discussing the image of God. It has suddenly become something we must strive to become or actualize, and we can fall painfully short in the process. The image, rather than being just a passive characteristic, a birthmark as it were, is also a declaration of life purpose, a binding agenda for action and a map for necessary growth which we as believers are obliged to follow. It is, in fact, the entire goal of the process of our sanctification. This is the *prescriptive* or *normative dimension* of the image-of-God concept.

The very nature of the mental health professions dictates that we must work at this prescriptive aspect of actualizing God's image in building our mental health professional identities in a way that few professions share quite so extensively. When we are reflecting on what we are to become, we must look beyond the de facto image and get a vision for what we are called to be; in our case, how we can actualize the image of God more clearly in our work in the mental health professions. We will explore three aspects of imaging that are relevant to the field of counseling, namely, actualizing the image of God's *roles* or *offices*, God's *character* and God's *concerns*.

Imaging the Offices of God

By *offices* we refer to the functional roles God assumes in interacting with his people. There are a number of these roles that are relevant to our work in the mental health field. Not all of his offices, however, are ours to assume; some may be impossible for us to assume. God's office as the King and sovereign Lord of the universe is an obvious example of this. Another would be his function as the Redeemer of humanity through sacrificing himself as the Lamb of God. But what are some of the roles he fills which are instructive to us and perhaps in some sense binding on our professional identities?

The first is that of God the Holy Spirit functioning as the *Paraclete*, the one who *draws alongside of us to help, comfort and encourage*. In some contexts (1 Jn 2:1), the concept of Paraclete means an advocate, one who pleads for us before the Father when we sin. In other contexts, the concept of Paraclete clearly takes on a more emotionally supportive meaning, as in 2 Corinthians 1 (especially v. 4) where we learn that God comforts us through the Holy Spirit so that we might be able to comfort others around us. In some contexts, the Paraclete helps concretely by equipping and providing to enable us to meet the deficiencies in our lives (as when he functions as the teacher who relieves our ignorance).

What rich instruction we can draw for our professional roles from this office that God discharges! Advocacy is a function counselors are called to fill from time to time, when we are dealing with persons who have been robbed of their choices, their hope or their rights. What a loop of beauty and purpose we have in suffering when we know that

God entered into our sufferings so that he might perfectly meet our needs, so that we in turn can give comfort to others, and in that process be ministering directly to Christ himself! The comforting thus flows in all directions when we image Christ and the Holy Spirit (or are allowed to be his image) by being paracletes ourselves, drawing alongside another with hope and comfort. This function adds new meaning and validity to the concept of the "wounded healer" that we hear so much of today (developed often in the writings of Henri Nouwen; see also Miller and Jackson, 1985; or Crabb, 1988). Finally, as providers of that which was lacking, we act as the image of God in comforting by taking part in making up what is lacking in the sufferer.

A second role or office of God which is instructive is his work as the *Reconciler.* Second Corinthians 5:18-21 instructs us directly that Christ reconciles each believer with God, and that we are in turn to become his agents of reconciliation, "ambassadors for Christ" (v. 20), who take seriously the call to draw others into reconciling relationships with the Father and the Son. The reconciliation called for by the gospel is not merely spiritual (God to person), however; the reconciliation that God works in our hearts is also intended to spill out into our human relationships as well, leading Christians to be bridges of healing between estranged persons wherever possible (Mt 5:24). Clearly, reconciliation between persons is designed to follow the spiritual reconciliation which the gospel brings between God and us.

There are two implications of this work of reconciliation. The first is the eternal value of the personal reconciliations which are so often achieved as a result of psychotherapy. The second is that evangelism will always play some role in counseling, because there should be some dimension of our professional lives which draws people toward reconciliation with God. This does not mean that counseling becomes a "scam" to lure to us emotionally distraught people who think they are going to be helped when our real motivation is to save their souls. Rather, Christian concern for the whole person will lead to a transparency for and centeredness on the Christ that could lead others to a saving knowledge of the gospel.

A third vital office of God is that of *Healer,* the "Great Physician." When the Lord's virtues are extolled in the Scriptures, his healing grace is often mentioned prominently, as in Psalm 103:2-4: "Praise the LORD, O my soul, and forget not all his benefits—who forgives all your sins and heals all your diseases, who redeems your life from the pit and crowns you with love and compassion." A narrow evangelicalism can focus exclusively on forgiveness of sins and neglect God's healing intent. Healing is an intimate part of God's identity in relating to his people. This implies that he has a heart of compassion for suffering and a passion for wholeness for his afflicted children which we would do well to cultivate.

The final office of God is that of his being the source of all wisdom; he is in fact the beginning of wisdom (Prov 1:7) and wisdom incarnate (Prov 1:20-33). Derek Tidball (1986) points out that before the coming of Christ, there were three types of "pastors" in ancient Jewish society: priests, prophets and wise men. We had never understood the term "wise men" to refer to an institutionalized role in Old Testament society. It seems to us that there are many parallels between the wise man role in ancient Jewish life and the role mental health professionals serve in contemporary American life. Tidball wrote, "The objective of the wise men was to provide down-to-earth counsel about the ordinary affairs of life. . . . Their approach was to consider, with steady logic, the truth which was hidden within human nature and creation in order to discover the regularities which could form the basis of their lives and counsel" (1986, p. 43). Certainly the provision of such wisdom is a prime duty of the psychotherapist. And it is vital to remember that true wisdom begins with "the fear of the LORD" (Prov 1:7).

Tidball suggests that the wise men did not often work according to explicit divine revelation in any direct sense, as they were grappling with practical matters which simply were not a preoccupation of God's revelatory energies. In other words, they dealt with matters for which no simple recourse to "the Bible says" was possible. Nevertheless, they were guided by the notion that "it is only a commitment to [God] which will reveal truth, as there can be no reality except that which he controls" (1986, p. 44). This need to ground wisdom in the word of God is further demonstrated by Jeremiah 8:8-9: "How can you say, 'We are wise, for we have the law of the LORD,' when actually the lying pen of the scribes has handled it falsely? The wise will be put to shame; they will be dismayed and trapped. Since they have rejected the word of the LORD, what kind of wisdom do they have?" Like the wise men of Israel, contemporary counselors must be cautious in delving into psychotherapeutic theory and practice to remain carefully, deliberately and courageously Christian in our core commitments, lest we merit the same condemnation that Jeremiah pronounced.

Unique spiritual resources are available to the Christian counselor and psychotherapist who is striving to live out the images of God's offices; resources for our ministry of growth and healing, such as prayer, the use of the Scriptures, the sacraments, fellowship and worship (cf. Foster, 1978). These resources must always be used judiciously, in recognition of the complex intricacies and dynamics of the personal and professional relationship of counselor to counselee; the diverse and varied ways that psychodynamics and faith can interact (cf. Fowler, 1984; Parks, 1986); the reality of healthy and unhealthy forms of religious experience; and the different personalities, world views, faith and value beliefs of counselor and counselee.

As Malony (1982) has warned, religious "God talk" and practice can be used and misused, so a concern for timing, tact and sensitivity must always be present (cf. Clinebell, 1965). Competent and committed clinicians will always attempt to assess accurately and examine the needs and wants of their clients prior to all interventions. Religious interventions that are not part of the societally defined role of the psychotherapist, and for which many therapists have not received formal training, should be cautiously used.

Counselors have a special obligation to intentionally live out the image of the comforting, healing, reconciling and wise God in their practice. Following and intentionally imaging his work is not an elective process if we claim the name of Christian. By learning all we can from how God himself has exercised these offices, we can be more faithful servants in this field.

Imaging the Character of God

We cannot image God's work without imaging his character, for God's work emanates from his character. Psychotherapy research seems to be converging on the finding that while psychotherapeutic technique per se is not unimportant, it is nevertheless the relationship with the client that carries the main power for at least initial change in the client (Patterson, 1985, chap. 13). The personal qualities of the therapist thus carry an inordinate potential for positive or negative impact on the client.

The list of personal traits we are called to "put on" in Colossians 3:12 are a powerful prescription for a healing influence on the life of another. We are called to "clothe yourselves with compassion, kindness, humility, gentleness and patience. Bear with each other and forgive . . . as the Lord forgave you." Even Patterson (1985, p. 91), a leading secular psychotherapist and theoretician, has described the essential character of an optimal therapeutic relationship as that of "love in the highest sense, or agape."

With Al Dueck of Mennonite Brethren Seminary and Siang Yang Tan of Fuller Theological Seminary, we recently presented a symposium in which we explored ten themes regarding the character of the therapist and her practice (Jones, Butman, Dueck and Tan, 1988). We suggested that the Christian counselor is called to virtues that are in contrast to those that might "pay off" in the professional world.

We are called to *compassion* as opposed to elitism. The lordship of Christ always issues forth with a compassion for the poor and downtrodden. A counseling practice that is established without a concrete concern for the poor is elitist and less than ideal. Guy (1987, p. 294) states that the truly outstanding clinician has something in addition to skill and expertise; he or she possesses "a deep sense of caring and compassion that results in a level of empathy and sensitivity that touches others in a very extraordinary way." We must in some way be committed to relieving human misery at a corporate as well as an individual level.

We are called to *servanthood* as opposed to superiority. Do we subtly elevate ourselves over our clients, or do we see ourselves when we look deeply into their lives? What is our ground motivation for practice? Christians are called to have servanthood as a ground motive, and this has special implications in therapeutic practice where control and power issues can so easily be intertwined with our practice.

We are called to *community* as opposed to isolation. We should seek out the give and take of life in unity with other believers. Since counselors are asking their clients to take an honest look at themselves and to make choices concerning how they want to change, it is crucial for counselors to be brutally honest with themselves. Because of the reality of self-deception, this cannot be done in isolation. It becomes difficult to "give yourself away" if you don't know who you are or what you really believe. Counselors must be rigorously committed to their own growth and development in the context of a confessional community if they expect to facilitate that process in others. Also, isolation is a major threat to the well-being of psychotherapists (Guy, 1987), but the radical call of the gospel for the establishment of community stands in opposition to this tendency.

We are called to *accountability* as opposed to independence and autonomy. Counselors should not be lone rangers operating by their personal idiosyncratic standards. Guy (1987) mentions independence as a major reason for attraction to the profession, yet we would argue that accountability, first to Christ and then to his church, is a vital dimension of Christian distinctiveness which makes independence as commonly conceived (e.g., "I walk to my own standard") destructive. If we are to speak the truth in love to others, we must find others who are willing to do the same for us. For some psychotherapists, this might involve careful supervision, personal therapy, the utilization of a spiritual mentor or director, or greater accountability to a local church.

We are called to *transparency* as opposed to impression management. We are called as Christians to be radically transparent to Christ within us in all aspects of life. The livelihood of counselors, though, often depends on impressing others so that they will refer clients to us. This increases the risk that the therapist will engage in impression management.

We are called to *love* as opposed to Rogerian positive regard. Positive regard supposedly accepts all and is totally indiscriminate. It must overlook evil and sin because it is based in the presumption of the worthiness of the person to be loved. God's love sees the negatives clearly and loves in spite of them. *Agape* love, while indiscriminate, is not relativistic and is wedded to a firm notion of the good for the beloved. Thus, true love can be strict or harsh in its pursuit of the good for the other.

We are called to *stewardship* as opposed to profit maximization. We should be seriously committed to the real effectiveness of the helping relationship rather than merely judging our success by the size of our referral base and our monthly gross.

We are called to *holiness* as opposed to anonymity or wholeness; holiness most basically applies to anything set apart for God's use, and we can be holy in this sense in spite of our own brokenness. A counselor who deserves to be called Christian, or an approach which is distinctively Christian, has to be grounded in a deep understanding of what it means to be intrapersonally or personally integrated. Tan (1987) describes this in terms of the servant's spirituality. As Carter and Narramore (1979, p. 117) have argued, "Unless we are open to the impact of a relationship with God in our lives and unless we are open to seeing our maladaptive ways of coping, we will find it necessary to shut ourselves off from certain sources of truth and block any real progress in integration. In fact, this is perhaps the biggest single barrier to integration."

We are called to *wisdom* as opposed to mere secular brilliance. Wisdom is practical intelligence applied to good and godly ends. The pursuit of wisdom is essential for the Christian therapist. We should be wise in God's eyes, even if that seems old fashioned, rather than seeking to dazzle with empty brilliance. As Foster (1978, p. 1) has lamented, superficiality is the curse of the modern age; what we need is people of depth.

Finally, we are called to *integrity* as opposed to mere ethical compliance. The fleshly person is merely constrained by ethical codes. The spiritual person should be transformed at a deep level by the Spirit and law of God and strive for a deep integrity that transcends mere compliance. Rather than ethics being a fence that barely constrains us, we should be exploring new frontiers of integrity and honesty in our practices.

Above all else, the Christian counselor should be characterized by a true depth of spirituality, the foundation for what Farnsworth (1985) has called "wholehearted integration." According to Tan (1987, pp. 36-37), such deep spirituality would have at least the following characteristics: (a) a deep thirst and hunger for God; (b) a love for God based on intimate knowledge of God, that leads naturally to worship and obedience; (c) being filled with the Holy Spirit and yielding to God's deepening work of grace in our lives and not to the flesh; (d) acknowledging and using the gifts of the Spirit for God's purposes and glory and manifesting the fruit of the Spirit; (e) developing biblical thinking and a world view that is consistent with God's perspective as revealed in the Scriptures; (f) being involved in spiritual warfare requiring the use of supernatural power and resources available only from God; and (g) being attuned to the "mystical" aspects of our faith that defy easy rational description. These will be the ultimate roots of the good we are able to do, or more accurately that God is able to do through us.

Imaging the Concerns of God

What are God's concerns? What does he care about deeply and passionately? In our contemporary parlance, what are his values? We are told clearly that God loves the world (Jn 3:16), and specifically his bride, the church. The book of Revelation is filled with imagery of the wedding feast of the King to his redeemed bride and the Song of Songs tells in passionate metaphor of God's pursuit of his beloved. But nowhere is this clearer than in Ephesians 5, where we are instructed about the Christ dying to cleanse his bride-to-be. A Christian counselor will thus passionately care for both the individual and the church.

At the individual level, good counseling or psychotherapy ought to seek to promote a client's spiritual and psychological maturity. We need to be clear about what we are trying to promote as counselors and psychotherapists, which requires us to examine not only the function of symptoms and sickness in a person's life, but the deeper meanings of the counselee's problems in living. As Foster (1978) has noted, the counselor is not unlike a spiritual guide in the process of deepening faith and understanding. Healers can take clients no further than they have been taken themselves. You can only love persons you know, and you can only love another if you have been deeply loved yourself. Clients can only grow if they have felt heard, understood, appreciated and valued. With the necessary skills, competencies and motivation, the process of growth and development can be facilitated.

Malony (1985) described a recent attempt to capture some of the essence of understanding mature spirituality in his "religious status interview." The eight dimensions of his semistructured interview include: (a) awareness of God, (b) acceptance of God's grace and steadfast love, (c) being repentant and responsible, (d) knowing God's leadership and direction, (e) involvement in organized religion, (f) experiencing fellowship, (g) being ethical and (h) affirming openness in faith. Together with the notions of spiritual wellness postulated by Carter (1985), Clinebell (1965) and White (1985), we have rich resources available to help us understand what constitutes healthy spirituality in the Christian counselor. And the development of such a faith is part of our most profound concerns.

But while God unquestionably loves individuals, there is a special status to the corporate church. It has its own identity that is more than the sum of its individual parts, and God's passion in a special way is for the corporate entity. Similarly, Christian mental health professionals must see the welfare of Christ's bride, the church, as a premier concern in their lives.

A focused and passionate concern for the welfare of the individuals in our caseloads or churches is not the same thing as concern for the church itself. Earlier we asserted that counselors are inescapably doing the work of the church in being agents of personal healing in the lives of our clients. If we are preoccupied exclusively with the individual impact of our work and not its corporate effect on the church, we may not have the effect of building up the body of Christ that we should have. This is not to argue that individual growth and healing is unimportant—it is in fact vital. But we live in an era when many influences are draining the vitality of the Western church. In the same way that those seeking to minister in the electronic media must grapple with the unintended fallout of utilizing a medium that specializes in unreality, superficial appearances and personal isolation, so also we in the mental health field must realize that not all of the effects of our work necessarily contribute to the benefit of the church. We need to ask hard questions about the corporate effects of our work.

Counseling that deserves to be called Christian will promote the kingdom of God in word and deed. It will stand in marked contrast, at times, to the modernity of Western culture. The church, not the profession, will be its source of accountability, as well as its well-spring for healing and helping. Its practitioners will be disciples, not independent practitioners or technicians, and its driving force will be shaped by the rituals and discernment of the confessional community (after Dueck, 1986).

Conclusion

There are many subtle and not-so-subtle influences that work against the Christian mental health professional effectively actualizing the image of the Father in his or her work. Psychotherapy is a culturally defined activity, and we all work in fashions that we have not adopted deliberately out of a desire to be an effective imager, but rather unreflectively by "going with the flow." In the give and take of daily life mental health professionals face many preoccupying concerns: there is fierce competition for the mental health dollar; interdisciplinary friction is rampant; financial stability for families and businesses (not just ideas) is at risk; and there is probably greater overall stress and insecurity than at any other time in recent history. In this context, counselors often feel already overloaded with the mundane concerns of maintenance and advancement of their practices and professional careers to take on the additional burdens of grappling with imaging God better.

But this is precisely what Christian counselors are called to do at this point in history. The Christian mental health establishment is far from being the effective handmaiden of the church that it ought to be. Pastors, when they are honest, often feel that they are mainly seen as a referral source by the mental health professional, people to be romanced by the psychotherapist to yield the obvious payoff of paying clients. Pastors are happy about the frequent positive outcomes of therapy, but are perhaps more skeptical about psychotherapy than they have been in past years. They are bombarded with "Christian Psychology Is Apostasy" literature on the one hand and "99 Reasons to Refer Your Parishioners to Us" literature on the other. Pastors are more aware than ever that it cannot be taken for granted that psychotherapy is advancing the cause of the church, because there is often too much slippage between therapy goals and the church's needs.

What are we advocating? Obviously, we must start with urging a renewed commitment to serving God and his church, a commitment to imaging the Father through our professional work. If this isn't a foremost commitment, than the rest hardly makes sense.

Second, we would advocate the need to think with Christian clarity about the theoretical approaches to understanding and changing people, which provide the background for all counseling practice. It is our prayer that this book represents an advancement of that enterprise.

Further, it is essential to be informed biblically and theologically about God's caring for his people and about the instruction he has given us for the care of souls in the church. Too much of what passes for integration today is anemic theologically or biblically, and tends to be little more than a spiritualized rehashing of mainstream mental health thought. The church has a rich corporate history in the field of pastoral care which we need to know about if we are to be Christian psychotherapists. Psychology was a division of practical theology long before it became a separate field and the pastoral care tradition has rich resources to digest.

Pastoral ministers were far from ineffective and uninsightful before the advent of Freud. The mental health professions often unwittingly believe and promulgate the fable that nothing significant occurred in the psychological care of persons before modern times— just look at the coverage in a typical introductory psychology text, where discussion of religion is typically paired with pictures of spinning chairs, straitjackets and inhumane insane asylums (Kirkpatrick and Spilka, 1989). But premodern pastoral care was not ineffective. Thomas Oden (1984), well-known pastoral theologian and former enthusiastic advocate of several psychotherapeutic methods, now calls himself a "classicist" and devotes his time to the study of the pastoral care techniques of Pope Gregory the Great (from the early so-called Dark Ages) and other historical pastoral care experts. The more we understand the rich history of pastoral care, the greater our appreciation for the richness of the Christian tradition for informing our contemporary practices will be.

Finally, we would recommend that Christian counselors be in explicit, ongoing dialog with responsible members of their own faith community about how best to be distinctively and appropriately Christian in their work. We can be dangerously myopic when we dialog only with other mental health professionals about these matters, because this lessens the chances that we will be able to see effectively beyond our disciplinary blinders. We know of several Christian psychologists who have formed accountability groups within their local churches. These groups of clergy and laypersons do not oversee or supervise their work at a specific level, but they were accountable to them at the broader level for the Christian distinctiveness and integrity of their functioning as therapists. We are impressed by their courage and openness in committing themselves to a deeper level of accountability than most of us would find "comfortable" or "convenient."

Christian counselors will probably arrive at a diversity of conclusions on how to be accountable for their Christian distinctiveness, but our concern is not so much with the conclusion as the process by which we get there. Have we engaged in an intentional dialog whereby we put in practice our desire to be responsive to and centered on the will of God and the welfare of the church over and beyond our individual professional welfare? That is the question we must seriously and regularly ask ourselves.

For Further Reading

Clebsch, W., and Jaekle, C. (1975). *Pastoral care in historical perspective*. New York: Jason Aronson.

Holifield, B. (1983). *A history of pastoral care in America*. Nashville: Abingdon.

Oden, T. (1984). *Care of souls in the classic tradition*. Philadelphia: Fortress.

Tidball, D. (1986). *Skillful shepherds: An introduction to pastoral theology*. Grand Rapids, MI: Zondervan.

Four excellent starting points in broadening one's understanding of the church's historical ministry in the "care of souls." Each has thought-provoking implications for rethinking the psychotherapeutic task.

References

Anderson, R. (1982). *On being human*. Grand Rapids, MI: Eerdmans.

Anderson, R. (1987). For those who counsel. Unpublished manuscript, Fuller Theological Seminary, Pasadena, CA.

Benner. D. (1983). The incarnation as a metaphor for psychotherapy. *Journal of Psychology and Theology, 11,* 287-294.

Carter, J. (1985). Healthy personality. In D. Benner (Ed.), *Baker encyclopedia of psychology* (pp. 498-504). Grand Rapids, MI: Baker.

Carter, J., and Narramore, B. (1979). *The integration of psychology and theology.* Grand Rapids, MI: Zondervan.

Clinebell, H. (1965). *The mental health ministry of the local church.* Nashville: Abingdon.

Crabb, L. (1988). *Inside out.* Colorado Springs: NavPress.

Dueck, A. (1986, January). The ethical context of healing. Paper presented for the J. Finch Symposium at Fuller Theological Seminary, Pasadena, CA.

Farnsworth, K. (1985). *Wholehearted integration.* Grand Rapids, MI: Baker.

Foster, R. (1978). *Celebration of discipline.* San Francisco: Harper & Row.

Fowler, J. (1984). *The stages of faith.* San Francisco: Harper & Row.

Guy, J. (1987). *The personal life of the psychotherapist.* New York: Wiley.

Jones, S.; Butman, R.; Dueck, A.; and Tan, S. (1988, April). Psychotherapeutic practice and the lordship of Christ. Symposium presented at the National Convention of the Christian Association for Psychological Studies, Denver, CO.

Kirkpatrick, L., and Spilka, B. (1989, August). The treatment of religion in psychology textbooks. Paper presented at the annual convention of the American Psychological Association, New Orleans, LA.

Malony, H. (1982, August). God-talk in psychotherapy. Paper presented at the annual convention of the American Psychological Association, Anaheim, CA.

Malony, H. (1985). Assessing religious maturity. In E. Stern (Ed.), *Psychotherapy and the religiously committed patient.* (pp. 25-34). New York: Haworth Press.

Miller, W., and Jackson, K. (1985). *Practical psychology for pastors.* Englewood Cliffs, NJ: Prentice-Hall.

Oden, T. (1984). *Care of souls in the classic tradition.* Philadelphia: Fortress.

Parks, S. (1986). *The critical years.* San Francisco: Harper & Row.

Patterson, C. (1985). *The therapeutic relationship: Foundations for an eclectic psychotherapy.* Monterey, CA: Brooks/Cole.

Tan, S. (1987). Intrapersonal integration: The servant's spirituality. *Journal of Psychology and Christianity, 6,* 34-39.

Tidball, D. (1986). *Skillful shepherds: An introduction to pastoral theology.* Grand Rapids, MI: Zondervan.

White, F. (1985). Religious health and pathology. In D. Benner (Ed.), *Baker encyclopedia of psychology* (pp. 999-1002). Grand Rapids, MI: Baker.

White, R. (1984). Salvation. In W. Elwell (Ed.), *Evangelical dictionary of theology* (pp. 969-971). Grand Rapids, MI: Baker.

Willard, D. (1990, August 20). Looking like Jesus. *Christianity Today,* pp. 29-31.

Subject Index

A-B-C format of RET, 176-77

Abnormality: Christian model, 33; psychoanalytic model, 71-73, 85-86; psychodynamic model, 100-102, 107-11; Jungian, 126-27, 135-37; RET model, 177-79, 188-92; cognitive-behavioral model, 205-6, 211-18, Adlerian model, 230-31, 239-40; reality therapy model, 245-46; Rogerian model, 259-60, 268-69; existential model, 287-88, 293-95; Gestalt model, 307-9, 317-18; TA model, 325-31, 339-42; family therapy model, 354-56, 368-69

Adlerian view of causality, 234

Adlerian view of religion, 231-33

"Adult," 325

Aesthetic approach to family therapy, 357-58

Aesthetic stage, 280

Agape love, 269-71

Amorality tendency, 206, 219-21

Anima, 123

Animus, 123

Anti-"thinking" philosophy, 315

Anxiety, 70-71

Archetypes, 123, 129-30

"As if" philosophy, 228

Assertiveness training, 151

Atomism: 158-59, 186-87, 198-99

Autism stage of development, 98

Autonomy, 267

Awareness of feelings, 267

Beck's cognitive therapy, 204-5

Behavior modification, 166-69, 199

Behavior modification and autistic children, 150

Behavioral social exchange therapy model, 357

Behavioral view of good and evil, 161-62

Behavioral view of motivation, 160-61

Bidirectional relationship with God, 110

Birth order (psychological position), 229

Chaining, 149

"Child," 325; adapted, 326; natural (free), 326; little professor, 326

Christian vocation of counseling: 402-5

Christianity and existential therapy, 289-93

Christianity and the world of thought, 18-20

Classical conditioning, 151-53

Cognitive and behavioral construction competencies, 201

Cognitive encoding strategies, 201

Cognitive restructuring, 207

Cognitive-behavioral view of the mind, 209-11

Collective unconscious, 120-24, 130

Collectivist view of persons, 361-63

Commitment to research, 273

Common-sense psychology, 237

Communication deviance, 354-55; double-bind, 354; mystification, 354; symmetrical relationships/one-upmanship, 354; complementary relationships, 354; triangulation, 355

Communications model, 356-57

Competence, 163-65

Compound nature, 45-46; tripartite, 45; bipartite, 45

Congruence of self, 265-66

Consequence, 163-64

Control beliefs, 40

Control theory of brain functioning, 244

Coping skills training, 207

Core personality tendencies, 380

Counseling, 13-14. See also Psychotherapy

Courage, 238

Dependence on therapist, 272

Depravity of persons, 268-69

Despair, 280

Determinism, 148, 155-58, 199-200

Directive confrontation, 310

Discouragement, 231

Disengagement, 355

Distorted standard of reality, 213

Dream analysis, 75, 127-28, 138, 311

Dynamic assumption, 67

Dysfunctional family system, 354

Eclecticism: nature of, 382-83; approaches to, 383-95; chaotic eclecticism, 384; pragmatic eclecticism, 384-90; metatheoretical or transtheoretical eclecticism, 390-93; theoretical integrationism, 393-95

Economic assumption, 68

Effectiveness of psychotherapy, 34-35

Ego defense mechanisms, 69

Ego psychology, 94

Ego states in TA, 325, 336-37

Electra conflict, 70

Ellis and atheism, 174

Empirical standard, 190-92

Empirical testing of psychodynamic model, 112

Enmeshment: 355

Environmentalism, 147-48

Equanimity, 185-86

Ethical stage, 280

Ethics in person-centered therapy, 263-64

Evil, 135-37, 334-35

Existential psychology,

278-79, 283-302
Existentialism, 283-85
Experiential model, 357
Extroversion, 124
Failure identity, 244
Faith of therapist, 111-12
Family system, 351;
  wholeness in, 351; in-
  terrelatedness of, 351;
  boundaries of, 351, 355;
  open or closed, 351; dynamic homeostasis of,
  351
Family systems therapy
  models, 356-60; and au-
  thority, 367; and values,
  368
Family therapy tech-
  niques, 359; reframing,
  359; symptom prescrip-
  tion, 359; paradoxical,
  359, 371; metaphors
  and parables, 359, 371;
  family genograms, 359
Fictional finalism, 228,
Fragmented internal
  sense of self, 98
Free association, 74
Games, 308, 329-30
Genetic assumption, 67
Gestalt therapy, 303-23;
  rules and games of, 311;
  exercises of, 311-12
Glasser's fundamental
  needs, 244
Goal of redeemed life,
  56-58
Goals, 296
Good-enough parenting,
  102
Guilt, 239-40; as existential manifestation, 286,
  294;
Habit, 164
Health: Christian model,
  33; psychoanalytic mod-
  el, 71, 82-85; psychodynamic model, 99-100,
  111-12; Jungian model,
  125-26, 133-35; RET
  model, 185-88; cogni-
  tive-behavioral model,
  205-6, 211-18; Adlerian
  model, 230, 236-239;
  reality therapy model,
  245-46; Rogerian mod-
  el, 258-59, 267-68; existential model, 285-87,

295-97; Gestalt model,
  307, 316-17; TA model,
  339-42; family therapy
  model, 352-54, 366-68;
Healthy family bounda-
  ries, 365
Hedonism, 174-75
"Here and now" empha-
  sis, 303, 307
Hermeneutical princi-
  ples, 40-42
Human motivations, 47-
  49, 55-56
Humanistic psychology,
  256-57, 262
Humanity in fallen state,
  49-56
Humanity in redeemed
  state, 56-58
Ideal self, 258
Idiographic emphasis,
  218, 238
Image of God in humani-
  ty, 43-44
Imaging God in therapy,
  405-14; the offices of
  God, 406-9; the charac-
  ter of God, 409-12; the
  concerns of God, 412-14
Immediacy, 310
Incongruity, 259-60
Individual psychology,
  229
Individualism in Jungian
  theory, 131-32
Inferiority, 229
Inferiority complex, 231
Integration of psychology
  and Christianity, 17-36;
  definition of, 19; ethical, 20; perspectival, 20;
  humanizer or Christian-
  izer of science, 20; destructive mode of, 20-21;
  constructive stages of,
  21-23; dangers of, 23-25;
  criticisms of the task of,
  25-30; methodology for
  Christian appraisal of,
  30-35
Internal regulatory ability, 305-6
Introjects, 97
Introversion, 124
Irrational beliefs, 177-79,
  188-91
Jung and Christianity,
  122-23, 129-31

Jungian teleology and
  causality, 122
Layers of deceit, 308-9;
  phony, 308; phobic,
  309; impasse, 309; im-
  plosive-explosive, 309
Levels of existence, 286;
  Umwelt, 286; *Mitwelt*,
  286; *Eigenwelt*, 286
Libertarian perspective of
  personal responsibility,
  105
Libidinal drive, 67
Life position, 328-29
Lifestyle, 229; composed
  of, self-concept, 229;
  self-ideal, 229; picture
  of the world, 229; ethical convictions, 229
Logical positivism, 146-47,
Logotherapy, 281-83, 292
Loving relatedness, 48
Marital relationship, 364-
  65
Meaning and creation of
  human beings, 42
Meaning and signifi-
  cance, 229, 289
Meichenbaum's cogni-
  tive-behavior therapy,
  203-4
Mischel's five person var-
  iables, 201-3
Multiple-level problems,
  210-11
Naturalism, 146-47, 154-
  55
Nature of sin, 50-54
Myers-Briggs Type Indi-
  cator (MBTI), 125, 132
Neo-Freudian theorists,
  91-93
Neurosis, 99, 134; as dis-
  couragement, 239;
Object relations, 94
Object representations,
  97
Oedipal conflict, 70
Operant and classical
  conditioning, 149-53,
  200
Operant learning, 149-51
Operant processes, 149-
  50
Optimism about growth/
  potential, 274, 334
Organismic valuing proc-
  ess, Rogerian, 258; Ge-

stalt, 305-6
Pain, 134
Paradoxical intention, 282
"Parent," 325; nurturing, 326; critical, 326
Peripheral personality tendencies, 380
Persona, 123
Personal responsibility, 234, 257, 263, 305, 318
Personal unconscious, 121, 123
Personality, Christian model, 32; psychoanalytic model, 77-80; psychodynamic model, 95-97, 105-9; Jungian model, 123-25, 132-33; behavioral model, 148-53, 158-65; RET model, 176-77, 181-85; cognitive-behavioral model, 200-205, 211-18; Adlerian model, 229-30, 236-39; reality therapy model, 244-45, Rogerian model, 257-58, 264-67; existential model, 285-87; Gestalt therapy model, 304-7; TA model, 325-31, 335-39; family therapy model, 350-54, 364-66
Personality disorder formation, 99
Person-centered therapy, 255-77
Person-environment interactionism, 214
Personhood and agency, 46-47
Phenomenology, 257, 299
Philosophical behaviorism, 146-48
Polarities, 309
Position-hunger need, 329
Pragmatic approaches to family therapy, 358
Pragmatic standard, 190-91; 303
Preventative community psychology, 227
Problem-solving training, 207
Psyche, 123
Psychoanalysis and deter-

minism, 64-65; 77
Psychoanalysis and religion, 74-77
Psychodynamic/object-relations therapy model, 357
Psychodynamics and internalized representations, 107
Psychodynamics and therapeutic relationship, 101-2
Psychological domain, 282
Psychosexual stages, 69-71; oral, 69; anal, 69; phallic, 70; latency, 70; genital, 70
Psychosis, 99
Psychosocial assessment, 70
Psychosocial model of pathology, 368
Psychotherapy, diversity of models, 11; psychoanalytic model, 73-76, 86-88; psychodynamic model, 102-4, 112-15; Jungian model, 127-28, 137-39; behavioral model, 153-54, 165-69; RET model, 179, 192-93; cognitive-behavioral model, 206-7, 218-22; Adlerian model, 231, 241-43; reality therapy model, 246-47, 249-50; Rogerian model, 260-61, 269-74; existential model, 288-89, 297-300; Gestalt model, 310-12, 318-21; TA model, 331, 342-44; family therapy model, 356-60, 369-71;
Psychotherapy and counseling, 13-14
Psychotherapy and friendship, 12-13
Rackets, 328-30
Reality therapy, 243-52; compatibility with Christianity, 247-49; and morals/ethics, 248-49
Reciprocal determinism, 200, 207-9
Reductionism, 147, 162-63, 199
Relational aspect of ther-

apy, 103-7; and psychodynamic models, 103-4; & *imago dei*, 108; & belief in God, 110-11
Relativism in Adlerian theory, 234-35
Relativism in Jungian theory, 131
Religious stage, 280
Reparenting, 343-44
Responsible dominion, 48
RET and emotions, 183-85
RET and rationality, 182-83
RET and the self, 176-77, 186-88
RET and values, 180-81, 190-91
Role-playing technique, 311
Scripts, and script analysis, 328-29
Self as defined by choices, 289
Self psychology, 94
Self-actualization, 257-58, 262, 264
Self-awareness, 314-15
Self-deception, 239
Self-efficacy, 203
Self-realization, 125
Self-regulatory systems and plans, 202
Separateness of human beings from God, 43
Separation and individuation stage of development, 98-99
Shadow, 124
Shaping, 149
Significance, drive for, 229
Sin and human freedom, 54-55
Sin and psychodynamic model, 106-7
Social interest functioning, 230
Social-cognitive theory, 203
Socialization process, 314
Somatic (physical) domain, 282
Spiritual domain, 282
Stimulus-hunger need, 328

Strategic family therapy model, 356
Strokes, 327
Strong family characteristics, 353
Structural analysis, 325-27
Structural assumption, 68
Structural family therapy model, 356
Structure-hunger need continuum, 328; withdrawal, 328; rituals, 328; pastimes, 328; activities, 328; games and rackets, 328-30; intimacy, 328
Subjective epistemology of psychodynamic theories, 96
Subjective stimulus values, 201-2
Subjectivism in existential therapy, 292-93; in Gestalt therapy, 313-14
Success identity, 244
Symbiotic stage of development, 98
Systematic desensitization, 152-53
Systemic philosophy, 363-64
Theology, liberation, 51
Therapist as facilitator, 269-70
Therapist congruence (genuineness), 260-61
Token economy, 150-51
Topographic assumption, 67
Transactional analysis, 327-28; complementary, 327; crossed, 327; ulterior, 327-28
Transactional analysis and concept of evil, 334-35
Transactional analysis and dichotomy of human beings, 335-36
Transactional analysis and secular salvation, 338-39
Transactional analysis, freedom and autonomy, 334
Transactional analysis language use, 332-33
Transference, 74
Transpersonal elements,

121
Unconditional positive regard, 258, 260-61, 269-72
Unfinished business, 308, 318-19
Unidirectional relationship with God, 108
Unity of person in therapy, 305
Value of human beings, 42-43
Value of self, 109-10
Vitality, 310

Author Index

Ackerman, 357
Adams, 18, 20, 21, 25, 26, 40, 164, 219, 241, 402
Adler, 224-46, 394
Allen, 21
Alston, 76
Altmaier, 14
Anderson, 56, 234-35, 404
Anderson and Guernsey, 350, 361, 364-66, 370, 372
Ansbacher and Ansbacher, 228, 232, 235, 239-40
Aquinas, 342
Arlow, 67
Arnold, 239
Backus, 179
Backus and Chapian, 179
Balswick and Balswick, 364-65
Bandura, 197, 200, 202-3, 207-9, 214, 394
Barlow, 389
Baruth and Manning, 232, 236
Bassin, Bratter and Rachin, 247
Batey, 332
Beavers, 353
Beck, 197, 204-5, 389, 393
Beck and Emery, 204
Beck, Rush, Hollon and Shaw, 197
Bednar, Burlingame and Masters, 360, 387, 389
Beels and Ferber, 359
Bellah, Madsen, Sullivan, Swindler and Tipton, 272, 313
Benner, 112, 300, 315, 405
Bergin, 180

Bergson, 283
Berkhof, 182
Berkouwer, 40, 236
Berne, 325, 328-29, 332-33, 335, 343
Bilezikian, 364, 368
Binswanger, Boss and Frankl, 283
Bloesch, 50-51
Bobgan and Bobgan, 20, 25-26, 28
Boghosian, 359, 371
Boivin, 155
Bonhoeffer, 181, 274-76
Bontrager, 332, 335, 337-38, 342, 344
Boszoremenyi-Hagy and Ulrich, 357
Bowen, 356
Boy and Pine, 256
Boyer, 139
Brenner, 67
Briggs, 198
Brink, 227-28, 232-33, 243
Brown, 147, 384
Browning, 10, 30, 65, 79-80, 83, 112, 131, 133-34, 136-37, 158-59, 162, 165-66, 262-66, 269, 305, 312-13
Brunner, 24, 56, 58, 283
Buber, 283
Buechner, 130
Bufford, 157, 163, 214, 218
Bugental, 283, 298-99
Buros, 125
Butman, 385
Calvin, 27, 84, 157
Campbell and Moyers, 120
Carkhuff and Anthony, 391, 393
Carlson, 139
Carter, 296-97, 413
Carter and McGoldrick, 351
Carter and Narramore, 411
Clebsch and Jaekle, 40, 180
Clinebell, 409, 413
Clouse, 161
Coles, 87
Collins, 384
Copans and Singer, 13
Corey, 75, 121, 124, 227, 230, 243, 247, 274, 283,

285, 308
Cosgrove, 162
Crabb, 65, 132, 219, 407
Craigie and Tan, 181, 188, 220
Curran, 353
Darwin, 160, 191
Deschenes and Shepperson, 359, 371
Desruisseaux, 86
DiClemente, McConnaughy, Norcross and Prochaska, 392
Dinkmeyer, Pew and Dinkmeyer, 231, 242
Dobson and Block, 198, 207
Dodgen and McMinn, 262
Doherty, 367
Dolby, 321
Domjam, 156
Donovan, 321
Dowd and Kelly, 238, 394
Dueck, 34, 410, 414
Dusay and Dusay, 333
Echeverria, 192
Edkins, 94
Edwards, 197, 213, 221
Egan, 391, 393
Elkin, Shea, Watkins, Imber et al., 114, 387, 389
Ellens, 270
Ellis, 173-78, 180-92, 197, 204, 388, 393
Ellis and Bernard, 173-75, 177, 181, 190
Ellis and Harper, 179
English and English, 382
Erikson, 94, 218, 228, 234, 237, 239-40
Erwin, 148
Eschenroeder, 184, 190-91
Evans, 20, 23, 29, 35, 46-47, 107, 147, 157, 190-92, 208, 211, 229, 234, 264-65, 279-81, 284, 297, 299
Fairbairn, 94
Farnsworth, 32, 35, 264, 412
Finch, 278, 285, 297
Finch and Van Dragt, 284, 286, 297
Fisch, Weakland and Segal, 356
Foley, 351

Ford and Urban, 67
Foster, 50, 138, 212, 296, 409, 412-13
Foster and Ledbetter, 28
Frank, 12
Frankl, 279, 281-83, 291-92
Freud, A., 94
Freud, S., 21, 66-71, 75-81, 83, 93, 109, 121, 129, 227-29, 256-57, 325-26, 415
Friedman, 284
Gaede, 266
Garfield, 12, 273, 393
Garfield and Bergin, 382-83
Gibson, 232
Gilkey, 42-43, 51
Glasser, 243-50
Goldenberg, 11-12, 356
Goldenberg and Goldenberg, 352, 355, 358-59
Goldfried, 394
Greenberg and Mitchell, 95, 102-3
Greenlee, 105, 108
Greer, 332
Greidanus, 20, 40-41
Grieger and Boyd, 187
Griffin, 136, 138
Grunlan, 364
Guntrip, 93, 99, 105, 107, 109-10
Gurman and Kniskern, 354, 360
Guy, 319, 410
Haavik, 238
Hackett, 76
Haden, 289-90
Haley, 356, 359, 367
Halgin, 381
Hall and Lindzey, 139
Hammond, Hepworth and Smith, 260
Hare-Mustin, 367-68
Harrington, 243
Harris, 325, 329
Hartmann, 94
Hauck, 180-81, 185, 187-88
Haughton, 332, 338, 341-42
Haule, 136
Hazelrigg, Cooper and Bourdin, 350, 357, 387
Hedlin, 319
Hedman and Kruus, 332-

33, 335-36, 341, 343
Hebel 284
Heidegger, 283, 287
Held, 383
Helson, 139
Hempelmann, 128, 134-35
Henderson, 106
Herrnstein, 160
Hersen and Bellack, 148
Hestenes, 56
Hester, 234
Hodges, 198
Holmes, 192
Holstege, 361
Homans, 136
Hubbard, 50
Huber, 232-33, 235, 241
Hughs, 125
Hume, 186
Hunt, 20
Hunt and McMahon, 20
Hurding, 10, 76-77, 79, 96, 130-32, 139, 291
Husserl, 257
Ivey and Authier, 391, 393
Jacobs, 274
Jacobson, 360
Jacobson and Margolin, 215
James, 332, 334, 338, 344
James and Jongeward, 325
James and Savary, 332, 335, 344
Janov, 59
Jewett, 44
Johnson, C., 365
Johnson, E., 53
Johnson, R., 95
Jones, E., Cumming and Horowitz, 12
Jones, J., and Wilson, 66
Jones, S., 19-20, 155, 165, 197, 242
Jung, 119-39
Kagan, 391
Kahoe, 243
Kanfer, 202, 216, 394
Kanter and Lehr, 353
Kaplan and Saccuzzo, 125
Kaufman, 284
Kaufmann, 121, 123, 127
Kazdin, 145
Keirsey and Bates, 125
Kelsey, 119, 136
Kemdall and Bemis, 206

Kernberg, 94, 387
Kierkegaard, 279-81, 283, 286, 289-90, 292, 297
Kilpatrick, 20
Kirkpatrick and Spilka, 24, 415
Kirwan, 96
Klein, 86
Klerman and Weissman, 114
Koch, 28-29
Koch and Leary, 29
Kohut, 94-95
Korchin, 13, 66, 71, 73-74, 80, 94, 256, 285, 299, 310, 349, 368
Kovel, 87, 121-22, 137, 274, 298, 369
Kreeft, 181, 211
Lake, 60, 96
Langsford, 368
Lapsley, 249
Lasch, 272
Lawrence, 334
Lawrence and Huber, 181, 189
Lazarus, 187, 206, 220, 384
Leith, 157
Levitsky and Perls, 311
Lewis, 47, 50, 129, 163, 165, 262, 341-42
Lewis, Gossetl and Phillips, 353, 365
Linn and Linn, 96
London, 11
Lovaas, 11, 150
Lovinger, 24
Lowenstein, 94
McDonald, 43-46, 50, 54, 58, 237
McFall, 215
MacIntyre, 132
McKeon and Piercy, 366
McLemore, 13, 57, 65-66, 88, 122, 133, 255, 267-68, 272, 298, 303, 314, 316-17, 320-21, 369
Maddi, 237, 380
Mahler, 98
Mahler, Pine and Bergman, 98
Mahoney, 388
Malony, 278, 294, 332, 334-35, 338, 343, 409, 413
Marks, 153
Marlatt, 200

Masters, Burish, Hollon, and Rimm, 145
Matarazzo and Wiens, 13
May, 283, 298
May and Yalom, 283, 285
Meichenbaum, 197, 203-4, 394
Meier, 272
Meissner, 74, 81
Menninger, 106
Miller and Dollard, 394
Miller and Jackson, 87, 320, 407
Minuchin, 355-56
Mischel, 197, 200-202, 215, 394
Mosak, 228-29, 238, 241
Mosak and Dreikurs, 230
Mullen, 279-80
Muller and Vande Kemp, 157
Munroe, 67, 73, 125
Myers, 240, 262
Narramore, 65, 79, 81-82, 85, 366
Neill, 21
Nelson-Jones, 382-83
Niebuhr, 51, 283
Nietzsche, 227, 283
Norcross, 279, 288, 298, 381-84, 386
Norcross and Prochaska, 383-84, 393
Nouwen, 407
Oakland, 76, 270
Oden, 40, 270, 334-35, 338, 340-41, 343, 415
O'Leary and Wilson, 145, 169, 389
Olson, Sprenkle and Russell, 353, 364, 387
Ortberg, 269-70
Pannenberg, 361-62
Parks, 300, 320
Parloff, London and Wolfe, 166
Pascal, 342
Patterson, 269, 357, 383, 391-92
Pavlov, 147, 151, 153
Pecheur, 212
Peck, 50, 65, 106, 268, 317, 320
Perls, 304-10, 312, 315-19
Perls and Shostrum, 310
Piercy and Sprenkle, 360, 364, 372, 388
Pine, 94

Piper, 163
Plantinga, 43-44, 157
Prochaska, 68, 72, 94, 264, 299, 351, 360, 362, 392
Prochaska and Norcross, 278, 396
Propst, 197, 212, 217, 219-21
Rachman and Wilson, 169
Rapaport, 94
Reuter, 332, 338
Rizzuto, 108-9
Roberts, 84, 183-86, 263, 265-66, 270-71, 290, 350, 370
Rogers, 21, 255-68, 271-74, 293, 305, 310, 386, 391
Rogers and Rablen (in Meador and Rogers), 258
Rozsnafszky, 243
Rychlak, 67, 125, 257, 283, 383, 396
Ryckman, 71, 120, 124
Salinger, 352, 364
Sanford, 119, 127, 138
Sartre, 283-84
Satir, 357
Schmidt, 179
Schreck, 350
Seamands, 96
Sharkey, 176, 186
Shuster, 54
Silverman, 71
Simkin and Yontef, 319
Skinner, 22, 30, 146-50, 156, 158, 160, 162, 165-66, 202-3, 207-9, 215, 363
Sloane. Staples, Cristol, Yorkston and Whipple, 387
Smedes, 35-36, 112, 270, 320, 366
Smith, 311, 382-83
Smith, Glass and Miller, 169, 384, 393
Solomon, 284
Sperry, 210
Spilka, Hood and Gorsuch, 24, 111
Sterner, 183, 188-89
Stinnett, 353
Stoker, 21
Stone, 101
Storr, 76-77, 82

Strupp and Binder, 11,
   272, 393
Stuart, 215
Swaggart, 26
Tan, 34, 167-68, 181, 197,
   213, 217, 220, 270, 389,
   410-12
Thielicke, 269
Thorndike, 147
Thurman, 179
Tidball, 408
Tillich, 51, 284, 286
Tisdale, 263, 267
Tweedie, 289-90, 292-94
Umphrey and Laird, 344
Uytman, 227
Vaihinger, 228
Van Belle, 256-57, 267
Vande Kemp, 10, 293
Vanderploeg, 105
Van Dragt, 285, 297
Van Leeuwen, 20, 29, 35,

81, 102, 123, 138, 146-47,
   165, 198, 236-37, 264,
   299, 352, 364, 368, 380
Vitz, 77, 84, 119, 126, 131-
   32, 256, 262-63
Vitz and Gartner, 78, 84
von Bertalanffy, 351
Wachtel, 394
Wagner, 265
Walen, DiGiuseppe and
   Wessler, 174-75
Wallace, 86
Walters, 76
Ward, 391
Watson, 147, 155
Weisz, Weiss, Alicke and
   Klotz, 169, 385, 388
Wessler, 188-89
Wheelis, 87
Whitaker, 357
White, 105, 404, 413
Whitehouse, 243

Winnicott, 102
Wolpe, 148, 152-53, 209
Wolterstorff, 25, 44
Woolfolk and Richard-
   son, 167, 206, 214, 219
Woollams and Brown,
   325
Woollams, Brown and
   Huige, 325
Workman, 96, 112-13
Wren, 208
Wynne, Jones and Al-
   Khayyal, 354
Yalom, 278-79, 283, 285,
   287, 299
Yankelovich, 314
Young, 247-48
Zajonc, 184
Zuk, 364
Zuriff, 156